MARX AND MODERN ECONOMIC ANALYSIS

Volume II

Marx and Modern Economic Analysis

Volume II: The Future of Capitalism and the History of Thought

Edited by G.A. Caravale

Professor of Economics
University of Rome

Edward Elgar

Published by
Edward Elgar Publishing Limited
Gower House
Croft Road
Aldershot
Hants GU11 3HR
England

Edward Elgar Publishing Company
Old Post Road
Brookfield
Vermont 05036
USA

British Library Cataloguing in Publication Data

Marx and modern economic analysis.
Volume 2, The future of capitalism and the history of thought
1. Economic analysis
I. Caravale, Giovanni A.
330

Typeset in Great Britain by Inhit Limited, Godalming, Surrey
and printed by Billing & Sons Ltd, Worcester
ISBN 1 85278 435 0 (2 volume set)

Contents

Preface

The 'last words' on Marx have been said too many times – the collection of essays presented here is not a further attempt in this direction. Rather, and more modestly, it reflects the desire to take bearings on some facets of the ongoing debate.

In particular, the aim of the collection is to evaluate, in the light of the results of modern economic analysis, some aspects of three groups of questions which appear of great significance in the field of Marxian Economics:

1. the relation between labour values, prices of production, and the notion of exploitation,
2. the 'law' of the falling rate of profit, and
3. the place of Marx in the history of economic thought.

The distinguishing feature of the collection is its attempt at the comparison of some conflicting interpretations of Marx in these areas (each of which is inevitably linked to a different general vision, or school, of political economy) without suggesting to the reader the choice of one specific interpretation. The main emphasis is on analytical and textual arguments, to the rigorous exclusion of ideological debates – though of course the non-ideological character of the analysis does not necessarily mean the absence of ideological-type implications.

These brief prefatory observations consist of an attempt at a sketchy, non-critical presentation of the main approaches and of the most substantive problems that emerge in the collection.

The first group of questions is dealt with in Volume I, and the second and third groups correspond, respectively, to Parts One and Two of Volume II. It must however be emphasized that, on account of frequent overlapping in the questions analysed, the placing of papers in one part rather than another implies a certain amount of arbitrariness – this is especially true for some papers presented in Volume I and the second part of Volume II.

The principal aim of Volume I is to compare two different views of the relation between values and prices of production, which may be called respectively the *traditional* and the *alternative* view. The traditional view sees the notion of exploitation as dependent on the possibility of an analytically legitimate 'passage' from labour values to prices in the general case of unequal organic composition of capital. In this perspective the notion of exploitation comes out to be fatally injured if the above mentioned passage – in the sense in which Marx conceived it – is logically disproved on the basis of the works of Dmitriev, Bortkiewicz and Sraffa. The alternative view, instead, sees the labour theory of value as performing an exclusively analytical role – as an 'instrument' whose place can be taken by a better one, if available, as (it is affirmed) is the case with Sraffa's theory of prices: the 'crisis' of the labour theory of value in this case would not touch upon the notion of exploitation which can continue to be at the centre of the (reconstructed) Marxian stage. A group of papers critically evaluate both the significance (analytical as well as historical) of the transformation problem and the soundness of the alternative view. The Marxian notion of exploitation is thus directly challenged. It seems important to emphasize that these two views of the relation between labour values and prices do not cover the existing spectrum of interpretations of Marx on this crucial ground. At least two significant positions are not presented systematically in the collection – although occasional references to these are present in some of the papers.

The first may be called the 'Anti-Sraffian Marxist Approach' (ASMA) and consists of the attempt to defend the core of Marx's value theory against the attack launched by adherents to the Sraffa-based Cambridge critique of orthodox value theory; these latter are criticized for setting apart the qualitative ('value form') aspects of the transformation problem, for ignoring the role of abstract labour, and for conflating 'causation' of prices and profits with their 'calculation'. Interestingly enough, and in a sense coherently with their general perspective, adherents to ASMA deny, or ignore, that Sraffa's analysis can be employed, as it is by some interpreters, for the defence of some of Marx's central concepts – for example, the notion of exploitation – in a theoretical context no longer founded on the labour theory of value (the stand taken by adherents to what has been indicated above as the alternative view).

The other significant position which is not systematically presented in this collection is usually indicated in the literature with the expression 'Analytical Marxism' (AM). This line of interpretation embeds Marx's theoretical problems in a general equilibrium setting (in a purely marginalist spirit equilibrium is defined in terms of optimizing behaviour of economic agents). The labour theory of value is rejected as an explanation of exchange since labour values can be defined only after the market, on the basis of equilibrium prices, has chosen which productive processes are profitable. Adherents to AM claim however to use the labour theory 'directly' as a theory of exploitation – from this viewpoint labour values are employed to prove the so-called Fundamental Marxian Theorem (the association between positive profits and the existence of surplus labour). The notion of exploitation of labour in a capitalist context comes to be strictly linked to the unequal distribution of property. In this context the need to argue the systematic relationship between prices and labour values totally disappears.

The papers in the first part of Volume II discuss the so-called 'law' of the falling rate of profit – one of the points with which the Marxian idea of the long-run tendency of capitalism to self destruction has been traditionally associated. These papers discuss various aspects of this significant part of Marx's theoretical reflection:

1. the special conditions that must be verified for the validity of the law, and the degree of likelihood of such conditions;
2. the different possible meanings of Marx's argument on this ground;
3. the extent to which the general position of a school of thought affects its interpretation of Marx on this score; and
4. Marx's views on the expansion of the financial sector and its impact on the growth path of the economy.

Although important differences exist among the various papers from the viewpoint of their basic perspective (which ranges from the neoclassical conception to the ASMA way of looking at the problem, passing through a series of more eclectic stands on the question) the general upshot of the contributions seems to be the necessity of the greatest possible caution in the attribution of the character of 'law' to Marx's argument on this ground. A fact of which Marx himself, anticipating his modern interpreters, appears to have been keenly aware.

Part Two discusses, on the other hand, some aspects of the questions relating to Marx's position in the history of economic thought with special reference to the works of Smith, Ricardo, Keynes and Kalecki. The two most important questions analysed in the papers presented in this part are:

1. the so-called 'continuity thesis' – the thesis that Classical and Marxian analyses are nothing but successive developments of the same theory; and
2. the connection between Marx's analysis and contemporary economic theory – the assessment of what elements, if any, of Marx's contribution are present in some of the most penetrating analyses relating to the functioning of modern economic systems.

The arguments offered by the papers on the former question amount to a strongly critical view of the 'continuity thesis' – existing analogies should not obliterate the differences in method, perspective and tools which characterize Classical and Marxian analyses. As to the latter problem, important points of contact are emphasized instead between Marx, Keynes and Kalecki especially from the viewpoints of the role of money, Say's law of markets and effective demand.

If and in so far as the essays here presented are seen to mirror the involvement of Marx's analysis in the crisis of economic theories, this collection would constitute a further reminder that, to use the expression applied by Joan Robinson to Keynes's contribution, we are 'left in the uncomfortable situation of having to think for ourselves' on a number of basic issues. Far from being an evil, this circumstance represents in fact the premise for a more mature way of looking at the functioning of contemporary economic systems and at the normative judgements on what should be done about it. In other words this collection might contribute to favour the systematic extension, to the realm of economic theorizing, of the 'sceptical' attitude of Michel de Montaigne who advocated, for all types of intellectual engagement, modesty, tolerance and refusal of dogmatism: 'au Gibelin,' he wrote in the *Essais*, 'j'estois Guelphe, au Guelphe Gibelin'.

G.A. Caravale,
University of Rome

Acknowledgements

The editor and the publisher wish to thank Dr Gary Mongiovi of St John's University, New York, USA, for his accurate and intelligent help in the linguistic revision of some of the papers written by Italian authors.

Chapter 2, 'Marx on the future of capitalism' by M. Blaug is a modified and updated version of the argument developed in *A Methodological Appraisal of Marxia Economics*, North Holland, 1983.

Chapter 9, 'Keynes and Marx' by Dudley Dillard appeared in the *Journal of Post Keynesian Economics*, Vol. VI, no. 3 and is reprinted by permission of M.E. Sharpe, Inc., Armonk, New York 10504.

Notes on contributors

Mark Blaug is Professor Emeritus of the Economics of Education at the University of London, Consultant Professor of Economics at the University of Buckingham and Visiting Professor of Economics at the University of Exeter. His publications include *Economic Theory in Retrospect* (1985) and *The Methodology of Economics* (1980). His first book was on *Ricardian Economics* (1958).

Giovanni A. Caravale is Full Professor of Economics at the University of Rome. He studied at the University of Rome and at Trinity College, Cambridge, and taught for several years at the University of Perugia. He is the author of numerous publications on the theory of growth, market structures, value and distribution, including *Il Credito al Consumo*, *Cicli Economici e Trend* and (with D. Tosato) *Ricardo and the Theory of Value, Distribution and Growth*. He recently edited the collection of essays *The Legacy of Ricardo* (1985).

Dudley Dillard is Professor Emeritus at the University of Maryland, College Park, where he has been a member of the Faculty since 1942 and served as Chairman of the Department of Economics from 1951 to 1975. His publications include *The Economics of John Maynard Keynes* and *Economic Development of the North Atlantic Community*. His present field of research is history of economic thought, and he is currently (1990) President-elect of the History of Economics Society.

Walter Eltis is Director General of the United Kingdom National Economic Development Office. From 1963 to 1988 he was Fellow and Tutor in Economics at Exeter College, Oxford. He is the author of *The Classical Theory of Economy Growth*, concerning the theories of economic growth of Quesnay, Smith, Malthus, Ricardo and Marx, and co-author (with Robert Bacon) of *Britain's Economic Problem: Too Few Producers* (1976).

Ben Fine is Professor of Economics at Birkbeck College, University of London. His books include *Marx's 'Capital'*, *Rereading 'Capital'* (with Laurence Harris) and, most recently, *The Coal Question: Political Economy and Industrial Change from the Nineteenth Century to the Present Day*. He has written widely on economic theory, the history of economic thought and Marx's economics. Current research interests include energy economics, privatization, changing patterns of consumption, female labour market participation, and the South African economy.

Warren S. Gramm is Professor of Economics at Washington State University. His primary interest is in history of economic thought. Representative of his recent published work are: 'Quality of Life and Allocation of Time Between Labour, Work and Leisure', *Journal of Economic Issues*, **XXI** (1), March, 1987, and 'The Movement from Real to Abstract Value Theory, 1817–1959', *Cambridge Journal of Economics*, **XIII** (2), June 1988.

David J. Hoaas is Assistant Professor of Economics at Centenary College in Shreveport, Louisiana, and Adjunct Assistant Professor and Member of the Graduate Faculty at Louisiana Tech. University–Barksdale Campus. He is the author of publications in the fields of public finance and the history of economic thought.

Samuel Hollander is a University Professor and Professor of Economics at the University of Toronto. He was elected Fellow of the Royal Society of Canada in 1976. He is the author of *The Sources of Increased Efficiency: A Case Study of Du Pont Rayon Plants* (1965), *The Economics of Adam Smith* (1973), *The Economics of David Ricardo* (1979), *The Economics of John Stuart Mill* (1985), and *Classical Economics* (1987); and is currently engaged on the economics of T.R. Malthus.

L.E. Johnson is Professor of Economics at Bemidji State University. He has previously served on the economics faculty at Cornell University, where he received his Ph.D. in 1975, Colgate University, and Wells College. He was a Visiting Scholar in the Dipartimento Di Teoria Economica e Metodi Quantitativi per ie Scelte Politiche at the University of Rome in 1987, and presently serves as Book Review Editor for the *Atlantic Economic Journal*. He is the co-author of the *Origins of Modern Economics: A Paradigmatic Approach* (1988), and has contributed numerous publications in labour economics, the history of economic analysis, and economic theory.

Ferdinando Meacci teaches Theory and Policy of Economic Growth at the University of Padua. He has been Visiting Professor of Economics at New York University and City University of New York. He is the author of several publications on the subjects of capital, technical progress and growth.

Sergio Nisticò graduated from the University of Rome where he now co-operates in the activity of the Chair of Economics in the Faculty of Political Sciences. He is the author of 'Prezzi Naturali e Conflitto Distributivo in Smith e Ricardo', *Studi Economici*, No. 36, 1988.

Roy J. Rotheim teaches in the Department of Economics at Skidmore College, New York. He was formerly Executive Editor of *Challenge Magazine*. His principal publications are in the areas of Post-Keynesian Economics and the Economics of Uncertainty.

Claudio Sardoni studied Economics at the Universities of Rome and of Adelaide, where he obtained the title of Doctor of Philosophy. He works at the University of Rome and also for the *Enciclopedia Italiana*, as Editor of a volume on the History of Economics in the 20th century. He is presently researching on the relationship between different market forms and effective demand. His main publications include *Marx and Keynes on Economic Recession* (1987) and several articles.

Mario Sebastiani is Professor of Economics at University of Rome II – 'Tor Vergata'. He was formerly Professor of Economics at the University of Perugia. He is the author of various works on Keynesian and post-Keynesian theories.

PART ONE THE FALLING RATE OF PROFIT AND THE FUTURE OF CAPITALISM

1 Marx and the falling rate of profit*

S. Hollander

Introduction

Marx considered his analysis of 'the tendency of the profit rate to fall as society progresses' to be 'one of the greatest triumphs over the *pons asini* of all previous political economy' (letter to Engels, 30 April 1868; in Marx and Engels 1988, p. 24). In *Capital* itself, the trend is represented as 'a logical necessity' flowing from 'the nature of the capitalist mode of production' (Volume III, p. 209). There can be no doubt about the high significance of the matter for Marx.

The analysis (*Capital*, Volume III, chapter 13) commences with an assumption of a given rate of surplus value s/v: the real wage basket per day and labour embodied therein, the length of work day and intensity of labour are all held constant (Volume III, pp. 207–8, 212–13; cf. p. 227). On this assumption, £100 of variable capital corresponds to the wages paid per period to a specific quantum of labour (or more accurately the value of these wages). As is common throughout *Capital* the rate of surplus value s/v is (initially) taken as 100 per cent – 'the labourers work daily as many hours for themselves, i.e., for the reproduction of their wages, as they do for the capitalist, i.e., for the production of surplus value' (p. 207). This given s/v, however, represents different rates of profit s/C according to the constant capital complement – again in terms of value – supporting labour. Thus:

c	v	S	$(c + v) = C$	$p' = s/C\%$
50	100	100	150	66⅔
100	100	100	200	50
200	100	100	300	33⅓
300	100	100	400	25
400	100	100	500	20

Marx observes that the profit rate p' (we shall call it R) declines because given s is calculated on a rising C (pp. 207–8). But Marx's usual practice

* My warm thanks to Carolyn Pitchik for taking me patiently through the mathematics (Appendix A), and to Lee Bailey, for his work on the computer (Appendix B).

is to work with a given C. It is preferable, therefore, to convert c and v to fractions of a total C of £100 value, thus:

c	v	s
33⅓	66⅔	66⅔
50	50	50
66⅔	33⅓	33⅓
75	25	25
80	20	20

The consequence of an increase in the c/v ratio (given s/v), is described in an important passage applying to the economy as a whole:

> If it is . . . assumed that this gradual change in the composition of capital is not confined only to individual spheres of production, but that it occurs more or less in all, or at least in the key spheres of production, so that it involves changes in the average organic composition of the total capital of a certain society, then the gradual growth of constant capital in relation to variable capital must necessarily lead to *a gradual fall of the general rate of profit*, so long as the rate of surplus-value, or the intensity of exploitation of labour by capital, remains the same. (p. 208)

It is apparent from his reference to average capital composition that in deriving the law of declining profits Marx presumes a solution to the transformation problem; the problems engendered by divergence between 'values' and prices of production are set aside. This, it has been shown recently, is a procedure with damaging consequences for the argument (e.g. Wolff 1979), but we shall assume the problem away in order to proceed with the main formulation – uniform composition would do the trick (cf. Dickinson 1956–7, p. 121n).

The assumptions of a constant s/v seems to be crucial to the case for a falling profit rate. This was how Joan Robinson (1942), and before her Bortkiewicz ([1907], 1952) approached the law. The assumption of constant s/v was essential to assure declining R, but raised insurmountable difficulties. For constant s/v, requires that rising productivity in the wage-goods industries – which implies increasing s/v – be exactly counterbalanced by rising commodity wages: 'Marx can only demonstrate a falling tendency in profits by abandoning his argument that real wages tend to be constant. This drastic inconsistency he seems to have overlooked, for when he is discussing the falling tendency of profits he makes no reference to the rising tendency of real wages which it entails' (p. 36). In fact, holding the real wage constant, and allowing for productivity increase, the rate of surplus value is unconstrained: for

$(v + s)$ is constant (with given labour time of given intensity), so that as v falls towards zero, s/v rises towards infinity. Robinson concludes: 'Marx's argument fails to establish a presumption that the rate of profit tends to fall' (p. 40). A similar objection will be found in Sweezy (1942, pp. 100–1) and Gillman (1956, p. 20); and we have a neat restatement of the Bortkiewicz–Robinson perspective in the charge that Marx failed to appreciate 'that the rate of surplus value is not only functionally but positively related to the very same process of mechanization that raises the organic composition of capital' (Blaug 1980, p. 46).

There are, on the other hand, those who deny Joan Robinson's contention, and go so far as to assert a *necessary* decline in R, on the basis of the absolute maximum to 'new value'. For example: 'an increase in the rate of surplus value cannot ultimately compensate for the rise in the organic composition of capital. That is, in the long run, the effect of the organic composition of capital will assert itself' (Cogoy [1973], 1987, p. 59). Similarly, Ronald Meek, in his well-known account, allows that while Marx was not justified in asserting (e.g. *Capital*, Volume III, p. 209) a continuous decline in R upon increase in c/v, his own arguments do allow one to say 'that there will eventually come a point beyond which no conceivable rise in the rate of surplus value – not even a rise to infinity – could possibly prevent the mass of surplus value produced by the given capital (and thus the rate of profit) from falling below its original level' (Meek 1967, p. 135). And Dickinson (1956–7) maintains that assuming (as he believed Marx did assume) s/v to be constant, the profit rate declines continuously; whereas allowing for increasing s/v simply introduces the possibility of an *initial* increase in R which is followed by a falling trend (p. 125). And he concludes his mathematical study thus: 'The sole value of an investigation such as this makes it impossible summarily to dismiss Marx's theory of the falling rate of profit as a mere chimera. Even though he left the proof of it in *Capital* mathematically incomplete, Marx's assertion that there was a connection between increasing organic composition of capital and a falling rate of profit was a sound intuition that a more rigorous method has largely justified' (p. 130).

In what follows, we shall take account of these sharply disparate views regarding the implications flowing from the characteristics of surplus value. We shall also consider Marx's basic assumption that an increase in the *technical* composition of capital – the 'physical' capital/labour ratio – is reflected in an increased *value* composition – the ratio of the value of constant capital to the value of variable capital (e.g. *Capital*, Volume III, p. 231).[1] For this assumption too has been subject to considerable criticism (e.g. Sweezy [1973], 1987). These tasks require that we first develop a framework to approach the issue – a framework faithful to Marx, and second that we get a firm grip on Marx's own position. It turns out that while the critics are correct that Marx failed to justify his case for a declining trend in the profit rate, the main reason offered for the failure – rising s/v – is inappropriate.

In the course of our analysis, which bears upon the contrast between Ricardian and Marxian economics, we consider the implications of allowing a differential impact of technology on the cost prices of wage-goods and capital-goods. Marx's case, it emerges rather unexpectedly, would be *strengthened* by assuming a relatively faster productivity increase in wage-goods production. Marx himself, however, did not take up this line of argument.

The conditions for falling *R*

The 'standard' formula for the Marxian profit rate is:

$$R = 100 \cdot s/(c + v) = 100 \frac{s/v}{(c/v) + 1}$$

where s, c and v refer to surplus, 'constant' capital and 'variable' capital, all in 'value' terms. This formula implies that both constant and variable capital are turned over once per period, i.e., that $(c + v)$ is the stock as well as the 'flow' of capital. Marx himself explicitly justified the simplification, as in the chapter on the formation of a general rate of profit:

> The magnitude of the actual value of [the] product depends on the magnitude of the fixed part of the constant capital, and on the portion which passes from it through wear and tear into the product. But since this circumstance has absolutely no bearing on the rate of profit, and hence, [on] the present analysis, we shall assume, for the sake of simplicity, that the constant capital is everywhere uniformly and entirely transferred to the annual product of the capitals (*Capital*, Volume III, p. 152).[2]

In the discussion of the falling profit rate, Marx also proceeds in this manner, obliging Engels to spell out the implicit assumption that 'capital is turned over in exactly one year' (p. 223; cf. p. 50 regarding the period of turnover of variable capital).[3]

While this is a useful formula it is more revealing if it is rewritten to specify explicitly the physical capital–labour ratio and the prices (values) of capital-goods and wage-goods. Moreover, we shall treat the variables in average terms (per unit of labour – say, the workday) rather than as totals. Selecting a day's labour as value unit, we have

$$R = 100 \cdot s/(c + v) = 100 \frac{L \cdot (\text{surplus per workday})}{L \cdot (\text{constant capital per workday}) + L \cdot (\text{variable capital per workday})}$$

$$= 100 \frac{L(1 - P_L)}{L \dfrac{(P_k K)}{L} + LP_L} = 100 \frac{(1 - P_L)}{\dfrac{P_k \cdot K}{L} + P_L}$$

where L is the number of workdays; $P_L < 1$ the value of the (given) commodity wage per day, the condition that labour embodied in the daily wage falls short of one day assuring a positive surplus; $(1 - P_L)$, the surplus generated per day; and $(P_k K)/L$ the value of constant capital per day.[4] Dividing through by P_L we obtain:

$$R = \frac{100 \cdot (1 - P_L)/P_L}{(P_K/P_L)(K/L) + 1} = \frac{100/P_L}{(P_K/P_L)(K/L) + 1} \cdot (1 - P_L)$$

The profit rate is thus the product of the *number of workdays employed per \$100 of capital invested*[5] and *surplus per day*.

Technical progress largely takes the form, for Marx, of raising K/L – say by a constant rate of increase α. Let the effect of such progress be to reduce (for simplicity without lag) the values of capital-goods, by β_K, and those of wage-goods, by β_L. We then have a time path for $R(n)$,

$$R(n) = L_{100}(n) \cdot [1 - P_L(1 - \beta_L)^n]$$

$$= \frac{\dfrac{100}{P_L(1 - \beta_L)^n}}{1 + \dfrac{P_K(1 - \beta_K)^n}{P_L(1 - \beta_L)^n} \cdot \dfrac{K}{L} \, (1 + \alpha)^n} \cdot [1 - P_L(1 - \beta_L)^n]$$

It is evident that a necessary (though insufficient) condition for falling R over time is falling L per \$100. For surplus per day is rising continuously towards 1, so that the product $L_{100}(1 - P_L)$ can fall only if L_{100} is falling.

We proceed to give the results for the *limit* to $R(n)$ – the 'ultimate' trend in the profit rate – with reference to three sets of situations: (1) $\beta_L = \beta_K$; (2) $\beta_L < \beta_K$, implying some check to the impact of new technology on the wage-goods sector relative to that on the capital-goods sector[6]; and (3) $\beta_L > \beta_K$. Since $\lim[1 - P_L(1 - \beta_L)^n]$ is 1, it does not enter into the calculation of $\lim R(n)$ – only L_{100} is relevant. (The details of the analysis are given in Appendix A.)

Uniform cost reductions (β) in capital- and wage-goods sectors: R tends to zero if $(1 - \beta)(1 + \alpha) > 1$, i.e., $\alpha > \beta/(1 - \beta)$ or $\beta < \alpha/(1 + \alpha)$ where α is the percentage annual increase in the technical capital–labour ratio or, in this case, in the organic composition of capital.

Non-uniform cost reduction ($\beta_L \neq \beta_K$):

$$\left[\frac{1 - \beta_K}{1 - \beta_L}(1 + \alpha)\right] \leqslant 1 \tag{1.1}$$

R tends to infinity.

$$\left[\frac{1 - \beta_K}{1 - \beta_L}(1 + \alpha)\right] > 1 \tag{1.2}$$

(i) $(1 - \beta_K)(1 + \alpha) \leqslant 1$, R tends to infinity.
(ii) $(1 - \beta_K)(1 + \alpha) > 1$, R tends to zero.

The first condition for ultimately falling R, which relates to the denominator in the expression

$$L_{100}(n) = 100 \frac{1/P_L(1 - \beta_L)^n}{1 + \dfrac{P_K(1 - \beta_K)^n}{P_L(1 - \beta_L)^n} \cdot K/L(1 + \alpha)^n},$$

implies that the value of capital-goods per labour unit relative to the value of the wage ($P_K K/P_L L$) – the 'value composition of capital' – is rising. (Where $\beta_K = \beta_L$ this condition *had* to be satisfied since the only force acting on the value composition is the rise in the capital–labour ratio, K/L.) In the event $\beta_K > \beta_L$, the ratio P_K/P_L declines, and should this decline outweigh the increase in the physical capital–labour ratio, $L_{100}(n) \to \infty$. However, with $\beta_L > \beta_K$ the upward pressure on the value composition is reinforced by a rising price ratio. But the denominator may rise less than the numerator. To avoid this outcome the second condition must be satisfied, namely $(1 - \beta_K)(1 + \alpha) > 1$ or $\alpha > \beta_K/(1 - \beta_K)$ – *the latter constituting in fact the sufficient condition for (ultimately) falling* $L_{100}(n)$.[7]

For a specific example of the case of uniform price reductions, we consider values for β of .03, .05, .09, and .091 with $\alpha = .10$:

β	$(1-\beta)(1+\alpha)$	$\lim_{n\to\infty} R(n)$
.03	$.97 \times 1.1 = 1.067 > 1$	0
.05	$.95 \times 1.1 = 1.045 > 1$	0
.09	$.91 \times 1.1 = 1.001 > 1$	0
.091	$.909 \times 1.1 = 0.9999 < 1$	∞

In brief, with the physical capital–labour rates rising at $\alpha = 0.1$ per period, the profit rate will (ultimately) decline for all β up to a value just short of .091; for higher β value, the trend is upwards. A detailed comparison between the cases, especially the speed of decline in the first three, can be made by reference to Appendix B, Figures 1.1(a)–(d).

In the case $\beta_K \neq \beta_L$ consider first $\beta_K = .09$, $\beta_L = .045$. Then

$$\left[\frac{1-\beta_K}{1-\beta_L}(1+\alpha)\right] = 1.048$$

and $(1-\beta_K)(1+\alpha) = 1.001$, so that R tends to zero. Needless to say, satisfaction of the second condition assures satisfaction of the first. But the opposite is not true. Thus with $\beta_K = 0.092$ and $\beta_L = .046$,

$$\left[\frac{1-\beta_K}{1-\beta_L}(1+\alpha)\right] = 1.047 > 1$$

but $(1-\beta_K)(1+a) = .999 < 1$ so that R tends to infinity. (See Appendix B, Figures 1.2(a)–(d).)

When we reverse the relative magnitudes of β_K and β_L, there occurs a startling transformation: in the case $\beta_L = .09$, $\beta_K = 0.045$, the decline in R now sets in much earlier and markedly so; and a similar pattern now also emerges for $\beta_L = .092$, $\beta_K = .046$. (For $(1-\beta_K)(1+\alpha) = .954(1.1) = 1.05 > 1$.) $\beta_L > \beta_K$ does not guarantee that $L_{100}(n)$ and therefore $R(n)$ tend to zero. (Thus $\beta_K = .0909$, $\beta_L = .091$, entails an ultimate decline in L_{100} and R; a slightly different configuration, $\beta_K = .09091$, $\beta_L = .091$, yields a continuous increase.) But $\beta_L > \beta_K$ does add to the pressures reducing L_n and R, and may transform a rising into a falling R trend. This result is not contingent upon the specific initial factor values or factor ratios selected. (For example: with

$K/L = 4$ and $P_K/P_L = 1$, almost the same pattern emerges as with the values in Appendix B, Figure 1.2, namely $K/L = .25$, $P_K/P_L = 20$.)

An ultimate decline in $R(n)$ does not, however, preclude an initially rising trend. Initial conditions do play a strategic role as far as concerns the entire course of $R(n)$. However, an upward trend is incompatible with an initial decline (see Appendix A).

Marx on the increasing rate of surplus value and the cheapening of constant capital

We shall draw upon the foregoing in our exegetical analysis of Marx's own position regarding the implications flowing from the nature of surplus value, and the behaviour of L per \$100. But before we can proceed to these tasks we must establish that Marx, who formulated his 'law' with constant s/v, makes it clear that he stood by the declining profit trend even in the event of rising s/v: 'the rate of surplus-value, at the same, or even a rising, degree of labour exploitation, is represented by a continually falling general rate of profit' (*Capital*, Volume III, p. 209). Or again in a useful summary of his position:

> The law of the falling rate of profit, which expresses the same, *or even a higher, rate of surplus value*, states . . . that any quantity of the average social capital, say, a capital of 100, comprises an ever larger portion of means of labour, and an ever smaller portion of living labour. Therefore, since the aggregate mass of living labour operating the means of production decreases in relation to the value of these means of production, it follows that the unpaid labour and the portion of value in which it is expressed must decline as compared to the value of the advanced total capital. Or: An ever smaller aliquot part of invested total capital is converted into living labour, and this total capital, therefore, absorbs in proportion to its magnitude less and less surplus-labour, *although the unpaid part of the labour applied may at the same time grow in relation to the paid part*. (pp. 211–12, emphasis added)[8]

Subsequently in the chapter, Marx frequently refers to a variation in the rate of exploitation 'through a drop in the value of wages due to an increase in the productiveness of labour' (as well as by lengthening or intensifying the working day) (p. 215; cf. pp. 218, 221), without suggesting that such variation threatened the law. It is regrettable that Marx failed to spell out the relevant constraints on surplus per man in the chapter entitled 'The law as such'. But it is already clear that, even in this chapter, he stood by the position that the profit rate declines *notwithstanding* an increasing rate of exploitation, a fact much emphasized by Ronald Meek (1967, p. 131) following Rosdolsky (1980, pp. 398–411).[9]

This conclusion may be reinforced by reference to the profit rate decline in the subsequent chapter on 'counteracting tendencies'. Here, allusions to extensions of the workday and intensification of labour (pp. 227–8) are followed by a most revealing observation regarding the reduced cost of producing wage-goods – increased '*relative*' surplus value:

> Moreover, it has already been demonstrated – and this constitutes the real secret of the tendency of the rate of profit to fall – that *the manipulations to produce relative surplus-value* amount, on the whole, to transforming as much as possible of a certain quantity of labour into surplus-value, on the one hand, and employing as little labour as possible in proportion to the invested capital, on the other, so that the same reasons which permit *raising the intensity of exploitation* rule out exploiting the same quantity of labour as before by the same capital. These are the counteracting tendencies, which, while effecting *a rise in the rate of surplus-value*, also tend to decrease the mass of surplus-value, and hence the rate of profit produced by a certain capital. (p. 228, emphasis added)

Or again: the 'same factors which raise the rate of relative surplus value, lower the mass of the employed labour-power' (p. 229). And yet more specifically:

> The tendency of the rate of profit to fall is bound up with a tendency of the rate of surplus-value to rise, hence with a tendency for the rate of labour exploitation to rise. . . . The rate of profit does not fall because labour becomes less productive, but because it becomes more productive. Both the rise in the rate of surplus value and the fall in the rate of profit are but specific forms through which growing productivity of labour is expressed under capitalism. (p. 234)

The foregoing position is further reiterated at the outset of the third chapter of the trio dealing with the profit rate decline – on 'internal contradictions of the law': 'We have just seen that even a rising rate of surplus-value has a tendency to express itself in a falling rate of profit' (p. 236). And subsequently in this same chapter the theme is again taken up in an elaboration of the development of the 'social productiveness of labour' (p. 242). Rising productivity manifests itself both in rising s/v – 'the reduction of the necessary labour time required for the production of labour-power' – and rising c/v – 'the decrease in the quantity of labour-power (the number of labourers) generally employed to set in motion a given capital'. These 'two movements not only go hand in hand, but mutually influence one another and are phenomena in which the same law expresses itself'.

Evidently the rising rate of exploitation alluded to here is *not* a 'counteracting tendency' in the sense of a 'disturbing cause' or change in *ceteris paribus* conditions, but a variation built into the process of rising K/L. Meek (1967, p. 136) defended Marx on these lines against the criticisms of Joan Robinson and others. But he does concede some validity to the complaint that Marx treats reductions in the value of constant capital – the 'cheapening' of constant capital – as a counter-acting cause incidental only to the law (see also Dickinson 1956–7, p. 123; Dobb 1959, pp. 99–100). The fact is, however, that just as Marx allows in stating the law for rising s/v due to reductions in v, so he allows for 'cheapening' of c, taking the position that despite such cheapening the value composition of capital can be expected to rise with increases in the technical composition, thus reducing employment per $100 of investment:

> the same development which increases the mass of the constant capital in relation to the variable reduces the value of its elements as a result of the increased productivity of labour, and therefore prevents the value of constant capital, although it continuously increases, from increasing at the same rate as its material volume, i.e., the material volume of the means of production set in motion by the same amount of labour power . . . [T]he same influences which tend to make the rate of profit fall, also moderate the effects of this tendency. (*Capital*, Volume III, p. 231)

Still, as we shall now see, there is this important difference between the allowances for rising s/v and for rising c/v – that the former has a sound rationale whereas the latter merely reflects a particular empirical estimate. It is also pertinent that Marx neglects the impact on c/v of rising productivity in the wage-goods sector (see below, pp. 19–20).

The limited impact of rising s/v

We shall return to the value composition and its trend after looking more closely at the rationale behind Marx's presumption regarding the limited impact of rising s/v or (for this amounts to precisely the same thing) the limits to surplus per unit of labour (say, per day).

In the *Grundrisse*, Marx states very clearly the limits to the rise in s as v per day falls. The passages explain an element of his rationale for a falling profit rate far more satisfactorily than do the formulations given in *Capital* itself:

> the smaller the fractional part of the [given] working day which forms the equivalent of the worker, which expresses necessary labour, the smaller is the increase in surplus value which capital obtains from [a given] increase of productive force. Its surplus value rises, but in an ever smaller relation to the development of the productive force. Thus the more developed capital already is, the more surplus labour it has created, the more terribly must it develop the productive force in order to realize itself in only smaller

> proportion, i.e. to add surplus value – because its barrier always remains the relation between the fractional part of the day which expresses *necessary* labour, and the entire working day. It can move only within these boundaries. The smaller already the fractional part falling to *necessary labour*, the greater the *surplus labour*, the less can any increase in productive force perceptibly diminish necessary labour; since the denominator has grown enormously. . . . The increase of productive force would become irrelevant to capital. . . . If necessary labour were 1/1000 and the productive force tripled, then it would fall to only 1/3000 or surplus labour would have increased by only 2/3000. (1973, pp. 340–1)

The point here is that each given successive cost reduction of, say, β per cent has a declining absolute impact on surplus per day; so that once the value of the wage basket has fallen to very low levels in consequence of the cumulative effect of the annual cost reductions, a further cost reduction of β per cent will have a negligible absolute impact on the surplus. (This reflects the simple fact that value per day is a constant and divided between surplus and necessary labour; though s/v rises to infinity as $v \rightarrow 0$, absolute s has an upper limit.) Consequently, as P_L falls by β per cent annually, we have surplus per day, $(1 - P_L)$, rising *at an ever decreasing* rate.

Subsequently, Marx asserts: 'as we have seen, relative *surplus value* rises much more slowly than the force of production, and moreover this proportion grows ever smaller as the magnitude reached by the productive force is greater' (1973, p. 422). This statement is acceptable if it is intended as the proposition that any given 'force of production', cutting costs by β per cent annually, will *ultimately* exceed the percentage impact on surplus per working day since the latter is continuously declining towards (though never reaching) zero.

The passages from the *Grundrisse* say nothing explicitly about the force of the (declining) rate of increase in surplus per man *relative to the fall in employment per \$100*, upon which, of course, depends surplus per \$100. This issue is broached in Part III of *Theories of Surplus Value* and Volume I of *Capital*:

> If the normal working-day remains the same, surplus labour can be increased relatively by reducing the necessary labour-time and reducing the prices of the necessaries which the worker consumes, in comparison with the development of the productive power of labour. But this very development of productive power reduces variable capital relative to constant. It is physically impossible that the surplus labour-time of, say, two men who displace twenty, can, by any conceivable increase of the absolute or relative [surplus] labour-time, equal that of the twenty. If each of the twenty men only work 2 hours of surplus labour a day, the total will be 40 hours of surplus labour, whereas the total life span of the two men amounts only to 48 hours in one day. (1971, p. 300)

> . . . the compensation of a decrease in the number of labourers employed, or of the amount of variable capital advanced, by a rise in the rate of surplus-value, or by the lengthening of the working-day, has impassable limits. Whatever the value of labour-power may be, whether the working-time necessary for the maintenance of the labourer is 2 or 10 hours, the total value that a labourer can produce, day in, day out, is always less than the value in which 24 hours of labour are embodied. . . . The absolute limit of the average working day – this being by nature always less than 24 hours – sets an absolute limit to the compensation of a reduction of variable capital by a higher rate of surplus-value, or of the decrease of the number of labourers exploited by a higher degree of exploitation of labour-power. This palpable law is of importance for the clearing up of many phenomena, arising from a tendency (to be worked out later on) of capital to reduce as much as possible the number of labourers employed by it, or its variable component transformed into labour-power, in contradiction to its other tendency to produce the greatest possible mass of surplus-value. (*Capital*, Volume I, pp. 305–6)

These passages insist that there are 'impassable limits' to the compensation for falling net value per $100 – i.e., falling employment per $100 – that can be generated by rising surplus per workday. They are important passages for they cover not merely the limits imposed on lengthening the working day – absolute surplus value – but those imposed on *relative* surplus value (in line with the *Grundrisse*).

A famous passage from Volume III, in the chapter on internal contradictions of the law, also touches on the issue of the relative strengths of the labour-reducing (and thus value-reducing) and surplus-increasing forces – on the one hand, *L* per $100 and, on the other, surplus per hour and thus surplus per $100:

> Inasmuch as the development of the productive forces reduces the paid portion of employed labour, it raises the surplus value, because it raises its rate [of surplus-value]; but inasmuch as it reduces the total mass of labour employed by a given capital [$100], it reduces the factor of the number by which the rate of surplus-value is multiplied to obtain its mass. Two labourers, each working 12 hours daily, cannot produce the same mass of surplus-value as 24 who work only 2 hours, even if they could live on air and hence did not have to work for themselves at all. In this respect, then, the compensation of the reduced number of labourers by intensifying the degree of exploitation has certain insurmountable limits. It may, for this reason, well check the fall in the rate of profit, but cannot prevent it altogether. (*Capital*, Volume III, p. 242)

The opening reference to reductions in the 'paid portion of employed labour' due to the 'development of the productive forces' might, in itself, be read as an illusion to the fall in *v* due to technical progress – reductions in the cost of producing wage-goods. Unfortunately, Marx proceeds to illustrate his contention that the profit rate decline is only checked and not prevented, by reference to the limited effects of extensions in the length of the working day. Now of course such extensions are constrained by the 'insurmountable limits' of nature (or by legislation). Marx seems to forget the impact of efficiency increase with which the passage apparently commences. This, however, is precisely the key issue; extensions of the working day or of the intensity of labour are merely sideshows because of their quantitative limits. But we need not stress this weakness, since Marx has said enough to make it clear that his proposition is intended to hold good generally – i.e., even if we assume working days of given length and intensity – once allowance is made for the impact upon v of new technology.

As we know from the earlier section on the conditions for falling R (pp. 6–8), declining R requires that L_{100} fall over time; for $(1 - P_L)$ is rising and a rising L_{100} would confirm an upward trend in R. Marx proceeded by taking for granted that L_{100} does indeed decline. On this assumption he is correct that R will fall (at least ultimately); because of the limits to compensation deriving from rising surplus per unit of labour, the relative impact of declining L per \$100 is constantly growing. R may yet rise at initial stages of the trend path notwithstanding falling L per \$100 should this decline be outweighed by the rising trend in surplus per man. But this Marx seems to have appreciated; at least he sometimes states that the law applies 'in the long run': 'The rate of profit could even rise if a rise in the rate of surplus-value were accompanied by a substantial reduction in the value of the elements of constant, and particularly of fixed, capital. But in reality, as we have seen, the rate of profit will fall in the long run' (*Capital*, Volume III, p. 225). Similarly, the 'long-period' property of the law emerges in the chapter on counteracting tendencies:

> We have thus seen in a general way that the same influences which produce a tendency in the general rate of profit to fall, also call forth counter-effects, which hamper, retard, and partly paralyse this fall. The latter do not do away with the law, but impair its effect. Otherwise, it would not be the fall of the general rate of profit, but rather its relative slowness, that would be incomprehensible. Thus the law acts only as a tendency. And it is only under certain circumstances *and only after long periods* that its effects become strikingly pronounced. (p. 233, emphasis added)

Of course, even assuming that our parameters β_K, β_L and α are such as to assure a fall in $L(n)$ (and thus in R) there is no guarantee that the decline will set in within a period of much interest to anyone: the 'long-run' may be very long indeed (cf. Dickinson 1956–7, p. 129; Meek 1967, p. 135). And the decline may be almost imperceptible – except to a computer calculating to 16 decimal places. This too seems to be implied in the foregoing passage.

The major problem, however, is that L per \$100 need not necessarily fall; Marx and his defenders, who insist on the ultimate *necessity* of a declining R, have put excessive weight on the limit to surplus per hour – itself a valid notion, at least within the 'value' framework. For, as we have seen, even a rising value composition – the condition is that $\frac{1-\beta_K}{1-\beta_L}(1+\alpha) > 1$ – does not *guarantee* falling L_n. But secondly, the value composition of capital may not rise despite an increase in the physical capital–labour ratio. (For example with $\beta_K = .091$, $\beta_L = .0455$ and $\alpha = .1$ the value composition rises; but with α at .05 the same β values yield a decline.)

It has, on the other hand, emerged from our analysis that the case for falling R is enhanced by assuming $\beta_L > \beta_K$. A lag in the impact of new technology on wage-goods, so it may be supposed, will put *downward* pressure on the profit rate, since the rise in s/v is muted.[10] But this is not the case. The opposite is true – a relatively unprogressive wage-goods sector implies a lower value composition than in the opposite case, for P_K/P_L is lower, and to that extent *stimulates* L per \$100 and R. In the next section we shall consider Marx's position regarding the relative progressiveness of the two sectors.

The implications of differential rates of cost decline

We note first a possibly relevant concession on Marx's part regarding the scope of his 'law'. In the course of his exposition Marx, as we know, insists that the rate of profit falls despite a rising s/v. But he also adds the proviso that uniform technical progress is the exception:

> *Outside of a few cases (for instance, if the productiveness of labour uniformly cheapens all elements of the constant, and the variable, capital), the rate of profit will fall, in spite of the higher rate of surplus value*, (1) because even a larger unpaid portion of the smaller total amount of newly added labour is smaller than a smaller aliquot unpaid portion of the former larger amount, and (2) because the higher composition of capital is expressed in the individual commodity by the fact that the portion of its value in which newly added labour is materialized decreases in relation to the portion of its value which represents raw and auxiliary material, and the wear and tear of fixed capital. (*Capital*, Volume III, p. 222)

Clause (1) relates to the limited impact of rising surplus per unit of labour; clause (2) alludes to the rise in value composition. And the case for falling R is said *not* to apply where $\beta_K = \beta_L$; $\beta_K \neq \beta_L$ is represented as a necessary condition for the argument.

What may Marx have intended by thus restricting the scope of his law of falling R? After all, a uniform rate of value decrease, i.e., constant P_K/P_L, does assure a rise in value (in this case organic) composition equal to α. (It is true though that L_n and R will not necessarily fall.) In the event $\beta_K > \beta_L$, P_K/P_L tends downwards checking the value composition and acting *against* a decline in L_{100} and R – a 'counteracting force'. The case for a falling L_N and R is, on the other hand, greatly strengthened by assuming relatively rapid progress in wage-goods production, i.e., $\beta_L > \beta_K$ and thus rising P_K/P_L. It cannot be ruled out that Marx intended by his restriction to limit his falling R to such cases. It is still possible on this view to incorporate the 'cheapening of the elements of constant capital' as a counteracting force to the decline in R; for the profit rate decline would be yet sharper should the capital-goods sector be unaffected by new technology. Whether or not this was Marx's intention, the notion that the value composition rises despite the impact of new technology upon the price of 'constant capital' can be more easily justified if we assume a relatively greater impact upon the price of wage-goods.

But this is inconclusive. We must look more closely at Marx's empirical evaluation of the relative impact of new technology. There is much discussion in *Theories of Surplus Value* (1861–3) regarding this issue. There are passages which suggest a faster rate of agricultural than industrial improvement under advanced capitalism – in contrast to early capitalism:

> In the period of the stormy growth of capitalist production, productivity in industry develops rapidly as compared with agriculture, although its development *presupposes* that a significant change as between constant and variable capital *has* already taken place in agriculture, that is, a large number of people have been driven off the land. Later, productivity advances in both, although at an uneven pace. But when industry reaches a certain level the disproportion must diminish, in other words, productivity in agriculture must increase relatively more rapidly than in industry. This requires: 1. The replacement of the easy-going farmer by the businessman, the farming capitalist; transformation of the husbandman into a pure wage-labourer; large-scale agriculture, i.e., with concentrated capitals. 2. In particular however: Mechanics, the really scientific basis of large-scale industry, had reached a certain degree of perfection during the eighteenth century. The development of chemistry, geology and physiology, the sciences that *directly* form the specific basis of agriculture rather than of industry, does not take place till the nineteenth century and especially the later decades. (1968, Part II, p. 110)[11]

On this view there had occurred or was actually underway a transition between the relative growth rates of productivity favouring agriculture.

However, as Perelman (1985) has pointed out, elsewhere in the same work a certain pessimism intrudes regarding prospects for agriculture under capitalist organization, with special reference to soil exhaustion:

> The development of productive power is not even. It is in the nature of capitalist production that it develops industry more rapidly than agriculture. This is not due to the nature of the land, but to the fact that, in order to be exploited really in accordance with its nature, land requires different social relations. Capitalist production turns towards the land only after its influence has exhausted it and after it has devastated its natural qualities. (1971, Part III, pp. 300–301)

Whether there occurred a 'sudden' change in viewpoint (Perelman, p. 470) is open to question. Marx may well have distinguished between shorter- and longer-run prospects. This seems to be the case in *Capital*. Here agriculture is represented as subject, to a peculiar degree, to labour-displacing technology – so much so that while aggregate industrial employment expands over time, agricultural employment declines: 'As soon as capitalist production takes possession of agriculture, and in proportion to the extent to which it does so, the demand for an agricultural labouring population falls absolutely, while the accumulation of capital employed in agriculture advances' (*Capital*, Volume I, p. 642; cf. Volume III, p. 622). At the same time, Marx warned of dangerous prospects ahead:

> all progress in capitalist agriculture is a progress in the art, not only of robbing the labourer, but of robbing the soil; all progress in increasing the fertility of the soil for a given time, is a progress towards ruining the lasting sources of that fertility. The more a country starts its development on the foundation of modern industry, like the United States, for example, the more rapid is this process of destruction. Capitalist production, therefore, develops technology and the combining together of various processes into a social whole, only by sapping the original sources of all wealth – the soil and the labourer. (Volume I, pp. 506–7)

Similarly, in Volume III, it emerges that while capitalism promotes agricultural technology it does so at the expense of (ultimate) exhaustion of the soil:

> The moral of history, also to be deduced from the observations concerning agriculture, is that the capitalist system works against a rational agriculture, or that a rational agriculture is incompatible with the capitalist system (although the latter promotes technical improvements in agriculture), and needs either the hand of the small farmer living by his own labour or the control of associated producers. (*Capital*, Volume III, p. 119)[12]

But even allowing for soil exhaustion (and assuming this implies a lag in agricultural productivity) it would still not be certain that wage-goods prices fall less rapidly than capital-goods prices. Raw materials constitute an important part of *constant* capital; to that extent any constraint upon the impact of new technology in the extractive industries acts to maintain the value composition of capital by raising P_K relative to P_L with a negative effect on R. Marx is explicit on this score:

> It is obvious that the quantity of raw material must increase proportionally with the productivity of labour; . . . [But] some kinds of raw materials, such as wool, silk, leather, are produced by animal *organic* materials, while *cotton*, *linen*, etc. are produced by vegetable organic processes and capitalist production has not yet succeeded, and never will succeed in mastering these processes in the same way as it has mastered purely mechanical or inorganic chemical processes. Raw materials such as skins, etc., and other animal products become dearer partly because the insipid law of rent increases the value of these products as civilisation advances. As far as coal and metal (wood) are concerned, they become much cheaper with the advance of production; this will however become more difficult as mines are exhausted, etc. (Marx 1971, pp. 367–8)

The question that remains is whether similar constraints keep up the value of *variable* capital – wage-goods. The argument in *Theories of Surplus Value* regarding the limits to increasing surplus value relative to falling employment (see above, p. 13) is followed immediately by the assertion that 'the value of labour-power does not fall in the same degree as the productivity of labour as capital increases'. This might mean no more than $\beta_L < \alpha$; but the assertion is justified in terms of the more rapid development of industry (cited above, p. 18) and this suggests $\beta_L < \beta_K$.[13] The evidence, therefore, is mixed, but on balance it seems fair to conclude that Marx viewed with some pessimism the relative prospects for agricultural technology under capitalism in the very long term.

But what to make of this weighting? One cannot easily escape the impression that Marx wished to avoid taking up the impact of wage-goods prices on R via the value composition of capital; it is the impact via the rate of surplus value – the limited impact – upon which he concentrates. Thus, in discussing the formation of a general rate of profit (*Capital*, Volume III, chapter ix), he writes that 'the organic composition of capital depends at any time on two circumstances: first, on the technical relation of labour-power employed to the mass of the means of production employed [our K/L]; secondly, on the price of these means of production [our P_K]' (p. 152) – P_L is entirely neglected. The chapter on countervailing influences to the law of falling R (Volume III, chapter xiv) alludes to falling wage-goods prices but allows for an impact on R only by way of the rate of surplus value: 'Since foreign trade partly cheapens the elements of constant capital, and partly the necessities of life for which the variable capital is exchanged, it tends to raise the rate of profit by increasing the rate of surplus-value and lowering the value of constant capital' (*Capital*, Volume III, p. 232). Marx seems to forget that v is the denominator not only of s/v but also of c/v; lowering the value of 'constant capital' says very little if the value of wage-goods is also falling. In the same chapter he refers to increasing relative surplus value (by way of reduction in wage-goods costs) as a force raising or maintaining the profit rate in a case where technology is such as not to require a higher K/L ratio: 'Everything that promotes the production of relative surplus value by mere improvement in methods, as in agriculture, without altering the magnitude of the invested capital, has the same effect [in raising the profit rate]' (*Capital*, Volume III, p. 228). Doubtless he intended to define instances where increasing K/L is not involved in order to assure the force of rising s/v undiminished by rising c/v; but again he neglects the fact that, even with given K/L, c/v rises with falling v. As a final example, consider the interesting complexity allowed by Marx, that a rise in productivity in the capital goods sector can affect R by raising s/v as well as by lowering c/v:

> If the decrease in the expenditure of constant capital is due to economies, etc., in lines of production whose products enter into the labourer's consumption, then this, just like the direct increase in the productivity of the employed labour itself, may lead to a decrease in wages due to a cheapening of the means of subsistence of the labourer, and may lead, therefore, to an increase in the surplus-value; so that the rate of profit in this case would grow for two reasons, namely, on the one hand, because the value of constant capital decreases, and on the other hand, because the surplus-value increases. (Volume III, p. 836)

Again the fall in v is allowed to act on s/v but not on c/v.

Marx's rather cavalier approach towards the determinants of c/v cannot be justified. If, as seems to be his position, the fall of materials' prices is ultimately destined to lag behind those of capital goods proper because of the exhaustibility of natural resources, then β_K (which relates to capital-goods proper as well as materials) will exceed β_L, so that P_K/P_L falls with a *positive* effect on R, via the lower value composition of capital.

Concluding comments

A necessary and sufficient condition for the tendency of the profit rate to decline within a Marxian framework is $(1 - \beta_K)(1 + \alpha) > 1$ or $\alpha > \beta_K/(1 - \beta_K)$, i.e., that the rate of increase in the physical capital–labour ratio exceeds β_K (the rate of decline in P_K) relative to $(1 - \beta_K)$, a ratio equalling the rate of increase of $1/(1 - \beta_K)$" (see note 7). This at first sight is a surprising property, since the rate of change in P_L, or β_L, does not appear at all. But of course β_L is relevant; for example, a sufficiently low β_L will assure

$$\frac{1 - \beta_K}{1 - \beta_L}(1 + \alpha) < 1,$$

i.e., falling value composition, rendering satisfaction of the necessary and sufficient condition impossible. We have seen that $\beta_L < \beta_K$ rather than the reverse can, *ceteris paribus*, transform a falling into a rising trend in R.

The condition in question concerns the behaviour of L_{100}, i.e., employment per \$100 of capital invested; the ultimate course of R depends on this alone and those criticisms of Marx which emphasize the fact that surplus per hour rises continuously as the value of wage-goods declines (i.e., that $s/v \rightarrow \infty$) are misplaced. But it is true that whether the condition is or is not satisfied is entirely an empirical matter; there is no a priori reason to justify a presumption in favour of falling R.[14]

There is first the fact, of which Marx himself was so well aware, that the very existence of a large stock of capital promotes capital-saving innovation (cf. Rosenberg 1976); there is no necessity for $\alpha > 0$. In this chapter, however, we have concentrated on the β_K–β_L relation, and have indicated that Marx himself seems to point to $\beta_L < \beta_K$ as a long-term prospect, having in mind the phenomenon of land exhaustion. This too mitigates against the falling profit rate tendency. All in all, Marx insisted, in deriving his 'law', upon rising c/v; his 'forecast' might have been valid for conditions pertaining at his time, but not for those of a more advanced capitalism – one utilizing on balance capital-saving technology and running into land-exhaustion problems.

Let us take a somewhat broader view of the latter issues. Marx objected to Ricardo for identifying R and its variations with s/v and its variations (e.g. *Capital*, Volume III, p. 45). There is good reason for the objection. For one thing, Ricardo erred seriously by neglecting the negative impact on R of secularly-rising material prices. (He was able to do so by an unstated assumption that materials are required only by industry; should materials be required in all sectors there is no way capitalists in any single sector can pass on the burden of rising costs to the consumer.) Marx also wished to avoid an analysis of R and its falling trend which turned on the implications flowing from land scarcity –

technological improvement was the order of the day within a capitalist organization.

The new model takes into account the impact upon R of a range of cost variation – the cost prices of capital-goods proper and materials as well as of wage-goods – and allows for cost reduction due to new technology. Marx apparently had in mind, at least for the distant future, a sluggish rate of decline of material and wage-goods prices compared with those of capital-goods in consequence of land exhaustion. He thus brings the land constraint back into the picture. He blames the phenomenon on capitalism not nature (see above, p. 18), although this is not altogether convincing since co-operative or peasant farmers must devote resources to avoid the problem. Schefold (1976) has pointed to the extract from *Theories of Surplus Value*, Volume III, pp. 367–8 (cited above, p. 19), as an indication that Marx, in order to assure rising c/v, 'retreat[ed] to a Ricardian explanation of the tendency of the rate of profit to fall', notwithstanding his 'scorn' for the technological determinism of Ricardo and Malthus. But this is not quite so. It emerges from our discussion that a differential against the extractive sectors – both materials and wage-goods production – has on balance a positive impact on R by reducing the value composition of capital. Any further constraint on the decline in wage-goods prices compared with those of materials acts further to maintain the profit rate, again by lowering c/v. It is true, however, that a *positive increase* in wage-goods costs must – whatever the levels of β_K and α – generate an ultimate fall in the profit rate.[15] There is nothing in Marx's theoretical model which precludes the 'classical' source of declining R.

Appendix A

Determination of limit $L_{100}(n)$

With uniform β_K and β_L the factor price ratio P_K/P_L is a constant, i.e., $(1 - \beta_K)$ and $(1 - \beta_L)$ cancel out in the denominator for $L_{100}(n)$. Now the numerator and denominator in the expression for L_{100} both approach ∞; to obtain the limit in this case requires that we take the limit of the derivative of the numerator relative to the derivative of the denominator. Rewriting L_{100} in logarithmic terms we have

$$L_{100}(n) = \frac{100/P_L\ [e^{-n\ln(1-\beta_L)}]}{1 + (P_K/P_L) \cdot (K/L)\ e^{n\ln(1+\alpha)}}$$

$$\lim_{n\to\infty} L_{100}(n)$$

$$= \frac{(100/P_L)(-\ln(1-\beta_L))}{(P_K/P_L)(K/L)} \cdot \lim_{n\to\infty} \frac{1}{[(1-\beta)(1+\alpha)]^n}$$

It follows that

$$\lim_{n\to\infty} R(n) = \lim_{n\to\infty} L_{100}(n) = 0$$

for $(1-\beta)(1+\alpha) > 1$; and ∞ for $(1-\beta)(1+\alpha) < 1$.

We turn to $\beta_L \neq \beta_K$. Again omitting

$$\lim_{n\to\infty} [1 - P_L(1-\beta_L)^n] = 1$$

in the calculation of $\lim_{n\to\infty} R$ we require

$$\lim_{n\to\infty} L_{100}(n)$$

$$= \lim_{n\to\infty} \frac{(100/P_L)\, e^{-n\ln(1-\beta_L)}}{1 + (P_K/P_L)\cdot(K/L)\, e^{n\ln(1-\beta_K)}\, e^{-n\ln(1-\beta_L)}\, e^{n\ln(1+\alpha)}}$$

Now

$$\lim_{n\to\infty} e^{n\ln(1-\beta_K)}\, e^{-n\ln(1-\beta_L)}\, e^{n\ln(1+\alpha)} = \lim_{n\to\infty} \left[\frac{1-\beta_K}{1-\beta_L}(1+\alpha)\right]^n$$

With $\dfrac{1-\beta_K}{1-\beta_L}(1+\alpha) < 1$, the limit of the denominator,

$$1 + (P_K/P_L)\cdot(K/L) \lim_{n\to\infty} \left[\frac{1-\beta_K}{1-\beta_L}(1+\alpha)\right]^n = 1.$$

Accordingly $\lim_{n\to\infty} L_{100}(n)$

reduces to $\lim_{n\to\infty} (100/P_L)\, e^{-n\ln(1-\beta_L)}$

or $\lim_{n\to\infty} 100/P_L(1-\beta_L)^n = \infty$. The profit rate tends upwards.

If, however, $\dfrac{1-\beta_K}{1-\beta_L}(1+\alpha) > 1$ then the limit to the denominator is ∞; since the limit of the numerator is also ∞ we must take the limit of the derivative of the numerator/derivative of the denominator:

$$\lim_{n\to\infty} \quad L_{100}(n)$$

$$= \frac{(100/P_L)(-\ln(1-\beta_L))e^{-n\ln(1-\beta_L)}}{(P_K/P_L)\cdot(K/L)\ln\left[\dfrac{1-\beta_K}{1-\beta_L}(1+\alpha)\right] e^{n\ln\left[\frac{1-\beta_K}{1-\beta_L}(1+\alpha)\right]}}$$

$$= \frac{(100/P_L)(-\ln(1-\beta_L))}{(P_K/P_L)\cdot(K/L)\ln\left[\dfrac{1-\beta_K}{1-\beta_L}(1+\alpha)\right]} \cdot \lim_{n\to\infty} \frac{1}{[(1-\beta_K)(1+\alpha)]^n}$$

It follows that

$$\lim_{n\to\infty} R(n) = \lim_{n\to\infty} L_{100}(n) = 0$$

for $(1-\beta_K)(1+\alpha) > 1$; and ∞ for $(1-\beta_K)(1+\alpha) < 1$.

Determination of R′(0)

$$R(n) = 100 \frac{\dfrac{1 - P_L(1-\beta_L)^n}{P_L(1-\beta_L)^n}}{1 + \dfrac{P_K}{P_L}\dfrac{(1-\beta_K)^n}{(1-\beta_L)^n} \cdot \dfrac{K}{L}(1+\alpha)^n}$$

$$= 100 \frac{[1 - P_L e^{n\ln(1-\beta_L)}]\ e^{-n\ln(1-\beta_L)}}{P_L\left[1 + \dfrac{P_K}{P_L} \cdot \dfrac{K}{L}\ e^{n\ln}\left[\dfrac{1-\beta_K}{1-\beta_L}(1+\alpha)\right]\right]}$$

$$= 100 \frac{e^{-n\ln(1-\beta_L)} - P_L}{P_L\left[1 + \dfrac{P_K}{P_L} \cdot \dfrac{K}{L}\ e^{n\ln}\left[\dfrac{1-\beta_K}{1-\beta_L}(1+\alpha)\right]\right]} = \frac{100}{P_L}\frac{f(n)}{g(n)}$$

Let $\tilde{R}(n) = f(n)/g(n)$. Then $\tilde{R}'(n)$

$$= \frac{[-\ln(1-\beta_L)\ e^{-n\ln(1-\beta_L)}]\left[1 + \dfrac{P_K}{P_L} \cdot \dfrac{K}{L}\ e^{n\ln}\left[\dfrac{1-\beta_K}{1-\beta_L}(1+\alpha)\right]\right] - [e^{-n\ln(1-\beta_L)} - P_L]\left[\dfrac{P_K}{P_L}\dfrac{K}{L} \cdot \ln\left[\dfrac{1-\beta_K}{1-\beta_L}(1+\alpha)\right] e^{n\ln}\left[\dfrac{1-\beta_K}{1-\beta_L}(1-\alpha)\right]\right]}{(g(n))^2}$$

The sign of $\tilde{R}'(n)$ will equal the sign of the numerator since the denominator $> 0\ \forall\ n$. Let $H(n)$ equal the numerator. Then

$$H(n) = -\ln(1-\beta_L)\,e^{-n\ln(1-\beta_L)}$$

$$+\frac{P_K}{P_L}\frac{K}{L}e^{n\ln\left[\frac{1-\beta_K}{1-\beta_L}(1+\alpha)\right]}$$

$$\left[P_L\ln\left[\frac{1-\beta_K}{1-\beta_L}(1+\alpha)\right] - \ln(1-\beta_L)e^{-n\ln(1-\beta_L)}\right.$$

$$\left. -\ln\left[\frac{1-\beta_K}{1-\beta_L}(1+\alpha)\right]e^{-n\ln(1-\beta_L)}\right]$$

$$H(0) = -\ln(1-\beta_L) + \frac{P_K}{P_L}\cdot\frac{K}{L}$$

$$\left[P_L\ln\left[\frac{1-\beta_K}{1-\beta_L}(1+\alpha)\right] - \ln[(1-\beta_K)(1+\alpha)]\right]$$

We shall now consider $H(0)$ in our three general cases (see above). The tendency for R ultimately to fall is assured by $\frac{1-\beta_K}{1-\beta_L}(1+\alpha) > (1-\beta_K)(1+\alpha) > 1$ – case 1.2(ii). But $H(0)$ may be either positive or negative, depending upon initial conditions. Thus $R(n)$ may initially increase, or may decline continuously. In the expression for $H(0)$, the first element $-\ln(1-\beta_L) > 0$ since $(1 - \beta_L)$ and $\ln(1-\beta_L) < 0$; this is true in all cases. The second element > 0 since $\frac{1-\beta_K}{1-\beta_L}(1+\alpha) > 1$ and its logarithm > 0. But from these must be deducted a positive number since $(1-\beta_K)(1+\alpha) > 1$ and $\ln[(1-\beta_K)(1+\alpha)] > 0$. The net outcome will depend on specific initial values.

Inspection of $H(0)$ indicates that $H(0) < 0$ – implying a continuous fall in R – requires $P_L(<1)$ sufficiently low to assure a negative multiplicand of $(P_K/P_L)\cdot(K/L)$. This is confirmed by rearranging $H(0)$ in the form

$$H(0) = -\ln(1-\beta_L) + \frac{P_K}{P_L}\frac{K}{L}$$

$$[P_L\ln[(1-\beta_K)(1+\alpha)] - P_L\ln(1-\beta_L) - \ln[(1-\beta_K)(1+\alpha)]]$$

$$= -\ln(1-\beta_L)\left[1+\frac{P_K K}{L}\right] + \frac{P_K K}{L}\,[\ln(1-\beta_K)(1+\alpha)]\left[1-\frac{1}{P_L}\right]$$

Given other values, there exists a P_L sufficiently low to assure that the second element in this expression is negative and outweighs the first (positive) element, i.e., $H(0) < 0$. It is also clear that if all else is fixed, there exists a β_L sufficiently high to assure that the first element preponderates, i.e., $H(0) > 0$.

Where $(1 - \beta_K)(1 + \alpha) < 1 < \dfrac{1 - \beta_K}{1 - \beta_L}(1 + \alpha)$ (*case 1.2(i)*), $\lim_{n \to \infty} R(n) = \infty$. In this case $H(0) > 0$ (so that $R'(0) > 0$) since here $(1 - \beta_K)(1 + \alpha) < 1$ and its log is < 0. There is also a continuous upward trend in R in case 1 where

$$(1 - \beta_K)(1 + \alpha) < \frac{1 - \beta_K}{1 - \beta_L}(1 + \alpha) < 1$$

Rearranging terms in $H(0)$, we have

$$H(0) = -\ln(1 - \beta_L) + \frac{P_K K}{L}$$

$$\left\{ \ln\left[\frac{1 - \beta_K}{1 - \beta_L}(1 + \alpha)\right] - \frac{\ln[(1 - \beta_K)(1 + \alpha)]}{P_L} \right\}$$

But

$$\ln\left[\frac{1 - \beta_K}{1 - \beta_L}(1 + \alpha) - \ln(1 - \beta_K)(1 + \alpha)\right] = -\ln(1 - \beta_L) > 0.$$

So that with $0 < P_L < 1$, the multiplicand of $P_K K/L > -\ln(1 - \beta_L) > 0$ and $H(0) > 0$. In this case of ultimately rising R there can be no initial decline.

Appendix B

The three curves in each graph in this Appendix portray L_{100} (top), R (middle), $1 - P_L$ (lower), with L_{100} and $(1 - P_L)$ reduced by a factor of 100 and 10 respectively for purposes of clarity. Figures 1.1(a)–(d) and 1.2(a)–(d) relate to the cases discussed. Figures 1.3(a) and (b) illustrate the impact of initial conditions on the full course of R; in this case a low P_K assures an initial rise in R.

Figure	K/L	P_K	P_L	α	β_K	β_L
1.1(a)	.25	10	.5	.1	.03	.03
1.1(b)	.25	10	.5	.1	.05	.05
1.1(c)	.25	10	.5	.1	.09	.09
1.1(d)	.25	10	.5	.1	.091	.091
1.2(a)	.25	10	.5	.1	.09	.045
1.2(b)	.25	10	.5	.1	.092	.046
1.2(c)	.25	10	.5	.1	.045	.09
1.2(d)	.25	10	.5	.1	.046	.092
1.3(a)	.25	10	.5	.1	.025	.05
1.3(b)	.25	.5	.5	.1	.025	.05

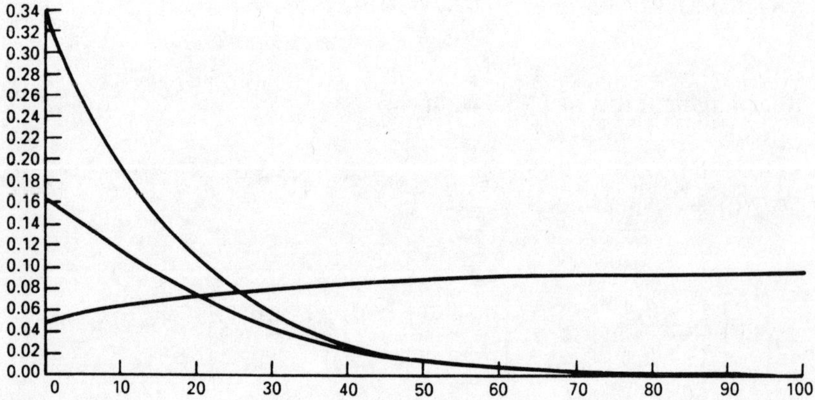

Figure 1.1(a)

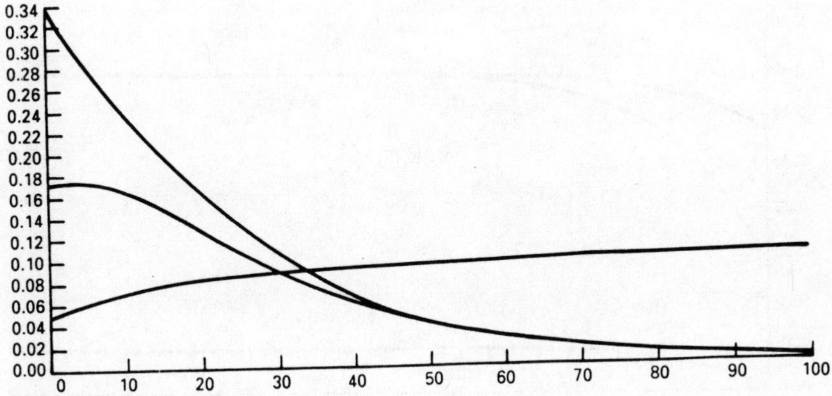

Figure 1.1(b)

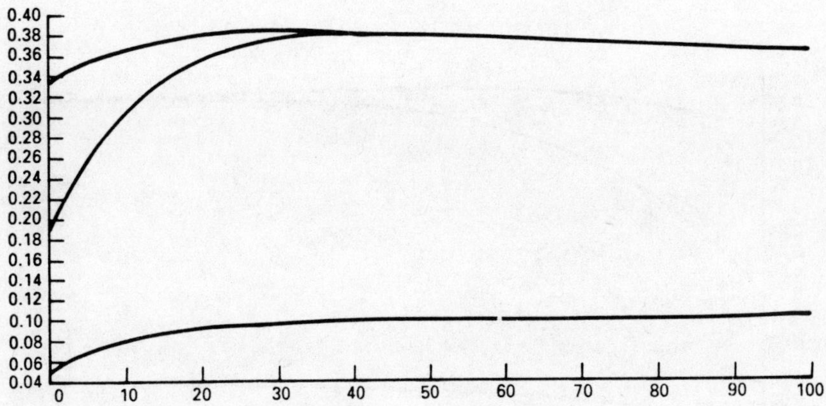

Figure 1.1(c)

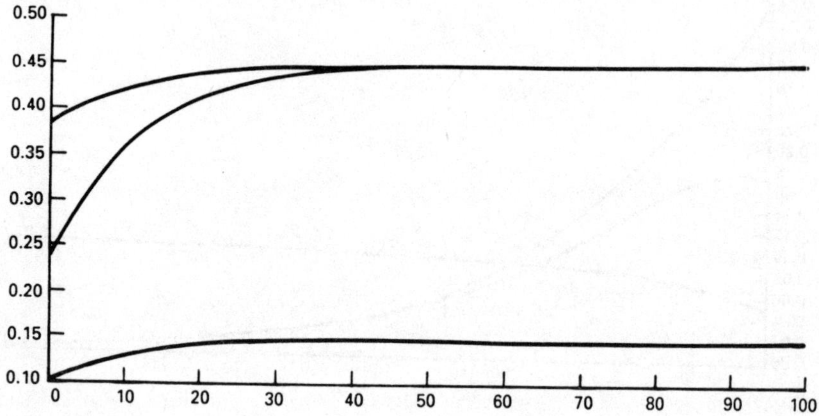

Figure 1.1(d)

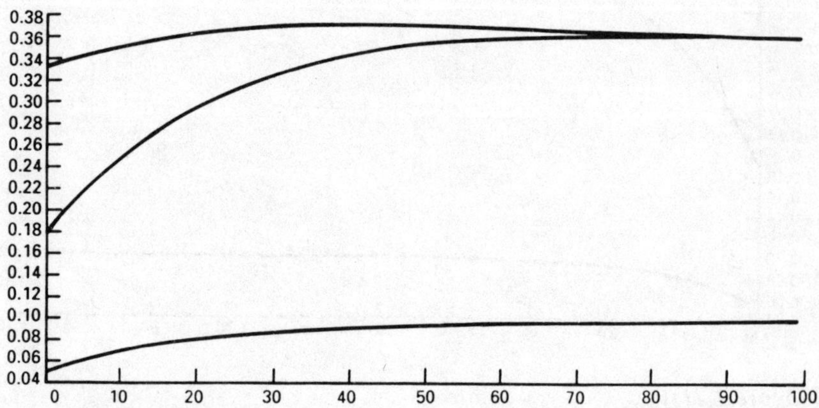

Figure 1.2(a)

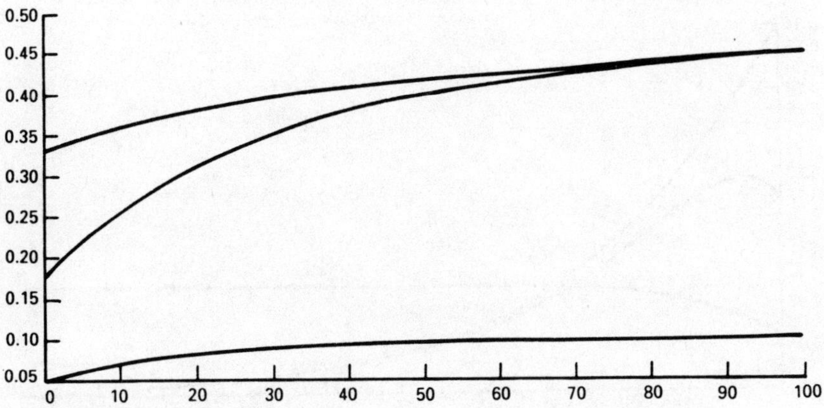

Figure 1.2(b)

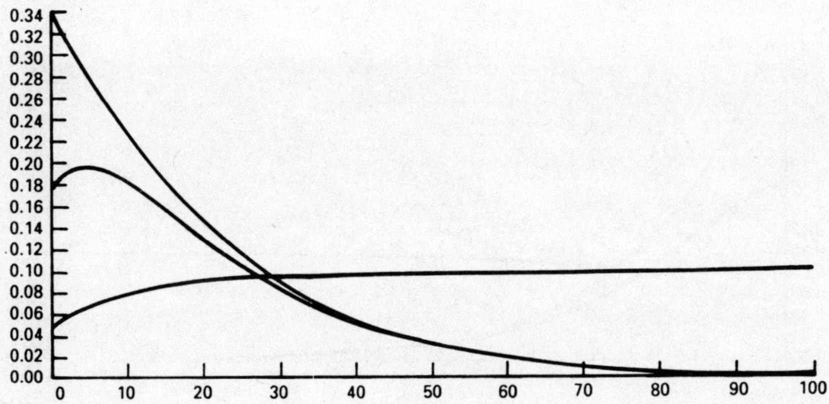

Figure 1.2(c)

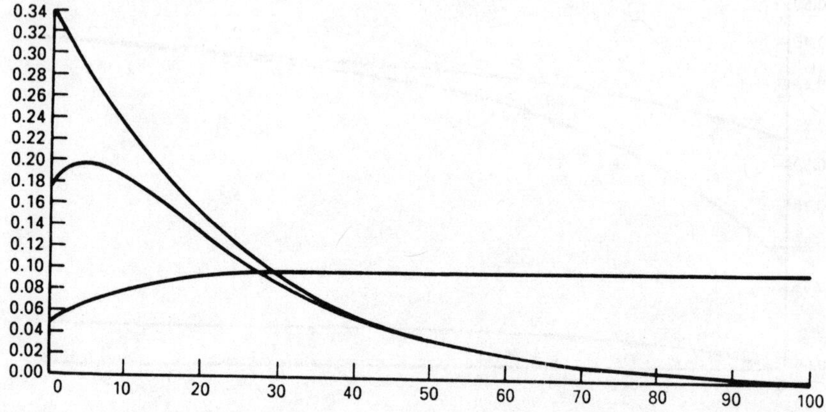

Figure 1.2(d)

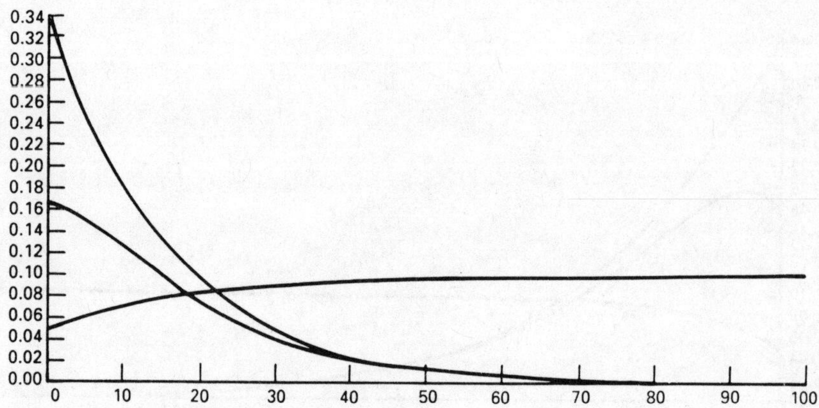

Figure 1.3(a)

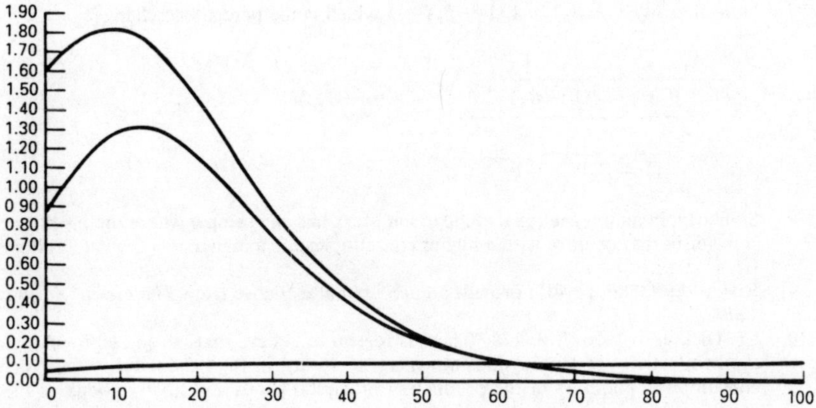

Figure 1.3(b)

Notes

1. A word here regarding definition: 'I call the value-composition of capital, in so far as it is determined by its technical composition and mirrors changes of the latter, the *organic composition* of capital' (*Capital*, Volume I, p. 612; cf. Volume III, p. 144). For much of what follows in this chapter the organic composition thus strictly defined is irrelevant because, following Marx, we have the values of capital goods and wage-goods varying differentially, so that changes in value-composition do not 'mirror' precisely changes in technical composition.
2. In proceeding with his formal transformation analysis Marx does include depreciation in his calculation of cost price, thus allowing for a difference between total and 'used up' capital. 'But', he repeats, 'this is immaterial to the rate of profit' (p. 154). In any event, cases where 'the entire constant capital [goes] into the annual product' are recognized in practice (p. 153).
3. The chapter dealing explicitly with the effect of the turnover on the rate of profit (Volume III, chapter iv) is an insertion by Engels.
4. The choice of value unit is arbitrary and one that Marx himself sometimes makes: 'If . . . e.g. £1 = 1 working day (no matter whether you think in terms of a day or a week, etc.), the working day = 12 hours, and the necessary labour (i.e., reproductive of the pay) = 8 hours, the wage of 30 workers (or working days) = £20 and the value of their labour = £30, the variable capital *per* worker (daily or weekly) = £2/3 and the value he creates = £1' (letter to Engels, 2 August 1862; in Marx and Engels 1985, p. 395).
5. The left-hand expression can be derived directly from the budget constraint:

$$P_L L + P_k K = 100$$

i.e., L per \$100 investment (written L_{100}) = $(100/P_L) - (P_K/P_L)K$. But K = gL where g is the technologically determined 'capital–labour' ratio. Therefore

$$L_{100} = (100/P_L) - (P_K/P_L)gL_{100} = \frac{100/P_L}{1 + (P_K/P_L)(K/L)}$$

6. Alternatively, let $\beta_L = \beta_K$ with $\alpha_L > \alpha_K$ implying the need for more constant capital per man to assure a given level of cost reduction.
7. Note that $\beta_K/(1 - \beta_K) = 1/(1 - \beta_k) - 1$ which is the percentage change:

$$\frac{\dfrac{1}{(1-\beta_K)^n} - \dfrac{1}{(1-\beta_K)^{n-1}}}{\dfrac{1}{(1-\beta_K)^{n-1}}}$$

8. Similarly, in an international comparison Marx has an example where the profit rate is lower in that country with a higher *c*/*v* ratio despite a higher *s*/*v* (*Capital*, Volume III, p. 212).
9. Rosdolsky (1980, p. 401) provides much textual evidence from *Theories of Surplus Value*.
10. Cf. Dickinson 1956–7, p. 128: 'There is reason to believe that, as an empirical fact, the productivity of labour does not increase so fast in the production of workers' consumption goods as in the production of capital-goods and luxury goods. If this is so . . . [the rate of surplus value] increases more slowly than we have assumed, and the point of diminishing [*R*] is reached with a smaller *K* than we have assumed.' Also Meek 1967, pp. 141–2): 'The initial rise in the rate of profit will be higher and the point of downturn will be later . . . the greater is the rise in productivity in the wage-goods industries relatively to that in the capital-goods industries.' Meek derives support from Rosdolsky (see 1980, pp. 407–8) who had pointed to 'certain additional reasons for [Marx's] belief that a rise in the rate of surplus value will not be sufficient to prevent the rate of profit from falling. For one thing, the increase of productivity in agriculture, will probably be less than its overall increase' (Meek, p. 134).
11. Cf. letter to Engels, 2 August 1862: 'a prerequisite for industry is the older science of mechanics, while the prerequisites for agriculture are the completely new sciences of chemistry, geology and physiology' (Marx and Engels 1985, p. 397).
12. On occasion, Marx seems actually to assume positive increases in costs; thus 'agriculture and the extractive industries' entail 'a decrease in labour productivity and, therefore, an increase in the number of employed labourers' (*Capital*, Volume III, p. 56).
13. This order of magnitude is further reinforced: 'An additional factor is that, as a consequence of landownership, agricultural products are expensive compared with other commodities, because they are sold at *their* value and are not reduced to their cost-price. They form, however, the principal constituent of the necessaries' (*Theories of Surplus Value*, Part III, p. 301). Marx is presumably basing himself here on a presumption that the organic composition in agriculture is low – itself an index of relative technological backwardness – so that value exceeds cost price, a differential which is not competed away by inflows of capital but absorbed by 'absolute' rent (cf. Marx and Engels 1985, p. 397). And there is allusion to a sort of diminishing returns applied, however, in a context of falling costs: 'Furthermore, if one-tenth of the land is dearer to exploit than the other nine-tenths, these latter are likewise hit "artificially" by this relative barrenness, as a result of the law of competition' (*Theories of Surplus Value*, Part III, p. 301).
14. The 'empirical' perspective is much emphasized by Sweezy. 'The increasing rate of surplus value was obvious to Marx but the dominant trend was the quantum leap in the organic composition – the transition in mid-century from "*manu*facture" to "*machine*facture" ' ([1973], 1987, p. 43; cf. also Sweezy 1968).
15. In this case even if $\dfrac{1-\beta_K}{1-\beta_L}(1+\alpha) < 1$, i.e., the value composition of capital tends to zero,

$$\lim_{n\to\infty} R(n) = \lim_{n\to\infty} \frac{\dfrac{1}{P_L(1+\beta_L)^n}}{1+\dfrac{P_K}{P_L}\dfrac{(1-\beta_K)^n}{(1+\beta_L)^n}\cdot\dfrac{K}{L}(1+\alpha)^n} = 0$$

since

$$\lim_{n\to\infty} \frac{1}{P_L(1+\beta)^n} = 0.$$

References

Blaug, M. (1980), *A Methodological Appraisal of Marxian Economics*, Amsterdam: North-Holland.

Bortkiewicz, L. (1907, 1952), 'Value and Price in the Marxian System', *International Economic Papers*, **2**.

Cogoy, M. (1973, 1987), 'The Falling Rate of Profit and the Theory of Accumulation', *International Journal of Political Economy*, **17**, pp. 54–74.

Dickinson, H.D. (1956–57), 'The Falling Rate of Profit in Marxian Economics', *Review of Economic Studies*, **24**, pp. 120–30.

Dobb, M. (1959), 'The Falling Rate of Profit', *Science and Society*, **23**, pp. 97–103.

Gillman, J.M. (1956), *The Falling Rate of Profit*, New York: Cameron Associates.

Marx, K., *Capital*, Volume I (1965); Volume III (1962), Moscow: Progress Publishers.

Marx, K., *Theories of Surplus Value*, Volume II (1968); Part III (1971), Moscow: Progress Publishers.

Marx, K. (1973), *Grundrisse: Foundations of a Critique of Political Economy*, New York: Penguin Books.

Marx, K. and F. Engels (1985), *Collected Works*, Volume 41, Moscow: International Publishers.

Marx, K. and F. Engels (1988), *Collected Works*, Volume 43, Moscow: International Publishers.

Meek, R.L. (1967), 'The Falling Rate of Profit', in *Economics, Ideology and Other Essays*, London: Chapman and Hall.

Perelman, M. (1985), 'Marx, Malthus and the Organic Composition of Capital', *History of Political Economy*, **17**, pp. 461–90.

Robinson, J. (1942), *An Essay on Marxian Economics*, London: Macmillan.

Rosdolsky, R. (1980), *The Making of Marx's 'Capital'*, London: Pluto Press.

Rosenberg, N. (1976), 'Marx as a Student of Technology', *Monthly Review*, **28**, pp. 56–77.

Schefold, B. (1976), 'Different Forms of Technical Progress', *Economic Journal*, **86**, pp. 806–19.

Sweezy, P.M. (1942), *The Theory of Capitalist Development*, New York: Oxford University Press.

Sweezy, P.M. (1968), 'Karl Marx and the Industrial Revolution', in R.V. Eagly (ed.), *Events, Ideology and Economic Theory*, Detroit, pp. 197–26.

Sweezy, P.M. (1973, 1987), 'Some Problems in the Theory of Capital Accumulation', *International Journal of Political Economy*, **17**, pp. 38–53.

Wolff, E.N. (1979), 'The Rate of Surplus Value, The Organic Composition, and the General Rate of Profit in the U.S. Economy, 1947–67', *American Economic Review*, **69**, (3), pp. 329–41.

2 Marx on the future of capitalism

M. Blaug

The doctrine that scientific theories must be judged in the final analysis by means of *a comparison between their empirical predictions and the facts of experience* was deeply embedded in mainstream British philosophy of science, as taught by William Whewell and John Stuart Mill, with which Marx was acquainted. However, Marx was also a disciple of Hegel, and Hegel did not always accept a purely empirical test as the final arbiter of scientific theories.

Despite the presence of other elements in Marx's thinking, however, I think it can be shown that Marx did adopt the standard approach to economic problems that united all the English classical economists from Adam Smith to John Stuart Mill: first, it was argued that a purely economic sphere of action could be legitimately isolated from the wider social context in which human action takes place; secondly, the subject of economics was conceived as an abstract, deductive science that moved by successive approximations from idealized assumptions about individual behaviour and the characteristics of economic institutions to the concrete phenomena of everyday reality; and, thirdly, it was held that the conclusions reached by this chain of reasoning should always be verified by appealing to whatever factual material was available. Our central interest lies in this dominant strand in Marx's work on economic problems. Nevertheless, we ought to spend a moment on those other elements in Marx's thinking that run in a different direction because these account for many of the difficulties which English and American readers experience when they read Marx.

What were Marx's views on his own economic methods? I wish that it were possible to point to his words for an unambiguous answer to that question. It is true that his writings are strewn with methodological remarks – unlike, say, Ricardo, he was hypersensitive to questions of method – but many of these provoke rather than clarify and the only occasion on which he wrote a sustained essay on 'The Method of Political Economy' in the *Grundrisse*, what emerges is both opaque and paradoxical (Marx 1975, pp. 71–82). Suffice it to say that his method seems to be made up of seven elements, of which the first is the hypothetico-deductive approach of the classical economists, to which we have already alluded. Let us simply list the remaining six:

1. A fundamental distinction, derived from Aristotle via Hegel, between the underlying 'essence' and the ordinary 'appearance' of things, from which it follows that the fundamental task of science is to pierce the veil of appearances so as to expose those inner essences.
2. A Hegelian 'vision', to use that favourite term of Schumpeter, according to which all abstract entities, whether natural or social, are conceived as made up of inner contradictory forces, both at the level of 'essence' and at the level of 'appearance', not to mention at the point of interaction between these two levels – this is what is popularly referred to as 'the dialectical method'.
3. Another Hegelian idea, overlapping the first two and yet adding extra dimension to the picture, which conceives of all entities as sets of internal relationships, having what is nowadays called a definite 'structure' (thus, when Marx says that 'capital' is a relation and not a thing, he means that the outward semblance of exchange ratios between commodities disguises what is really a social relationship between people, thereby combining the philosophy of relationism with the essence/appearance distinction and with the dialectical method).
4. An 18th-century Scottish historical method, which sees social change as initiating in changing 'modes of production', consisting of both technological forces and the property relations between social classes, which changes in the 'base' are then reflected in a 'superstructure' of ideas and institutions, including scientific ideas – this is what Engels called 'the materialist conception of history'.
5. A logico-historical thesis, or what I would prefer to call 'an anti-genetic thesis', again having its roots in Hegel, which argues that the logical status of abstract concepts reverses the actual course of historical development (in other words, the 'essence' of social institutions is grasped, not by examining their origins, but by examining their mature forms at the highest stage of their evolution).
6. A theory of truth which dissolves the Humean is/ought distinction by the concept of *praxis* as the ultimate test of a social theory, particularly the *praxis* of the 'proletariat' fulfilling its historical mission by ushering in socialism.

The last of these will give us a great deal of trouble because it threatens to dissolve, not just the Humean distinction between a domain of empirical facts and a domain of ethical values, but also the very notion from which we started, namely, that the predictions of a social theory can be, and must be, put to a detached scientific test.

Taking all seven propositions together, we have more or less the sum of what other commentators have discerned as Marx's method.[1] I shall resist the temptation to comment at length on each of these propositions but we really must pause to consider essentialism, relationism, and the dialectical method, that is, the first three on our list. All three may be regarded as powerful heuristic postulates, or algorithms for solving problems, and as such they are unobjectionable. A social theory should not be praised or condemned for resorting to such postulates; it should be judged on its fruits and not on its metaphysical sources of inspiration. Nevertheless, it has been argued by Popper that essentialism has damaging effects on social theories because it encourages an anti-empirical tendency to solve problems by the use of definitions. For Plato and Aristotle, knowledge or 'science' begins with observations of individual cases and proceeds by simple enumeration until one has grasped by intuition that which is universal in them – their 'essence' – which is then enshrined in a definition of the phenomenon in question. This doctrine that it is the aim of science to discover the true nature or essence of things and to describe them by means of definitions had an enormous influence on western thought right up to the 19th century and Popper (1957, pp. 26–34; also 1976, pp. 18–21, 197–8) contrasts this brand of 'methodological essentialism' with the 'methodological nominalism' that came into scientific debates with Newton, according to which the aim of science is to describe *how* things behave in various circumstances with the aid of universal laws, and not to determine *what* they really are.

There can be no doubt that Marx was a thoroughgoing essentialist. The three volumes of *Capital* are simply peppered with statements of the essence/appearance distinction, endlessly reiterating the view that the task of political economy is to expose the inner 'essence' of things that is always masked by their outward 'appearances' (for example, Marx 1976, pp. 168, 421, 433, 677, 679, 714; and 1909, pp. 56, 198, 199, 209, 367, 815).[2] It is his adherence to the doctrine of essentialism that accounts for Marx's steadfast belief in the two-tier approach to money prices and money profits: the domain of prices must rest on an underlying domain of values because competitive prices are only epiphenomena, which cannot themselves explain anything. And, of course, he was right. Prices must be explained in terms of an underlying technology, a set of motives ascribed to economic agents, and a rudimentary structure of economic institutions. Is this not the method of orthodox economics? In other words, there is nothing peculiarly Marxian about the essence/appearance distinction. Where we may quarrel with Marx is on the question whether the nature of the 'essence' of prices is only to be found in the domain of values, as if no other 'essence' will suffice. Thus, when Marx dismissed virtually every economist after Ricardo as a 'vulgar' economist, meaning one who skimmed the surface of things and never penetrated to their inner connections, he was simply equating the doctrine of essentialism with his own labour theory of profits.

Adherents of essentialism are inclined to settle substantive questions by reaching for a dictionary – usually a dictionary of their own making. Marx too was very prone to this tendency. Having adopted the labour theory of profits, he was forced to confront the question whether all living labour creates surplus value, regardless of how or by whom it is employed. He asserted that profits are only created by 'production' and not by 'circulation', which is true by definition of 'circulation' as a zero-sum game, and this led him to view that only labour employed in production, or what he called 'productive labour', creates surplus value, 'unproductive labour' being in effect paid out of the profits created by 'productive labour'. He decided, however, that the packing, storing and shipping of goods is part of 'production', whereas all the commercial functions of middlemen and of course the merchandising functions of retailers are part of 'circulation', in consequence of which a lorry-driver is 'productive' if he is transporting goods from the factory to the warehouse but he is 'unproductive' if he is merely moving goods from a middleman to a retailer. Marx wrote hundreds of pages on these questions, pondering the issue as to whether school teachers and lawyers could ever be considered 'productive' workers, not all of which are free from inconsistencies. But the point I wish to make about his writings on the subject is simply that he always reaches a decision as to what is or is not 'productive labour' by applying the definition that 'productive labour is labour that creates surplus value'. The problem had considerable importance for him because, obviously, the size of the 'productive' labour force governs the total surplus value that is created, which governs the total profits that are available for distribution among capitalists, which in turn determines the rate of profit in the price system. Nevertheless, it never occurred to him to ask whether any empirical observations could ever assist him in deciding which labour is 'productive' and which is 'unproductive'. Thus, he conceded that any reduction in the 'time of circulation' of goods would act to raise the money rate of profit (Marx 1909, pp. 329–30) but this did not lead him to abandon the view that the merchandising function is always 'unproductive'. Marxists (e.g. Gough 1972, and Mandel in Marx 1978, pp. 38–46) have ever since followed Marx's policy of categorizing labour as productive or unproductive by manipulating definitions, never once asking: How do we *know* that we have arrived at the correct definition? In recent years, for example, British Marxists have debated the question as to whether state employees are 'productive' workers (see Fine and Harris 1976, pp. 154–9), not by looking at what state employees actually do, but by unravelling the taxonomic question whether the state actually produces or whether is merely 'realizes' surplus value.

Marxism has paid a heavy price for its commitment to the methodology of essentialism. Thus, when Marx in the second volume of *Capital* invented the now so familiar Harrod–Domar technique of stating the necessary conditions for smooth economic expansion or balanced growth, he spoiled what could have been a major contribution to economic thought by expressing the necessary conditions entirely in terms of labour values, instead of the money prices that actually govern the inducement to invest. In consequence, he failed to notice that his arithmetic examples of smooth exponential growth involved purely arbitrary rates of capital accumulation. His disciples always found it difficult to square this picture of feasible steady-state growth with Marx's other analyses of the falling rate of profit and the crisis-ridden nature of capitalism. For 40 years, they heatedly debated the meaning of Marx's so-called 'reproduction schema' – a debate known as the 'breakdown controversy' – and all this time none of them recognized that the whole debate was beside the point because it was entirely carried out in terms of the value system of Volume I from which nothing can ever be deduced about the motives for capital accumulation. The 'breakdown controversy' is an instructive story of the dangers of 'essentialism' with its tendency towards the reification of the concepts of value and surplus value.[3]

The same anti-empirical note is struck in the now ongoing debate about 'the labour reduction problem'. Marx argued that 'socially necessary' labour costs are countable in units of common, abstract labour, skilled labour being counted as so many multiples of common labour. These multiples must be construed as purely technical conversion coefficients and not as wage rates, because it is obviously illegitimate to invoke prices in what purports to be an explanation of how prices are determined. So long as labour is only differentiated in terms of acquired skills, there is no problem: we can assume that such skills are being produced in a separate training industry, in which case labour skills are simply more means of production that are produced and reproduced at the going rate of profit. In other words, the time-consuming production of skilled labour raises no difficulties for the labour theory of value that are not also raised by the time-consuming production of machines. The argument breaks down, however, the moment we concede that labour is also differentiated in terms of 'ability', regardless of whether those ability differences are inborn or whether they are due to family rearing. Such 'ability' differences simply cannot be interpreted either as given technical coefficients or as the outputs of a notional industry that is governed by the principle of equal profitability. Marx himself invoked what we have called the 'anti-genetic thesis' to justify the principle of calculating labour costs in the common denominator of abstract labour: labour may have been heterogeneous in the past but capitalism tends constantly to erode all differences between types of labour by the introduction of skill-saving processes, so that purely homogeneous, raw labour represents the appropriate abstraction that corresponds to capitalism at its highest stage of development.

Now, undoubtedly, factor substitution acts to overcome shortages of skilled labour by a continuous process of deskilling, but, on the other hand, technical progress frequently acts in the opposite direction by raising the skill requirements of new products and processes. It is a moot question whether the labour force has in fact become more or less differentiated in the process of industrialization, but certainly the educational explosion of the last 35 years suggests the very opposite of Marx's belief in the increasing homogenization of labour. This is not a question we can settle here but what is striking is that the facts, whatever they are, are totally ignored in Marxist contributions to the labour reduction problem.

When Böhm-Bawerk and Hilferding discussed these issues at the turn of the century, very little was known about the structure of wages and particularly the personal characteristics of workers in relation to differential rates of pay. But since then we have witnessed the rise of human capital theory, which has generated a vast body of evidence about the determinants of the distribution of earnings in terms of such individual characteristics as age, education, occupation, family origins, and even measured IQ at an early age. And yet when we examine the numerous writings of Marxists in recent years on the labour reduction problem,[4] we do not find a single reference to this new source of data with which to test Marx's conjecture that capitalism tends historically to reduce all types of labour to raw, undifferentiated labour. Moreover, the new data strongly suggests that the rate of return to the training industry, which of course includes the whole of the formal educational system, is not in fact equalized with the rate on profit on business capital (Blaug 1976, pp. 838–9), implying that the labour reduction problem is not solved by simply disregarding all 'ability' differences between workers. Besides, these 'ability' differences, whether due to nature or to nurture, show up in all the regressions that have poured out of the human capital research programme (Blaug 1976, pp. 842–3), in which case the classic Marxist solution to the labour reduction problem falls to the ground.

Some radical American economists with Marxist leanings contend that the labour market under capitalism is always segmented into non-competing sexual, racial and ethnic groups, so that there are as many rates of surplus value as there are segments in the labour market, with some workers exploiting others (Bowles and Gintis 1977, 1978). Whether true or not, here at least is an attempt to reformulate the labour reduction problem in terms of observable phenomena. But more orthodox Marxist economists show no similar inclination to relate their theoretical discussions to recent empirical research, preferring instead to go on mouthing Marx's own cryptic remarks about the inevitable tendency of capitalism to strip concrete labour of all of its differentiating characteristics.[5]

We turn now to the dialectical method, which friend and foe alike regard as the hallmark of Marx's approach to social problems. It is difficult to know how seriously to take Marx's use of Hegelian dialectics but it certainly inspired him powerfully to see conflict where others saw only harmony and the reconciliation of opposing interests. He actually claimed no more than that he 'coquetted' with Hegel's modes of expression for the purpose of 'setting traps' for his more philistine readers (Marx 1976, pp. 102–3). At any rate, why should we take much notice of the inner contradictions of capitalism when we learn that even the elliptical motions of planets around the sun are nothing but the resolution of the 'contradiction' between rectilinear motion and the centripetal force of gravity (Marx 1976, p. 198). Marx's destructive 'contradictions' are so frequently merely 'contradistinctions', or else mutually counteracting forces that may as easily coexist in stable as in unstable equilibria. Indeed, the classical economist's habit of pronouncing economic 'laws' that may be offset by 'disturbing causes' was tailormade for Marx's use of the dialectical method: when evidence fails to confirm a fundamental law, he chalks this up as proof that the disturbing causes are at work, thus exemplifying once again the inner 'contradictions' that will eventually disrupt and destroy capitalism.

I must explain that I am in no way decrying the role of tendency-laws in economics.[6] The classical economist's notion of 'disturbing causes' that are said to be capable of contradicting the predictions of economic theories is echoed in the modern economists' appeal to *ceteris paribus* clauses that are invariably attached to general economic propositions or statements of economic 'laws'. There is a widespread impression that *ceteris paribus* clauses abound in the social sciences but rarely occur in the physical sciences. Nothing could be further from the truth, however. A scientific theory that could entirely dispense with *ceteris paribus* clauses would in effect achieve perfect closure, that is, inclusion of all the variables that could make any difference to the phenomena being studied. It is doubtful whether even Newtonian mechanics achieved such perfect closure and completeness. It might be said, therefore, that just about all theoretical propositions in both the natural and the social sciences are in fact statements of tendency-laws. Nevertheless, there is a world of difference between most tendency statements in physics and chemistry and virtually all such statements in economics and sociology, the difference residing in the fact that physicists and chemists usually specify the magnitude of the amount of the distortion which results from the *cetera* that are held *pares*. In the social sciences, however, it is common to encounter tendency statements with unspecified *ceteris paribus* clauses – a sort of catch-all for everything that is unknown – or if specified, specified only in qualitative rather than quantitative terms, which may not help very much when we come to test for the existence of the underlying tendency.

I conclude, therefore, that tendency-statements in economics may be regarded as promissory notes that are only redeemed when the *ceteris paribus* clause has been spelled out and taken into account, preferably in quantitative terms. Unless they are so redeemed, the argument will fail to produce a refutable prediction even in terms of the direction of the total change being predicted, much more in terms of the magnitude of that change.

Marx's defence of the famous 'law' of the tendency of the rate of profit to decline fails to meet these methodological standards. He said that the law was subject to five 'counteracting causes', and he went on to spell out what these were – we may summarize them under three headings as: (1) increases in the productivity of labour in excess of increases in wages, (2) the introduction of capital-saving innovations, and (3) the expansion of foreign trade. What he gives us, therefore, is one negative rate of change, expressing the basic 'law' of the falling rate of profit, and five offsetting, positive rates of change; clearly, the joint outcome of these six rates of change could go either way. Furthermore, Marx (1909, p. 277) made it clear that four of the five counteracting causes to the falling rate of profit are themselves induced by the fall, which is like saying that we can never observe the operation of the tendency of the rate of profit to decline without simultaneously observing the operation of these counteracting influences.

In the circumstances, there seems little point in even asking whether he would ever have contemplated an empirical refutation of his law of the falling rate of profit. It must be recalled, of course, that he did not invent that law (just as he did not invent the concept of the recurrent business cycle, nor the idea that the size of business firms will increase in the course of economic progress – both of these are found in John Stuart Mill). What he was doing was to provide a wholly new and rather surprising explanation of a standard classical doctrine. It was surprising because in Ricardian theory, the rate of profit tends to decline because the growth process runs into the barrier of non-augmentable natural resources, and to this barrier there is only one offset, namely, technical progress with a land-saving bias, whose likely occurrence cannot be predicted from terms within Ricardian theory. Marx refused to regard land as a non-reproducible factor in limited supply and he struggled instead to attribute falling profits directly to the process of mechanization. Since he did not distinguish between factor substitution and technical change, he produced a somewhat paradoxical theory in which the rate of profit tends to fall, not because there is too little technical progress, but because there is too much, or, at any rate, too much of the labour-saving type. The air of paradox that hangs over these propositions is aggravated by his inclination to argue that the falling rate of profit is accompanied by constant and even falling wages – all this in a model in which there is no primary, non-reproducible factor other than labour, in which the introduction of new methods is solely motivated by the money rate of profit, and in which there is no irreversible technical change, such that old processes previously discarded cannot be taken up again. This thesis, associating the law of the falling rate of profit with a vaguely expressed law of the impoverishment of the working class, is simply untenable and it is not made any more tenable by linking it with another one of Marx's great ideas, the so-called 'industrial reserve army' of the unemployed whose function it is to keep wages from rising in a boom.

The theory of surplus value, you will recall, rests on the notion that the value of labour-power is determined, like that of all other commodities, by the amount of total labour embodied in its production, that is, the amount of labour embodied in the wage-goods that workers consume. Once values are suitably transformed into prices, Marx relies on the standard mechanism of demand and supply to keep short-run market prices in line with long-run equilibrium prices. But in Marx this mechanism does not apply to labour-power because labour-power is not produced by households in accordance with rational cost calculations. Hence, Marx had to find some other mechanism to keep market wages from drifting above the value of labour-power and his answer to that problem was the concept of the 'industrial reserve army'. For him, capitalism and full employment are incompatible except for brief moments at the peak of a business cycle. It is obvious that this mechanism of wage rates fluctuating inversely with the level of unemployment, reminiscent of something like the Phillips Curve, is a dynamic theory. Furthermore, it is predicated in turn on an inverse relationship between the wage rate and the profit rate, that is, on a fairly stable investment demand function that is negatively inclined throughout its entire length.

Here, by the way, is another logical flaw in the labour theory of profits, for it now appears that this theory requires specific dynamic assumptions which take us out of the value system of Volume I of *Capital* where the analytical context is strictly that of static equilibrium, or, at least, balanced growth in a steady state.[7]

To return to the law of the falling rate of profit. Marx defined the rate of profit to be a positive function of the rate of surplus value and a negative function of the organic composition of capital, from which it follows immediately that he was really talking about the value rate and not the money rate of profit. He thought that there were no limits to the increase of the organic composition of capital, whereas increases in the rate of surplus value were subject to an upper bound; hence, the value rate of profit had to fall sooner or later. Unfortunately, the rate of surplus value is not only functionally but positively related to the very same process of mechanization that raises the organic composition of capital, and it is now generally agreed that Marx became thoroughly confused by the problem of reckoning in labour-time as the process of capital accumulation proceeds.[8] The conclusion of a falling *value* rate of profit depends essentially on what happens to the labour-time required to produce wage-goods as against the labour-time required to produce investment goods and products consumed by capitalists and landlords, and there is nothing in Marx's arguments that suggests an answer to that question. The more serious difficulty is that the money rate of profit need not fall just because the value rate of profit is falling. Since indirect labour is accumulated and embodied into the final product at one rate in the value system and at quite another, lower rate in the price system, any change in the technology of producing capital goods cannot affect the value rate and the money rate of profit in the same way. In general, there is no reason to expect that the trends in these two rates will even have the same sign (Wolff 1979). Of course, Marx himself was convinced that the two rates would rise and fall together because he had indeed transformed values into prices by setting the first rate equal to the second. If, as we have argued in our first lecture, this is both arbitrary and mathematically incorrect, we end up by concluding that Marx simply had no coherent theory of the falling *money* rate of profit.

Once again, we see how fundamental is the transformation problem to Marxian economics. Even now we frequently witness attempts to test his law of the falling rate of profit by invoking data on the capital–labour ratio and on the ratio of profits and wages – I have indulged in this pastime myself – which is to pretend that we can cross over effortlessly from the value system to the price system. But the organic composition of capital is not the same thing as the capital–labour ratio measured in constant prices, and the rate of surplus value is not the same thing as the relative shares of profits and wages in national income.

The money rate of profit has shown no persistent trend in advanced capitalist economies for over 100 years and there is no doubt that this fact would have seriously disturbed Marx, particularly as the trendless rate of profit has been accompanied by a persistent upward trend in real wages. Marx made other predictions about the future course of capitalist development – the increasing severity of recurrent unemployment, the increasing amplitude of business cycles, the steady concentration of capital in ever-larger business units, the ever-widening geographical extension of the capitalist mode of production, the growing polarization of society into two classes, and the continued alienation of both workers and capitalists from production, from society, and from themselves[9] – all of which are either corollaries of the law of the falling rate of profit, or *ad hoc* prophecies that are simply tacked on to his system.[10] If the law of the falling rate of profit is a dead letter, so are virtually all of his other predictions.

Some Marxists of the Old Left have stoically accepted the empirical refutation of Marx's analysis of competitive capitalism, insisting, however, that all the improvements of living standards under capitalism over the last century are due, not to the operation of spontaneous economic forces, but to trade union pressures and the independent intervention of the state (Meek 1967, pp. 108–10, 117–28). But many younger Marxists remain recalcitrant, denying that Marx's laws can ever be expected to reveal themselves in the realm of appearances, and proposing indeed to reformulate the law of the declining rate of profit as 'the law of the tendency of the rate of profit to fall *and* of the tendency for counteracting influences to operate' (Fine and Harris 1976, pp. 162–3; also Hodgson 1977, pp. 97–8; Fine and Harris 1977, pp. 113–17; and Fine and Harris 1979, pp. 61–5), thus flatly rejecting the requirement that tendency-laws in economics must be stated so as to be falsifiable at least in principle.

We may grant that admiration for Marx's predictions is subject to long waves that correspond almost perfectly with the long waves of the capitalist system (Bronfenbrenner 1970). In the 1930s, Marx's predictions of the growth of big business and the hard-core of chronic unemployment struck contemporaries as remarkable forecasts of the long-term evolution of capitalism. In the post-war euphoria of the 1950s and 1960s, however, the virtual disappearance of business cycles and the continued resilience of small- and medium-sized business enterprises threw doubt even on these last remaining predictions of the Marxian system. It is not surprising, therefore, that the 1970s have seen a reaffirmation of virtually all of Marx's concrete forecasts of long-term trends under capitalism. But the fact remains that few of the predictions follow logically from the structure of the Marxian theory of capital accumulation, which is simply over-determined: it is a pot-pourri of elements that can be endlessly permuted and combined to rationalize virtually any set of events (Howard and King 1975, chapter 6 and Harris 1978, pp. 282–3). Any moment now, we keep being told, the definite, coherent Marxist theory of accumulation for the current phase of monopoly capitalism will emerge from the mêlée of Marxist discussions – and still we wait, 112 years after the publication of Volume I of *Capital*. However, apart from the fairly trite idea that monopoly capitalism destroys the equalization of the rate of profit, raising profits in the monopolized sector at the expense of the competitive sector, nothing of any significance has been added to the original Marxist model.[11] Compared to these meagre accomplishments, even the admittedly unsatisfactory orthodox theory of oligopoly looks impressive.

Marx never wrote an exposition of his methodology, nor did his work receive the sort of criticism in his own lifetime that might have led him to defend and explain his methodology. We cannot, therefore, be sure how he would have reacted to the fact that so few of his predictions have actually materialized: capitalism has survived and it has survived at growth rates that are generally higher than those achieved in the 19th century. What is clear is that Marx would have regarded the continued survival of capitalism as posing a serious challenge to Marxist theory. He had, as I have said before, a complex attitude to the question of truth in social theory because he fondly believed that he had found in the concept of the 'proletariat' a philosopher's stone that would somehow unite theory and practice, making effective social action inspired by a theory the ultimate test of the validity of that theory. This is what is meant by the doctrine of *praxis*, according to which Marxism can only be refuted, not by empirical facts on wage rates, profit rates, and the like, but by the failure of the proletariat in advanced capitalist countries to overthrow the system.

The mystical and essential doctrine of *praxis* has posed serious problems to Marx's followers: they have been reluctant to simply ignore the apparent refutations of so many of Marx's predictions because that would be tantamount to obscurantism; at the same time, they have been embarrasssed to defend Marxism simply as a rationalization of the belief that western capitalism must sooner or later break down. As for the doctrine of *praxis*, they were no doubt aware that it amounts to turning majority opinion into *the* criterion of scientific validity. And so, whenever Marxists come to state the grounds on which economic and social theories ought to be validated, we hear a great deal about capturing the 'essence' of the problem as it comes to be reflected in the social experience of men, but very little about predictions, and the verification or falsification of predictions.[12] Above all, Marxists consistently evade the fundamental question that Popper has taught us to pose to all adherents of theories: Marxists, are there any events, which, if they were to occur, would make you abandon Marxism?

I said that Marxists consistently evade that fundamental Popperian question but I have actually discovered two exceptions to that rule. The first is contained in an authoritative and comprehensive reply to Popper's critique of Marx by Maurice Cornforth, a well-known British Marxist philosopher of the Old Left; the second is found in the introduction to a new translation of Volume I of *Capital* by Ernest Mandel, a leading figure in the Fourth International originally founded by Trotsky. I must first explain that Popper agrees that no scientific theory can ever be conclusively refuted because adverse results can always be explained away as due to faulty measuring instruments or, more generally, as due to the absence of the appropriate antecedent conditions. What distinguishes science from non-science in Popper is not so much the proposition that scientific theories ought to be falsifiable in principle, but rather that the development of these theories ought to be subject to a set of methodological rules that forbid what he calls 'immunizing stratagems': 'immunizing stratagems' are those adjustments to a theory whose only purpose is to protect the theory against repeated refutations and mounting anomalies.[13]

Popper argues that Marxism is indeed a scientific theory, or rather a scientific research programme; however, it has been falsified by the course of events and only the constant resort to 'immunizing stratagems' have kept it alive for so long. He gives Marx credit for correctly foreseeing the inherent technical dynamism of the capitalist system and the equally inherent tendency of that dynamism to be constantly associated with periodic business slumps (Popper 1962, II, pp. 193, 194, 196) – curiously enough, he fails to mention 'concentration and centralization of capital', one of Marx's more remarkable predictions.[14] But he leaves no doubt that Marx's other economic predictions of growing impoverishment, mounting unemployment, and ever more violent business fluctuations have all been glaringly refuted (Volume II, pp. 183, 189, 193). In Popper's view, however, it is only when the failure of Marx's economic predictions are coupled with the failure of his political predictions that we can judge the Marxist system in the round. Many of Marx's political predictions, unlike at least some of his economic ones, simply do not follow logically from his premises (Volume II, pp. 138–9, 140–1, 146). In particular, the tendency of Marx's followers to identify the socialist revolution that Marx foresaw with the Russian Revolution is a typical example of the use of an 'immunizing stratagem'. The Russian Revolution was the product, not of the contradictions of advanced capitalism, but of industrial infancy, agricultural backwardness, and a power vacuum created by the defeat in war (Volume II, pp. 109, 349). To cite the Russian Revolution as confirming Marxist theory is, according to Popper, to turn Marxism into a metaphysical doctrine that culminates in the empty prophecy that, somehow, some day, there will be a revolution somewhere (Volume II, p. 326).

With these observations in mind, let us now take up Cornforth's (1972, pp. 31, 32, 37) reply to the gauntlet thrown down by Popper:

> If uninterrupted economic development were to be combined with capitalist enterprise and capitalist profit, then Marx's theory would be falsified . . . Marxists can, it is true, readily account for the socialist revolution starting in Russia. But if it had started, say, in the Far East or in Central Africa, or if it had never started at all, that could not have been accounted for, and really would have falsified Marxism. But it did start, and started where Marxism permitted it to start . . . So far it [Marxism] has not been falsified but confirmed.

What needs to be explained is how Cornforth can find Marxism confirmed while accepting as much of Popper's methodology as he does. The clue lies in that part of Popper's philosophy of science that he does not accept, namely, the ban on 'immunizing stratagems'. Cornforth (pp. 33–4, 40–1) holds it to be a virtue of Marxism that its fundamental propositions are so framed as to accommodate the widest range of possible events, although on Popper's arguments it is precisely this that weakens rather than strengthens the Marxist claim to science: if Marxism is a living science, it should not hesitate to submit itself to really severe tests.

Thus, to give one more example, Cornforth vigorously endorses what Marx called 'the absolute general law of capital accumulation': 'in proportion as capital accumulates, the situation of the worker, be his payment high or low, must grow worse' (Marx 1976, pp. 798–9). 'Like all other laws', Marx added, 'it is modified in its workings by many circumstances', but we search in vain in his writings for any list of what these circumstances are. Undeterred by the idea of an economic tendency-law offset by an unspecified number of countervailing forces, Cornforth (1972, pp. 193–4) explains the significance of the 'absolute general law' in these words:

> Marx certainly did maintain that all those hopeful people (like Dr. Popper himself) who think that improvements in living standards can go on and on under capitalism, so that everything will get better and better and eventually all poverty, unemployment, class differences and war will simply disappear are blind to the operation of 'the absolute general law'.

In short, so long as poverty, unemployment, class stratification and war persist under capitalism, Marx is confirmed, whatever the logical structure of his argument and whatever the time-scale of his predictions. Clearly, this is an open invitation to invent 'immunizing stratagems' without limit, which virtually reduces Marxism to the fortune-telling practices of gypsies.

Similarly Mandel (Marx 1976, p. 24) accepts Popper's challenge head-on and yet hedges his bets by selecting predictions that simply do not discriminate between Marxism and many other competing explanations:

> In fact, it would be very easy to 'prove' Marx's analysis to have been wrong, if experience had shown for example, that the more capitalist industry develops, the smaller and smaller the average factory becomes, the less it depends upon new technology, the more its capital is supplied by the workers themselves, the more workers become owners of their factories, the less the part of wages taken by consumer goods becomes. . . . If, in addition, there had been decades without economic fluctuations and a full-scale disappearance of trade unions and employers' association . . . then one could indeed say that *Capital* was so much rubbish and had dismally failed to predict what would happen in the real world a century after its publication.

But, on the contrary, Mandel (Marx 1976, p. 23) declares:

> It is precisely because of Marx's capacity to discover the long-term laws of motion of the capitalist mode of production in its essence . . . that his long-term predictions – the laws of accumulation of capital, stepped-up technological progress, accelerated increase in the productivity and intensity of labour, growing concentration and centralization of capital, transformation

> of the great majority of economically active people into sellers of labour-power, declining rate of profit, increased rate of surplus value, periodically recurrent recessions, inevitable class struggle between Capital and Labour, increasing revolutionary attempts to overthrow capitalism – have been so strikingly confirmed by history.

However, 50 pages later Mandel admits that 'contrary to what Marx expected', capitalism was overthrown, not in America or Europe, where 'the proletariat was most strongly developed numerically and economically', but in Russia and China 'where the bourgeoisie was weakest (p. 85). This was, no doubt, one of Marx's slight oversights for which, of course, he must be pardoned!

Cornforth and Mandel notwithstanding, I would argue that what has been refuted in Marxism is not so much the specific economic predictions, although here too there are fewer hits than misses, as the general conception of how capitalism would gradually come apart at the seams. We are now as far away from Marx as Marx was from Adam Smith and if Marx's picture of what was soon to happen to capitalism is looked at in the cold light of a century of development, the gap between prognosis and reality is actually so large as to be ludicrous. In appraising Marxian economics, let us not forget that Marx died almost a century ago and that what his followers have managed to do, or not to do, with his ideas in that time is all that really matters if Marxism is to be judged as a progressive rather than an ossified scientific research programme.

The heart of Marx's vision was, after all, his concept of the proletariat as a new class of impoverished, wage-dependent workers created by the power-driven factories of the Industrial Revolution. The factory system concentrated large numbers of men, women and children under a single roof and harnessed them to the discipline of machine-paced labour, thus unwittingly fostering among them the consciousness of being members of a group with interests different from, and frequently in conflict with, the owner-managers of factories. At the same time, the pressures of competition and the constant necessity to stay ahead of rivals, compelled the factory owners to cut wages, or at least to resist their upward drift, and to lengthen hours of work as much as possible. Thus, capitalism generated increasing misery amidst increasing plenty, which would inevitably weld workers together even if the alienating experience of factory life failed to do so. Moreover, competition tended to destroy itself because larger business units would always outpace and swallow up smaller units. Hence, society would increasingly polarize into two classes: an ever-diminishing class of haves and an ever-increasing class of have-nots. In these circumstances, the proletariat would grow more conscious of its identity with every passing day. In short, the proletariat was, or would soon become, the subversive class *par excellence* that simply could not fail to seize the rich fruits of this new social system by political means, so as to distribute them to the many rather than to the few.

All this was a remarkable forecast in 1867, which, I do not doubt for one moment, would have fully persuaded me had I been among the first readers of the first volume of *Das Kapital*.

However, this vision of capitalism, doomed by the very key to rapid economic growth that it had discovered – private property in the means of production – already struck many contemporaries as unrealistic before the turn of the century when Eduard Bernstein launched his revisions of Marx. Karl Kautsky's replies to Bernstein, disputing Bernstein's evidence of rising living standards and reinterpreting Marx's law of impoverishment as a statement about relative shares,[15] began the degeneration of the Marxist research programme, which continues to this day. But Bernstein's revisionism was as nothing compared to the blow that the First World War gave to the notion of the proletariat as an alienated, revolutionary class that never could be seduced by appealing to its love of fatherland. Of course, Lenin had a ready explanation for the patriotic response of workers throughout Europe: it was the treason of socialist leaders and the bribery of the 'aristocracy of labour' out of the windfalls of imperialist exploitation that accounted for the events of 1914. But in truth, the workers had voted with their feet against class and in favour of nation, and most socialist leaders (except Bernstein, the revisionist) simply saved their political skin by going along with working-class opinion.

The next blow to Marx's vision was the Russian Revolution. Russia was very near to being the most backward country in Europe and its proletariat in 1917 could at most have numbered 10 per cent of the total population. Even Lenin could only justify a proletarian revolution under these circumstances by appealing to the imminence of international revolution, followed by fraternal aid from western socialist countries. War Communism shattered these hopes and the retreat to NEP simply registered that fact. When Lenin died, the policy of 'socialism in one country' marked the final demise of Marx's vision: a theory of historical change that posited, if it posited anything at all, the primacy of economic over political forces was now to be read backwards to mean the very opposite.

One could continue in this vein. The Great Depression of the 1930s and the rise of Fascism seemed finally to realize the prophecies of Marx, even if in a distorted form, and we may forgive the fellow-travellers of that generation who moved to the left as they read what at the time must have appeared as the handwriting on the wall. Wrong again! The capitalist world emerged out of the Second World War to enter, against the predictions of Marxists and orthodox Keynesians alike, a 25-year period of expansion that was as unprecedented as had been the earlier slump of the thirties. Marxism died out as an intellectual force in the West, but elsewhere it received yet another dramatic transformation. Mao Tse Tung made a revolution, not just without a proletarian majority and a developed capitalist technology, but without any proletariat at all and with a level of technology that England had surpassed in the 17th and Russia in the 19th century. Nevertheless, the Chinese strategy of revolution-among-peasants-before-revolution-among-workers was carried forward under the banners of Marxism. Lastly, the boom of the 1960s completed the circle by promoting students, academics, women, blacks, the oppressed people of the Third World, and even criminals in capitalist prisons – anyone but factory workers – as the new revolutionary element that would soon overthrow capitalism. In the name of Bakhunin? No, in the name of Marx, the young Marx, Marx the humanist, who had not yet read and studied Adam Smith and David Ricardo. And, finally, in the 'stagflation' of the 1970s, we are told to go back once again to the old Marx, not so much for his economic as for his sociological insights.

What a wonderful story is the history of Marxism, refuted again and again, and revised again and again – not by its enemies but by its friends. This is a familiar story in the history of economic thought. It happened to Ricardo before Marx and it happened to Keynes in our own lifetime. Perhaps there are still some among you who think that economic theories can be decisively refuted by the historical record and that there is no need for Popperian rules that positively forbid arbitrary revisions of a theory to accommodate growing anomalies and repeated refutations. If so, study the history of Marxism and consider the error of your ways.

Notes

1. For a small sample, see Sweezy (1942, chapter 1), Wolfson (1966, chapter 1), Meek (1967, pp. 93–112, 154–7), Ollman (1971, chapters 2, 3), Meek (1973, pp. 146–56), Howard and King (1975, chapter 2), Mandel in Marx (1976, pp. 17–25), Meek (1977, pp. 128–30, 134–45), Morishima and Catephores (1978, pp. 201–7), Kolakowski (1978, I, pp. 312–24; III, pp. 264–80, 297–300), and, particularly, Walker (1978, chapter 8).
2. This has been noticed by many commentators, most of whom take it as prima facie evidence of Marx's profoundity (e.g. Geras 1972; Howard and King 1975, pp. 39–45; Oakley 1976, pp. 414–15; Sowell 1976, pp. 65–9; and Rosdolsky 1977, pp. 561–70).
3. Elements of the story can be found in Sweezy (1942, chapter 11), Georgescu-Roegen (1960), and Desai (1979, pp. 151–71).

4. See Rowthorn (1974), Roncaglia (1974), and Steedman (1977, chapter 7), who cite many other authors.
5. See, e.g., the curiously one-sided historical treatment of Braverman (1974).
6. The following discussion of tendency-laws raids Blaug (1980, chapter 2).
7. Sweezy (1942, pp. 84–5n) candidly admits that 'Marxists have generally overlooked the logical difficulties involved in applying the law of value to the commodity labor power', adding that Oskar Lange was the first to point out the implications of the problem for Marx's theoretical structure. This was in 1935, 52 years after Marx's death! Once again, we see evidence that all through the Golden Age of Marxism, Marxists simply failed to understand the logical structure of Marxian economics.
8. For a survey of the latest discussions on Marx's law of the falling rate of profit, see Hodgson (1974b), Christiansen (1975), and Steedman (1977, chapter 9).
9. There is no time to explore the multi-faceted meaning of this theory of 'alienation'. But see Plamenatz (1975), who traces the pre-Marxian history of this theory and considers its validity as a proposition about capitalism as distinct from a proposition about industrialization and urbanization.
10. For a veritable compendium of Marx's predictions, counting 153 in all, of which about half are economic predictions occurring in the four volumes of *Capital*, see Gottheil (1966), and for a perfect example of the ambiguities of some of Marx's predictions, see Rosdolsky (1977, pp. 300–3) on the law of impoverishment of the working-class and Cutler, Hindess, Hirst and Hussain (1977, I, chapters 4, 6) on the law of the falling rate of profit.
11. See Mandel (1975), which exhibits all the worst features of dogmatic Marxism, adopting both Marx's erroneous method of transforming values into prices and the arbitrary investment behaviour built into Marx's reproduction schema, while sternly chastizing other Marxists for misinterpreting the words of the Master. Thus, when posing the question whether 'permanent arms economy' in late capitalism can raise the rate of profit, his answer runs entirely in terms of the tendency of defence expenditures to raise rather than to lower the average organic composition of capital in the economy as a whole, irrespective of how these expenditures are financed. For a brief but trenchant critique of Mandel, see Desai (1979, pp. 204–6), and for a more general critique of Marxist analyses of 'permanent arms economy', see Bleaney (1976, chapter 12).
12. See, e.g., Sweezy (1942, p. 20), Dobb (1945, pp. 127–8, 131; 1973, pp. 25, 36), Meek (1967, pp. 128, 142), Geras (1972, pp. 94–5), Medio (1972, pp. 318–19), Harris (1978, p. 51), and Junankar (1982, pp. 150–1).
13. For an extended discussion of Popper's methodology, see Blaug 1980, chapter 1.
14. It must be said that Popper's cogent critique of Marx is not always satisfactory with respect to Marxian economics. For one thing, Popper (1962, Volume II, pp. 168–70, 181–9, 329) gives much more attention to the law of impoverishment and the notion of increasingly severe business cycles than to the law of the falling rate of profit, and he never explicates the theoretical underpinnings of the latter as the foundation-stone of all of Marx's other 'laws of motion'. For another, his examination of Marx's theory of value (Volume II, pp. 170–7, 344) is open to the charge of being simplistic, ignoring as it does the transformation problem, while equating 'exploitation' in Marx to low wages and long working hours.
15. The story of Bernstein's revisionism has been frequently told but never better than by Kolakowski (1978, Volume II, chapter 4). The whole of Kolakowski's book can be warmly recommended as a breath-taking survey, conceived on a vast scale, of the steady degeneration of Marxism over a period of almost 100 years.

References

Althusser, L. and E. Balibar (1970), *Reading Capital*, London: New Left Books.

Baumol, W.J. (1974), 'The Transformation of Values: What Marx "really" meant (an interpretation)', *Journal of Economic Literature*, **12**, (1), pp. 51–62.

Baumol, W.J. and A.S. Blinden (1979), *Economics, Principles and Policy*, London: Harcourt Brace Jovanovich.

Bell, P.F. (1977), 'Marxist Theory, Class Struggle, and the Crisis of Capitalism', in J. Schwartz (ed.), *The Subtle Anatomy of Capitalism*, Santa Monica: Goodyear Publishing Company.

Blaug, M. (1971), 'The Classical Economists and the Factory Acts – A Re-examination', in A.W. Coats (ed.), *The Classical Economists and Economic Policy*, London: Methuen & Co.

Blaug, M. (1973), *Ricardian Economics*, Westport: Greenwood Press.

Blaug, M. (1975), *The Cambridge Revolution: Success or Failure?* London: Institute of Economic Affairs.

Blaug, M. (1976), 'The Empirical Status of Human Capital Theory: A Slightly Jaundiced Survey', *Journal of Economic Literature*, **14**, (3), pp. 827–55.

Blaug, M. (1978), *Economic Theory in Retrospect*, 3rd ed., Cambridge: Cambridge University Press.

Blaug, M. (1980), *The Methodology of Economics*, Cambridge: Cambridge University Press.

Bleaney, M.F. (1976), *Underconsumption Theories*, London: Lawrence and Wishart.

Blundell-Wignall, A. (1976), 'On Exposing the Transformation Problem', *Australian Economic Papers*, Dec., pp. 277–88.

Bose, A. (1975), *Marxian and Post-Marxian Political Economy*, London: Penguin Books.

Bose, A. (1980), *Marx on Exploitation and Inequality. An Essay in Marxian Analytical Economics*, Oxford: Oxford University Press.

Bowles, S. and H. Gintis (1977), 'The Marxian Theory of Value and Heterogeneous Labour: A Critique and Reformulation', *Cambridge Journal of Economics*, **1**, (1), pp. 173, 192.

Bowles, S and H. Gintis (1978), 'Professor Morishima on Heterogeneous Labour and Marxian Value Theory', *Cambridge Journal of Economics*, **2**, (1), pp. 311–14.

Braverman, H. (1974), *Labor and Monopoly Capital*, New York: Monthly Review Press.

Brewer, A. (1984), *A Guide to Marx's Capital*, Cambridge: Cambridge University Press.

Bronfenbrenner, M. (1970), 'The Vicissitudes of Marxian Economics', *History of Political Economy*, **2**, (2), pp. 205–24.

Bronfenbrenner, M. (1971), *Income Distribution Theory*, London: Macmillan.

Bronfenbrenner, M. (1973), 'Samuelson, Marx, and their Latest Critics', *Journal of Economic Literature*, **2**, (1), pp. 58–64.

Buchanan, A.E. (1982), *Marx and Justice. The Radical Critique of Liberalism*, London: Methuen.

Christiansen, J. (1975), 'Marx and the Falling Profit Rate', *American Economic Review*, **66**, (2), pp. 20–6.

Cleaver, H. (1979), *Reading* Capital *Politically*, Texas: University of Texas Press.

Cohen, G.A. (1979), 'The Labour Theory of Value and the Concept of Exploitation', *Philosophy and Public Affairs*, **8**, (4); reprinted in *The Value Controversy*, I. Steedman (ed.), London: Verso, 1981, pp. 202–23.

Conway, D. (1987), *Farewell to Marx. An Outline and Appraisal of His Theories*, Harmondsworth: Penguin.

Cornforth, M. (1972), *The Open Philosophy and The Open Society*, 2nd ed., London: Lawrence and Wishart.

Cutler, A. and B. Hindess, P. Hirst, A. Hussain (1977), *Marx's Capital and Capitalism Today*, 2 vols, London: Routledge & Kegan Paul.

Desai, M. (1974), *Marxian Economic Theory*, London: Grey-Mills.

Desai, M. (1979), *Marxian Economics*, 2nd ed., Oxford: Basil Blackwell.

Dobb, M. (1945), *Political Economy and Capitalism*, New York: International Publishers.

Dobb, M. (1973), *Theories of Value and Distribution since Adam Smith*, Cambridge: Cambridge University Press.

Eatwell, J. (1975), 'Sraffa's Standard Commodity and the Rate of Exploitation', *Quarterly Journal of Economics*, **89**, (4), pp. 543–56.

Elster, J. (1985), *Making Sense of Marx*, Cambridge: Cambridge University Press.
Fine, B. (1977), 'The Concept and Origin of Profit', in F. Green and P. Nore (eds), *Economics: An Anti-Text*, London: Macmillan.
Fine, B. and L. Harris (1976), 'Controversial Issues in Marxist Economic Theory', in R. Miliband and J. Saville (eds), *The Socialist Register 1976*, London: The Merlin Press.
Fine, B. and L. Harris (1977), 'Surveying the Foundations', in R. Miliband and J. Saville (eds), *The Socialist Register 1977*, London: The Merlin Press.
Fine, B. and L. Harris (1979), *Rereading Capital*, London: Macmillan.
Foley, D. (1986), *Understanding Capital. Marx's Economic Theory*, Cambridge MA: Harvard University Press.
Georgescu-Roegen, N. (1960), 'Mathematical Proofs of the Breakdown of Capitalism', *Econometrica*, **28**, pp. 225–43.
Geras, N. (1972), 'Essence and Appearance: Aspect of "Fetishism" in Marx's Capital', *New Left Review*, in R. Blackburn (ed.) (1970), *Ideology in Social Science*, London: Fontana/Collins.
Geras, N. (1985), 'The Controversy about Marx and Justice', *New Left Review*, 150, March/April, pp. 47–85.
Gottheil, F.M. (1966), *Marx's Economic Predictions*, Evanston, USA: Northwestern University Press.
Gough, I. (1972), 'Marx's Theory of Productive and Unproductive Labour', *New Left Review*, **76**, pp. 47–72.
Harris, D.J. (1978), *Capital, Accumulation and Income Distribution*, London: Routledge & Kegan Paul.
Hodgson, G. (1974a), 'The Theory of the Falling Rate of Profit', *New Left Review*, **84**, pp. 61–3.
Hodgson, G. (1974b), 'Marxian Epistemology and the Transformation Problem', *Economy and Society*, **3**, (4), pp. 357–92.
Hodgson, G. (1977), 'Papering Over the Cracks', in R. Miliband and J. Saville (eds), *The Socialist Register 1977*, London: The Merlin Press.
Hodgson, G. (1982), *Capitalism, Value and Exploitation*, Oxford: Martin Robertson.
Hollander, S. (1981), 'Marxian Economics as "General Equilibrium" Theory', *History of Political Economy*, **13**, (1), pp. 121–55.
Howard, M.C. and J.E. King (1975), *The Political Economy of Marx*, Harlow: Longman Group.
Howard, M.C. and J.E. King (1976), 'Introduction', in *The Economics of Marx*, London: Penguin Books.
Hunt, I. (1986), 'A Critique of Rolmer, Hodgson and Cohen on Marxian Exploitation', *Social Theory and Practice*, **12**, (2), Summer, pp. 121–71.
Johnson, O. (1969), 'The "Last Hour" of Senior and Marx', *History of Political Economy*, **1**, (2), pp. 359–69.
Junankar, P.N. (1982), *Marx's Economics*, Oxford: Phillip Allan.
Kolakowski, L. (1978), *Main Currents of Marxism*, 3 vols, Oxford: Clarendon Press.
Lange, O. (1968), 'Marxian Economics and Modern Economic Theory', in D. Horowitz (ed.), *Marx and Modern Economies*, London: Macgibbon & Kee.
Linder, M. (1977), *Anti-Samuelson*, 2 vols, New York: Urizen Books.
Maguire, J.M. (1978), *Marx's Theory of Politics*, Cambridge: Cambridge University Press.
Mandel, E. (1968), *Marxist Economic Theory*, London: Merlin Press.
Mandel, E. (1975), *Late Capitalism*, London: New Left Books.
Marx, K. (1909), *Capital III*, edited by Friedrich Engels, Chicago: Charles H. Kerr.
Marx, K. (1963), *Theories of Surplus Value*, edited by S. Ryazanskaya, 3 vols, Moscow: Progress Publishers.
Marx, K. (1975), *Karl Marx: Texts on Method*, edited by Terrill Carver, Oxford: Basil Blackwell.
Marx, K. (1976), *Capital I*, introduced by Ernest Mandel, London: Penguin Books.
Marx, K. (1978), *Capital II*, introduced by Ernest Mandel, London: Penguin Books.

Medio, A. (1972), 'Profits and Surplus Value: Appearance and Reality in Capitalist Production', in E.K. Hunt and J.G. Schwartz (eds), *A Critique of Economic Theory*, London: Penguin Books.

Meek, R.L. (1967), *Economics and Ideology and Other Essays*, London: Chapman and Hall.

Meek, R.L. (1973), *Studies in the Labour Theory of Value*, 2nd ed., London: Lawrence and Wishart.

Meek, R.L. (1977), *Smith, Marx, and After*, London: Chapman and Hall.

Morishima, M. (1973), *Marx's Economics: A Dual Theory of Value and Growth*, Cambridge: Cambridge University Press.

Morishima, M. (1974), 'The Fundamental Marxian Theorem: A reply to Samuelson', *Journal of Economic Literature*, **12**, (1), pp. 71–4.

Morishima, M. and G.C. Catephores (1978), *Value Exploitation and Growth*, London: McGraw-Hill.

Nuti, D.M. (1977), 'The Transformation of Labour Values into Production Prices and the Marxian Theory of Exploitation', in J. Schwartz (ed.), *The Subtle Anatomy of Capitalism*, Santa Monica, USA: Goodyear.

Oakley, A. (1976), 'Two Notes on Marx and the "Transformation Problem" ', *Economica*, **43**, (172), pp. 411–18.

Ollman, B. (1971), *Marx's Conception of Man in Capitalist Society*, Cambridge: Cambridge University Press.

Pasinetti, L. (1977), *Lectures on the Theory of Production*, London: Macmillan.

Plamenatz, J. (1975), *Karl Marx's Philosophy of Man*, Oxford: Oxford University Press.

Popper, K.R. (1957), *The Poverty of Historicism*, London: Routledge & Kegan Paul.

Popper, K.R. (1962), *The Open Society and its Enemies*, 2 vols, 4th ed., London: Routledge & Kegan Paul.

Popper, K.R. (1976), *Unended Quest: An Intellectual Autobiography*, London: Fontana/Collins.

Robinson, J. (1942), *An Essay on Marxian Economics*, London: Macmillan.

Roemer, J. (1981), *Analytical Foundations of Marxian Economic Theory*, Cambridge MA: Cambridge University Press.

Roemer, J. (1982), *A General Theory of Exploitation and Class*, Cambridge MA: Harvard University Press.

Roemer, J. (1985), 'Should Marxists be Interested in Exploitation?', *Philosophy and Public Affairs*, **14**, (1), pp. 30–65.

Roncaglia, A. (1974), 'The Reduction of Complex Labour to Simple Labour', *Bulletin of the Conference of Socialist Economists*, **9**, pp. 1–12.

Roncaglia, A. (1978), *Sraffa and the Theory of Prices*, Chichester: Wiley.

Rosdolsky, R. (1977), *The Making of Marx's 'Capital'*, London: Pluto Press.

Rowthorn, B. (1974), 'Skilled Labour in the Marxian System', *Bulletin of the Conference of Socialist Economists*, **8**, pp. 25–45.

Samuelson, P.A. (1966), 'A Modern Treatment of the Ricardian Economy: 1. The Pricing of Goods and of Labor and Land Services', in J.E. Stiglitz (ed.), *The Collected Scientific Papers of Paul A. Samuelson 1*, Cambridge MA: MIT Press.

Samuelson, P.A. (1972), 'Understanding the Marxian Notion of Exploitation: A Summary of the so-called Transformation Problem between Marxian Values and Competitive Prices', in R.C. Merton (ed.), *The Collected Scientific Papers of Paul A. Samuelson 3*, Cambridge MA: MIT Press.

Samuelson, P.A. (1976), *Economics*, 10th ed., New York: McGraw-Hill.

Samuelson, P.A. (1977), 'Reply on Marxian Matters' (*Journal of Economic Literature*, 1973); 'Marx as a Mathematical Economist: Steady-state and Exponential Growth Equilibrium', in A. Metzler, G. Howich and P.A. Samuelson (eds), *Trade, Stability and Macroeconomic Essays in Honor of Lloyd*; 'Insight and Detour in the Theory of Exploitation: A Reply to Baumol' (*Journal of Economic Literature*, 1974), all in H. Nagatani and K. Crowley (eds), *The Collected Scientific Papers of Paul A. Samuelson 4*, Cambridge MA: MIT Press.

Schumpeter, J.A. (1942), *Capitalism, Socialism and Democracy*, Oxford: Oxford University Press.

Schumpeter, J.A. (1954), *A History of Economic Analysis*, Oxford: Oxford University Press.

Seton, F. (1976), 'The "Transformation Problem" ', in M.C. Howard and J.E. King (eds), *The Economics of Marx*, London: Penguin Books.

Shaikh, A. (1977), 'Marx's Theory of Value and the "Transformation Problem" ', in J. Schwartz (ed.), *The Subtle Anatomy of Capitalism*, Santa Monica: Goodyear.

Sowell, T. (1976), 'Marx's *Capital* after One Hundred Years', in M.C. Howard and J.E. King (eds), *The Economics of Marx*, London: Penguin Books.

Steedman, I. (1977), *Marx After Sraffa*, London: New Left Books.

Steedman, I. (1981), 'Ricardo, Marx, Sraffa, in The Value Controversy', ed., I. Steedman *et al.*, London: Verso.

Sweezy, P. (1942), *The Theory of Capitalist Development*, New York: Oxford University Press.

Walker, A. (1978), *Marx: His Theory and its Context*, London: Longman.

Weston, J.F. (1970), 'The Profit Concept and Theory: A Restatement', in I.H. Rima (ed.), *Readings in the History of Economic Theory*, New York: Holt, Rinehart & Winston.

Wiles, P.J.D. (1977), *Economic Institutions Compared*, Oxford: Basil Blackwell.

Wolff, E.N. (1979), 'The Rate of Surplus Value, the Organic Composition, and the General Rate of Profit in the U.S. Economy, 1947–67', *American Economic Review*, **69**, (3), pp. 329–41.

Wolff, R.P. (1984), *Understanding Marx. A Reconstruction and Critique of Capital*, Princeton NJ: Princeton University Press.

Wolfson, M. (1966), *A Reappraisal of Marxian Economics*, New York: Columbia University Press.

Wolfson, M. (1971), *Karl Marx, Columbia Essays on Great Economists 3,* New York: Columbia University Press.

Wolfstetter, E. (1973), 'Surplus Labour, Synchronised Labour Costs and Marx's Labour Theory of Value', *Economic Journal*, **83**, pp. 787–809.

Wright, E.O. (1979), 'The Value Controversy and Social Research', *New Left Review*, **116**, pp. 53-82.

3 The falling rate of profit debate in Marx: alternative lines of interpretation*

L.E. Johnson, Warren S. Gramm and David J. Hoaas

Karl Marx's doctrine of the falling rate of profit has stimulated considerable debate (Brewer 1984, p. 145; Fine and Harris 1979, p. 58).[1] Moreover, the debate is seen by many as a critical aspect of the broader controversy regarding Marx's economics since it represents one of his basic tenets concerning the laws of motion of capitalism in general, and the self-limiting nature of capitalist expansion in particular.[2] With regard to the law's importance in evaluating the scientific content of Marx's analysis, Laibman (1982, p. 95) notes:

> Its advocates contend that Marx's law of the falling rate of profit is the central immanent contradiction of capitalism; to abandon it would be to remove the objective necessity of capitalist crisis and socialist revolution. Marxist political economy then becomes another form of radical populism, and socialism a utopian rather than a scientific concept. Critics, on the other hand, deny this interpretation, suggesting that this is too narrow and fatalistic a view of capitalism's eminent contradiction one which denies the involvement of class struggle and consciousness in that contradiction.

Our aim in this chapter is to determine the extent to which well-defined alternative lines of interpretation have emerged from the flood of research on Marx's law of profit. We are not concerned with questions of textual exegesis (Stigler 1965, pp. 447–50). As such, no attempt is made to defend a particular line of interpretation, nor to provide an alternative reconstruction of Marx's doctrine.

In part, the problem of identifying alternative lines of interpretation regarding Marx's law of profit results from the vast amount of literature. The matter has been further complicated by differing views regarding the phenomena to which the law is intended to apply. For example, does it refer to movements in an actual rate as opposed to the potential

* Some of the material contained in this chapter was presented at the 1988 Atlantic Economic Society meetings. It also reflects views contained in 'The Legacy of Ricardo: A Review Article' (Johnson 1988). Still other aspects emerged from the series of lectures Johnson delivered to the Dipartimento di Teoria Economia e Metodi Quantitativi per le Scelte Politiche of the University of Rome in 1987. The authors wish to thank Professor Giovanni A. Caravale for his many helpful suggestions.

and underlying rate of profit, or does it refer to the price rate as opposed to the value rate of profit?[3] Moreover, problems of textual exegesis emerge from the different approaches in Volumes I and III of *Capital*.

In our view, however, an important source of difficulty also results from the fact that the debate has been carried on at three distinct, though admittedly interrelated, levels of abstraction.[4]

First, Marx's law of profit has been discussed in the context of his theory of cycles and the problems of sectoral disproportionality, under-consumption, and cyclical instability. At this level of abstraction the self-limiting nature of capitalism is a purely endogenous process (Brewer 1984, pp. 149–50; Wolff and Resnick 1987, pp. 189–92).

At a second level of abstraction, the law is presented in the context of Marx's theory of secular crisis. The primary emphasis here involves its relationship to rise in the organic composition of capital, the rate of exploitation, structural unemployment, monopolization of capital, and the subsistence wage doctrine. At this level the self-limiting nature of capitalism is also endogenous.

Finally, the law has been placed in the broader meta-economic context of the natural law of historical change, and its relationship to class struggle, alienation, and immizeration. At this level of abstraction, the self-limiting nature of the capitalist system results from both endogenous and exogenous forces (Elster 1988, p. 74).

In this chapter we focus on the law of profit as it relates to Marx's secular theory of crisis. We argue that at this level of abstraction there are four well-defined lines of interpretation, and that these alternatives present similarities to the methodological evolution that has characterized the current Ricardian controversy.

The state of the Ricardian controversy

Our interest in these matters, indeed the importance of the subject itself, involves its methodological dimensions. On the one hand, the evolution of alternative lines of Ricardian interpretation reflects the differing analytical and ideologically competing schools of modern economic analysis (Caravale 1985, p. ix; Johnson 1988, p. 792). On the other hand, the current Ricardian debate arguably mirrors the methodological alternatives for the study of the history of economics in general (Maneschi and Thweatt 1987, p. 806).

Continuing debate regarding various aspects of Ricardo's analysis began in his own lifetime (Stigler 1958, p. 362),[5] and remains a source of controversy (Johnson 1984, pp. 50–9; 1988 p. 781).[6] The current Ricardian controversy originated with Sraffa's publication of Ricardo's collected works (Sraffa 1951),[7] and was further stimulated by the publication of *Production of Commodities by Means of Commodities* (Sraffa 1960), where Sraffa argued that Ricardo's 'invariable measure of value' was an attempt to expand the basic logic of the corn model (Blaug 1985, pp. 3–4). As a result, diverse reconstructions have appeared on various aspects of Ricardo's thought.[8]

The result of this rush of new literature has been the emergence of three fairly well-defined lines of Ricardian interpretation (Johnson 1988, pp. 781–96).[9] The first is the 'neo-classical New-View',[10] which employs the objectivist methodological model[11] (Johnson 1980, pp. 53–4; 1988, pp. 787–8; Johnson and Ley 1988, pp. 14–16). Here Ricardo is placed in a continuum originating with Adam Smith and running through J.B. Say, Leon Walras, and Alfred Marshall. This rejects the view that the 1870s and the development of the neo-classical paradigm represented a revolution in economics (Hollander 1985, p. 13). This reconstruction is static. Ricardo's focus, like that of the neo-classicists, is presumed to be allocative efficiency in the context of a price-auction general equilibrium market framework. With this interpretation there is no separation of prices and outputs, consumer demand impacts on product prices and factor returns, and there is a clear interdependence between commodity and resource markets (Hollander 1985, pp. 16–17). All prices are determined endogenously and are variable, including the real wage rate. The major focus in this reconstruction is on the nature and role of short-run market equilibrium adjustments (Blaug 1985, p. 4), rather than on the classical natural equilibrium (Caravale 1985, pp. vii, 130–2). The role of opportunity costs and derived factor demand in a cost-price theory of value play a key role in this line of interpretation (Hollander 1985, pp. 18, 20–2, 29, 30). Finally, there are no class antagonisms present (Johnson 1988, pp. 784–6).

A second line of Ricardian reconstruction is the 'Sraffa-based' interpretation.[12] This approach focuses on the role of natural equilibrium and an exogenously determined natural wage. This interpretative line is also static. Prices and quantities are determined separately in a one-way causal chain in the context of a constant level of output and technology. The 'fundamental theorem of distribution' involves an inverse wage rate–profit rate. The key class relationship in Ricardo then centres on capitalists and workers. This reconstruction places Ricardo in a direct Ricardo–Marx–Sraffa continuum. Hence, it provides a non-paradigmatic form of objectivism,[13] and represents a frontal assault on neo-classical New-View (Garegnani 1985, pp. 87–9, 94–6).

Finally, a third interpretive line has emerged which may be termed the 'neo-Sraffa' view.[14] In this reconstruction, Ricardo's analysis is presented in the context of a dynamic, natural equilibrium growth path which defines the distributive relationships between rent, the rate of profit, and the given real wage rate (Caravale 1985, pp. 129, 135–6, 140, 143). The system's expansion and distributional features are described as a series of natural equilibrium positions along a growth path, which represents a centre of gravity toward which the system is continually pulled. Once this path has been specified, the fundamental theorem of distribution becomes the inverse relationship between diminishing returns in agriculture – increasing labour content of corn – and the rate of profit. As such, the key class antagonism is between landlords and capitalists, and not between workers and capitalists as in the Sraffa-based reconstruction (Caravale 1985, p. 168). Like the Sraffa-based view, the focus is on natural equilibrium with an exogenously determined real wage, but there is no separation of prices and quantities. In the neo-Sraffa approach, Ricardo is placed within the classical paradigm of political economy (Johnson 1980, pp. 55–60; 1983, pp. 1097–1107; 1988, pp. 789–90; Johnson and Ley 1988, pp. 25–38, 89–116).

A number of points of method emerge from the current Ricardian debate. First, the traditional objectivist interpretation of Ricardo is alive and well, but has been pushed to a logical extreme in the neo-classical New-View. Second, the traditional relativist view[15] (Johnson 1980, pp. 53–4; Johnson and Ley 1988, pp. 16–19) has evolved into a non-paradigmatic version of objectivism in the hands of the Sraffa advocates. Finally, the neo-Sraffa line of interpretation, in many respects, employs a paradigmatic framework[16] and represents a synthesis of the two objectivist lines (Johnson 1988, pp. 791–2).

Marx's law: the traditional relativist approach

One interpretative approach to Marx's law of profit applies the relativist methodological model. Here Marx's law is generally placed in the context of classical political economy. Thus, relativist interpreters generally present Marx's law and related theory of the secular crisis in a framework of historical dynamics (Baumol 1959, pp. 6–9; Morse 1961, pp. 237–9; Schumpeter 1963, pp. 963–7, 1160–1), rather than dynamics defined in the sense of modern growth theory (Samuelson 1948, pp. 8–10, 284–5, chapter XI; Harrod 1948; Frisch 1935, pp. 100–5). Moreover, Marx's law is seen as a reaction against the explanations provided by his classical predecessors for the secular fall in the general rate of profit. In particular, these writers contend that Marx's law was derived as an alternative to the Ricardian explanation based on decreasing returns to social scale (Dobb 1959, p. 99; Foley 1986, chapter 8; Hunt 1979);[17] that Marx emphasized instead the necessity for capitalists to accumulate and innovate if they are to survive the rigours of competition (Balinky 1970, pp. 127–8).

The relativist definition of profit, and therefore, the rate of profit in Marx is consistent with the general classical conception. As such, it is an aggregative, general economy-wide average rate (Balinky 1970, p. 125) based on a residual theory of the profits (Baumol 1959, p. 16) as a class income share, though the definition of the components of this residual are unique to Marx's own analysis. Hence, it represents a rate of return to capitalists as an economic class rather than a return to capital as productive factor.[18] Certainly there is no implication of profits as a neo-classical opportunity cost of entrepreneurship.

Finally, relativists see the law of profit in Marx within the context of the political economist's overriding concern with capitalism's capability for long-run maximization[19] of total social welfare (Johnson 1983, p. 1105; Johnson and Ley 1988, pp. 89–90). Thus, Marx's law is treated as part of the general classical concern for the interdependency between the basic issues of economic growth and the class income distribution, in the context of a natural equilibrium (Landreth and Colander 1989, p. 185), though this aspect of their argument has never been clearly and consistently specified.

In the relativist line of interpretation, Marx's law of the falling rate of profit is neither a theoretical nor empirical proposition; rather it is tautological or definitional in nature (Hunt 1979, p. 205; Robinson 1966, p. 36). The tautology has its origins in Marx's labour theory of the source of value. This maintains that surplus value can be created only by hours of socially necessary abstract labour power embodied in produced goods. Surplus value is then generated only from variable capital, while the rate of profit is based on all capital (Hunt 1979, pp. 203–6). Therefore, an increase in the organic composition of capital will generate a fall in the rate of profit as long as the rate of surplus value remains constant or rises by a less than equal proportion to the organic composition.

At least two alternative strains of relativism have emerged (Meek 1967, pp. 129–42). With some exceptions, one group of interpreters might be termed the 'early Cambridge' relativists. These writers argue that if Marx's law is viewed as a tautology, it must be understood in the context of a constant rate of exploitation (Robinson 1966, p. 36). This view leads to a de-emphasis of the countervailing influences,[20] which create potential offsets to the law. Moreover, these writers tend to argue that Marx's law has explanatory meaning only in the context of an appropriate theory of aggregate demand (Robinson 1966, p. 42); that without such a theory it is not critical or even necessary to Marx's theory of secular crisis (Dobb 1959, p. 101; Moszkowska 1935; Robinson 1966, pp. 35–42; Sweezy 1968).

On the other hand, what may be termed the 'orthodox' relativists, of which there are numerous permutations, contend that Marx never intended to confine his law of profit to situations in which the rate of exploitation was assumed constant (Balinky 1970, pp. 127–9; Cogoy 1973; Fine and Harris 1979, pp. 61–5; Hunt 1979, pp. 204–6; Landreth and Colander 1989, p. 185; Meek 1967, p. 134; and Yaffe 1972). These interpreters emphasize the countervailing influences on Marx's law, pointing out the conditions under which these forces do or do not result in its violation. At the very least they see the law as a taxonomical device for identifying various forces that could, at any time, be producing results opposite from the actual historical trend of the rate of profit (Hunt 1979, p. 205). Ultimately, however, orthodox relativists – though for different reasons – argue that secularly the law tends to hold.

Despite the fact that the relativists generally see Marx's law of profit as a definitional or axiomatic proposition, and irrespective of their views regarding its primacy in Marx's theory of secular crisis, these writers all see that Marx's law was part and parcel of his understanding of the laws of motion of capitalist expansion.

Depending on the relativist strain to which one refers, several difficulties emerge with Marx's law of profit in its definitional form. First, there are a number of problems presented in the countervailing forces. These include the facts: (1) that certain of these influences may result in a fall in the organic composition; (2) that they may cause an increase in the rate of exploitation in the context of a constant organic composition of capital; or (3) that they may lead to an increase in both the organic composition of capital and the rate of exploitation, hence the possibility that the latter will increase at a greater than equal proportion to the former (Balinky 1970, pp. 130–3). The last two possibilities are the ones most interpreters have focused on, since they appear to violate the secular trends which define Marx's view of capitalist expansion and contraction.

Most of these difficulties, as well, indeed, as the relevance of Marx's law, are eliminated if one accepts the early Cambridge version. That is, if Marx's law requires a constant rate of exploitation, it thereby abstracts from distributional changes, from indirect effects of the rising technical composition of capital, and the effects of price and wage changes (Fine and Harris 1979, p. 62).

However, such is not the case for the orthodox relativist. A number of solutions have been presented by these writers in defence of Marx's law. Some of these analyses have argued that there are simply practical limits to the capitalist's ability to increase the rate of exploitation (Hunt 1979, p. 204; Meek 1967, p. 133). Once those limits are reached, the validity of the law will re-establish itself. Others have centred their argument on the distinction between relative and absolute exploitation, emphasizing the primacy of relative exploitation as the cause of secular increases in the rate of exploitation. Still others have simply shifted the ground of the debate by moving to another level of abstraction. On the one hand, some have shifted their definition of the law to Marx's theory of cycles (Fine and Harris 1979, p. 71). In some instances emphasis is placed on the tendency of the value rate of profit to fall and the interdependence between the process of production and exchange. Here careful distinction is made between the organic composition of capital and value of the composition of capital.[21] In this variant of the orthodox approach, it is then argued that Marx's law depends on the organic composition, while the countervailing influences depend on the value of the composition of capital (Fine and Harris 1979, pp. 58–65). In other instances, primary emphasis is on the actual rate of profit in relation to cycles to show that no inconsistency exists (Cogoy 1973; Yaffe 1972). On the other hand, some have shifted the focus to the historical relationship between the law of profit and the immizeration of the working class, hence the process of historical change.

The connection between real wages and the validity of Marx's law creates a second problem. One difficulty concerns the law's relationship to the wage share that accrues to labour. Given a constant rate of exploitation, with an increase in the organic composition of capital, the resulting increase in productivity will cause the real wage share to increase in a constant proportion to an increasing output. Marx's law then results in an increase in real wages, which appears to be inconsistent with his view of the matter (Robinson 1966, p. 36). On the other hand, the real wage contradiction is sometimes presented in terms of the wage rate. If the rate of profit is determined by the marginal productivity of capital, with a fixed technology the increase in the organic composition of capital will result in the fall in the rate of profit as capital per man increases. However, the marginal productivity of labour will rise; since competition among capitalists causes the real wage to equal labour's marginal product, the wage rate will rise as the rate of profit falls (Robinson 1966, pp. 36–7).

The problem of the relationship of Marx's law to a rising wage share presents a difficulty only for the early Cambridge writers who have insisted that the rate of exploitation remain constant. Even here the problem disappears once it is admitted that Marx was concerned with the direction of change in relative rather than absolute shares. The problem of an increasing real wage share, of course, is of no consequence for orthodox relativists who reject the assumption of a constant rate of exploitation.

A rising real wage rate is likewise little problem to the relativist interpreter of Marx's law of profit. On the one hand, the marginal productivity theory of wages is completely at odds with Marx's analysis of value (Robinson 1966, p. 38). Moreover, the difficulty is eliminated by many relativist interpreters who argue that the subsistence wage doctrine in Marx emanates from the same forces that lead to his law of profit, the creation of the reserve army as a result of the rising organic composition of capital. Finally, many relativists also judge that while Marx thought that the real wage rate tended toward subsistence, his doctrine was based on a culturally rather than biologically defined notion of subsistence.

The traditional objectivist interpretation of Marx's law of profit

A second traditional line of interpretation of Marx's law of profit is based on the objectivist methodological model. In this reconstruction, Marx's law is placed in the context of neo-classical production theory employing a constant returns to scale production function (Blaug 1986, p. 250; Dickinson 1956–57). As such, the law of profit is evaluated either in an essentially static framework, or within the dynamics of conventional growth theory. Moreover, there is no attempt in the objectivist reconstruction to relate Marx's law to any notion of a classical natural equilibrium. Hence, objectivist interpreters typically place Marx's analysis in general, and his law of profit in particular, outside of the development of mainstream economic analysis. In paradigmatic terms, Marx's economics necessarily lies outside the classical paradigm of political economy, representing a non-paradigmatic alternative to mid-19th century orthodoxy.

With the objectivist approach, the law of profit in Marx is neither a definitional nor tautological proposition. On the contrary, these writers base the law on a functional relationship between the rate of profit and the organic composition of capital (Blaug 1986, p. 246; Dickinson 1956–57, p. 125). Objectivists do not impute a neo-classical opportunity cost notion to the rate of profit. They do, however, define it as a return to capital as opposed to a return to capitalists as an economic class. Finally, objectivist interpreters, like relativists, define the rate of profit as an aggregative variable.

The objectivist interpretive line has focused on the problem of distinguishing between changes in technology, and changes in the aggregate technique of production. As one would expect, this was a problem that did not concern Marx since he typically treated innovations as being embodied in new investment (Blaug 1986, pp. 243–50). The objectivist concludes that for movements along the production function, in the face of a constant technology, an increase in the organic composition of capital will result in a fall in the rate of profit. This result obtains since output per man rises less than in proportion to capital per man along the production function. For, as capital increases, assuming its efficient employment, an increase in the capital–output ratio will cause a fall in the marginal productivity of capital and the rate of profit (Robinson 1966, pp. 36–7).

However, once technological change is introduced, Marx's law becomes subject to qualification in the objectivist framework. Now the validity of the law depends on the nature of the technological change. If technological change is labour saving, the natural assumption for Marx to make (Robinson 1966, p. 36) and indeed, necessary for his theory of the reserve army and the subsistence wage doctrine (Baumol 1959, p. 30), it results in an increase in the organic composition, hence in the fall in the profit rate. Here, the capital-absorbing effects of the innovation govern the degree to which wages rise as capital increases (Blaug 1986, pp. 250–1). If wages rise as fast as output per man, relative shares are unaffected and the rising capital–output ratio alone leads to a fall in the rate of profit. The Marxian law, therefore, is based upon a very rapidly rising capital–output ratio, which implies that technical change is heavily slanted toward labour-saving improvements. If, on the other hand, the technological change is capital saving or Harrod-neutral, Marx's law no longer is valid.

In summary then, the objectivist reconstruction of Marx's law is functionally rather than definitionally grounded; it depends on the nature of the production function instead of the definition of the value components of output. As such, the objectivist approach does not require a labour theory of the measure of absolute value in the social accounting sense of that term (Johnson 1984, p. 50).

However, despite its advantages, this approach begs a number of broad interpretive questions. First, despite the fact that the nature of the production function is specified and the functional relationship between the profit rate and the organic composition is established, it is not clear that objectivists have avoided the definitional basis of Marx's law. It still can be argued that the whole objectivist apparatus requires the acceptance of the labour theory of the source of value (while a labour theory of the measure of absolute value is not required). In a word, a rise in the organic composition of capital will not functionally lead to a falling rate of profit under any circumstance unless the only source of surplus value is embodied labour.

Second, one wonders if the 'Magnificent Dynamics' of Marx's theory of secular crisis, of which his law of profits was an important part, can be adequately understood in the context of neo-classical statics, or even with the conventionally-defined dynamics of modern growth theory. With the objectivist derivation of Marx's law, the ties that Marx so emphatically emphasized between the rate of profit, technological unemployment, the monopolization of capital (Baumol 1959, p. 31), the reserve army, and the subsistence wage doctrine are at the very least tenuous.

Finally, even though the rate of profit is defined as a macroeconomic aggregate, the objectivist approach which places Marx's law in the context of neo-classical production theory is questionable. Many interpreters have noted that Marx's entire theory of value is intended to exclude the idea of attributing productivity to capital, as well as the concept of incremental productivity of any productive factor (Robinson 1966, pp. 37–8).

The neo-classical New-View of Marx's law

During the past decade a third line of reconstruction of Marx's law of profits has emerged, which may be termed the 'neo-classical New-View'. This approach also employs the objectivist model, but pushes it to its logical extreme. In the neo-classical New-View, Marx's law is placed in the context of neo-classical microeconomic general equilibrium theory. Thus, the law of profit is couched in terms of allocative efficiency, rather than its relationship to the long-run problems of growth, distribution, and the resulting effects on total social welfare with which the classical political economists were primarily concerned. As such, the New-View presents Marx's law in a purely short-run static framework. Here the focus is exclusively on competitive market equilibrium, rather than classical long-run natural equilibrium analysis. Finally, the rate of profit in the New-View interpretation is a microeconomic rate, which is defined as a late neo-classical opportunity cost.

This interpretation of Marx's law has its origins in the Okishio theorem (Okishio 1961). With this theorem it is argued that, assuming a constant real wage, it is impossible for an increase in the organic composition of capital to generate a fall in the equilibrium rate of profit. Van Parijs (1980, p. 10) summarizes Okishio's theorem as follows:

> Under competitive capitalism, a profit-maximizing individual capitalist will only adopt a new technique of production . . . if it reduces production cost per unit or increases profits per unit at going prices. A technical innovation which satisfies this condition . . . enables the capitalist to get (temporarily) a transitional rate of profit higher than the initial general rate in the economy . . . [T]he generalization of the technique within the industry and capital movements between industries will [equalize] the rates of profit throughout the economy. . . . [I]t is completely impossible for the general rate of profit to fall as a result of a viable technical innovation if real wages are kept constant.

Initially, exception was taken to Okishio's theorem (Shaikh 1978). Shaikh argued that Okishio looked only at rates of profit (total profit/total investment) instead of profit margins (total profit/total cost), and these will differ in the absence of fixed capital. In Shaikh's purely competitive model, by distinguishing between the rate of profit and the profit margin[22] it becomes possible to introduce viable (cost reducing) innovations which will cause a fall in the rate of profit.[23]

However, the attack on Marx's law originated by Okishio was again picked up by van Parijs who traced the arguments regarding the validity of the law from its early Marxist origins to the work of Shaikh (1978).[24] He argued that with a proper definition of the organic composition of capital (van Parijs 1980, pp. 3–4) and the assumption that the ratio of the means of production grows faster than the amount of labour employed, a rise in the organic composition of capital can lead to a fall in the equilibrium rate of profit. For this to occur, however, one of the following three conditions must hold: (1) a fall in the length of the working day; (2) a rise in the real wage; or (3) an increase in the embodied labour requirement of the means of subsistence. The first two present a profit-squeeze approach to the falling rate of profit; the third is the typical Ricardian view. Van Parijs argues that while all these could result in a falling rate of profit, they are non-Marxian and should be ignored in evaluating Marx's law. Holding the above factors constant, van Parijs concludes that the most that can be demonstrated is that the maximum rate of profit must fall. The maximum rate of profit, however, is not the equilibrium rate, and changes in the maximum rate may have no implications for the equilibrium rate since the maximum rate of profit may fall while the equilibrium rate is rising, or vice versa.

The neo-classical New-View has received its most complete and recent articulation by Roemer (1979, 1981, 1988). Roemer (1981, p. 112) summarizes the problem as follows:

> For the most part discussion of the Marxian falling rate of profit (FRP) theory is marked by lack of attention to microeconomic detail . . . Briefly, the profit-maximizing urge of capitalists directs them to replace workers with

> machinery, which raises the organic composition of capital, which lowers (or produces a tendency to lower) the profit rate . . . It claims to deduce a macroeconomic phenomenon, itself quite beyond the ability of any individual capitalist to realize from the anarchic (competitive) behavior of atomized economic units.[25]

Roemer then believes that the appropriate approach to Marx's law is to postulate the microeconomic behaviour of capitalists concerning technical innovation that may lead to a falling rate of profit (Roemer 1981, pp. 113–14). A von Neumann general equilibrium model is employed wherein Roemer assumes that: (1) fixed capital can wear out at different rates; (2) joint production of output occurs; and (3) production processes can have different periods of production. With regard to improvements in technology, Roemer assumes that innovations take the form of inventing new processes, but not new commodities and that inventions and innovations are 'free' non-economic goods (Roemer 1981, p. 130). In equilibrium it is possible for the system to reproduce itself by operating only those processes that achieve the maximum rate of profit. Moreover, this rate will be unique and equal to the von Neumann rate, which is the minimum rate of profit derived from sales of commodities for which all prices are greater than or equal to zero (Roemer 1981, pp. 125–6).

Using this model, Roemer addresses the Okishio theorem, and concludes that 'if real wages are assumed fixed, then rational innovation never leads to a falling rate of profit, regardless of complications introduced by fixed capital, differential turnover times, and so on' (p. 130).[26] He then addresses several other propositions concerning the falling rate of profit. As noted earlier, in response to Okishio's theorem some have contended that although the actual rate of profit rises, the maximum rate of profit falls. The proposition that mechanization lowers the maximum rate of profit implies that sooner or later the actual rate of profit must fall. Roemer disagrees, arguing that the maximal rate of profit is of no consequence for what happens to the actual rate (1981, pp. 115–16).[27] Others have argued that if the organic composition of capital rises over time as a consequence of technical change, then, all other things being equal, the value of the rate of profit also will fall. Again Roemer disagrees, under the assumption that the real wages remain fixed; in that case the surplus always will rise sufficiently to more than offset the rise in the organic composition of capital, under the assumed competitive scenario (1981, pp. 118–19). Finally, some have attempted to rescue Marx's law by claiming that competitive innovations will cause the profit margin to rise, but the profit rate will fall if large amounts of fixed capital are involved. Roemer argues that the criterion of innovation with which these models burden capital is incorrect; they ignore the costs of fixed capital (except for depreciation). Any capitalist considering an innovation that involves fixed capital must amortize its costs (1981, pp. 122–3).

In summary, Roemer argues that with a constant real wage there are no grounds for a falling rate of profit theory in a competitive equilibrium environment.[28] If the rate of profit falls in a changing real wage model, it is a consequence of the class struggle that follows technical innovation, not because of innovation itself.[29]

The elegantly formulated neo-classical general equilibrium models employed in the New-View, presents an interpretive line that appears to be fundamentally anti-Marxian. Marx's theory of secular crisis, of which his law of profit is a part, is forced into the totally static framework of neo-classical general equilibrium analysis. One must question the use of a subjective, individualistic, allocative efficiency welfare model to reconstruct the Marxian analysis of the secular expansion of capitalism. The latter, in complete contrast, involves the large questions of economic growth, distribution, and the maximization of total social welfare (Johnson 1983, pp. 1104–7; Johnson and Ley 1988, pp. 89–90, 112–16).

How legitimate is it for the New-View interpreters to employ an analytical construct that implicitly assumes an atomistic and harmonistic view of society and the economy, when the classical political economists, including Marx, adhered to a pluralistic view of society and a class conflict view of the economy? Finally, the notion of profit and the rate of profit employed in the neo-classical New-View seems antithetical to Marx's understanding. The relevance of their results is subject to serious question. Whether one relates the rate of profit in Marx to the share accruing to the capitalist class, or as a direct return to capital, it clearly is based on a residual theory of profits. It refers to an aggregate, economy-wide rate, rather than the opportunity cost rate utilized in the New-View reconstruction.

The Sraffa-based interpretation of Marx's law of profit

A final line of reconstruction of Marx's law of profit which appears to be emerging is the 'Sraffa-based' interpretation.[30] This approach has its origins in early Cambridge relativism, along with the work of others such as Sweezy (1968). Its recent development, however, owes most to the analysis of Himmelweit (1974), and Hodgson (1974), and in some specific respects to the work of Steedman (1972, 1975, 1976, 1977).

The Sraffa-based interpretation places Marx in a direct non-paradigmatic objectivist continuum running of Ricardo, Marx, and Sraffa.

These writers put Marx's law in the context of a secular tendency toward natural equilibrium (Fine and Harris 1979, p. 71). Moreover, like other political economists, Marx's law is placed in the setting of pluralistic view of society and a class conflict view of the economy; still, the Sraffa-based interpreters analyse this tendency with a static price of production model, which utilizes Sraffa's standard commodity.[31] As such, Marx's law is analysed in terms of given levels of output and technology – meaning the state of the arts, not the matrix of technical coefficients of production.[32]

Basic to the Sraffa-based reconstruction of Marx's law is the 'fundamental theorem of distribution', which posits an inverse real wage rate–profit rate relationship (Fine and Harris 1979, p. 26; Steedman 1977, p. 127). Rather than being functionally or definitionally based on the organic composition of capital, the rate of profit is functionally related to the wage rate, hence it is related to the profit share and the return to capitalists as an economic class. Though the proponents of the Sraffa-based view are concerned with the actual rate of profit, they define it, nevertheless, as an aggregate, economy-wide rate.

This interpretive line of Marx's law discounts distinctions between the valuc composition of capital, tcchnical composition, and the organic composition of capital (Steedman 1977, pp. 132–3).[33] Thus, their concern is whether or not the net effect of the law in relation to the countervailing tendencies creates a secular fall in the actual rate of profit (Fine and Harris 1979, p. 66). They conclude that Marx's law of profit does not hold, since a rise in the technical composition of capital does not necessarily lead to an increase in the organic composition of capital. Moreover, even if it does, it will not necessarily cause a fall in the actual rate of profit.

In a price of production model, with a given level of technology, but with changing technical coefficients of production, it can be established that there is an inverse relationship between the wage and the actual rate of profit (Sraffa 1960). Therefore, these writers conclude that a wage increase is generally associated with a fall in the actual rate of profit. In one version of the Sraffa-based reconstruction, with a given real wage, technical progress will raise not lower the actual rate of profit; 'technical regress can result only from worsening conditions in the production of . . . raw materials. [then] With a given real wage, a falling rate of profit can . . . result only from the increasing niggardliness of nature' (Steedman 1977, p. 129). Other commentators, however, argue that the rate of profit is 'equally determined' by higher wages stemming from the class struggle and technically-based increases in productivity (Fine and Harris 1979, pp. 26–7). Irrespective of differences in the particulars, the Sraffa-based interpretation concludes that the element of truth in Marx's law is that a rise in the technical composition of capital may involve a fall in the maximum attainable rate of profit, that is, the rate that would exist if wages were equal to zero. As long as wages are greater than zero, Marx's law would not hold (Fine and Harris 1979, pp. 68–70).

There are appealing, innovative features of the Sraffa-based reconstruction. However, both specific technical objections and numerous more broadly-based problems have been orchestrated in the literature regarding this interpretive view. First, as noted above, doubts must arise concerning any reconstruction, such as the Sraffa-based approach, which utilizes a static framework to analyse the historical dynamics of Marx's system, of which the law of profit is a part. Second, it may be argued that the crucial nature of the distribution problem for Marx involved the secular direction of change in relative class shares. Yet the Sraffa-based reconstruction portrays the distribution problem as one involving the determination of the size of absolute shares from a fixed value of output.

Third, others have questioned the notion of competition employed in the Sraffa-based view in contrast to that employed by Marx (Fine and Harris 1979, p. 69). The Sraffa-based reconstruction limits the role of competition to the equalization of profit and wage rates, the determination of the level of wages, and provision of incentives for cost reduction. It can be argued, however, that for Marx, competition provided the stimulus to accumulate. It was then the driving force, the independent variable for the expansion of the capitalist system. The wage rate was the dependent variable. In the Sraffa-based view, the causation appears to be just the opposite – wage changes are the strategic factor. Fourth, and directly related, critics of the Sraffa-based reconstruction argue that there is no motive provided for accumulation, nor can there be in the type of static construct that they employ.

Fifth, still other interpreters find that the Sraffa-based approach focuses exclusively on the distributional class struggle in the sphere of exchange. As such, it fails to appreciate the interdependences and contradictions between the processes of production and exchange, which are created by Marx's law in relation to the countervailing influences. Finally, there is criticism by those who see Marx's law as a theory of the tendency of the secular decline in the rate of profit, which was *logically* deducible from his general theoretical structure. This is incompatible with the statement of the law in the Sraffa-based approach, which is seen by some to present its opposite, the *sine qua non*, of an *empirical* proposition predicting the fall in the actual price rate of profit (Fine and Harris 1979, p. 71).

Conclusion

Conclusions regarding the importance of the debate over Marx's law of profit might well be drawn at two distinct levels of enquiry. On the one hand, there are the implications of methodological evolution of the controversy. On the other hand, there is the question of specific analytical and textual contents of the debate.

In this chapter our focus has been on the first level of enquiry. We have attempted to determine the extent to which well-defined alternative interpretations of Marx's law of profit can be identified, and the degree to which these reconstructions parallel those that have emerged from the current Ricardian controversy. In this effort our focus has been on Marx's law as it relates to his theory of secular crisis, and we identify four such interpretations.

One distinct reconstruction of Marx's law is the traditional relativist interpretation. Here Marx's general analysis, including the law of profit, is placed in the context of classical political economy where it represents one aspect of Marx's concern with economic growth, distribution, and the maximization of total social welfare over time. Employing a framework of historical dynamics, relativists see Marx's law as a reaction to previous classical explanations of the falling rate of profit. In the relativist reconstruction, the rate of profit represents a macroeconomic aggregate based on a residual theory of the profit share, which accrues to the capitalist class. As such, the law of profit is placed in the context of a pluralistic view of society and a class conflict view of the economy. Moreover, Marx's law represents a definitional proposition which emerges from the secular trend in the composition of capital.

The evolution of the traditional relativist view of Marx's law differs from its evolution in the current Ricardian debate. This difference results from the fact that there have been two strains of the relativist reconstruction of Marx's law. On the one hand, orthodox relativists argue that Marx's law was never intended to apply to the limiting case of a constant rate of exploitation. These writers see the law of profit as a crucial component in Marx's theory of secular crisis. Unlike the methodological evolution in the Ricardian controversy, the orthodox version of relativism remains alive and well today. On the other hand, the Early Cambridge relativists argue that Marx's law must be interpreted in the context of a constant rate of exploitation, where it is concluded that the law of profit is not a crucial component of Marx's theory of secular crisis. This relativist strain has, however, evolved in a manner similar to its evolution in the Ricardian debate for it has emerged as an alternative and competing form of objectivism in the hands of the recent Sraffa-based reconstruction.

The Sraffa-based reconstruction represents a second interpretive approach to Marx's law. Marx's analysis in general, and the law of profit in particular, are placed in a non-paradigmatic objectivist continuum from Ricardo to Sraffa. The law of profit in Marx is placed in a static – Sraffa inspired – price of production model. The nature and validity of Marx's law then is dependent on the Ricardian theorem of distribution, which posits an inverse relationship between the wage and profit rate. In the Sraffa-based reconstruction the rate of profit is an aggregative, economy-wide price rate and is functionally related to the wage. It is, however, based on a residual theory of profits and is seen as a return to the capitalist class. The Sraffa-based reconstruction concludes that Marx's law does not, in general, hold in the face of a constant real wage.

A third interpretive line of Marx's law is the traditional objectivist approach. Here, the law of profit is placed in the context of neo-classical production theory employing a static or conventionally-defined dynamic analytical framework. Consequently, Marx's analysis in general, and the law of profit in particular, is seen to represent a non-paradigmatic or heterodox alternative to the development of mainstream economics. With this approach the rate of profit is an aggregate, economy-wide rate of return to capital, and its validity is judged in terms of a functional relationship between the rate of profit and the organic composition of capital. By clearly distinguishing between changes in the aggregate technique of production and changes in technology, they conclude that Marx's law will hold in the face of a constant level of technology. However, once technological change is admitted, increases in the organic composition of capital will cause the rate of profit to fall only if the technological change is labour saving.

As was the case with the current Ricardo debate, the traditional objectivist view of Marx's law has been pushed to its logical extreme by the advocates of the neo-classical New-View; the fourth distinct reconstruction of the law of profit. In this interpretation, Marx's law is placed in the short-run static framework of neo-classical microeconomic general equilibrium analysis employing an atomistic view of society and a harmonistic view of economic activity. Consequently, the Marx's law is evaluated in terms of allocative efficiency instead of growth, distribution, and the maximization of social welfare. The rate of profit in Marx is, therefore, defined as a microeconomic rate of return on capital in an opportunity cost sense. These writers conclude that Marx's law will not hold in the face of a constant real wage, and if the law of profit holds in a changing real-wage model, it is a result of the class struggle not a rising organic composition of capital.

As noted above, there has been a number of differences in the methodological evolution of alternative lines of interpretation in the current Ricardian controversy and the debate regarding Marx's law of profit. In addition, it is also the case that while a neo-Sraffa line of interpretation employing the paradigmatic methodological model emerged in the Ricardian debate, no such reconstruction has surfaced in the Marxian law of profit controversy. In spite of these methodological dissimilarities, however, it still appears to be true that the debate over the meaning and validity of Marx's law mirrors the analytically and ideologically competing schools of present-day economic analysis, and to a significant extent reflects the methodological alternatives employed in the study of the history of our discipline.

At the second level of enquiry a different judgement regarding the importance of the debate concerning Marx's law of profit might be reached. Many outstanding scholars have pondered the nature and significance of Marx on profits. The falling profits controversy runs on since Smith and Ricardo. A fundamental element is highlighted in the distinction between big and little questions. Joan Robinson has noted how Marshall changed the value question from Ricardo's concern for 'the distribution of total output between wages, rent and profit' to the 'little question' concerning the price of eggs and tea. She noted regretfully that the little question 'kept Marshall's pupils preoccupied for fifty years' (1973, p. 26). A similar pattern of the allocation of scarce intellectual resources and an analogous change in the question may be what is at stake in the debate over Marx's law of profit. For example, Roemer and others reduce the argument to the microeconomic general equilibrium framework. They ignore Marx's central focus on the large question of the laws of motion of capitalism. The distinction is clearly drawn by Robinson as she sets the scene for the constructive blending of classical political economy and Keynesian economics. Reading Sraffa's 'Introduction' to Ricardo's *Principles* caused her:

> to see that the concept of the rate of profit . . . is essentially the same in Ricardo, Marx, Marshall and Keynes; while the essential difference between these, on the one side, and Walras, Pigou and the latter-day textbooks on the other, is that the Ricardians are describing an historical process of accumulation in a changing world, while the Walrasians dwell in timeless equilibrium where there is no distinction between the future and the past. (1973, p. 247)

In her *Essay*, Robinson found that the falling rate of profit thesis suffered from both basic logical inconsistencies and lack of contact with the problem of aggregate demand. She characterized Marx's search for the law of profit as a 'false scent' (1966, p. 42). There is presented here an instructive parallel with the problem of 'transforming value into price'. In Robinson's judgement neither relationship was necessary for Marx's elucidation of the 'big' question (p. 22). In the latter case, out of the lines of Eugen von Böhm-Bawerk, Marx is rejected by his enemies. Ironically, in the case in hand, he is substantively rejected by his friends.

Notes

1. For example, see Armstrong and Glyn 1980; Catephores 1973; Clawson 1983; Cogoy 1973; Coram 1986; Dickinson 1956–57; Dobb 1959, 1972; Elster 1985, 1988; Fine and Harris 1979, p. 58; Foley 1986; Gillman 1957; Glyn 1973; Harris 1983; Himmelweit 1974; Hodgson 1974; Laibman 1982; Meek 1967; Nakatani 1980; Okishio 1961; Robinson 1966; Roemer 1979, 1981, 1988; Shaikh 1978; Steedman 1972, 1975, 1976, 1977; Sweezy 1968; Van Parijs 1980, 1983; Yaffe 1972.
2. For standard examples of this view, see Adelman 1961, pp. 81–90; Backhouse 1985, p. 120; Balinky 1970, pp. 127–33; Blaug 1985, p. 245; Brewer 1984, pp. 145–55; Burtt 1972, p. 153; Eagly 1974, p. 111; Ekelund and Hebert 1983, pp. 241–3; Freedman 1961, pp. 110–47; Gouverneur 1983, p. 98; Hunt 1979, pp. 203–6; Landreth and Colander 1989, pp. 180–94; Lekachman 1959, pp. 221–5; Mandel 1968, pp. 166–70; Oser and Brue 1988, pp. 182–3, 188; Pribram 1983, p. 257; Rogin 1956, pp. 346–50, 369–93; Roll 1963, p. 285; Sardoni 1987, p. 64; Schumpeter 1963, p. 652; Sowell 1985, pp. 130–2; Spiegel 1971, p. 473.
3. This difficulty has been referred in the context of the 'empirical' versus 'abstract' tendency in the rate of profit (Fine and Harris 1979, p. 64).
4. Though the levels are defined differently than ours, the problem of arguing at different levels of abstraction has been clearly recognized by some interpreters. For example, see Fine and Harris 1979, pp. 62–4.
5. For example, interpretations regarding Ricardo's use of the labour theory of value during his own lifetime included the views of James Mill, Malthus, McCulloch, and Torrens to mention just a few of the major combatants.
6. Beginning with Bailey's analysis such early writers as J.S. Mill, Coleman, Marshall, Hamilton, Hollander, Cannon, and Cassels made important contributions to the debate.
7. For example, the post-Sraffa literature on Ricardo's use of the labour theory of relative price has become very extensive. Some of the early post-Sraffa contributors would include: Blaug 1956, pp. 41–58; 1958; Bose 1964, pp. 722–5; Chowdhary 1957, pp. 1–11; Dickinson 1957, pp. 144–8; Dillard 1953, pp. 94–101; Gillman 1954, pp. 151–60; Gordon 1959, pp. 462–72; Hutchison 1952, pp. 415–32; 1953, pp. 263–73; Johansen 1963, pp. 89–103; Minakata 1964, pp. 1–18; Robertson 1957, pp. 171–86; Robinson 1954, pp. 141–51; Stigler 1952, pp. 187–207; 1958, pp. 357–67.
8. Matters have been complicated by the proliferation of Ricardo-like models, which may or may not represent Ricardo's meaning (Brems 1960, pp. 74–86; Pasinetti 1960, pp. 78–98; Samuelson 1959, pp. 1–35, 217–31).
9. This view is consistent with that expressed by Caravale (1985, pp. vii–viii).
10. See Casarosa, 1974, 1976, 1978, 1985; Costa 1977, 1985; Hicks and Hollander 1977; Hollander 1971, 1973, 1975, 1976, 1977a, 1977b, 1977c, 1979, 1983a, 1983b, 1984, 1985.

11. The objectivist methodological model sees the time path of orthodox economics as a continuous, rather linear positively sloping function. Such a view is based on four basic propositions, including: (1) modern economic theory is the appropriate evaluative criterion by which to judge past economic analysis; (2) economic analysis proper is the only appropriate subject matter for study; (3) economic theory has changed primarily because of scientific activity; and (4) economic ideas have progressed from poorer to better economics.
12. See Eatwell 1975, 1977; Garegnani 1960, 1970, 1982, 1983a, 1983b, 1985; Roncaglia 1978, 1985.
13. Here we refer to the objectivist methodological model, where, however, the benchmark of modern economic theory is not the neo-classical orthodoxy, but rather a modern heterodox theoretical alternative (Johnson and Ley 1988, pp. 144–53).
14. For example, see Caravale 1985; Caravale and Tosato 1974, 1980; Porta 1985; Rosselli 1985; Tosato 1985.
15. The relativist methodology is also based on four basic propositions, including: (1) economic ideas of the past must be evaluated in terms of the time and context out of which they arose; (2) that the broader area of economic doctrines is the appropriate subject matter; (3) economic ideas have changed in response to changes in the environment in which economists have worked and lived; and (4) there has been no necessary progression from poorer to better economics. The time path for mainstream economics is therefore not seen as continuous or linear.
16. In the paradigmatic model the intellectual progress of mainstream economic analysis is as consisting of three stages of scientific change: (1) the paradigm stage defined by the practice of normal science; (2) the crisis stage typified by the recognition of anomalies; and (3) the pre-paradigm stage in which competing bodies of analysis vie for professional acceptance. The overall time path of mainstream economic analysis is then seen to be positive, linear, and continuous in the paradigm stages, non-linear and or non-continuous in the crisis and pre-paradigm stages.
17. Ricardo's task was to create a theory of growth and distribution based on a postulated growth-induced increase in the embodied labour content of agricultural goods relative to manufactured goods – an increase that was due to decreasing returns to social scale in agriculture (as distinct from diminishing returns to variable proportions) as population growth required the use of additional, but qualitatively less productive lands (Barnett and Morse 1963, pp. 51–71). In his theory, this led to a concurrent increase in agricultural prices relative to the prices of manufactured goods; to a consequent relative upward trend in the class income shares of wages and rent compared to profits and, finally, to a stoppage of accumulation and growth as the profit share fell too low to motivate further capital formation.
18. This was, of course, the approach of all of the political economists. For example, Smith's early reference to profits makes it clear that he views profits as a legitimate reward to capitalists for risk. 'In exchanging the complete manufacture either for money, for labour, or for other goods, over and above what may be sufficient to pay the price of materials, and the wages of the workmen, something must be given for the profits of the undertaker of the work who hazards his stock in this adventure' (Smith 1937, p. 48).
19. By maximization we do not mean maximization of a mathematical function as in neo-classical welfare analysis. Rather, we refer to what may be properly termed 'relative-systemic maximization' since the political economists were concerned with whether or not a capitalist economy achieved more satisfactory levels of total social welfare than some alternative system (Hutchison 1978, p. 11).
20. Specifically, Marx argued that capitalists would take steps to reverse these trends as follows (Hunt 1979, pp. 204–5; Foley 1986, pp. 133–4): (1) the rate of exploitation may rise as a result of a fall in the value of labour-power with the rising productivity of labour; (2) the depression of wages below the value of labour-power in cases in which capitalists can gain a temporary advantage in their bargaining with workers; (3) the general increase in labour productivity will lower the value and price elements

of constant capital; (4) the emergence of unemployment as workers are displaced by technical change; and (5) foreign trade may make possible cheaper elements of constant capital or cheaper means of subsistence.

21. There are really three concepts that have been distinguished here. The first is the 'technical composition of capital', which refers to the ratio of the mass of means of production consumed per production period to the mass of wage-goods. It is a physical or material ratio not measurable by a single index. The second is the 'value composition of capital', which is the technical composition of capital measured in terms of current values of the means of production and the wage-goods consumed, hence the ratio of constant to variable capital. Finally, the third concept is the 'organic composition of capital', which is the ratio of constant to variable capital measured at their original values (Fine and Harris 1979, p. 59).
22. Semmler also criticizes the Okishio theorem. His complaint also is that Okishio fails to properly distinguish between the profit margin and profit rate. With innovation, the cost-minimizing technique may lead to one of three events (Semmler 1984, p. 451): (1) an increase in the profit margin and the rate of profit; (2) an increase in the profit margin but an unchanged rate of profit; and (3) an increase in the profit margin and a decrease in the profit rate. This final case is consistent with the Marxian case of falling rate of profit. For this to occur the cost decreasing effects of a new innovative technique must be smaller than the effect resulting from an increasing amount of investment per unit of output (p. 452).
23. Van Parijs (1980, p. 11) points out that capitalists in Shaikh's model would have to behave irrationally to adopt a capital-intensive technique which gave them a rate of profit which was lower than the general rate. Under competitive capitalism the profit-maximizing capitalist must use technical innovations which yield a rate of profit superior to the initial general rate. The Okishio theorem could not be violated by Shaikh. The only case when the Shaikh propositions are plausible is the case of oligopoly (Armstrong and Glyn 1980).
24. For a comment on van Parijs see Clawson (1983). Here Clawson challenges not the conclusions found by van Parijs but the assumptions of his model.
25. This was a point emphasized by van Parijs (1983) in his reply to Clawson (1983).
26. Laibman (1982) uses a constant rate of exploitation assumption in contrast to the constant real wage assumption of Okishio.
27. The shift to a discussion of the maximum rate of profit as opposed to the actual rate of profit came about because of the work of Shaikh (1978). In addition to Roemer, the work of Nakatani (1980) also criticizes Shaikh's conclusions.
28. Coram (1986, p. 266) notes that some may find fault with the work of Roemer (1979, 1981) because it deals with a price rate of profit not a pure labour theory of value rate of profit. Coram claims to show that the organic composition of capital does not increase with technological change and that the value rate of profit will not fall (p. 271). As such, Coram's work should be considered an extension of Roemer's results.
29. Salvadori (1981) takes exception to Roemer's claim that in equilibrium the general rate of profit converges with the von Neumann rate (Salvadori 1981, p. 60).
30. The Sraffa-based reconstruction has also been referred to as the neo-Ricardian view (Fine and Harris 1979, pp. 65–72).
31. However, Sraffa's standard commodity could not be used for intertemporal comparisons of the social product because it was tied to a given technology and product mix.
32. We distinguish here between changes in the level of technology meaning the state of the arts, and changes in the technical coefficients of production. Changes in the level of technology results in a change in the dimensions of the production matrix itself, while changes in the technical coefficients of production results only in changes in the configuration of the vector spaces within the same dimensional matrix.
33. For those that focus on the distinction between the value of the composition of capital and the organic composition of capital, the general conclusion is that changes in the organic composition and the technical composition of capital are directly

proportional, while changes in the value of the composition of capital are not. On the other hand, it is claimed that the Sraffa-based interpretation sees the distinctions between the value composition of capital and the organic composition of capital as a simple quantitative issue of two different index numbers (Fine and Harris 1979, p. 59).

References

Adelman, I. (1961), *Theories of Economic Growth and Development*, California: Stanford University Press.

Armstrong, P. and A. Glyn (1980), 'The Law of the Falling Rate of Profit and Oligopoly: A Comment on Shaikh', *Cambridge Journal of Economics*, **4**, (1), pp. 69–70.

Backhouse, R. (1985), *A History of Modern Economic Analysis*, New York: Basil Blackwell.

Balinky, A. (1970), *Marx's Economics*, Lexington, Massachusetts: D.C. Heath.

Barnett, H.J. and C. Morse (1963), *Scarcity and Growth*, Baltimore: The Johns Hopkins Press.

Baumol, W.J. (1959), *Economic Dynamics*, New York: Macmillan Company.

Blaug, M. (1956), 'The Empirical Content of Ricardian Economics', *The Journal of Political Economy*, LXIV, (1), February, pp. 41–58.

Blaug, M. (1958), *Ricardian Economics*, New Haven: Yale University Press.

Blaug, M. (1985), 'What Ricardo Said and What Ricardo Meant', in G.A. Caravale (ed.), *The Legacy of Ricardo*, Oxford: Basil Blackwell.

Blaug, M. (1986), *Economic Theory in Retrospect*, Cambridge: Cambridge University Press.

Bose, A. (1964), 'The Labour Approach and the Commodity Approach in Mr. Sraffa's Price Theory', *The Economic Journal*, LXXIV, 295, September, pp. 722–5.

Brems, H. (1960), 'An Attempt at a Rigorous Restatement of Ricardo's Long-Run Equilibrium', *Canadian Journal of Economics and Political Science*, XXVI, (1), February, pp. 74–86.

Brewer, A. (1984), *A Guide to Marx's Capital*, Cambridge: Cambridge University Press.

Burtt, E.J. Jr (1972), *Social Perspectives in the History of Economic Theory*, New York: St Martins Press.

Caravale, G.A. (1985), 'Diminishing Returns and Accumulation in Ricardo', in G.A. Caravale (ed.), *The Legacy of Ricardo*, Oxford: Basil Blackwell.

Caravale, G.A. and D.A. Tosato (1974), *Un modello ricardiano di sviluppo economico*, Turin: Boringhieri.

Caravale, G.A. and D.A. Tosato (1980), *Ricardo and the Theory of Value, Distribution and Growth*, London: Routledge and Kegan Paul.

Casarosa, C. (1974), 'La teoria ricadiana della distribuzione e dello sviluppo economico', *Rivista de Politica Economica*, 44, pp. 959–1015.

Casarosa, C. (1976), 'Imposte e destribuzione del reddito nell'analisi ricardiana', *Geornale degli Economisti*, 35, pp. 171–200.

Casarosa, C. (1978), 'A New Formulation of the Ricardian System', *Oxford Economic Papers*, 30, pp. 38–63.

Casarosa, C. (1985), 'The "New View" of the Ricardian Theory of Distribution and Economic Growth', in G.A. Caravale (ed.), *The Legacy of Ricardo*, Oxford: Basil Blackwell.

Catephores, G. (1973), 'Some Remarks on the Falling Rate of Profit', *Bulletin of the Conference of Socialist Economists*, **II**, (5), spring.

Chowdhary, M.K. (1957), 'Development of Labour Theory of Value', *The Federal Economic Review*, **IV**, (1), January, pp. 1–11.

Clawson, P. (1983), 'A Comment on Van Parijs' Obituary', *The Review of Radical Political Economics*, **15**, (2), pp. 107–110.

Cogoy, M. (1973), 'The Fall in the Rate of Profit and the Theory of Accumulation: A Reply to Paul Sweezy', *Bulletin of the Conference of Socialist Economists*, **II**, (7), Winter.

Coram, B.T. (1986), 'Marx, Roemer and the Theory of the Falling Rate of Profit', *Australian Economic Papers*, **25**, (41), pp. 265–71.
Costa, G. (1977), 'La convergenza allo stato Stazionario di un'economia di tipo ricardiano', in F. de Cindio and P. Sylos Labini (eds), *Saggi di Economia in Onore di Antonio Pesenti*, Milan: Giuffre.
Costa, G. (1985), 'Time in Ricardian Models: Some Critical Observations and Some New Results', in G.A. Caravale (ed.), *The Legacy of Ricardo*, Oxford: Basil Blackwell.
Dickinson, H.D. (1956–57), 'The Falling Rate of Profit in Marxian Economics', *The Review of Economic Studies*, **24**, (2), February, pp. 120–30.
Dickinson, H.D. (1957), 'The Labour Theory of Value', *Scottish Journal of Political Economy*, IV–VI, (2), June, pp. 144–8.
Dillard, D. (1953), 'Ricardo in Retrospect', *Journal of Economic History*, XIII, (1), pp. 94–101.
Dobb, M. (1959), 'The Falling Rate of Profit', *Science and Society*, **23**, (2), Spring, pp. 97–103.
Dobb, M. (1972), *Political Economy and Capitalism*, London: Routledge Press.
Eagly, R.V. (1974), *The Structure of Classical Economic Theory*, London: Oxford University Press.
Eatwell, J. (1975), 'The Interpretation of Ricardo's Essay on Profits', *Economica*, **40**, pp. 260–82.
Eatwell, J. (1977), 'The Irrelevance of Returns to Scale in Sraffa's Analysis', *Journal of Economic Literature*, **15**, pp. 61–8.
Ekelund, R.B. Jr and R.F. Hebert (1983), *A History of Economic Theory and Method*, New York: McGraw-Hill.
Elster, J. (1985), *Making Sense of Marx*, Cambridge: Cambridge University Press.
Elster, J. (1988), *An Introduction to Karl Marx*, Cambridge: Cambridge University Press.
Fine, B. and L. Harris (1979), *Rereading 'Capital'*, New York: Columbia University Press.
Foley, D.K. (1986), *Understanding Capital, Marx's Economic Theory*, Cambridge, Massachusetts: Harvard University Press.
Freedman, R. (ed.) (1961), *Marx on Economics*, New York: Harcourt, Brace and World.
Frisch, R. (1935–6), 'On the Notion of Equilibrium and Disequilibrium', *Review of Economic Studies*, III, pp. 100–5.
Garegnani, P. (1960), *Il capitale nelle teorie della distribuzione*, Milan: Giuffre
Garegnani, P. (1970), 'Heterogeneous Capital, the Production Function and the Theory of Distribution', *Review of Economic Studies*, **37**, pp. 407–36.
Garegnani, P. (1982), 'On Hollander's Interpretation of Ricardo's Early Theory of Profits', *Cambridge Journal of Economics*, **6**, pp. 65–77.
Garegnani, P. (1983a), 'Ricardo's Early Theory of Profits and Rational Foundation: A Reply to Professor Hollander', *Cambridge Journal of Economics*, **7**, pp. 175–8.
Garegnani, P. (1983b), 'The Classical Theory of Wages and the Role of Demand Schedules in the Determination of Ricardian Prices', *American Economic Review*, pp. 309–13.
Garegnani, P. (1985), 'The "New View" of the Ricardian Theory of Distribution and Growth', in G.A. Caravale (ed.), *The Legacy of Ricardo*, Oxford: Basil Blackwell.
Gillman, J.M. (1954), 'Comments on the Labor Theory of Value', *Science and Society*, XVIII, (2), pp. 151–60.
Gillman, J.M. (1957), *The Falling Rate of Profit*, London: Dobson.
Glyn, A. (1973), 'Productivity, Organic Composition and the Falling Rate of Profit – A Reply', *Bulletin of the Conference of Socialist Economists*, **II**, (6), winter.
Gordon, D.F. (1959), 'What Was the Labor Theory of Value?', *American Economic Review*: papers and proceedings, XLIX, (2), May, pp. 462–72.
Gouverneur, J. (1983), *Contemporary Capitalism and Marxist Economics*, Totowa, New Jersey: Barnes and Noble.
Harris, D.J. (1983), 'Accumulation of Capital and the Rate of Profit in Marxian Theory', *Cambridge Journal of Economics*, **7**, (3–4), pp. 311–30.
Harrod, R.F. (1948), *Towards a Dynamic Economics*, London: Macmillan and Company.

Hicks, J.R. and S. Hollander (1977), 'Mr. Ricardo and the Moderns', *Quarterly Journal of Economics*, **91**, pp. 351–65.
Himmelweit, S. (1974), 'The Continuing Saga of the Falling Rate of Profit – A Reply to Mario Cogoy', *Bulletin of the Conference of Socialist Economists*, **III**, (9), Autumn.
Hodgson, G. (1974), 'The Theory of the Falling Rate of Profit', *The New Left Review*, **84**.
Hollander, S. (1971), 'The Development of Ricardo's Position on Machinery', *History of Political Economy*, **3**, pp. 105–35.
Hollander, S. (1973), 'Ricardo's Analysis of the Profit Rate, 1813–1815', *Economica*, **40**, pp. 260–82.
Hollander, S. (1975), 'Ricardo and the Corn Profit Model: A Reply to Eatwell', *Economica*, **42**, pp. 188–202.
Hollander, S. (1976), 'Ricardianism, J.S. Mill, and the Neo-Classical Challenge', in J.M. Robson and M. Laine (eds), *James and John Mill: Papers on the Centenary Conference*, Toronto: University of Toronto Press.
Hollander, S. (1977a), 'Ricardo and the Corn Laws: A Revision', *History of Political Economy*, **9**, pp. 1–47.
Hollander, S. (1977b), 'Smith and Ricardo: Aspects of the Nineteenth Century Legacy', *American Economic Review*, **67**, pp. 37–41.
Hollander, S. (1977c), 'The Reception of Ricardian Economics', *Oxford Economic Papers*, **20**, pp. 221–57.
Hollander, S. (1979), *The Economics of David Ricardo*, Toronto: University of Toronto Press.
Hollander, S. (1983a), 'Professor Garaegnani's Defense of Sraffa on the Material Rate of Profit', *Cambridge Journal of Economics*, **7**, pp. 167–74.
Hollander, S. (1983b), 'On the Interpretation of Ricardian Economics: The Assumption Regarding Wages', *American Economic Review*: papers and proceedings, **73**, pp. 314–18.
Hollander, S. (1984), 'J.S. Mill on "Derived Demand" and the Wage-Fund Treaty Recantation', *Eastern Economic Journal*, X, January–March, pp. 87–98.
Hollander, S. (1985), 'On the Substantive Identity of the Ricardian and Neoclassical Conceptions of Economic Organization: the French Connection in British Classicism', in G.A. Caravale (ed.), *The Legacy of Ricardo*, Oxford: Basil Blackwell.
Hunt, E.K. (1979), *History of Economic Thought: A Critical Perspective*, Belmont, California: Wadsworth Publishing Company, Inc.
Hutchison, T.W. (1952), 'Some Questions About Ricardo', *Economica*, XIX, (76), November, pp. 415–32.
Hutchison, T.W. (1953), 'Ricardo's Correspondence', *Economica*, XX, (79), August, pp. 263–73.
Hutchison, T.W. (1978), *On Revolution and Progress in Economic Knowledge*, Cambridge: Cambridge University Press.
Johansen, L. (1963), 'Labour Theory of Value and Marginal Utilities', *Economics of Planning*, III, (2), September, pp. 89–103.
Johnson, L.E. (1980), 'A Neo-Paradigmatic Model for Studying the Development of Economic Reasoning', *Atlantic Economic Journal*, VIII, (4), December, pp. 52–61.
Johnson, L.E. (1983), 'Economic Paradigms: A Missing Dimension', *Journal of Economic Issues*, XVII, (4), December, pp. 1097–111.
Johnson, L.E. (1984), 'Ricardo's Labour Theory of the Determinant of Value', *Atlantic Economic Journal*, XII, (1), March, pp. 50–9.
Johnson, L.E. (1988), 'The Legacy of Ricardo: A Review Article', *Rivista Internazionale Di Scienze Economiche E Commerciali*, XXXV, (8), August, pp. 781–96.
Johnson, L.E. and R.D. Ley (1988), *Origins of Modern Economics: A Paradigmatic Approach*, Needham Heights, Massachusetts: Ginn Press.
Laibman, D. (1982), 'Technical Change, the Real Wage and the Rate of Exploitation', *The Review of Radical Political Economics*, **14**, (2), pp. 95–105.
Landreth, H. and D.C. Colander (1989), *History of Economic Theory*, New York: Houghton Mifflin Co.

Lekachman, R. (1959), *A History of Economic Ideas*, New York: Harper and Row.
Mandel, E. (1968), *Marxist Economic Theory*, Vol. I, New York: Monthly Review Press.
Maneschi, A. and W.O. Thweatt (1987), 'The Legacy of Ricardo: A Book Review', *Southern Economic Journal*, January, pp. 805–7.
Meek, R.L. (1967), 'The Falling Rate of Profit', in his *Economics and Ideology and Other Essays*, London: Chapman and Hall.
Minakata, K. (1964), 'A Note on Ricardo's Theory of Value', *Kobe University Economic Review*, pp. 1–18.
Morse, C. (1961), 'A Note on Static, Dynamic, and Historical Analysis', *Southern Economic Journal*, XXVII, (3), January, pp. 237–9.
Moszkowska, N. (1935), *Zur Kritik moderner krisentheorien*, Prog: Kacha.
Nakatani, T. (1980), 'The Law of the Falling Rate of Profit and the Competitive Battle: Comment on Shaikh', *Cambridge Journal of Economics*, **4**, (1), pp. 65–8.
Okishio, N. (1961), 'Technical Change and the Rate of Profit', *Kobe University Economic Review*, **7**, pp. 85–99.
Oser, J. and S.L. Brue (1988), *The Evolution of the Economic Thought*, New York: Harcourt, Brace and Jovanovich.
Pasinetti, L. (1960), 'A Mathematical Formation of the Ricardian System', *The Review of Economic Studies*, XXVII, (73), February, pp. 78–98.
Porta, P.L. (1985), 'The Debate on Ricardo: Old Results in New Frameworks', in G.A. Caravale (ed.), *The Legacy of Ricardo*, Oxford: Basil Blackwell.
Pribram, K. (1983), *A History of Economic Reasoning*, Baltimore: The Johns Hopkins University Press.
Robertson, H.M. (1957), 'The Ricardo Problem', *South African Journal of Economics*, XXV, September, pp. 171–86.
Robinson, J. (1954), 'The Labour Theory of Value: A Discussion', *Science and Society*, XVIII, (2), spring, pp. 141–51.
Robinson, J. (1966), *An Essay on Marxian Economics*, New York: St Martins Press.
Robinson, J. (1973), 'An Open Letter from a Keynesian to a Marxist', *Collected Economic Papers*, Vol. 4, Cambridge MA: MIT Press.
Roemer, J.E. (1979), 'Continuing Controversy on the Falling Rate of Profit: Fixed Capital and Other Issues', *Cambridge Journal of Economics*, **3**, (4), pp. 379–98.
Roemer, J.E. (1981), *Analytical Foundations of Marxian Economic Theory*, New York: Cambridge University Press.
Roemer, J.E. (1988), *Free to Lose: An Introduction to Marxist Economic Philosophy*, Cambridge, Massachusetts: Harvard University Press.
Rogin, L. (1956), *The Meaning and Validity of Economic Theory*, New York: Harper and Brothers.
Roll, E. (1963), *A History of Economic Thought*, Englewood Cliffs, New Jersey: Prentice-Hall Inc.
Roncaglia, A. (1978), *Sraffa and the Theory of Prices*, London: John Wiley.
Roncaglia, A. (1985), 'Hollander's Ricardo', in G.A. Caravale (ed.), *The Legacy of Ricardo*, Oxford: Basil Blackwell.
Rosselli, A. (1985), 'The Theory of the Natural Wage', in G.A. Caravale (ed.), *The Legacy of Ricardo*, Oxford: Basil Blackwell.
Salvadori, N. (1981), 'Falling Rate of Profit With a Constant Real Wage: An Example', *Cambridge Journal of Economics*, **5**, pp. 59–66.
Samuelson, P.A. (1948), *Foundations of Economic Analysis*, Cambridge: Harvard University Press.
Samuelson, P.A. (1959), 'A Modern Treatment of the Ricardian Economy: I; The Pricing of Goods of Labor and Land Services', *The Quarterly Journal of Economics*, LXXIII, (1), February, pp. 1–35.
Samuelson, P.A. (1959), 'A Modern Treatment of the Ricardian Economy: II; Capital and Interest Aspects of the Pricing Process', *The Quarterly Journal of Economics*, LXXIII, (2), May, pp. 217–31.

Sardoni, C. (1987), *Marx and Keynes on Economic Recession*, New York: New York University Press.

Schumpeter, J.A. (1963), *History of Economic Analysis*, New York: Oxford University Press.

Semmler, W. (1984), 'Marx and Schumpeter on Competition, Transient Surplus Profit and Technical Change', *Economie Appliquée*, **37**, (3–4), pp. 419–55.

Shaikh, A. (1978), 'Political Economy and Capitalism: Notes on Dobb's Theory of Crises', *Cambridge Journal of Economics*, **2**, pp. 233–51.

Smith, A. (1937), *An Inquiry into the Nature and Causes of The Wealth of Nations*, New York: The Modern Library.

Sowell, T. (1985), *Marxism Philosophy and Economics*, New York: William Morrow.

Spiegel, H.W. (1971), *The Growth of Economic Thought*, Englewood Cliffs: Prentice-Hall.

Sraffa, P. (ed.) (1951), *The Works and Correspondence of David Ricardo*, Cambridge: Cambridge University Press.

Sraffa, P. (1960), *Production of Commodities by Means of Commodities: Prelude to a Critique of Economic Theory*, Cambridge: Cambridge University Press.

Steedman, I. (1972), 'Marx on the Rate of Profit', *Bulletin of the Conference of Socialist Economists*, **I**, (4), Winter.

Steedman, I. (1975), 'Positive Profits with Negative Surplus Value', *Economic Journal*, **85**, March.

Steedman, I. (1976), 'Positive Profits with Negative Surplus Value: A Reply', *Economic Journal*, **86**, September.

Steedman, I. (1977), *Marx After Sraffa*, London: NLB.

Stigler, G.J. (1952), 'The Ricardian Theory of Value and Distribution', *The Journal of Political Economy*, LX, (3), June, pp. 187–207.

Stigler, G.J. (1958), 'Ricardo and the 93% Labor Theory of Value', *American Economic Review*, XLVIII, (3), June, pp. 357–67.

Stigler, G.J. (1965), 'Textual Exegesis as a Scientific Problem', *Economica*, XXXII, (128), November, pp. 447–50.

Sweezy, P.M. (1968), *The Theory of Capitalist Development*, New York: Monthly Review Press.

Tosato, D. (1985), 'A Reconsideration of Sraffa's Interpretation of Ricardo on Value and Distribution', in G.A. Caravale (ed.), *The Legacy of Ricardo*, Oxford: Basil Blackwell.

Van Parijs, P. (1980), 'The Falling-Rate-of-Profit Theory of Crisis: A Rational Reconstruction by Way of Obituary', *The Review of Radical Political Economics*, **12**, (1), pp. 1–16.

Van Parijs, P. (1983), 'Why Marxist Economics Needs Microfoundations: Postscript to an Obituary', *The Review of Radical Political Economics*, **15**, (2), pp. 111–24.

Wolff, R.D. and S.A. Resnick (1987), *Economics: Marxian versus Neoclassical*, Baltimore: The Johns Hopkins University Press.

Yaffe, D. (1972), 'The Marxian Theory of Crisis, and the State', *Bulletin of the Conference of Socialist Economists*, **I**, (4), Winter.

4 The organic composition of capital and the falling rate of profit*

Ferdinando Meacci

Introduction

Marx's 'magnificent dynamics' contains three theories: the falling-rate-of-profit theory (FRPT), the falling-rate-of-profit theory of crisis (FRPTC), and the falling-rate-of-profit theory of the breakdown (FRPTB). While the problems addressed by these theories are different, their interdependence, based as it is on Marx's concept of the rate of profit, makes all of them dependent on the same crucial notion. This is the organic composition of capital (OCC). Following in the wake of J. Robinson (1942) and Sweezy (1942), whose contributions mark the beginning of modern Marxian economics, Dickinson (1957), Gillman (1957), Okishio (1961), Blaug (1960, 1980), Meek (1967), Rosdolski (1968), Morishima (1973), Hodgson (1974), Steedman (1977), Roemer (1977, 1979), Shaikh (1978), J. Robinson (1978), Fine and Harris (1979), Harris (1983), I. Hunt (1983) and others have been contributing to an actual shift of attention away from the FRPTB (which appealed so much to a previous generation of economists) on to the FRPT and the role that the OCC plays within this theory. It is doubtful, however, whether these discussions, marked as they are by minor or major controversies, diverging interpretations and different viewpoints, have cast any new light on a subject that Marx himself had left in an unpolished and even obscure state.

For instance, while some authors have argued that the OCC (interpreted by some as the 'value' composition, and by others as the 'technical' composition) is more liable to fall than to rise and others that what is liable to decline is the 'value' as opposed to the 'price' rate of profit (or the 'maximum' as opposed to the 'actual' rate, or profit 'rates' as opposed to profit 'margins'), the distinction between the 'truth-value' and the 'predictive record' of Marxian economics (Blaug 1980, p. 1) has been largely neglected. Thus, owing to the role that the OCC plays in the FRPT, the failure to keep the truth-value of the FRPT apart from its predictive record has gone hand in hand with the failure to do

* I wish to thank Ian Steedman, who acted as discussant of a first draft of this paper at the 1988 meeting of the History of Economics Society, and Giovanni Caravale for their helpful criticisms and suggestions. The usual disclaimer applies.

the same with the OCC notion. This tendency has in turn been more fostered than thwarted by the recent struggle between 'fundamentalism', an approach whereby the FRPT is developed from the nature of capital itself, and 'functionalism', an approach whereby the FRPT is deduced from phenomena that are unrelated to the nature of capital and to the state of its composition.

Unlike most recent contributions, this chapter attempts to investigate the truth-value of the FRPT by following a 'fundamentalist' approach. However, in contrast to most fundamentalist contributions, the purpose of this chapter is not to uphold the FRPT on the basis of the OCC notion. It is rather to evaluate the inner consistency of the FRPT by questioning the significance of the OCC notion itself. This task will be carried out by focusing on the *qualitative* aspects of Marxian concepts as well as on their relationships and differences. No regard will be paid, therefore, to issues such as the formalization or quantification of those concepts or to the specific question of whether the ratio the OCC results in – or the rate of profit to which it leads – has *actually* risen or fallen in the past or shall rise or fall in the future. Furthermore, since the purpose of the chapter is to tackle the FRPT from within and since this will be done with regard to the context of 'capital in general' rather than of 'one capital in relation to another', no attention will be devoted to Marx's theory of value or to the problems relating to the transformation of values into prices.

The chapter is divided into two parts. The first deals with the OCC from the *static* point of view, the second from the *dynamic*: while the former is concerned with the concepts of capital on which the OCC is based, the latter deals with technical progress and with the forms that this phenomenon must take for the OCC to behave in the manner pointed out by Marx.

While a characteristic feature of the chapter is to tackle the OCC in the light of the distinction between *individual* and *social* capital, its most general implication is that Marx's handling of this distinction is flawed by his conception of social capital as the interaction of all individual capitals in their capacity to generate or to attract *surplus value* rather than as the source from which the *national revenue* annually flows.

Capital

The labour process and the valorization process as wealth-creating and value-determining processes

To grasp the true nature of the distinction between *constant* and *variable* capital (henceforth: the c-v distinction) on which the OCC is based, one should first start from Marx's anatomy of a capitalist economy as consisting of the 'labour process' (*Arbeitsprozess*) and the 'valorization process' (*Verwertungsprozess*) (*Capital*, Volume I, chapter 7).

Going back to the distinction between value and wealth (Ricardo 1821, chapter XX) and to the fact that the former notion relates to the exchange of individual commodities in terms of each other (exchange value), the latter to their power of satisfying human wants (use value), the two processes can be interpreted in the sense that the labour process is related to the creation of wealth while the valorization process is confined to the determination (and, given Marx's theory of exploitation, distribution) of value. The former is as crucial from the point of view of society (i.e., with regard to the formation of national revenue) as the latter is from the point of view of an individual capitalist (i.e., with regard to the formation of surplus value).[1]

Unlike his predecessors' theories of capital, Marx's theory is mostly concerned with the place of capital within the valorization process. This is evident in *Capital*, Volume I, where Marx's theory of capital is launched on the assumption that money, 'the ultimate product of circulation', is said to be also 'the first form of appearance of capital'; and in *Capital*, Volume II, where Marx deals with (the circuit of) what is here called 'money capital' as something that 'divides itself in two parts, one of which purchases labour-power, the other means of production'. The part that purchases labour-power is called 'variable capital', the other part 'constant capital' (*Capital*, Volume I, chapter 8). Thus, the following distinction:

1. Labour (L) and means of production (Mp) are factors of the process of the creation of wealth (labour process).
2. Constant capital (C) and variable capital (V) are factors of the process of the determination (and distribution) of value (valorization process).

This distinction is consistent not only with Marx's point of departure (money capital)[2] and initial definitions of the two kinds of capital[3] but is also confirmed by the fact that the role played by the different components of C (machinery and materials) is the same (however different is the way in which this role is played) when it comes to the determination of value while it is different when it comes to the creation of wealth.[4] Conversely, since, in talking about the different way in which the value of different components of C is transferred to the product, Marx points out that by C he usually means 'the value of the means of production actually consumed in the course of production'

(*Capital*, Volume I, p. 321) – which is *not* the amount of money capital embodied in these means – special attention should be paid to two different ways in which the c-v distinction and the OCC notion may be conceived of. One way consists in regarding it from the point of view of the *investment* of *money* capital (whereby a sum of money is said to be laid out either in the form of means of production or in the form of labour-power); the other consists in regarding it from the point of view of the *consumption* of *invested* capital (whereby a given value of these means is said to be transferred to a given product). Whence Marx's own distinction between capital *invested* and capital *consumed*[5] (a distinction of the utmost importance when fixed capital comes under discussion)[6] and the resulting conclusion that whether it comes to the investment of money capital or the consumption of invested capital it is *individual* capital with which Marx is essentially concerned.[7]

Technical composition, value composition and the OCC

While the distinction between capital invested and capital consumed is reinforced in modern Marxian economics, the difference between C-V and Mp-L is weakened or obscured. For instance, while talking about Marx's OCC and his 'obscure terminology', J. Robinson (1942, chapter 2; 1951–80, *passim*) first notes that 'he uses one set of symbols for two meanings' and then proposes to write C and V 'for constant and variable capital in their aspects as divisions of the stock of capital' and c and v 'when they appear as elements in gross income'. Although J. Robinson (1978) eventually changed her mind about the V component of this distinction, the fact still remains that while her c and v clearly imply the notion of capital *consumed*, her C and V are not as clearly related to the notion of capital *invested*. For, instead of regarding C as money capital 'turned into' (invested in) Mp, and V as money capital 'turned into' L (thus keeping C and V apart from Mp and L), she usually identifies C with Mp and V with L as though the real contrast were between Mp and L, on the one hand, and c and v, on the other, rather than between C and V (valorization process), and Mp and L (labour process). Indeed, not only may Mp and L change without any change – or even with opposite changes – in C and V but the Marxian rule is that the difference between C and V rises more slowly than the difference between Mp and L as the process of accumulation unfolds (*Capital*, Volume I, p. 774).[8]

The distinction between C-V and Mp-L, however, is eventually more important than the distinction between C-V and c-v, for while the latter distinction implies different versions of the OCC depending on whether this is measured in terms of stocks (C-V) or of flows (c-v) the former is essential to the OCC notion itself. In fact, on the one hand, it is known that one thing is the *technical* composition (TC), another the *value* composition (VC) and that the OCC is the VC 'in so far as this is determined by its technical composition and mirrors the changes in the latter' (*Capital*, Volume I, p. 762; see also Volume III, p. 245); on the other, TC is related to Mp and L as much as VC is to C and V.[9] This is why changes in VC may not coincide with – and may indeed be misunderstood for – changes in TC (regardless of whether changes in the *price* composition do or do not coincide, and are or are not misunderstood for, changes in the *value* composition).[10] This is also why Marx introduced the OCC notion as the name given to the VC 'in so far as this is determined by the TC and reflects it', it being understood that a change in TC is more crucial than a change in VC for changes in the productivity of social labour result from changes in TC (not in VC) regardless of whether these changes are or are not associated with changes in VC and regardless of whether this association is or is not of the cause-effect type (Marx 1905, Volume III, pp. 275–89; 379–84).[11]

It should be pointed out, however, that in so far as a change in VC 'reflects' a change in TC (i.e., in so far as a change in the OCC occurs), either the rate of surplus value or the rate of wages, or both, must change as a result of the change in the productivity of social labour necessarily associated with a change in TC. The two rates, however, are assumed constant in Marx's FRPT. Although untenable, as for instance J. Robinson (1942) and Sweezy (1942) first pointed out, this assumption is nonetheless unavoidable within Marx's system of thought, for otherwise it follows, as will be argued below, that surplus labour, far from being always spent 'for the capitalist', may indeed be spent 'for the worker himself' even under the capitalist rules of the game.

The c-v distinction, the f-c distinction, and the turnover period of capital

The difference between the value-determining process and the wealth-creating process is not only essential to the distinction between C and V (in the sense that the latter makes sense, unlike the distinction between Mp and L, within the former process), but is also implied – though in a different sense – by the distinction between *fixed* and *circulating* capital (henceforth: f-c distinction).

Marx's treatment of the f-c distinction is developed in Volume II of *Capital* and is introduced by his statement that the fixed and circulating forms of capital are 'two new forms which capital obtains as a result of the *circulation* process, and which affect the form of its turnover' (p. 236). This circulation process is regarded by him, first, as the 'change of hands' that money capital and commodity capital undergo in their leaving and returning to their points of departure; and, at a later stage, as the 'transfer of value' that goes from the means of production to their products regardless of whether a 'change of hands' is or is not implied by this transfer. Leaving aside the fact that the circulation process is not exactly the same thing in the two cases, Marx ends up by regarding the f-c distinction as arising exclusively within the circulation of *value* and by basing it on whether the value of productive capital is transferred only gradually (fixed capital) or once and for all (circulating capital) to the product (*Capital*, Volume II, pp. 239–40).

Thus, in Volume I the c-v distinction is developed in the light of the fact that the transfer of value from the objective (Mp) and subjective (L) factors of the labour process implies a preservation of value for the objective and a creation of surplus value for the subjective factors. In Volume II the f-c distinction is considered a variant of the c-v distinction in the sense that the former is used to determine not so much which of the two forms of capital creates surplus value but how each of the two forms contributes to the determination of the value of a given product.[12]

But the role of the f-c distinction as distinct from the c-v distinction is confined by Marx not only to the fact that C consists of a circulating as well as of a fixed part while circulating capital consists of a variable as well as of a constant part. It is also extended to the fact that capitals of equal size tend to give different rates of profit not only according to the difference in their compositions but also 'according to their period of circulation in so far as this is determined by the ratio of fixed capital to circulating capital and also by the various periods of reproduction of the different sorts of fixed capital' (Marx 1905, Volume II, p. 28). Accordingly, Marx's FRPT should be formulated not only in the prevailing sense that the rate of profit tends to fall as C rises relatively to V but also in the more accurate sense that this rate tends to fall either as C rises relatively to V, while the ratio of fixed to circulating capital remains constant, or as the ratio of fixed to circulating capital rises while C remains constant relatively to V. The latter sense is first introduced in Chapters 15 and 16 of Volume II of *Capital* where the difference in turnover periods is referred to the distinction between capital *advanced* and capital *applied*, and is later developed in (Engel's) Chapter 4 of Volume III where the profit rates of two capitals of the same percentage composition with the same rate of surplus value and the same working day are said to 'vary inversely as their turnover times' (*Capital*, Volume III, p. 165).

Now, although Marx himself acknowledges in Chapter 15 that he is there considering only the turnovers of circulating capital 'and not those of fixed capital' (p. 354), the fact remains that 'all capital is circulating capital' (p. 238; see also *Grundrisse*, p. 620). This implies (1) that the relationship between a fixed capital and a circulating capital turning over once in a year is the same as the relationship between the latter and a circulating capital turning over *n* times in a year; and (2) that just as a reduction (increase) in the turnover time of circulating capital raises (lowers) the rate of profit (*Capital*, Volume III, p. 163), likewise a change in the turnover time of capital in general (all the more so when this change results from a conversion of circulating into fixed capital) should be assumed to bring about an opposite change in the rate of profit.[13]

Modern treatments of the difference between the f-c and the c-v distinctions

The difference between the f-c distinction and the c-v distinction as well as the role that the former should play in the FRPT is somewhat neglected in modern Marxian analysis. One exception is provided by Steedman (1982) and another by I. Hunt (1983). Although Steedman's contribution is oriented less than Hunt's to the problems raised by that difference with regard to the OCC and the FRPT, it seems worthwhile to devote to it some preliminary attention for it raises some crucial points that go to the heart of the OCC and of the FRPT itself.

Steedman

Steedman's treatment of this issue is, on the one hand, embedded in a broader discussion of some criticisms raised by Marx against Ricardo and arises, on the other, from Steedman's specific discussion of whether Marx's charges that 'Ricardo ignored constant capital' (1982, p. 116) are well-founded. Granted that this is not the place to go into Steedman's broader discussion, we can still profit from his assessment of Marx's assessment of Ricardo by focusing on the first link of this chain, i.e., on Steedman's views of Marx. In this regard, Steedman develops his arguments by identifying C with 'non-wage capital' (so that the Marxian question he tries to answer is 'Did Ricardo ignore non-wage capital?') while his answer is that Ricardo did *not* ignore non-wage capital 'at least when considering the economy as a whole'. If C consists of non-wage capital it does not follow, however, that non-wage capital is C in the very sense in which – as Marx maintains – if C consists of Mp this does not mean that Mp is C even under the capitalist rules of the game (whence his distinction, discussed above, between VC and TC). In fact the identification of C with non-wage capital as such implies the identification of the c-v distinction with the Mp-L distinction and, therefore, of the valorization process with the labour process. Which in turn implies, owing to Ricardo's own distinction between wealth (the essential object of the labour process) and value (the essential element of the valorization process), that the contrast is here less between Marx and Ricardo than between Steedman on the one hand and Marx plus Ricardo on the other.[14]

Steedman's approach, however, is noteworthy for it takes explicitly into account what is usually neglected in the FRPT discussions, i.e., the two points of view – that of an individual and that of the economy as a whole – from which all problems of capital can be addressed. However, after showing that 'Ricardo did not ignore non-wage capital at the economy level' although he frequently referred '*only* to fixed capital and to wages', Steedman concludes that 'in the (impossible) case of there being no raw materials' the f-c distinction and the c-v distinction do coincide. But this seems to be misleading regardless of whether the discussion is conducted from the point of view of an individual (hence within the value-determining process) or of the economy as a whole (hence within the wealth-creating process). For even if one adopts Marx's view of the f-c distinction as a variant of the c-v distinction within the value-determining process, the two distinctions remain nonetheless different in a Marxian framework: the former is exclusively focused on the transfer of value, while the latter also implies the process of the creation of surplus value. Moreover, if one drops Marx's own interpretation of the f-c distinction the latter turns out to be dealt with by Ricardo first within the value-determining process (in his chapter *On Value*) and later on within the wealth-creating process (as for instance in his chapter *On Machinery*).[15] In this sense the issue of whether raw materials are or are not to be taken into account in the f-c distinction presents itself as the more sophisticated issue of whether (1) the adopted point of view is that of the individual or of the economy as a whole and (2) raw materials require a longer or shorter time of reproduction than wage goods.

If one adopts the point of view of the economy as a whole along with the assumption that raw materials require a shorter time of reproduction than wage goods, it turns out that raw materials eventually disappear as a component of circulating capital and simply become a *transitory aspect of wages*. This follows not only from the fact that if the labour bestowed on the maintenance of fixed capital 'may be considered as really expended on the commodity manufactured' (Ricardo 1821, p. 39), the same should hold true for the labour bestowed on the production of raw materials embodied in 'the commodity manufactured' itself; but also from some important passages on the distinction between value and wealth in Marx's *Theories of Surplus Value* (Volume II, pp. 414ff, 470ff, 535ff). Here Marx, in referring to Ricardo's famous statement that 'the labour of a million of men in manufactures will always produce the same value but will not always produce the same riches', first objects that Ricardo would be right 'if the capital advanced consisted only of variable capital'. He then asserts that, in the case where the capital advanced consists of C as well as of V (here taken, it seems, in their 'material aspect'), it remains nonetheless true that 'a large part of the capital laid out annually, which appears to be C from the standpoint of the individual capitalist or the particular sphere of production, resolves itself into V from the standpoint of society or of the capitalist class' during the same period (ibid., pp. 414–15). Which amounts to saying that, once the circulating part of C (or at least that part of C whose circulation takes one year) is assumed away as a transitory aspect of V, Ricardo's famous statement is nonetheless wrong for it assumes away even that fixed part of C which, far from disappearing at the aggregate level when the same period is considered, does indeed change from one branch of production to another.

It should be pointed out, however, that Marx's objections to Ricardo's statement are framed within a point of view which is different from the one adopted by Ricardo himself. Whilst Ricardo's passage implies a *diachronic* view of the reproduction process (a view whereby any part of C may be regarded as a transitory aspect of V over different periods), Marx's criticism displays a *synchronic* view of the same process (a view whereby C and V are considered side by side within the same period). Marx is indeed aware that the two views may coexist, at least when he points out (*Grundrisse*, p. 737) that the fixed and circulating forms of capital can be viewed either as 'changing forms of the same capital in different phases of its turnover' or as 'two different modes of existence of capital' at the same time (they can be viewed, that is, either as complementary or as alternative forms of 'capital in general'). But he seems to confine this insight to the f-c distinction as though the c-v distinction were exclusively associated with the synchronic view. Yet just as the circulating part of C vanishes when one ascends with Marx from one branch of industry to the economy as a whole within the same period, likewise the fixed part of C should vanish as well (so that C vanishes altogether) as one moves diachronically from one period to the next.

Marx fails, however, to reach this conclusion. In fact, as the decisive element of his c-v distinction is not the turnover period of capital, likewise the central target of his system of thought is not the capital of the whole nation (i.e., social capital as the source of national revenue) even when, in Part 3 of Volume II of *Capital*, he deals with what is here called 'total social capital' (*Gesellschaftliches Gesamtkapital*).[16] Indeed when Marx, as quoted by Steedman, says that 'Ricardo has far too great an instinct for logic not to be sensitive to this [i.e., that Ricardo's f-c distinction is nothing but Marx's c-v distinction], and he therefore just lets this part of the capital [i.e., raw materials] disappear', it eludes him that what Ricardo is sensitive to is not what Marx himself believes it to be. In particular, it is the role of social capital in the wealth-creating process and the role of the f-c distinction itself within this process – something Marx was rather insensitive to – which accounts for the disappearance of raw materials when Ricardo's approach to capital occurs within the latter process. Likewise what Marx, as quoted by Steedman again, says about Ricardo (i.e., that 'he is, therefore, only right in the *one* case where the total capital equals the variable capital; a presupposition that pervades all his, and Adam Smith's, observations regarding the capital of society as a whole') may be turned against Marx himself by arguing that he [Marx] is, therefore, right only in the case where the total capital does *not* equal the variable capital, a presupposition that pervades all his observations regarding the capital of individual capitalists.

I. Hunt

That the difference between the f-c and c-v distinction is essential to a proper understanding of the OCC is implied by I. Hunt (1983). After noting that one thing is the 'value', another the 'organic' composition of capital, Hunt distinguishes between a *flow* and a *stock* notion of the OCC in the sense that 'any increase in the OCC defined in terms of capital stocks can be expressed in terms of changes in the flow OCC and the turnover period of capital' (p. 134). He then explains his preference for the 'flow' notion in that the latter can be easily associated with changes in the turnover period of capital (TPC). Whence the following possibilities:

1. an increase in OCC may be compounded by an increase in TPC;
2. an increase in OCC may take place without any increase in TPC;
3. an increase in TPC may take place without an increase in OCC.

From Marx's treatment (mentioned above) of the difference between capital invested and capital consumed, it should follow, however, that the 'flow' and 'stock' notions are less two alternative ways of expressing the same concept than two alternative ways in which the same concept can be used to solve different problems. For the *value* of a particular commodity is one thing, the *annual rate of profit* of the capital advanced for the production of this commodity is another, and the volume of *employment* provided by the capital thus advanced is still another. While the 'flow' notion (with the associated concept of capital consumed) seems to fit in with the problem of value, the 'stock' notion (with the associated concept of capital invested) seems to be more suitable for tackling the problems of unemployment and of the rate of profit. Conversely, it should be noted that the turnover periods of circulating, fixed and total (circulating + fixed) capital are entirely different things, as are the turnover periods of an individual capital and of social capital. As far as the latter is concerned, its turnover period must increase whenever the OCC is assumed to rise. For, on the one hand, all increases in OCC reflect increases in TC, and, on the other, the productivity of social labour associated with TC cannot increase *for long* without an increase either in the gestation period of new machines or in their lifetime or both: which implies in all cases a secular rise in TPC. Hence a clash in Marx's FRPT, based as the latter is on the analysis of secular tendencies as well as of a constant TPC.

Leaving aside Marx's synchronic view of the reproduction process mentioned above, his reluctance to assign to the TPC a crucial role in his FRPT may result from the fact that the notion of TPC is strictly related to the f-c distinction rather than to the c-v distinction. But one sense in which the two distinctions differ from each other is that the f-c distinction (hence TPC itself) applies to individual capital in a different sense than it does to social capital. For what turns over in the circulation of an individual capital is value whereas wealth is what turns over in the circulation of social capital. Furthermore, when the point of view of social capital is adopted, not only does the ratio of fixed to circulating capital become more suitable than the OCC for expressing how much capital is laid out in the 'wrong' form and how much in the 'right' form of wages (Hicks and Hollander 1977) but the very notion of TPC becomes more significant than the ratio of fixed to circulating capital itself in that a change in TPC may occur (as when circulating capital is converted into fixed capital) even though no change in the amount of total capital takes place. Indeed, when this level of observation is associated with the diachronic view, all capital appears as circulating capital or, to put it differently, all capital appears as either circulating or fixed depending on whether the length of TPC is equal to or longer than a predetermined span of time (year). Under these circumstances the ultimate impact of the accumulation process turns out to be a lengthening of the turnover period of social capital rather than an increase in the average of many individual OCCs.

Technical progress

Unity and contradictions in Marx's analysis of unemployment and of the falling rate of profit. Relations with Ricardo

Once the static nature of the OCC is put into perspective, attention should be focused on its dynamic behaviour. Since technical progress is the force that comes to the fore when this point of view is adopted, a step backward is needed again to investigate how Marx deals from the outset with this force.

Marx's analysis of technical progress is carried out in strict connection with his analysis of accumulation in Volume I of *Capital* and is based on the notions of 'necessary' and 'surplus' labour as well as on the shift that takes place in the balance between these two kinds of labour as the process of innovation unfolds. Marx applies the term 'relative' to the surplus value resulting from a shortening of necessary labour without any prolongation of the working day (year), and his analysis of technical progress essentially becomes an analysis of the 'particular methods of producing relative surplus-value' (*Capital*, Volume I, Part 4). The first thing worth noting in this connection is that however much these methods (classified by Marx in the three broad categories of co-operation, manufacture and large-scale industry) may be interpreted as a progressive manifestation, at different stages of the process of accumulation, of Smith's principle of the division of labour, they turn out to be something different in Marx's system of thought. For unlike Smith, whose analysis is grounded in the process of the formation of wealth (the number of pins *produced* being more relevant to him than the number of pins *appropriated* as a result of the innovation). Marx's analysis of these methods is here framed *a fortiori* within the process of the determination of value owing to his notion of relative surplus value.

This quid pro quo is particularly evident in Marx's famous equalization of the rate of surplus value to the ratio of surplus labour to necessary labour. For whilst the latter distinction may be conceived of as arising within the wealth-creating process and is actually compatible with any theory of value, surplus labour is defined by Marx within the valorization process as 'labour time for the capitalist'. The result is that he eventually makes unthinkable what on the contrary has occurred hitherto, i.e., that a lengthening of surplus labour *along with* a shortening of the working day (year) is a phenomenon which is just as possible as the fact that surplus labour can be eventually turned, in spite of the capitalist rules of the game, into labour time *for the worker himself*, i.e., into labour time devoted to the production of luxuries for the worker's own consumption.

Marx's ambiguities about value and wealth are not confined, however, to his treatment of technical progress as such. They return when he comes to deal with the most advanced form of this phenomenon, i.e., with the employment of machinery (and related unemployment of labour), as well as with 'the expression, peculiar to the capitalist mode of production, of the progressive development of the social productivity of labour' (*Capital*, Volume III, p. 319), i.e., with the tendency for the general rate of profit to fall.

Let us first consider Marx's treatment of the former issue as developed in his famous chapter *Machinery and Large-Scale Industry* in Volume I of *Capital*. Here, despite Marx's earlier acknowledgement of the 'great difference' that exists between the machine 'as a factor in the formation of value and as a factor in the formation of the product' (Volume I, p. 509), most of the argument focuses on the 'great difference' that also exists between 'the value of a machine and the value transferred in a given time by the machine to the product'. This tendency reflects itself in the first analytical problem tackled in this chapter, i.e., the problem concerning the change in the value of a particular commodity resulting from the mechanization of its production, as well as in the second analytical problem of the same chapter, i.e., the displacement of workers induced by the introduction of machinery. Since the latter problem is approached by focusing on the *motives* that induce capitalists to introduce the new machines as well as on the *effects* that their introduction brings about in those branches (or regions) where they are employed, its solution implies, as for the motives, that the price of new machines must be lower than the price of the labour that they displace. And, as for the effects, that the quantity of labour displaced is always more than the quantity of labour employed in producing the machines (the difference between the two prices being proportionately less than the difference between the two quantities) (*Capital*, Volume I, p. 508ff). Whence Marx's conclusion that the introduction of machinery necessarily results, under the capitalist rules of the game, in an increase in exploitation and unemployment, it being understood, with regard to unemployment, that the *virtual* and the *actual* displacement of workers[17] are two things as different as are, with regard to exploitation, the *natural* and the *artificial* increase in productivity.[18]

The phenomena of unemployment and exploitation are taken up again in the famous chapter of *Capital* titled *The General Law of Capitalist Accumulation*. Here the causes and effects of mechanization are discussed in terms of the causes and effects of a rising OCC. From a distance, this chapter not only appears to be linked to the chapter on machinery just discussed, it also seems to be instrumental along with the latter in setting the stage for Volume III of *Capital* and particularly for a crucial proposition of this Volume, i.e., that the tendency of the rate of profit to fall is a 'self-evident necessity deriving from the nature of the capitalist mode of production' (*Capital*, Volume III, p. 319). Indeed the 'necessity' of this law, along with the 'unity' of Marx's thought, results from the fact that while everything conspires to increase the OCC (as shown in Volume I) this increase necessarily implies a decline in the rate of profit (as shown in Volume III).

From a greater distance, however, Marx's approach to the phenomena of unemployment and exploitation turns out to change as he moves from the chapter on machinery to the chapter on the general law of capitalist accumulation. For, on the one hand, what was a *micro* approach in the former becomes a *macro* approach in the latter chapter; on the other, not only is this chapter the place where Marx introduces the OCC notion but the OCC with which this chapter deals is the 'composition of social capital' defined by Marx as the 'average' composition of individual capitals. Now while an average of individual compositions is nothing in itself but an average of different numbers, it should be remarked that in the context of the distinction between individual and social capital the latter may be regarded as the set of all individual capitals only if value is (again) mistaken for wealth. For, on the one hand, the (initial and final) substance of capital changes as one moves from the individual to the social point of view (it is value in the former, wealth in the latter case); on the other, the difference between wealth and value being *not* a matter of degree, social capital cannot be regarded as a sum of exchange-values. Accordingly, the 'general' rate of profit, defined by Marx as the average of all rates holding in sectors of different composition, turns out to be marred by the same ambiguities embodied in the 'composition of social capital' itself and in turn appears as nothing more than an average of different numbers.

However, it should not be overlooked that the law of the falling rate of profit is said by Marx to be 'double-edged' in the sense that it implies a decline in the *rate* along with a simultaneous increase in the absolute *mass* of profit (*Capital*, Volume III, p. 326). Accordingly, when Marx comes to discuss in Volume III the two effects of a rising OCC as dealt with in Volume I, i.e., a rising unemployment and the falling value of commodities, this double-edge is specified in the sense that a rising OCC does not imply either an absolute fall in V (pp. 322–6) or a percentage fall in the value of commodities more than proportional to the percentage rise of the total quantity produced (pp. 335–8).[19] An absolute fall in V, however, seems to be implied in a tacit assumption of Marx's analysis of machinery as developed in Volume I, i.e., that the machines introduced in a particular branch are *already built* in another branch,[20] while the contrast between the two percentage changes mentioned in Volume III is denied by the other tacit assumption of Volume I, i.e., that output be *constant* as new machines replace the old in any branch.[21] The assumption of constant output, however, is consistent with Marx's tendency to focus on value rather than on wealth. The first thing that should come to mind and be first discussed with respect to the wealth-creating process is whether the introduction of machinery is or is not *output expanding* (hence whether the displacement of workers is accordingly of the virtual or of the actual kind) rather than whether it is or it is not *labour-saving* (hence whether the value of the product in terms of the labour embodied in it decreases or increases with the introduction of the new machines).

Curiously enough, when Marx comes to the 'compensation theory' (CT) he, on the one hand, acknowledges that 'as a matter of fact' output increases after the introduction of new machines and that accumulation may well proceed 'on the existing technical basis' (*Capital*, Volume I, pp. 570, 578); on the other, he expresses himself again in terms of machines that are introduced in a particular branch. As a result, the framework of Ricardo's chapter *On Machinery*, which seems to provide the example by which Marx attempts to prove the CT wrong,[22] is altered in a counter-productive way. For his 'capitalist' is viewed as a producer, amongst others, of a particular commodity who dismisses part of his workers and purchases from someone else the machine that replaces them (whereas the corresponding group of Ricardo's workers is employed in the production of the machine itself). Conversely, Ricardo's chapter *On Machinery* seems to be understood by Marx as though its topic were the same as that of Ricardo's chapter *On Value*, i.e., as though Ricardo's chapter on machinery were concerned with, in Marx's own terms, 'an exception to the law of value' (*Capital*, Volume II, p. 293) whereas it can be argued that this chapter is rather about 'an exception to the law of wealth'.[23]

Accordingly, when Marx says with regard to a labour-saving innovation that 'a part of the capital, instead of being set free, is here locked up in such a way as to cease to be exchanged for labour-power' (*Capital*, Volume I, p. 565), the capital here considered as 'locked up' should be understood as *money* capital rather than as *variable* capital. For the object of its purchase is an 'instrument of labour', i.e., something that belongs to another capitalist and for the production of which a *new* variable capital *was* invested in the past. In this sense, what Marx argues against the CT (i.e., that, if the workers that have been thrown out of work in a given branch find it in another this takes place 'only through the agency of a new, additional capital which is seeking investment, and in no way through the agency of the capital that was already functioning previously and was then converted into machinery': *Capital*, Volume I, p. 567), seems to be consistent only if the 'new capital' is intended as a new *will* to invest the means of subsistence that have been set free by the labour-saving innovation rather than as new *means* of subsistence i.e., as wage goods that are produced *ex novo* after the innovation and were unavailable prior to it.[24]

The capital-saving approach to the OCC

The issue of whether a rising OCC is a *necessary* or just a *possible* phenomenon has been dealt with in modern Marxian economics along with the parallel issue of whether a falling rate of profit is a necessary or only a possible feature of the capitalist mode of production.[25] While the latter issue has been largely settled in the sense that any fall in the rate of profit occurs for reasons unrelated to the nature of capital itself (whence the development of the so-called *profit-squeeze approach* to the FRPT), the former has been solved in the similar sense that a rise in the OCC is simply a possibility and that its decline is more likely than its increase (whence the development of what might be called the *capital-saving approach* to the OCC).

While a discussion of the profit-squeeze approach is beyond the scope of this chapter, the capital-saving approach is well reflected in Hodgson's (1974) criticism of Yaffe's (1972) isolated defence of Marx. According to Hodgson, who is here concerned with the tendencies vs. countertendencies issue, 'there is no less justification to assert that the reduction in the value of elements of constant capital is the underlying tendency, and the increase in the OCC is a counteracting influence or isolated case' (1974, p. 62). It should be noted, however, that far from arguing (unlike Marx who devotes most of Volume I of *Capital* to doing the opposite) why 'there is no less justification', Hodgson eventually joins Yaffe in mistaking the OCC for the VC. For while Yaffe (1972, p. 196) asserts that both the TC and the OCC must increase 'although the latter will not increase as quickly as the former' (thereby confusing the TC and VC roots of the OCC notion), Hodgson (1974, p. 70) starts from Garegnani's assertion that there is no simple relation between 'output per man' and 'capital per man' (Garegnani 1970) in order to conclude that 'there is no basis, therefore, for asserting that increased productivity is generally associated with an increased OCC'. But Garegnani's 'capital per man' has little to do with Marx's OCC, not only because the OCC is the VC *in so far as* it reflects the TC; but also because changes in 'output per man' are impossible beyond a certain point without corresponding changes in TC unless 'output per man' is confused with the wage rate (whose level depends on how the product is distributed rather than on how it is produced). On the other hand, however similar Marx's VC may appear to Garegnani's 'capital per man', it should not be overlooked that the 'value' of Marx's VC is measured (unless the value composition of capital is mistaken for its price composition) in terms of the labour embodied in C (without regard, as Hodgson remarks, to labour embodied at different dates) and not in terms, as the moderns imply, of future profits discounted back to the present or of past costs capitalized at the going interest rate.

As for the capital-saving approach, it should first be pointed out that capital-saving innovations must be shown to *necessarily* recur in order for Marx's analysis of a rising OCC to be proved wrong (Yaffe 1972). Moreover, if 'it is a logical fallacy to infer from the fact that some feature x is necessary while another feature is not, to the necessity of having more of x than of y' (van Parijs 1980), it does not follow that having more of y (capital-saving) than of x (labour-saving) is a necessity. Conversely, when Blaug (1960) in developing this approach goes so far as to distinguish between 'fixed-capital-saving' innovations and 'circulating-capital-saving' innovations, he does not go far enough to notice that a necessary condition for the second kind of innovations to occur is frequently a fixed-capital-using innovation.[26] Blaug's contribution, however, is noteworthy for he maintains that innovations may be considered labour- or capital-saving depending on whether they are looked at from the point of view of a particular sector or of the economy as a whole (see also Roemer 1979); and also that the issue of whether unemployment is or is not associated with technical progress depends on whether the process of accumulation is of the deepening or of the widening kind. While the second issue is settled by Blaug in the sense that no unemployment occurs when the capital-widening effects outweigh in the whole economy the capital-deepening effects of particular sectors, the first implies that what is saved from the point of view of the whole economy is not the capital or labour saved in a particular branch. It is indeed the capital or labour saved in this branch less the additional capital or labour used in other branches as a condition for the saving to occur in the initial branch.

Unfortunately, once the effects of innovations are considered across all branches of production, one should come to a conclusion that Blaug failed to reach, i.e., that the ultimate result of the *majority* of innovations is, as implied by Böhm-Bawerk with regard to the greater frequency of 'lengthening' (capital-using) as compared to 'shortening' (capital-saving) inventions,[27] an increase in the TPC for the economy as a whole. Indeed on this point Böhm-Bawerk falls into line with Marx although, of course, their more general views remain as far apart as possible. For while both authors would regard the modern categories of 'neutral' and 'capital-saving' innovations as a *possible* rather than as the *prevailing* form of technical progress, the predominance of capital-using innovations is derived by Marx from the fact that this phenomenon is the only way by which capitalists can reap a greater relative surplus value from a *given* output, whereas Böhm-Bawerk argues that this is the only way by which society can reap a *greater* output from a given amount of labour and length of working day (year).

All this brings us back to the wealth-creating process as distinct from the value-determining process and to the macro as distinct from the micro approach discussed above. However, as we ascend with Böhm-Bawerk to the macro level and as we focus with him on the wealth-creating process, we might discern not only what he has in common with Marx but also where both authors are surpassed by their criticized (in the case of Marx) or neglected (in the case of Böhm-Bawerk) predecessors. For, once this level of analysis is reached, it should be realized, as argued above, that what is liable to increase as the process of accumulation unfolds is the fixed-to-circulating rather than the constant-to-variable capital ratio.

Conclusions

The foregoing discussion has run along two interwoven lines of thought; one relates to authors, the other to arguments. While the former line has shown Marx's thinking about the OCC, unemployment and the rate of profit to differ from – or to be unsatisfactory for other reasons than – what it has been thought to be by some of his critics, the other has shown the unity of Marx's arguments as they run from Volume I to Volume III of *Capital*, i.e., from the simple notion of money capital to the complicated conclusions about the falling rate of profit. Looking from within this unity consists in the fact that Marx's arguments about the OCC, unemployment and the rate of profit are all based on the neutral notion of the development of the productivity of social labour. Looking from without, Marx's unity consists in the fact that all his arguments seem to be aimed at the crucial question, raised by Smith and others, whether the phenomenon of the development of the productivity of social labour resulting from the accumulation of capital does or does not lead to a permanent improvement of the conditions of the working class. In this sense Marx's arguments about the OCC may be summarized as follows:

1. The development of the productivity of social labour is necessarily associated with an increase in TC (which may or may not be mirrored by an increase in VC).
2. The development of the productivity of social labour or, similarly, an increase in the OCC results in a tendency for unemployment to increase and for the rate of profit to fall.
3. Contrary to Smith who maintains that increases in the 'real price of labour' naturally result (despite the competition between workers and the conspiracies of capitalists) from the accumulation of capital (primarily because the associated increases in the productivity of labour prevent the labour cost per unit of output from rising at the expense of profit as accumulation goes on: see Smith 1776, Book I, chapter 8), Marx's conclusion is that the development of productivity necessarily leads to two evils: for the working class in the first place (rising unemployment); for the capitalist mode of production in the end (falling rate of profit).

Despite its unity, this chain of reasoning is not devoid of its own contradictions. These seem to result from Marx's neglect or misapplication of some important distinctions with which he was not altogether unfamiliar. One is the distinction between value and wealth. Another is the distinction between diachronic and synchronic views of the reproduction process. Still another is the more general distinction between individual and social capital, the latter being the source of national revenue rather than the set of all individual capitals in any of their (money, commodity or productive) forms. The difference between the classics' f-c distinction and Marx's own c-v distinction lies somewhere in between. Although Marx, unlike most modern economists, devoted careful attention to this difference, its treatment in his work is as unsatisfactory as the treatment of the above distinctions. For not only is the f-c distinction confined by Marx to the value-determining process; but his inability to apply this distinction to the wealth-creating process seems in turn to result from his failure to assign to social capital and to the associated process of the reproduction of national revenue the same central place reserved for these notions in the system of thought of his predecessors. On the other hand, if the problems of capital are tackled from the point of view of the capital whose 'sole end and purpose' is 'to maintain and augment the stock which may be reserved for immediate consumption', i.e., the stock which 'feeds, clothes, and lodges the people' (Smith 1776, Book II, p. 283), it turns out that C, V and the OCC eventually lose their own identities whilst the older notions of fixed capital, circulating capital and the fixed-to-circulating capital ratio come to the fore again with circulating capital presenting itself as the wages fund. From this general point of view it also turns out that a rise in the average OCC appears rather as a lengthening of the turnover period of social capital while technical progress becomes a force whose prevailing impact is a lengthening of the turnover period of social capital rather than a rise in the average OCC.

Notes

1. In this chapter the terms 'value' and 'wealth' will be used as synonymous with the terms 'exchange value' and 'use value'. It should be noted, however, that this is more than a terminological convention owing to the different role that the two notions of value play within the theory of capital. In fact, as it will be argued in the text, exchange values are as essential to the concept of individual capital as use values are to the concept of social capital (as well as to the related concept of national revenue). On the association between individual capital and exchange values, on the one hand, and between social capital and use values, on the other, see Marx himself (1905, Volume III, p. 337). For a further discussion of the distinction between individual and social capital see Meacci (1989a, 1989b).
2. 'The means of production on the one hand, labour-power on the other, are merely the different forms of existence which the value of the original capital assumed when it lost its monetary form and was transformed into the various factors of the labour process' (*Capital*, Volume I, p. 317).
3. 'That part of capital, therefore, which is turned into means of production, i.e. the raw material, the auxiliary material and the instruments of labour, does not undergo any quantitative alteration of value in the process of production. For this reason, I call it the constant part of capital, or more briefly, constant capital. On the other hand that part of capital which is turned into labour-power does undergo an alteration of value in the process of production. It both reproduces the equivalent of its own value and produces an excess, a surplus-value, which may itself vary, and be more or less according to circumstances. I therefore call it the variable part of capital, or more briefly, variable capital' (*Capital*, Volume I, p. 317).
4. Indeed, while from the point of view of the value-determining process the two components of C differ not with respect to the role that they play (for it equally consists in the transfer of their value to the product) but with respect to the way in which they play their role, from the point of view of the wealth-creating process it is their role – not the way in which it is played – that differs. Here, as Marx points out, the increase of the machinery component presents itself as a *condition* while the increase of the materials component is a *consequence* of the increasing productivity of labour (see *Capital*, Volume I, p. 773). For a related discussion of the relationship between money capital on the one hand and C and V on the other as well as between C and V on the one hand and 'the appropriation of the labour process by capital' and 'the labour process itself' on the other, see Marx's 'Results of the Immediate Process of Production', in *Capital*, Volume I, p. 941ff.
5. For a detailed discussion of this distinction see Marx's *Theories of Surplus Value* and particularly his chapter on Cherbuliez (Volume III, p. 362ff).
6. About the importance of fixed capital within Marxian economics, see Shaikh's (1978) criticism of Okishio's (1961) attack on Marx's FRPT. See also Roemer (1979).
7. This seems to be the case even when, as in *Capital*, Volume II, Part 3, Marx turns to 'the reproduction and circulation of total social capital'. In this connection see

the text below and particularly note 16. For a brief discussion of the relationship between the wealth-creating and value-determining processes, on the one hand, and the modern theory of joint products, on the other, see below, note 15.

8. This phenomenon is called by Marx 'relative cheapening of machinery' (1905, Volume III, p. 221).
9. 'The composition of capital is to be understood in a twofold sense. As value, it is determined by the proportion in which it is divided into constant capital, or the value of the means of production, and variable capital, or the value of labour-power, the sum total of wages. As material, as it functions in the process of production, all capital is divided into means of production and living labour-power. This latter composition is determined by the relation between the mass of the means of production employed on the one hand, and the mass of labour necessary for their employment on the other. I call the former the value-composition, the latter the technical composition of capital' (*Capital*, Volume I, p. 762).
10. The difference between TC and VC turns out to be even greater when one considers the raw material content of C. For a discussion of the role of raw materials in Marx's OCC as well as of the relationship between the latter and population growth (two problems that lie outside the scope of this chapter) see Perelman (1985). Perelman's paper, however, is not focused on the OCC as such and does not tackle the analytical problem of the price composition as distinguished from the value composition which is implied in several passages on raw materials in Marx's *Theories of Surplus Value* (see also *Capital*, Volume III, chapter 6). For a discussion of the distinctions between VC, TC and the OCC (though not between the price composition and the value composition) and for an attempt to link VC and TC to, respectively, a *cyclical* and *secular* falling rate of profit see Groll and Orzech (1987). For an extension of this discussion to the more general level of the relationships between production, exchange and distribution see Fine and Harris (1979).
11. It is interesting to note that the misunderstanding about TC and VC (as well as about C-V and Mp-L) reappears in the ratio of *dead* to *living* labour (RDL): a sophisticated proxy for the OCC. The use of this ratio has recently become so fashionable that van Parijs (1980), after noting that the OCC 'can be understood in at least two ways' – i.e., as the VC and the RDL – calls the former a 'textbook variant' and the latter a 'modern variant' of the FRPT. But, what can be understood in at least two ways – i.e., as TC and VC – is 'the composition of capital' as distinct (see note 9 above) from the OCC (which, on the contrary, can be understood in just one way once TC is distinguished from VC). It should furthermore be noted, with regard to the RDL and particularly to its denominator, that since 'the mass of living labour' is one thing, 'the value of this mass' (*Capital*, Volume III, p. 246) is another, and since V is assumed by Marx himself to be 'an index' of the living labour that it sets in motion rather than of the dead labour embodied in it (*Capital*, Volume III, pp. 245–6), the denominator of the RDL should be intended as the *mass* of living labour rather than as the *value* of this mass. This is, however, the contrary of what is usually implied in the 'modern variant' of the OCC. See, for instance, Morishima (1973, pp. 35–6) and Steedman (1977, pp. 132–6). It should be noted, however, that this ambiguity belongs to Marx in the first place. Compare, for instance, his passages as cited in this note with those quoted in note 9 above as well as with Marx's definition of V at the beginning of his analysis of the schemes of reproduction in *Capital*, Volume II, pp. 471–2. Finally, it should also be noted that the further variant of the OCC known as the 'capital-output ratio measured in value terms' (in terms, that is, of the labour embodied in the two variables of this ratio) is still more perplexing than Marx's ambiguous definitions of the 'active component' of the OCC itself. For, on the one hand, the capital–output ratio appears to be a version of Marx's notion of the VC rather than of the OCC (the magnitude of the capital–output ratio may indeed rise, fall or remain unchanged as TC, hence the productivity of social labour, increases); on the other, it is a crucial proposition of Marxian economics that the value of

labour-power is *not* equal to the value created by it (which in turn is not the same thing as labour-power itself).

12. Whence Marx's statement that 'it is not just the slower or more rapid return that makes a means of production into fixed capital, but rather the specific manner in which it gives up value to the product' (*Capital*, Volume II, p. 304) as well as the other whereby 'it is not the worker's means of subsistence that acquire the characteristics of circulating capital in contrast to fixed capital. As it is also not his labour power, but rather the portion of the value of the productive capital that is spent on it, that has this characteristic in the turnover in common with some components of the constant part of the capital and in contrast with other parts' (*Capital*, Volume II, p. 245). The relationship and differences between the f-c distinction and the c-v distinction are discussed at greater length in Meacci (1989a).
13. Although Marx asserts that what is decisive for the rate of profit to fall is not a change in the ratio between fixed and circulating capital but a change in the turnover period of capital (*Capital*, Volume III, pp. 250–2), it should be noted that the latter change turns out to be a necessary result of the former when the turnover period is referred to total (fixed + circulating) capital rather than to just one of its two components. On this point see also below, pp. 94–5.
14. It should be noted, however, that Ricardo's treatment of this distinction is generally more consistent than Marx's not only with respect to the latter's ambiguous definition of the process of production as the 'unity' of the labour process and the valorization process (*Capital*, Volume I, p. 304; pp. 978–9, 991, *passim*) but also because Marx often fails to notice *which* of the two processes is being dealt with by Ricardo, or *when* it is that Ricardo's analysis shifts from the one to the other. For instance, in a passage concerning Ricardo's famous definition of capital, Marx first notes that 'the consumption of the means of subsistence is actually no more than an incident in the labour process, like the consumption of coal by the steam-engine, of oil by the wheel, of hay by the horse', and then rightly observes that 'it is in keeping with this that Ricardo lists "food and clothing" alongside raw materials and tools, as things which "give effect to labour" and hence serve as "capital" in the labour process'. He immediately adds, however, that 'the means of subsistence that the worker consumes are commodities that he has *purchased*' so that as soon as they pass into his hands 'they cease to be capital' (*Capital*, Volume I, p. 1004). Now, whilst by the expression 'in keeping with this' Marx rightly implies – thus stressing Ricardo's consistency – the context of the labour process as a wealth-creating process (i.e., as argued in the text above and implied in Ricardo's own definition of capital based as this is on the notion of the 'wealth of a country', the context of social capital itself), by the last two sentences Marx suddenly shifts to a point of view whereby what 'ceases to be capital' is, properly speaking, *money* (i.e., *individual*) capital while what labour consumes turns out to be simply what a worker 'has purchased'.
15. For a discussion of this change of focus in Ricardo's *Principles* see Meacci (1985) as well as the text below, pp. 99–100. It is interesting to note that Marx's tendency to neglect the wealth-creating process to the advantage of the value-determining process (which is particularly evident in his reformulation of Ricardo's chapter on machinery discussed below) seems to reappear in Steedman's (and Sraffa's) notion of fixed capital as a special kind of joint product (Steedman 1977, chapter 10). In fact, once joint products are distinguished (as in Steedman 1977, p. 137, n. 2) from *pure* joint products (which are in effect a frequent result of the wealth-creating process as distinct from the value-determining process) and once fixed capital is (consistently) considered as a kind of non-pure joint product, it should be acknowledged that the process with which this notion of fixed capital is compatible is the value-determining process rather than the wealth-creating process. This is in compliance not only with Malthus's observation (quoted by Marx and by Steedman himself, ibid., p. 140) that 'if we reckon the *value* of the fixed capital employed as a part of the advances, we must reckon the remaining *value* of such capital at the end of the year as a part of the annual return' (emphasis added); but also with Marx's

own remark that 'a machine participates in every labour process as a whole, but enters into the simultaneous process of valorization only in parts' (*Capital*, Volume I, p. 312, n. 2). (A statement that is in turn related not only to the distinction between the two processes just mentioned but also to the difference between the Mp-L, C-V and c-v distinctions discussed above on pp. 88–9.) In this connection it should also be noted that the English translation of the passages of *Capital* where Malthus's observation is quoted is misleading. For while the German text clearly refers to the two sides of the calculation as the 'Seite des vorgeschossnen *Werts*' and the 'Seite des Produkten*werts*' (emphasis added), the English text refers to the latter as the side of the *product* rather than as the side of the *value* of the product.

16. 'What we now have to consider,' Marx points out at the beginning of Part 3, 'is the circulation process of the individual capitals as components of the total social capital, i.e. the circulation process of this total social capital' (*Capital*, Volume II, p. 430). In the same place money capital is mentioned again as 'a component of the total social capital': a further proof that Marx's 'total social capital' is taken to be the grand total of all individual capitals whatever their (money, commodity or productive) forms (whether, that is, they are sources of, or magnets for, surplus value). This is in contrast, however, with the un-Marxian notion of social capital considered as the source of national revenue. The distinction between social capital and the set of all individual capitals is reiterated in the text (see also note 14, above).
17. 'If someone says that 100 million people would be required in England to spin with the old spinning-wheel the cotton that is now spun with mules by 500 000 people, this does not mean that the mules took the place of those millions who never existed. It means only that many million workers would be required to replace the spinning machinery. If, on the other hand, we say that in England the power-loom threw 800 000 weavers onto the streets, we do not refer to existing machinery, which would have to be replaced by a certain number of workers, but to an actually existing number of workers who were in fact replaced or displaced by the looms' (*Capital*, Volume I, pp. 555–6).
18. The distinction between 'the increased productivity which is due to the development of the social process of production, and that which is due to the exploitation by the capitalists of that development' is emphasized by Marx, for instance, in *Capital*, Volume I, p. 547.
19. 'In actual fact, the fall in commodity prices and the rise in the mass of profit on the increased mass of cheapened commodities is simply another expression of the law of the falling profit rate in the context of a simultaneously rising mass of profit' (*Capital*, Volume III, p. 338).
20. This assumption comes neatly to the surface in Marx's discussion of Everett's first wool-shearing machine (*Capital*, Volume I, p. 554). In saying that this machine 'was set on fire by 100 000 people who had been thrown out of work', Marx fails for instance to enquire whether amongst those who set the machine on fire were the workers who had built it and who presumably were about to build new ones or the workers of other sectors who had already purchased or were about to purchase its products.
21. Indeed while Marx's analysis of machinery conforms to his familiar bias towards the process of the determination of value (whereby products, hence machines themselves, are considered as given in quantity and the problem is restricted to what determines the values of commodities in terms of each other), Marx himself asserts as an 'absolute law' that 'if the total quantity of the article produced by machinery is equal to the total quantity of the article previously produced by handicraft or by manufacture, and now made by machinery, then total labour expended is diminished' (*Capital*, Volume I, p. 570).
22. That Ricardo's chapter on machinery is the source of inspiration for Marx's chapter on *Machinery and Large-Scale Industry* is implied, *inter alia*, by a number of

references to Ricardo's chapter such as those mentioned by Marx on pages 516, 532 n. 72, 557 n. 18, 565 n. 34 of the edition of *Capital* here in use.

23. On this point, as well as on why Ricardo does say 'a capitalist' (1821, p. 388) but does not mean exactly what he says, see Meacci (1985).
24. It should finally be noted that the far-reaching implications of two phenomena mentioned by Marx in the context of his criticism of CT, i.e., the output-expanding qualities of new machines and the capital-widening aspect of investment, are usually neglected in his own theory except, perhaps, for the first paragraph of the chapter on *The General Law of Capitalist Accumulation*. The process of capital widening, however, is here mentioned (along with its beneficial effects on the wages of labour) as a sort of introduction to the subsequent paragraph, where it is stated that the process of accumulation 'goes beyond this phase' (ibid., p. 772). It is interesting to note that the latter paragraph, the remainder of the chapter and the 'Law' itself are then developed by Marx as though this statement could *not* in turn be applied to phases of capital deepening as well. Which is not the case, however, with the part of the chapter on *Machinery and Large-Scale Industry* devoted to the CT for it is here admitted that the process of deepening the 'existing technical basis' is 'constantly interrupted by periods of rest' (ibid., p. 578).
25. For an overview of the debate and of its evolution see van Parijs (1980).
26. This remark is not only in Marx's spirit. It is also in compliance with the recent trend of investment and particularly with the energy-saving bias that was triggered by the two oil shocks of the 1970s.
27. Böhm-Bawerk's argument is most clearly developed in his *Further Essays on Capital and Interest*. See particularly *Essay I*, pp. 1–23 and *Essay II*, pp. 24–33 in Huncke and Sennholz (eds) (1959, Volume 3).

References

Blaug, M. (1960), 'Technical Change and Marxian Economics', in M. Blaug (1986).

Blaug, M. (1980), *A Methodological Appraisal of Marxian Economics*, Amsterdam: North-Holland.

Blaug, M. (1986), *Economic History and the History of Economics*, London: Wheatsheaf Books.

Bradley, I. and M. Howard (eds) (1982), *Classical and Marxian Political Economy*, London: Macmillan.

Caravale, G. (ed.) (1985), *The Legacy of Ricardo*, Oxford: Basil Blackwell.

Dickinson, H.D. (1957), 'The Falling Rate of Profit in Marxian Economics', *Review of Economic Studies*, **24**, pp. 120–30.

Fine, B. and L. Harris (1979), *Rereading 'Capital'*, New York: Columbia University Press.

Garegnani, P. (1970), 'Heterogeneous Capital, the Production Function and the Theory of Distribution', *The Review of Economic Studies*, **37**, pp. 407–36.

Gillman, J.M. (1957), *The Falling Rate of Profit*, London: Dobson.

Groll, S. and Z.B. Orzech (1987), 'Technical Progress and Values in Marx's Theory of the Decline in the Rate of Profit: an Exegetical Approach', *History of Political Economy*, **19**, pp. 591–613.

Harris, D.J. (1983), 'Accumulation of Capital and the Rate of Profit in Marxian Theory', *Cambridge Journal of Economics*, **7**, pp. 311–30.

Hicks, J.R. and S. Hollander (1977), 'Mr. Ricardo and the Moderns', *Quarterly Journal of Economics*, **91**, pp. 351–69.

Hodgson, G. (1974), 'The Theory of the Falling Rate of Profit', *New Left Review*, **84**, pp. 55–82.

Huncke, G.D. and H.F. Sennholz (eds) (1959), *Capital and Interest*, 3 vols, North Holland: Libertarian Press.

Hunt, I. (1983), 'An Obituary or a New Life for the Tendency of the Rate of Profit to Fall?', *Review of Radical Political Economics*, **15**, pp. 131–48.

Marx, K. (1867), *Capital*, Volume I, Harmondsworth: Penguin, 1976.

Marx, K. (1885), *Capital*, Volume II, Harmondsworth: Penguin, 1978.

Marx, K. (1894), *Capital*, Volume III, Harmondsworth: Penguin, 1981.

Marx, K. (1905), *Theories of Surplus Value*, 3 vols, London: Lawrence & Wishart, 1969.

Marx, K. (1939), *Grundrisse*, Harmondsworth: Penguin, 1973.

Meacci, F. (1985), *Ricardo's Chapter on Machinery and the Theory of Capital*, in G. Caravale (ed.) (1985).

Meacci, F. (1989a), 'Different Divisions of Capital in Smith, Ricardo and Marx', *Atlantic Economic Journal*, **17**, pp. 13–21.

Meacci, F. (1989b), 'Irving Fisher and the Classics on the Notion of Capital: Upheaval and Continuity in Economic Thought', *History of Political Economy*, **21**, pp. 409–24.

Meek, R. (1960), 'The Falling Rate of Profit', in R. Meek (1967), pp. 129–42.

Meek, R. (1967), *Economics, Ideology and Other Essays*, London: Chapman and Hall.

Morishima, M. (1973), *Marx's Economics: A Dual Theory of Value and Growth*, Cambridge: Cambridge University Press.

Okishio, N. (1961), 'Technical Change and the Rate of Profit', *Kobe University Economic Review*, **7**, pp. 85–99.

Perelman, M. (1985), 'Marx, Malthus and the Organic Composition of Capital', *History of Political Economy*, **17**, pp. 461–90.

Ricardo, D. (1821), *On the Principles of Political Economy and Taxation*, in P. Sraffa (1951).

Robinson, J. (1942), *An Essay on Marxian Economics*, London: Macmillan.

Robinson, J. (1951–80), *Collected Economic Papers*, Oxford: Basil Blackwell.

Robinson, J. (1978), 'The Organic Composition of Capital', *Kyklos*, **31**, pp. 5–20.

Roemer, J.E. (1977), 'Technical Change and the "Tendency of the Rate of Profit to Fall" ', *Journal of Economic Theory*, **16**, pp. 403–24.

Roemer, J.E. (1979), 'Continuing Controversy on the Falling Rate of Profit: Fixed Capital and Other Issues', *Cambridge Journal of Economics*, **3**, pp. 379–98.

Rosdolski, R. (1968), *The Making of Marx's 'Capital'*, London: Pluto Press.

Shaikh, A. (1978), 'Political Economy and Capitalism: Notes on Dobb's Theory of Crisis', *Cambridge Journal of Economics*, **2**, pp. 233–51.

Smith, A. (1776), *An Inquiry into the Nature and Causes of the Wealth of Nations*, Campbell and Skinner (eds), Oxford: Clarendon Press, 1976.

Sraffa, P. (1951), *The Works and Correspondence of David Ricardo*, Cambridge: Cambridge University Press.

Steedman, I. (1977), *Marx after Sraffa*, London: New Left Books.

Steedman, I. (1982), 'Marx on Ricardo', in I. Bradley and M. Howard (eds) (1982).

Sweezy, P.M. (1942), *The Theory of Capitalist Development*, New York: Oxford University Press.

Van Parijs, P. (1980), 'The Falling-Rate-of-Profit Theory of Crisis: a Rational Reconstruction by Way of Obituary', *Review of Radical Political Economics*, **12**, pp. 1–16.

Yaffe, D. (1972), 'The Marxian Theory of Crisis, Capital and the State', *CSE Bulletin*, **4**, pp. 5–58.

5 On the falling rate of profit*

Ben Fine

Marx's theory of the law of the tendency of the rate of profit to fall (LTRPF) has been extremely controversial, in terms of its validity, its interpretation and its significance. In this chapter, an attempt will be made to outline Marx's law and to answer some of the criticisms that have been levelled against it. In much of the literature, Marx's analysis has been treated too simplistically as a set of algebraic propositions that have been asserted to be correct, incorrect or somewhere in between. On the other hand, Marx's contribution has often been removed to the realm of high philosophy, in which the law takes on the character of an abstract truth, something derived from the logic of capital itself.

In the algebraic-type treatments, commonly referred to as Sraffian or neo-Ricardian,[1] given technical relations of production (usually specified by an input–output matrix) are used to establish an inverse relation between the rate of profit and the level of real wages.[2] Accordingly, the rate of profit can only fall if wages rise or, in case of availability of new technology, if wages rise by more than appropriately measured productivity increase. In this perspective, increased wages are the source of both changing technology (capital deepening in response to higher wages) and, if great enough, a falling rate of profit.[3] This represents a rejection of what is perceived to be Marx's view that changes in technology, and capital deepening, are the source of falling profitability.

The more abstract treatment, usually referred to as fundamentalist or as the capital-logic school, takes accumulation of capital as its starting point and, significantly, there seems to be no such basis in the Sraffian treatment for which production with constant returns can take place at any scale of output. Accumulation is then associated with the transformation of the conditions and nature of production which are deemed inevitably to lead to falling profitability. As production develops, increased surplus value is sought through the displacement of living, direct labour by dead, indirect labour embodied in and through the use

* This chapter is an expanded and revised version of a chapter included in *Marx's 'Capital'* (Fine 1989) and draws heavily on the approach developed jointly with Laurence Harris (Fine and Harris 1979) where a critical assessment of the literature up to that point is also presented.

of machinery within the factory system. Emphasis is placed on the contradiction between living labour as the source of (surplus) value and its decreasing use relative to the mass of dead labour (constant capital) employed. As it were, the capitalist system bites the very hand that feeds it.

The position adopted here differs from both of these, admittedly parodied, extremes. The argument is, however, a complex one, depending upon conceptual rather than algebraic argument. As a result, the structure of the analysis is summarized first and is followed by a more detailed account containing elaboration and justification. A brief final section draws some general conclusions.

Summary of the argument point by point

1. Marx's LTRPF is based upon a fundamental conceptual distinction between the organic composition of capital (OCC) and the value composition of capital (VCC).
2. Each of these is derived from the technical composition of capital (TCC). Marx's notion of the TCC seems straightforward. In conventional terms, it is the physical capital–labour ratio. In principle, both capital and labour inputs are not homogeneous so that the TCC as a 'ratio' is better seen as vector of material inputs relative to a vector of (differentiated) labour inputs. However, Marx has a specific theory of how production develops under capitalism. The use of machinery leads to a rise both in fixed capital and in raw materials relative to living labour. These can be measured in value terms.
3. On the basis of the rising TCC, the OCC measures the results of accumulation by exclusive reference to the sphere of production, i.e. surplus value creation, whilst the VCC reflects this process in the sphere of exchange, i.e. (surplus) value realization or formation as productivity increase is reflected in changing (reduced) values. Thus, whilst both the OCC and the VCC are measured by C/V, where C is constant and V is variable capital, there is a difference between the two. For the OCC takes no account of the reducing values of inputs brought about by increasingly intensive machine production whilst the VCC does reflect these value changes.
4. The rise of the OCC associated with the specifically capitalist methods of production is the source of the law as such, whilst the formation of the VCC is associated with the counteracting tendencies (CTs). These two tendencies are essential and underlying aspects of the accumulation process which interact to form more

complex economic phenomena, but only for that stage of development of capitalism for which machine production is predominant.

5. This implies that the LTRPF (and the CTs) is an abstract law in that it does not give immediate predictions about movements in the rate of profit. In other words, it is not an empirical law in this narrowly predictive sense, but it does provide the basis on which more complex and immediate economic phenomena can be studied by the inclusion of further historical and logical analysis.
6. The presentation of Marx's LTRPF in this way leads to a complete contrast with the understanding and criticism of it associated with Okishio and which has been taken up by the Sraffian school of economics. Because this latter analysis employs comparative statics, which is based on equilibrium analysis, it treats the accumulation process as one which engenders a harmonious interaction between production and circulation. Consequently, the theory can be characterized as the dialectical opposite of Marx's. On the other hand, the fundamentalist approach locates and confines the contradictions of capitalist accumulation within the sphere of production alone and fails to recognize the significance of the contradictory relationship between the production and realization of surplus value.

The compositions of capital

In Volume I of *Capital*, Marx examines the specifically capitalist method of production, i.e., the systematic way in which capitalism seizes and transforms the labour process.[4] In its earliest stages, capitalism utilizes the methods of production that it has inherited from pre-capitalist modes and expands by reliance upon the production of absolute surplus value. At a more developed stage, relative surplus value is produced through the introduction of machinery to displace living labour in the production process. This is the real subordination of labour to capital, as opposed to the mere formal subordination associated with the earlier stage, since labour is now controlled and utilized within production according to the changes and pressures dictated by the logic of capitalism.[5]

Marx argues that the capitalist development of production through the use of machinery inevitably leads to a rising technical composition of capital (TCC), the mass of raw materials in use relative to the mass of living labour. On the one hand, there is the use of the machinery itself, which tends to displace the labourer. On the other hand, machinery allows production to proceed more quickly and intensively, so that a worker will work up more raw materials into final products in a given time. For example, in spinning there will be an increase in the spindles and the cotton used per worker. It should be noted that Marx did not suggest that technical progress had to take only this form – of what the neo-classical orthodoxy would call capital-deepening – only that this is the systematic tendency of capitalist production.

The rising TCC that accompanies accumulation can be measured by a single index only in so far as a mass of heterogeneous raw materials (and living labour) is reduced to a common denominator. For orthodox theory, this is an index number problem. In Marx's theory, the values of commodities are the basis on which the TCC can be measured. This is not simply the choice of one index rather than another. It reflects his previously-developed proposition in the opening chapters of *Capital* that value, understood as socially necessary labour time, is a legitimate category of analysis for a commodity-producing society, since such a society brings different concrete labours into equivalence with each other, thereby creating value relations within that society as a social relation.[6] Consequently, it is legitimate to measure the TCC in value terms, not for convenience with the drawbacks associated with any index number, but as the expression of the changing conditions of production in terms of the social (and value) relations in which they are embodied. In other words, the measurement of the TCC by values is not a more or less convenient and arbitrary index of changing production conditions, but an analytical and conceptual examination of part of the accumulation process.

These comments are borne out when the ways of constructing the value measure of the TCC are analysed. Marx substantially discusses the composition of capital in Volume III of *Capital* and in the three parts of *The Theories of Surplus Value*, although the discussion in the latter is less developed.[7] He does so in the context of three apparently unconnected issues – the transformation problem, the law of the tendency of the rate of profit to fall, and the theory of (absolute) agricultural rent. Although only the first of these is under discussion in this chapter, elsewhere it has been argued (Fine 1986) that Marx develops a consistent theory of the composition of capital over all three areas of study.

Marx carefully distinguishes between the value and organic compositions. In the literature, these have rarely been distinguished and the two have been used interchangeably,[8] usually according to the terminology adopted by Marx for the subject under consideration.[9] For both, the algebraic definition has been denoted by C/V, but this begs the question of what values are used to reduce the heterogeneous bundle of raw materials (in the case of C) and of living labour (in the case of V) to a single value dimension. This is a pertinent problem in this context, since the whole analysis is concerned with accumulation, in which the production of relative surplus value is motivated by the wish to reduce, i.e., to change, the values of commodities.

Before dealing with this problem in the 'dynamic' context of accumulation, it is useful for expositional purposes to distinguish the VCC and the OCC in a 'static' context. Consider, for example, the production of jewellery. Let us suppose that exactly the same labour process is used to produce both silver and gold rings. Both production processes will have the same TCC, since this measures the mass of raw materials to living labour. But the production of gold rings will involve a higher VCC since it uses raw materials of a higher value. To reflect the lack of difference in the production processes from the technical point of view, Marx defined the OCC as equal for the two sectors. It is supposed to measure the TCC in value terms, leaving aside the differences created by the greater or lesser value of the raw materials employed. Thus for Marx (1971, p. 145), using the example of copper and iron as raw materials in place of gold and silver:

> For instance, certain work in copper and iron may require the same ratio of labour power to mass of means of production. But since copper is more expensive than iron, the value relation between variable and constant capital is different in each case, and hence also the value composition of the two. The value composition of capital, in as much as it is determined by, and reflects, its technical composition, is called the organic composition.

Thus, value compositions differ according to the respective values of the raw materials worked up into final commodities. On the other hand, the organic composition captures differences in the methods of production, in the way, as the word organic suggests, that the commodities are put together. Thus, Marx (1972, p. 382) notes, '[b]y the organic composition of productive capital. By this we mean the technological composition.'[10]

The differences in the value composition create some difficulty in measuring the OCC, since the appropriate values at which to define the ratio of C to V are not specified. Should we, for example, use the value of gold, the value of silver or something in between for the definition? This is a problem created by the attempt to make the distinction in a static context. It is only when production processes are changing that the distinction between the OCC and the VCC has any significance, for otherwise the TCC alone is adequate to specify the equivalence or otherwise between production processes from the organic point of view.

Let us consider another example. Suppose that there is a reduction in the value of steel, but otherwise nothing else changes. Then the VCC in any one sector will change according to the relative content of steel in the production of its constant capital and in the value of labour power. Given an equal composition of the various skills of labour between sectors, then the VCCs will vary according to their relative use of steel. Nevertheless, the OCCs across the sectors have remained unchanged, because there has been no change in the TCCs. The OCC simply measures changes in production in value terms and so is only of interest, as distinct from the VCC, when the TCC is changing. Then, it can measure something distinct from the VCC, which measures changes in the TCC only after account has been taken of the changing values of commodities, as they are realized in exchange. The two examples given above only serve to explain the difference between the VCC and the OCC. They do not have much significance in themselves.

The matter is different once we begin to consider changing conditions of production. Marx argued that, at its developed stage, capitalism involves accumulation through the production of relative surplus value with the use of machinery to displace living labour. This results in a rising TCC which can be measured in value terms by the OCC from the point of view of changes in production alone. Raw materials and labour power enter the production process with definite values and this leads to a definite ratio of constant to variable capital, according to the extent that labour is coerced to transform inputs into outputs. If we were to put it chronologically, the OCC measures the TCC at the 'old' values prevailing prior to the renewal of the production process.

This results, however, in a change (reduction) in the values of commodities. When these enter the market, correspondingly new values are established in the form of market values. The VCC is measured at this stage. Necessarily, it takes account of the TCC from the point of view of the change both in the OCC and in the values of commodities as they are realized in the sphere of exchange. To put it chronologically, the VCC is measured at the 'new' rather than at the 'old' values.

The description of the difference between the VCC and the OCC in terms of new and old values is slightly misleading, since the distinction is conceptual rather than chronological. At any moment in time, some capitals will be entering the production process as others will be leaving it. What the distinction does is to draw upon and build a separation between the spheres of production and exchange. In production, the two classes of capital and labour confront each other over the process of production and, as accumulation proceeds, so there is a tendency for the OCC to rise. In exchange, capitalists confront each other as competitors in the process of buying and selling and, as accumulation proceeds, so there is a tendency for values to be reduced and for the VCC to rise less than the OCC. It is the interaction of these processes, as understood in the structural separation between production and exchange, which is the concern of Marx's LTRPF.

The thrust of the distinction between the OCC and the VCC suggested here can be best brought out, by way of summary, by comparison with the one offered by Groll and Orzech (1987). They argue that Marx's distinction is important and define the OCC along the lines that the VCC has been defined here. It is, however, almost perceived to correspond to the equilibrium values (prices of production, more exactly) corresponding to underlying production conditions. They then define the VCC by reference to a re-evaluation of the OCC at prices that diverge from values due to cyclical movements. In other words, the OCC is derived from production alone, as expressed through its corresponding prices, and the VCC is defined by exchange-based deviations from this. Here, however, it is argued that both the OCC and the VCC are derived from production but that the former incorporates technical change on the basis of untransformed values, whereas the latter incorporates transformed values also.

The Law as Such and the counteracting tendencies

Marx's treatment of the LTRPF occupies three chapters in Volume III of *Capital*. The first is entitled 'The Law as Such', Chapter XIII. It contains what appears to be a simple algebraic derivation of falling profitability. Since the rate of profit may, in value terms, be written as $r = e/\,(\text{OCC} + 1)$, where e is the rate of surplus value, a fall in r is immediate from the previously-derived rising OCC, provided there is no rise in e. From the previous discussion, it should be clear that this law cannot be interpreted as a prediction about empirical movements in the rate of profit, since discussion of the OCC is restricted to changes in the production process without any reference to changes in the values of commodities. This explains why the constant value of e is not so much an assumption, as an expression of the unchanging values of commodities during production, so that there is no reduction in the value of labour power.

Marx's second chapter (XIV) deals with the counteracting tendencies, CTs. These fall into two types. There are those that follow from the changes in values, resulting from the rising OCC. If we write $r = S/(C + V)$, it follows that anything that reduces C or V and anything that increases S tends to increase r. The production of relative surplus value tends to do all of these by increasing productivity and reducing the value of C, V (whether directly in the wage-goods sector or indirectly through its use of lower valued raw materials) and increasing *S* through the reduction of *V*. These changes in the values of commodities are synonymous with the formation of the VCC.

In addition, Marx considers CTs of a less systematic variety, which do not follow directly and of necessity from accumulation, such as the paying of lower wages to those pulled into backward employment from the reserve army of labour, the cheapening of raw materials and wage-goods through foreign trade, and the formation of joint-stock companies which, by virtue of their large mass of less risky capital, yield a lower rate of return than the general rate of profit. This group of CTs does not follow of necessity from the rising OCC, even though they can be seen to be necessary, if contingent, results of capitalist development. Marx appears to lump them together with the others without separating them analytically. This may be explained by the lack of final preparation of Volume III for publication. In addition, Marx's list of CTs follows closely that of J.S. Mill's, suggesting that he had yet to rework his material properly. Mill's treatment of the law follows that of Ricardo and is based upon the declining productivity of agriculture, rather than the increasing productivity of all sectors as for Marx.

It is this treatment of the CTs by Marx which makes it appear as though he is dealing with immediate movements in *r* as a numerical counterweight to the law as such. Certainly, the CTs are presented at a more complex level of analysis than the law for, as we have seen, they involve the formation of the VCC which incorporates changes both in production and exchange. However, like the law, the CTs should not be seen as factors of empirical weight directly governing movements in the rate of profit, but as embodying those processes that transform the changing conditions of production into movements in exchange.

The internal contradictions of the law

In the previous section, both the law and the CTs are interpreted as being directed at capturing abstract, underlying processes rather than as predicting immediate movements in the rate of profit. This follows from a more general interpretation of a law or tendency in this way. For example, when it is argued that there is a *tendency* for rates of profit to be equalized across sectors as a result of capital mobility, this should be seen, not as a prediction of equal rates of profit, but as one process amongst others governing capital accumulation. It is only in orthodox economics that this tendency is seen as an actuality, so that an equilibrium can be constructed in which all profit rates are equalized. In contrast, for Marx, laws and tendencies have to be located in the context of the more complex form in which they manifest themselves.

In this case, the tendency for the rate of profit to be equalized has to be set against the competition between capitalists to differentiate their rates of profit from the average, whether this be through accumulation to increase productivity, the paying of lower wages, or whatever.

This is the basis on which Marx's third chapter on the LTRPF should be examined, aptly named 'The Internal Contradictions of the Law'. He examines the law and the CTs as a contradictory unity of underlying tendencies which gives rise to more complex empirical phenomena. Consequently, the analysis is more concerned with the antagonistic coexistence of the law and its CTs than with the prediction of movements in the rate of profit. The two tendencies cannot be added together algebraically to give a rise or fall in the rate of profit according to which of the two is the stronger.[11] Rather, it is concerned with the contradictions between the production and circulation of (surplus) value as the process of value creation and formation proceeds on the basis of existing values, even as these are reduced by the accumulation of capital. In dramatic terms (Marx 1971, pp. 248–9):

> These two elements embraced by the process of accumulation, however, are not to be regarded merely as existing side by side in repose . . . They contain a contradiction which manifests itself in contradictory tendencies and phenomena. These antagonistic agencies counteract each other simultaneously . . . These different influences may at one time operate predominantly side by side in space, and at another succeed each other in time. From time to time the conflict of antagonistic agencies finds vent in crises.

That the LTRPF concerns the interaction of abstract tendencies is implicitly confirmed by Marx's analysis of the internal contradictions. There is little or no discussion of movements in the rate of profit, and a much greater concern throughout the three chapters concerned with the ability of the economy to be able to accumulate the mass of surplus value that it has been able to produce. There is a greater focus on whether accumulation can be sustained than on whether it generates a higher or lower rate of profit.

In this light, the CTs can be reinterpreted. If the reduction in the values of constant and variable capital have been realized, then this is indicative of the translation of changes in conditions of production into the sphere of exchange. On the other hand, the formation of joint-stock companies, the exploitation of the reserve army of labour, and the opening up of foreign trade become conditions conducive to a continuing accumulation, irrespective of the rate of profit at which they occur.

The consideration of the LTRPF as an abstract law also should not deny it any empirical significance. As we have seen, Marx's main conclusion is that the law and CTs cannot exist side by side in harmony, but must at times give rise to crises. This requires careful interpretation, for there is certainly no axiomatic derivation of the necessity of crises, just as there is no axiomatic derivation of a falling rate of profit. Rather, Marx is pointing to the *immanent* possibility of crises, just as he had done previously in Volume II of *Capital* as a result of the more narrow potential of disjuncture between sale and purchase on the basis of unchanging values. For the LTRPF, however, a source of disjuncture is identified in the accommodation in exchange of changing values from production.

This leads to further empirical implications of the LTRPF, for it suggests that crises which owe their origins to developments in the sphere of production will, nevertheless, break in the sphere of circulation. This is one reason why the LTRPF is liable to lead empirically to actual falls in the rate of profit. As the accumulation process falters, the mass of profit realized tends to be set against an unchanging mass of fixed capital, so that profitability declines. But this need not be so. If, for example, as a result of bankruptcies, large masses of capital are depreciated or bought up by surviving capitalists at rock bottom prices, then the rate of profit may even rise as a result of the ensuing crisis.

This point illustrates that the falling rate of profit has been something of a fetish in the literature, whatever the position adopted in relation to Marx's own analysis. The focus has been on whether theory can produce a fall in the rate of profit or not, by whatever mechanism, whether it be a rising OCC or by a rise in wages at the expense of profits. Once the rate of profit falls, it is presumed that the economy collapses into crisis as a result of deficient investment on the part of capitalists, this in turn leading to deficient demand for potential output as in Keynesian theory. In this perspective, there is a complete separation between the theory that yields the fall in profitability and the theory of the results of that fall, i.e., between the cause and the course of the crisis.

It cannot, however, even be presumed that a fall in profitability results in a crisis. There may be a reduced incentive and capacity to accumulate in terms of reward, but some reward is better than none. Continuing accumulation may be necessary to preserve existing (fixed) capital and, most important of all, falling profitability acts as a coercive competitive force. Consequently, as capitalists attempt to restore profitability, they may accumulate at a faster rate than previously!

For Marx, the generation of crises through proximate falls in the rate of profit is a possibility, but this does not offer a penetrating analysis of the cause and course of crises. If the LTRPF is understood as the combination of contradictory tendencies uniting production and exchange, then the examination of these tendencies, at the more complex level of their interaction, opens the way to an analysis of crises linked to and based upon the accumulation process.

At the general level, this requires an analysis of value production and formation in exchange in a much wider context than is presented in the opening chapters of *Capital*. There, the category of value is understood as a social relation which establishes an equivalence between different types of concrete labour, thereby creating the category of abstract labour. There will be different skills of labour as well as different types of labour. Within each sector, there can be different levels of productivity. But commodity equivalence through exchange is a melting pot that reduces all of these labours to the common denominator of value. With accumulation and the competition to reduce values, socially necessary labour time (SNLT) in each sector becomes the centre around which individual values in the sector revolve.

This creates a new task for value and it is one which is intimately related to the LTRPF. Since accumulation leads to a reduction in SNLT, the whole concept of value appears to be at risk, for we are attempting to utilize a category whose quantification through labour time of production is upset as soon as it is established. This is not so, however, once we recognize that the equivalence established between different types of labour is extended through time to labours of different productivity. The OCC, for example, is constructed on the basis of equivalence for previously established values, whereas the formation of the VCC is the process of establishing those values in the wake of the changing production conditions associated with the rising OCC.

In short, Marx's LTRPF (and CTs) is an abstract law concerning contradictory tensions in the accumulation process which in turn reflect the distinction between the OCC and the VCC. The articulation of the two, reflects the unity of production and exchange as accumulation proceeds and production conditions are transformed. In this light, the axiomatic proof of an empirical fall in the rate of profit does not appear to be Marx's intent.

This interpretation, and its contrast with that of others, can be illustrated by reference to Figure 5.1. The fundamentalists adopt a similar structure of analysis but assert that the LTRPF must predominate in an empirical sense over the CTs to yield falling profitability. The Sraffian approach would reject this structure of analysis since accumulation does not appear to be imperative within their theory, and the rising TCC is perceived to be a contingent consequence of rising

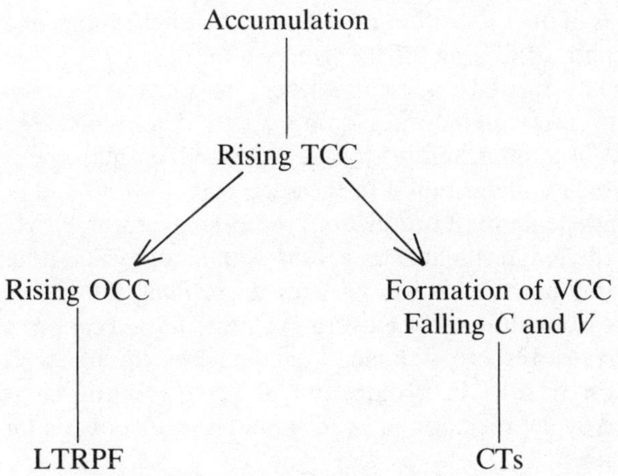

Figure 5.1 The Law as Such and Counteracting Tendencies

wages rather than as an initiating causal factor.[12] However, were this schema to be accepted, the stance adopted would be that there is no reason for the LTRPF to outweigh the CTs and, if it does, this is because of wage increases.

What these two views share in common is the notion of the LTRPF and CTs as being on the two sides of a balance, with the two schools differing about which side, if any, the balance comes down. In contrast, here it has been argued that the LTRPF and the CTs cannot be so simply combined but that each is a product of the accumulation process whose simultaneous weight gives rise to crises when they cannot be mutually accommodated.

Fixed capital and money[13]

We can go no further than this without specifying the nature of the interaction between the law and the CTs. This can be done by extending the logical analysis of the mechanisms by which value relations are expressed in exchange or by specifying particular historically-developed conditions in which accumulation takes place. Here, two examples of the former type of analysis are briefly embarked upon.

It is apposite to study fixed capital in this context since, by definition, it passes value on to commodities over a time which exceeds the production period. It is during this time that there is a reduction both in the replacement value of this portion of constant capital, as productivity rises in the sector producing fixed capital, and in the value passed on to commodities by the fixed capital, as productivity rises in the sector where it is in operation. Let us consider the implications of this in terms of the length of lifetime of the fixed capital.

The value passed on by machinery to the raw materials that are worked up into commodities is only partly determined by the physical condition of the machinery. It is also dependent upon the formation of SNLT which is determined in the sector as a whole and is, to a large extent, independent of production by any single capital. From this point of view, the longer the machinery lasts, the more value it has preserved over its lifetime. There is a pressure to prolong the life of machinery for this reason, although the overall value produced cannot be increased by this means. If there is an increase in machine durability, for whatever reason, this results in a reduction in SNLT, as the constant capital preserved by depreciation of fixed capital is spread over a larger mass of commodities.

The previous paragraph analyses the turnover of fixed capital from the point of view of its use value in value production. We now look at the value of fixed capital from the point of view of its own production. With the accumulation of capital, there tends to be a reduction in the value of the machine, due to productivity increases in the sector producing it as well as through productivity increase in the raw materials with which it is made. In addition, there are liable to be improvements in the quality of machinery. As a result, from the point of view of the exchange value passed on in the circulation process, the lifetime of the machinery should be reduced to a minimum. This is so that its value can be preserved in the commodities produced before it is incapable of adding positively to SNLT.

If these two factors are put together, it is found that there are pressures both to increase and to reduce the durability of fixed capital. The formation of turnover time, in practice, will reflect the equivalence created between the values of old, continuing fixed capital and the new fixed capital. For orthodox theory, this conflict is resolved harmoniously within vintage models by the smooth renewal of fixed capital through the market mechanism. For Marxist theory, there can be violent movements in the value relations connecting old and new fixed capital so that the renewal of fixed capital tends to follow a self-reproducing cycle.

The second example of further logical development of the LTRPF is to be found in the analysis of the value of money. In the early chapters of Volume I of *Capital*, Marx demonstrates how money acts as the social means of measuring value in its property of general equivalent. As already observed, once accumulation is proceeding, the measure of value now has to perform the task of establishing an equivalence between 'old' and 'new' values. Whether it does so on the basis of a formal convertibility with a (gold) commodity money or not, we will show that there are competing pressures on changes in the value of money. Since $1 + r = (C + V + S)/(C + V)$, it follows that profitability is increased the greater is output relative to capital advanced. However, in monetary terms, output is evaluated at prices formed at a different time than those for inputs and this is necessarily so, except by way of accident, since there has been an intervening change in values because of changing conditions of production. From the point of view of production of other commodities, there is pressure for the value of money to remain the same, so that the value of advanced capital is preserved in output, i.e., that the value of output or new values is assessed on the market-place at the same values as the value of inputs or old values. From the point of view of circulation, however, and for the renewal of accumulation, there is pressure for the value of money to increase so that the value of capital advanced is reduced, this reflecting the reduced values that have been achieved in the previous period of production. This corresponds to the new values asserting themselves as SNLT at the expense of the old values.

Once again, it is the interaction of these two competing factors which establishes an equivalence between old and new values. In the previous example, it did so through the formation of the turnover time of fixed capital. In this case, it is the value of money that must emerge. According to orthodox theory, this can be done by the market mechanism with the two factors cancelling each other out to yield an equilibrium level of prices corresponding to full employment (or below full employment for Keynesian theory). For Marxist theory, there can be no such presumption and the value of money is subject to sharp fluctuations which correspond to and intensify crises of production. This is quite independent of whether the conditions of production of gold are relevant in establishing a value for this commodity which does itself diverge from the value that money represents in the process of exchange.

Although Marx laid the theoretical foundations for examining fixed capital in Volume II of *Capital*, he did not take his analysis much further. It is far from clear how this can be done, otherwise than by an empirical study of the differing conditions of production. This lack of analysis is not reproduced in the case of the formation of the value of money. In his study of banking capital in Volume III, Marx provides a sophisticated extension of his theory of money by a logical analysis of the forms of capital in exchange and by a corresponding empirical analysis of the British banking system. In the cases of both fixed capital and money, then, it can be shown that the LTRPF provides a framework within which each can be analysed but that to do so requires further theoretical and empirical analysis.

A response to Okishio[14]

The major criticism of Marx's theory of the LTRPF has evolved in recent years as a result of a theorem proved by Okishio (1961). Informally, he argued that the rate of profit cannot fall unless real wages rise, given a wider availability of techniques of production. In other words, a falling rate of profit is contingent upon rising wages. In Okishio's interpretation of Marx, new techniques of production become available to capitalists who adopt them if they are more profitable than existing techniques at prevailing prices of production. Once these new techniques are generalized across the sectors concerned, this will result in a new set of prices of production and a new rate of profit, equalized across sectors. It is not only in the sectors where there has been innovation that prices will change, because their, presumably lower, prices will be passed on to the sectors in which those commodities are used as inputs or as part of the wage. Okishio asks whether the capitalists, acting blindly to increase individual profitability by introducing new techniques, can paradoxically lead the system to a lower rate of profit. Not surprisingly, he comes up with a negative answer, unless real wages are increased, and concludes that Marx is incorrect. To put his result formally, suppose production conditions are initially denoted by A and these are improved to B. Let initial prices be a vector $\mathbf{p}$ and new prices be $\mathbf{q}$, initial rate of profit r and new rate of profit s. Then for a given real bundle of wage-goods w, s is greater than r.

It is important to recognize that Okishio's theorem, whatever its merits in interpreting (and in refuting) Marx, is an exercise in comparative statics, i.e., that it compares one position of economic equilibrium with another. These equilibria are constructed on the basis of a linear input–output technology, denoted by the matrices A and B. This use of comparative statics is already a peculiarity in the context of the subject of enquiry. For, if we are concerned with movements in the rate of profit as a source of crises, then it is inappropriate to adopt an equilibrium approach. If we move from one equilibrium to another we cannot be analysing crises whatever happens to the rate of profit. There is one exception and this is if the movements in the rate of profit are considered independently of, but as the source of, subsequent crises. This approach was discussed in the previous section. Here it comes up with the result that, first, we move from one equilibrium to another. Second, if the rate of profit falls, we have a crisis. Otherwise we do not.

It is not clear, however, why the equilibrium, even with a lower rate of profit, would suddenly collapse into crisis.

This raises the much more interesting question of the movement between the two equilibria, rather than their comparison. This has not been analysed very much in the wake of the Okishio theorem, but it is motivated by the description of the way in which new techniques are introduced. By examining this process, it is apparent that, far from interpreting Marx's LTRPF, the approach associated with Okishio is its dialectical opposite! This is one reason why Marx may have blessed his analysis with the name of a law, since he saw the function of science to penetrate beneath the surface of appearances, in this case as they occur in the minds of individual capitalists and, presumably, academic economists such as the followers of Okishio.

Initially, an individual capitalist adopts a more advantageous technique of production, whether this be obtained through superior access to finance or technology. At initial prices p, this capitalist makes a higher rate of profit than the average level. Let this be denoted by $t > r$. From the perspective of the *individual* capitalist, the introduction of a new technique is associated with an increase in the rate of profit. This contrasts with Marx's analysis of the rising OCC which leads to a tendency for falling profitability for *social* capital, since the evaluation of inputs and outputs at old values will lead to declining profitability.

Now, consider the generalization of the new technique to all capitalists in the sector and the formation of new equilibrium prices and profit rate. It can be shown by techniques similar to those employed by Okishio that $t > s > r$. In other words, the capitalist who had an original advantage finds that it is eroded as the source of the advantage is generalized across all other capitalists. The process of reducing prices, as a result of the introduction of the new technique, is one of reducing the rate of profit for the individual capitalist that had the initial advantage. Price formation out of technical change acts for the *individual* innovating capitalist as a pressure reducing the rate of profit. In contrast, for Marx, the process of price (VCC) formation out of technical change is a counteracting tendency to falling profitability for *social* capital, since it leads to a reduction in the value of constant and variable capital.

Now, put the two processes, of introducing new technology and of generalizing it to form new prices, together. Throughout, the processes for Okishio are immediate empirical phenomena. They interact to form algebraically a simple sum of effects that leads overall to a rise in profitability for the economy as a whole. Moreover, the two disequilibrium processes combine to cancel each other out and leave the system in harmonious equilibrium. Because of this, in the context of comparative statics, those who follow the Okishio approach never distinguish between the VCC and the OCC. Instead, they rely exclusively upon an equilibrium notion of the VCC which, nevertheless, is given the name organic composition. By contrast, for Marx, the law and the CTs are underlying, abstract, tendencies whose interaction is not some simple algebraic sum but a crisis-ridden path of accumulation.

Nevertheless, Okishio's result is a powerful one, since empirically the rate of profit can only fall if wages rise. This is allowed for in Marx's law. For, at old values, the value of labour power will represent an increasing bundle of wage-goods as a result of productivity increase. This could precipitate a crisis, but, in general, accumulation prospers with rising real wages, as measured by the level of consumption as opposed to the value of labour power. If real wages remain the same, then there is a reduction in the value of labour power and an increase in the rate of surplus value. These are CTs for Marx. That they exist, as a result of accumulation, does not guarantee the absence of crisis.

Concluding remarks

A number of propositions follow from the preceding analysis. The first is that Marx's analysis of falling profitability depends on a distinction being made between the organic and value compositions of capital. Second, the LTRPF only applies to the capitalist mode of production when it has reached the machine stage of the modern factory system. Third, the law only lays down a method for analysing the process of accumulation, one that stresses the contradictory unity between the spheres of production and exchange, with the former as the determinant, since in it lies the source of surplus value. Accordingly, fourth, the LTRPF represents the culmination of Marx's theory of capital accumulation, combining a complex series of propositions concerning production and exchange. As such, this cannot be properly understood as an equilibrium problem within comparative statics nor as focusing primarily on distributional conflict. Finally, this theory provides a starting point rather than a substitute for an analysis of the historically developed conditions in which accumulation takes place.

Notes

1. It is possible to distinguish between the Sraffian and the neo-Ricardian schools even though they are often treated as the same. The former, as represented by Steedman (1977) for example, focuses on the distributional relations between capital and labour by rejecting the labour theory of value, whereas the latter retains the labour theory of value as a 'sociology' of capitalism, as in Armstrong *et al.* (1978).
2. The Sraffian system is notable for having no role for money so that real and money wages are synonymous for a given numeraire.

3. These propositions have a notable affinity to neo-classical theory.
4. See especially, Part IV of Volume I of *Capital*.
5. See the 'missing' Chapter 6 of *Capital*, Marx (1976).
6. For a discussion of value in these terms see Elson (1979) for example.
7. The *Theories of Surplus Value* was compiled prior to the three volumes of *Capital* of which only the first was completed for publication. See Oakley (1983).
8. This is most forcibly argued in Fine (1983) in the context of the transformation problem. See also Fine (1979) for the importance of the distinction between the OCC and the VCC in the context of agricultural rent.
9. For an exception, see Groll and Orzech (1987) who carefully distinguish the OCC and the VCC in the specific context of the LTRPF and provide a partial survey of those who have made the distinction. But for a competing view to theirs, see Fine (1988) and later in this chapter.
10. There are many references to the TCC, the OCC and the VCC in *Capital* and the *Theories of Surplus Value*, although the latter does not explicitly use the term value composition. Throughout, the usage is consistent with the interpretation offered here, subject to the incompleteness of the material concerned.
11. That the LTRPF and the CTs are both simultaneous products of accumulation tends to invalidate the idea that a crisis requires the 'mobilization' of the counteracting tendencies (as if to outweigh the law as such), a formulation popular with, for example, Holloway and Picciotto (1978) in specifying the role of the state.
12. Sraffians would not accept the value calculations on which this argument is based, preferring to depend upon price calculations.
13. The discussion of fixed capital draws heavily on Weeks (1982) and that of money is loosely drawn from the approach of Foley (1986).
14. This section draws heavily on Fine (1982).

References

Armstrong, P. *et al.* (1978), 'In Defence of Value – a Reply to Ian Steedman', *Capital and Class*, (5).

Elson, D. (1979), *The Representation of Labour in Capitalism*, London: CSE Books.

Fine, B. (1979), 'On Marx s Theory of Agricultural Rent', *Economy and Society*, **8**, (3).

Fine, B. (1982), *Theories of the Capitalist Economy*, London: Edward Arnold.

Fine, B. (1983), 'A Dissenting Note on the Transformation Problem', *Economy and Society*, **12**, (4).

Fine, B. (1986), 'Introduction', in B. Fine (ed.), *The Value Dimension: Marx versus Ricardo and Sraffa*, London: Routledge and Kegan Paul.

Fine, B. (1989), *Marx's 'Capital'*, 3rd ed., London: Macmillan.

Fine, B. (1990), 'On the Composition of Capital: a Comment on Groll and Orzech', *History of Political Economy*, **22**, (1), Spring.

Fine, B. and L. Harris (1979), *Rereading 'Capital'*, London: Macmillan.

Foley, D. (1986), *Understanding 'Capital': Marx's Economic Theory*, Cambridge: Harvard University Press.

Groll, S. and Z. Orzech (1987), 'Technical Progress and Values in Marx's Theory of the Decline in the Rate of Profit: an Exegetical Approach', *History of Political Economy*, **19**, (4).

Holloway, J. and S. Picciotto (1978), *State and Capital: a Marxist Debate*, London: Edward Arnold.

Marx, K. (1971), *Capital*, Volume III, London: Lawrence and Wishart.

Marx, K. (1972), *Theories of Surplus Value*, Part II, London: Lawrence and Wishart.

Marx, K. (1976), *Capital*, Volume I, Harmondsworth: Penguin.

Oakley, A. (1983), *The Making of Marx's Critical Theory: A Bibliographical Analysis*, London: Routledge and Kegan Paul.

Okishio, N. (1961), 'Technical Change and the Rate of Profit', *Kobe University Economic Review*, **7**.
Steedman, I. (1977), *Marx after Sraffa*, London: New Left Books.
Weeks, J. (1982), *Capital and Exploitation*, London: Edward Arnold.

6 Marx on the unproductiveness of the financial sector and its tendency to grow*

Walter Eltis

Employment to provide financial services has grown at astonishing rates in all western economies since the Second World War. In the United Kingdom the proportion of the labour force which provides financial services and insurance rose from 6.0 per cent in 1971 to 10.4 per cent in 1987, so the remarkable situation has been arrived at where almost one worker in ten is now needed to look after the financial and commercial transactions of the other nine. The situation in the United States is similar and the financial and commercial sectors of all the leading western economies have increased sharply as Table 6.1 shows.

Table 6.1 Share of total employment in banking, insurance and financial services (%)

	1971	1987
United States	6.9	11.1
Canada	4.9	10.5
United Kingdom	6.0	10.4
France	5.5	8.6
Japan	4.9	7.4
West Germany	4.7	6.8

Source: OECD

Marx regarded such employment as unproductive, and he believed that the payment of the workers involved had to be financed from the surpluses generated in the productive sector of the economy – in his analysis, those engaged in commodity production. He insisted that a larger commercial and financial sector would be associated with a lower overall rate of surplus and therefore a lower rate of profit in the economy as a whole.

Is some variant or derivative of Marx's argument still valid? Is it

* I am grateful to Chris Moir and Luci Francis of the National Economic Development Office for the preparation of the data in this chapter.

actually efficient for modern economies to employ up to one worker in ten to provide financial services for the other nine and, if this fraction is higher than it needs to be, will extra workers in these activities actually derive their livelihoods from surpluses generated elsewhere with the result that they reduce the net return on capital in industry and agriculture as Marx suggested? In this chapter, Marx's argument will be presented first and its possible relevance to the modern world will then be considered.

The role of the financial and commercial sector in *Capital*

Marx explained why the commercial and financial sector was unproductive, in the sense that it played no part in the generation of surplus value, in Volumes II and III of *Capital*. He divided capital in the economy's financial sector into two 'sub-species': 'commercial capital' concerned with the financing of actual business transactions associated with production, and 'money-dealing capital', concerned with such matters as share flotations, portfolio management and financial transactions within the banking system, and these will be considered in turn.

In Marx's analysis, commercial transactions involve no more than changes in titles of ownership to commodities, and these cannot create any net addition to the aggregate value of output, which is all created through commodity production in industry and agriculture. Capitalists devote a good deal of time to commercial transactions, but these merely change the ownership of economic values that have already been created in industry and agriculture, without adding to them:

> the time during which the capitalist buys and sells, prowls around the market, forms a necessary part of the time in which he functions as a capitalist, i.e. as personified capital. It forms a part of his business hours . . . all that is involved in these acts is the conversion of the same value from one form into another – from the commodity form into the money form, and from the money form into the commodity form . . . If the commodities are sold at their values, then the amounts of value in the hands of both buyer and seller remain unchanged; it is only the form of existence that has altered. If the commodities are not sold at their values, then the sum of converted values remains unaffected; what is a plus for one side is a minus for the other. (Volume II, p. 207)

Marx insists that any profits or surplus value that the commercial sector obtains must originally derive from surpluses earned in industry and agriculture:

> Commercial capital is nothing more than capital functioning within the circulation sphere. The circulation process is one phase in the reproduction process as a whole. But in the process of circulation, no value is produced,

> and thus also no surplus-value. The same value simply undergoes changes of form. Nothing at all happens except the metamorphosis of commodities, which by its very nature has nothing to do with the creation or alteration of value. If a surplus-value is realized on the sale of the commodity produced, this is because it already existed in the commodity. . . .
>
> Since commercial capital does not itself produce any surplus-value, it is clear that the surplus-value that accrues to it in the form of the average profit forms a portion of the surplus-value produced by the productive capital as a whole. (Volume III, pp. 392, 395)

What Marx says about the unproductive nature of commerce does not apply to storage, transport, distribution and retailing, for he regards these as ancillary elements in the production process which in each case add value to the physical products which emerge directly from agriculture and industry. It is only commercial transactions which involve mere changes of ownership that are unproductive, and where profits must be derived from true surplus value that is created elsewhere. He writes at considerable length about the service sector activities that are, in essence, productive:

> The purely commercial costs of circulation (i.e. excluding the costs of dispatch, transport, storage, etc.) are the costs that are necessary to realize the value of the commodity, whether transforming it from commodity into money or from money into commodity – to effect its exchange. In this connection we ignore completely any eventual production processes that continue during the act of circulation and can exist quite separately from commerce as such; as for instance the transport industry proper and the dispatch of goods can be completely separate from trade, as branches of industry, and actually are so. Goods for purchase and sale may also be kept in docks and other public storage areas . . . The haulier, the railway director and the shipowner are not 'merchants'. (Volume III, p. 402)

It is actual commercial transactions between merchants that are unproductive and he likens these to equally unproductive disputes in the law courts where much energy and labour time is expended to ascertain who actually owns particular items of capital or property. These involve high costs in a modern economy, but no value is actually created by such struggles for the title deeds to property:

> business transactions between buyer and seller . . . in which each side seeks to get the better of the other. It is businessmen who face each other here, and 'when Greek meets Greek then comes the tug of war'. The change of state costs time and labour-power, not to create value, but rather to bring about the conversion of the value from one form into the other, and so the reciprocal attempt to use this opportunity to appropriate an excess quantity of value does not change anything. This labour, increased by evil intent on either side, no more creates value than the labour that takes place in legal

> proceedings increases the value of the object in dispute. (Volume II, pp. 207–8)

Marx uses similar reasoning to insist that insurance is equally unproductive:

> Insurance companies, for example, divide the losses of individual capitalists among the capitalist class. But this does not prevent the losses thus adjusted from being losses as before, from the standpoint of the total social capital. (Volume II, p. 215)

Despite the fact that commercial transactions add nothing to the value of output as a whole, Marx entirely accepts that they are indispensable to the total economic process.

> The merchant, by . . . carrying on the functions of capital in the circulation sphere after the productive capitalist has ceased to do this, simply takes the place of the industrial capitalist. The labour-time that these operations cost is being employed on necessary operations in the reproduction process of capital, but it does not add any extra value. (Volume III, p. 403)

There are, moreover, efficiency advantages if commercial transactions are handled by specialist commercial companies:

> As a result of the division of labour, the capital that is exclusively concerned with buying and selling is smaller than it would be if the industrial capitalist had to conduct the entire commercial part of his business himself. (Volume III, p. 388)

Some of these advantages correspond to the benefits from the division of labour in industry to which Marx attributed great significance in Volume I of *Capital*:

> A well-defined division of labour in the commercial office, where one person keeps the books, another the cash-box, a third writes letters, this one buys, another sells, that one travels, etc., spares a tremendous amount of labour-time, so that the number of workers involved in wholesale trade is in no way proportionate to the comparative scale of the transactions. In commerce, in fact, far more than in industry, the same function takes the same amount of labour-time whether it is performed on a large or small scale. Thus concentration historically appears in commerce earlier than in the industrial workshop. There are also the expenses for constant capital. A hundred small offices cost infinitely more than one big one, a hundred small warehouses more than a big warehouse. (Volume III, p. 409)

Marx sums up the advantages industrial producers obtain from the existence of a separate commercial sector:

> Commercial capital . . . in so far as it contributes towards shortening the circulation time, . . . can indirectly help the industrial capitalist to increase the surplus-value he produces. In so far as it helps to extend the market and facilitates the division of labour between capitals, thus enabling capital to operate on a bigger scale, its functioning promotes the productivity of industrial capital and its accumulation. In so far as it cuts down the turnover time, it increases the ratio of surplus-value to the capital advanced, i.e. the rate of profit. And in so far as a smaller part of capital is confined to the circulation sphere as money capital, it increases the portion of capital directly applied in production. (Volume III, pp. 392–3)

However, because of the advantages from the division of labour to which Marx refers, the size of the commercial sector will fall in relation to the output of the economy as a whole as a country's capital stock grows:

> The more the scale of production grows, the greater are industrial capital's commercial operations, although the increase is by no means in the same proportion. (Volume III, p. 413)

> The developed capitalist mode of production, compared with earlier conditions, has a double effect on commercial capital; the same amount of commodities are turned over with a smaller amount of actually functioning commodity capital; while on account of the more rapid turnover of this commercial capital and the greater speed of the reproduction process on which it depends, the ratio of commercial capital to industrial capital is reduced. (Volume III, p. 425)

The costs of the commercial sector will moreover be reduced because wages and salaries will fall as commerce expands:

> The commercial worker proper belongs to the better paid class of wage-labourer; he is one of those whose labour is skilled labour, above-average labour. His wage however has a tendency to fall, as the capitalist mode of production advances, even in relation to average labour . . . because the division of labour within the commercial office means that only a one-sided development of ability need be produced and that much of the cost of producing this ability is free for the capitalist, since the worker's skill is rather developed by the function itself, and indeed is developed all the more quickly, the more one-sided the function becomes with the division of labour. (Volume III, p. 414)

In addition, the commercial education that society provides will reinforce the tendency for well-qualified employees to become available at a lower real cost to employers:

> basic skills, knowledge of commerce and languages, etc., are reproduced ever more quickly, easily, generally and cheaply, the more the capitalist

> mode of production adapts teaching methods, etc. to practical purposes. The general extension of popular education permits this variety of labour to be recruited from classes which were formerly excluded from it and were accustomed to a lower standard of living. This also increases supply, and with it competition. With a few exceptions, therefore, the labour-power of these people is devalued with the advance of capitalist production; their wages fall, whereas their working ability increases. (Volume III, pp. 414–15)

It is a well-known feature of the Marxist theory of education that anything commercially useful that workers are taught will raise the profits of their employers and not their own wages and salaries. Engels offers the example of clerks versed in several languages who can be obtained very cheaply in London.

> We can give an example of this prognosis, written in 1865, of the fate of the commercial proletariat since this time, in the form of the hundreds of German clerks skilled in all commercial operations and in three or four languages, who are offering their services in vain in the City of London for a weekly wage of 25 shillings – well below the wage of a skilled mechanic. (Volume III, p. 415)

Marx's account of how the economy's commercial sector grows in order to finance necessary business transactions (the present interpretation is similar to Ian Gough's) cannot explain the enormous growth in employment in the financial sectors of all western economies in the late 20th century, for he predicted that employment in commercial activities to finance production and distribution would diminish in relation to employment in industry and agriculture. If it is not the financing of actual business transactions that has produced this growth, what has? Of his two categories of financial capital, 'commercial capital' has been considered so far. Can expansion in his other category, 'money dealing capital', explain the enormous growth of the financial sector in the late 20th-century?

A first clue is provided by Marx's account of how, as capitalism develops, the wealth of non-producers grows:

> as a nation advances in the career of wealth, a class of men springs up and increases more and more, who by the labours of their ancestors find themselves in the possession of funds sufficiently ample to afford a handsome maintenance from the interest alone. Very many also who during youth and middle age were actively engaged in business, retire in their latter days to live quitely on the interest of the sums they have themselves accumulated. This class, as well as the former, has a tendency to increase with the increasing riches of the country, for those who begin with a tolerable stock are likely to make an independence sooner than they who commence with little. Thus it comes to pass, that in old and rich countries, the amount of

> national capital belonging to those who are unwilling to take the trouble of employing it themselves, bears a larger proportion to the whole productive stock of the society, than in newly settled and poorer districts. (Volume III, pp. 483–4)

> As material wealth increases, the class of money capitalists grows. On the one hand there is an increase in the number and wealth of the retired capitalists, the rentiers; and secondly the credit system must be further developed, which means an increase in the number of bankers, money-lenders, financiers, etc. (Volume III, pp. 642–3)

This significant development will naturally lead to growth in the number of City firms concerned with portfolio management to assist rentiers to manage their growing financial wealth.

A further factor which greatly contributes to the wealth and employment provided by the financial sector is the development of credit which, according to Marx, provides extensive possibilities for speculation from which the clever can gain fortunes from the less astute without any parallel productive activity. He quotes gleefully from J.W. Gilbart's, *The History and Principles of Banking* (1834):

> It is the object of banking to give facilities to trade, and whatever gives facilities to trade gives facilities to speculation. Trade and speculation are in some cases so nearly allied, that it is impossible to say at what precise point trade ends and speculation begins . . . Wherever there are banks, capital is more readily obtained, and at a cheaper rate. The cheapness of capital gives facilities to speculation, just in the same way as the cheapness of beef and of beer gives facilities to gluttony and drunkenness. (Volume III, p. 532)

and he naturally improves on Gilbart:

> a tremendous number of . . . bills represent purely fraudulent deals, which now come to light and explode; as well as unsuccessful speculations conducted with borrowed capital, and finally commodity capitals that are either devalued or unsaleable or returns that are never going to come in. (Volume III, p. 621)

> With the development of interest-bearing capital and the credit system, all capital seems to be duplicated, and at some points triplicated, by the various ways in which the same capital, or even the same claim, appears in various hands in different guises. The greater part of this 'money capital' is purely fictitious. With the exception of the reserve fund, deposits are never more than credits with the banker, and never exist as real deposits. In so far as they are used in clearing-house transactions, they function as capital for the bankers, after these latter have lent them out. The bankers pay one another reciprocal drafts on these non-existent deposits by balancing these credits against each other. (Volume III, p. 601)

Further possibilities for fraudulent gains (and consequent high employment in firms that achieve them) are provided by speculation and flotations of equity shares associated with joint-stock companies which developed extensively in the second half of the 19th-century.

> On the basis of capitalist production, a new swindle with the wages of management develops in connection with joint-stock companies, in that, over and above the actual managing director, a number of governing and supervisory boards arise, for which management and supervision are in fact a mere pretext for the robbery of shareholders and their own enrichment. (Volume III, p. 514)

> Profits and losses that result from fluctuations in the price of these ownership titles, and also their centralisation in the hands of railway magnates etc., are by the nature of the case more and more the result of gambling, which now appears in place of labour as the original source of capital ownership, as well as taking the place of brute force. This kind of imaginary money wealth makes up a very considerable part not only of the money wealth of private individuals but also of banking capital, as already mentioned. (Volume III, p. 609)

An interesting development which may more than any other explain the growth of wealth in the financial sector is the very clearly stated proposition that financial capitalists, and therefore those they employ, gradually obtain control over a growing fraction of the wealth of productive industrial capitalists. They do this by having the financial resources (which industrial capitalists lack) to buy up shares and take over companies when industry is under financial pressure at crisis points in the trade cycle:

> We have seen how, in the bad phases of the industrial cycle, the rate of interest may rise so high that it temporarily swallows up profits entirely for some branches of business, particularly those unfavourably located. At the same time, the prices of government paper and other securities fall. This is the moment when money capitalists buy up this devalued paper on a massive scale, as it will soon go up again in the later phases, and even rise above its normal level. They will then sell it off, thereby appropriating a part of the public's money capital. Those securities that are not sold off yield a higher interest, since they were bought below their price. But all the profit which the money capitalists make, and which they turn back into capital, they transform first of all into money capital for loan. Thus we already have an accumulation of this money capital as distinct from the genuine accumulation – even if the accumulation of its off-shoot – when we simply consider the money capitalists, bankers, etc. themselves, as the accumulation of this particular class of capitalists. And this must grow with each extension of the credit system, as it accompanies the genuine expansion of the reproduction process. (Volume III, pp. 634–5)

These developments led Marx to suggest that the money capitalists will actually be able to exploit the original exploiters of labour – the industrial capitalists who create society's surplus value or profit by paying workers less than the true value of their labour power – and acquire control over increasing fractions of a nation's wealth:

> the money capitalist makes the savings of other people into his capital, and the credit that the reproductive capitalists give one another, and that the public give them, he makes into his own source of private enrichment. The final illusion of the capitalist system, that capital is the offspring of a person's own work and savings, is thereby demolished. Not only does profit consist in the appropriation of other people's labour, but the capital with which this labour of others is set in motion and exploited consists of other people's property, which the money capitalist puts at the disposal of the industrial capitalist and for which he in turn exploits him. (Volume III, p. 640)

Engels tells a vivid story of how this mechanism for the appropriation of industrial wealth into the financial sector operates:

> Directly after the February revolution [of 1848], when commodities and securities in Paris were extremely devalued and totally unsaleable, a Swiss merchant in Liverpool, Mr E. Zwilchenbart (who related this to my father), sold whatever he could for cash, travelled to Paris, and went to Rothschild with the proposal to do a joint deal. Rothschild stared at him fixedly and then rushed up to him and said, grasping him by both shoulders: 'Do you have money in your pocket?' – 'Yes, Baron'. – 'Then you're the man for me!' – And they both made a handsome profit. (Volume I, p. 599)

Marx's suggestion that financial capitalists will gradually achieve control over an increasing fraction of the industrial capital stock is developed by the great Austrian Marxist economist, Rudolf Hilferding in *Finance Capital: A Study of the Latest Phase of Capitalist Development* (1910) which has been described as a continuation of *Capital*.

Hilferding follows Marx in suggesting that those who control financial capital – in early 20th-century Austro-Hungary and Germany, undoubtedly the banks – are bound to exercise increasing power over industrial capital:

> The . . . relative independence of bank credit from ordinary commercial credit gives the banker certain advantages. Every merchant and industrialist has commitments which must be honoured on a specified date, but his ability to meet these obligations now depends upon the decisions of his banker, who can make it impossible for him to meet them by restricting credit . . . Once the credit system has attained a certain degree of development, the utilisation of credit by the capitalist enterprise becomes a necessity, imposed upon it by the competitive struggle . . . the enterprise becomes tied to the bank. In this relationship the bank is the more powerful party. The bank always

> disposes over capital in its liquid, readily available, form: money capital. The enterprise, on the other hand, has to depend upon reconverting commodities into money. Should the circulation process come to a halt, or prices fall, the enterprise will require additional capital which can only be obtained in the form of credit. Under a developed credit system, an enterprise maintains its own capital at a minimum; any sudden need for additional liquid funds involves obtaining credit, and failure to do so may lead to bankruptcy. It is the bank's control of money capital which gives it a dominant position in its dealings with enterprises whose capital is tied up in production or in commodities. The bank enjoys an additional advantage by virtue of the fact that its capital is relatively independent of the outcome of any single transaction, whereas the fate of the entire enterprise may depend entirely upon a single transaction. (pp. 92–5)

The financial sector will acquire growing wealth which will increase the pressure it can exert:

> credit develops in such a way as to place at the disposal of industry not only the whole capital reserves of the capitalist class but also the major part of the funds of the non-productive classes. In other words, present-day industry is carried on with an amount of capital far exceeding that which is owned by the industrial capitalists. With the development of capitalism there is also a continual increase in the amount of money which the non-productive classes place at the disposal of the banks, who in turn convey it to the industrialists. The control of these funds which are indispensable to industry rests with the banks, and consequently, with the development of capitalism and of the machinery of credit, the dependence of industry upon the banks increases. (p. 224)

The banks and financial capital can only obtain increasing profits if industrial capitalists get less, as the sum of surplus value available to the two together is limited. Because of the advantages of the financial sector which have been referred to, it can be expected to gain at the expense of industrial profits:

> Commercial profit, however, is part of the total surplus value generated by production. Other things being equal, the larger the share which falls to commercial capital, the smaller will be the share of industrial capital. Thus there exists a conflict of interest between industrial and commercial capital. These conflicting interests lead to a struggle which ends with the victory of one of the parties and the subordination of the other in a relation of dependence. In any such struggle between capitalist interests, the deciding factor is the relative strength of the capitals involved, but this should not be conceived in purely quantitative terms. The whole preceding discussion shows that the form of the capital is also important. Other things being equal, control over money capital assures superiority, because both industrialists and merchants become increasingly dependent upon money capital as the credit system develops. (pp. 210–11)

Gradually, as increasing returns lead to industrial and commercial concentration, the nation's industrial and financial capital will be controlled by a smaller number of very powerful individuals and families who will own both industrial and financial companies:

> the bank disposes of bank capital, and the owners of the majority of the shares in the bank dominate the bank. It is clear that with the increasing concentration of property, the owners of the fictitious capital which gives power over the banks, and the owners of the capital which gives power over industry, become increasingly the same people. As we have seen, this is all the more so as the large banks increasingly acquire the power to dispose over fictitious capital. We have seen how industry becomes increasingly dependent upon bank capital, but this does not mean that the magnates of industry also become dependent on banking magnates. As capital itself at the highest stage of its development becomes finance capital, so the magnate of capital, the finance capitalist, increasingly concentrates his control over the whole national capital by means of his domination of bank capital. Personal connections also play an important role here. (p. 225)

In the last resort it will be the financial capital element in this conglomerate wealth which will exercise the dominant influence. Hilferding sees a cycle in which financial capital was dominant over society's productive forces in the medieval world, and it has become dominant again in the early 20th-century, with an intervening period in which the power and influence of industrial capital was the greater of the two:

> With cartelization and trustification finance capital attains its greatest power . . . A cycle in the development of capitalism is completed. At the outset of capitalist production money capital, in the form of usurers' and merchants' capital, plays a significant role in the accumulation of capital as well as in the transformation of handicraft production into capitalism. But there then arises a resistance of 'productive' capital, i.e. of the profit-earning capitalists – that is, of commerce and industry – against the interest-earning capitalists. Usurer's capital becomes subordinated to industrial capital. As money-dealing capital it performs the functions of money which industry and commerce would otherwise have to carry out themselves . . . The utilisation of capital and the continual expansion of credit gradually brings about a complete change in the position of the money capitalists. The power of the banks increases and they become founders and eventually rulers of industry, whose profits they seize for themselves as finance capital, just as formerly the old usurer seized, in the form of 'interest', the produce of the peasants and the ground rent of the lord of the manor. (pp. 225–6)

Hilferding believes that a touch of Hegel will help his readers to comprehend the nature of this cyclical process; his 20th-century successors are equally ready to believe that occasional equations will illuminate their underlying argument:

> The Hegelians spoke of the negation of the negation: bank capital was the negation of usurer's capital and is itself negated by finance capital. The latter is the synthesis of usurer's and bank capital, and it appropriates to itself the fruits of social production at an infinitely higher stage of economic development. (pp. 225–6)

The important line of argument of Marx and Hilferding that financial capitalists obtain control over an increasing fraction of industrial capital contributes to a possible explanation of the rapid relative growth of the financial sectors of modern western economies. If the financial sectors contain what are in effect supervisory boards of directors which exercise the ultimate control over the disposal of a high fraction of a nation's capital between companies, it will follow that those who work in these sectors will be exceptionally highly remunerated and the numbers employed to undertake research into takeover targets etc., for finance capital, will all the time grow.

The other thread in Marx's argument which contributes to an explanation of the growing share of wealth and employment in the financial sectors of economies is that the accumulated financial wealth of non-producers will increase so that the resources required to manage consequently expanding share portfolios will grow.

Nonetheless, because the resources required to arrange and supervise the commercial transactions directly concerned with production should diminish, there is no clear implication in Marx's work that the financial sectors of economies need have any tendency to grow in relation to output as a whole.

The growth of the financial sectors of western economies in the late 20th-century

At first sight it appears surprising that in the United States and the United Kingdom, the most financially-developed western economies, the financial sectors provide employment for approximately one worker in ten. These employees are, moreover, more highly paid than workers in general. The 10.7 per cent of workers in the financial sector in the United States in 1986 received 14.2 per cent of the total wage and salary bill, while in the UK the 10.0 per cent received 13.1 per cent of wages and salaries. The near identity of these developments in the two countries, and the quite similar growth in employment in financial services in all the major western economies, suggest that these are underlying trends which are not peculiar to the institutions of any one country. The economies with the highest levels of per capita national income, the United States and Canada, have the largest financial sectors, while the UK although having a lower per capita national income than Germany, has a larger financial sector for well-known historical reasons. How far does the growth that has been occurring fit into Marx's categories?

Table 6.2 suggests that the main growth in employment in the UK from 1971 to 1988 has been in business services and in banking and finance. These amount quite largely to the provision of extra commercial services, a category of activity where Marx predicted an eventual declining trend in the ratio of total employment. In practice, of course, the range of transactions between businesses has been becoming increasingly complex with the result that the extent of financial activity has risen greatly. Marx wrote of the benefits that manufacturing companies can derive from the potential scale economies in financial companies which enable them to look after manufacturers' financial transactions more cheaply. There are therefore efficiency gains in the handling of necessary but not materially productive financial activities by specialist financial sector companies. The range of services that these provide has increased greatly since the 19th-century with recent developments in computer and information technology and the sheer range of financial interconnections between businesses.

The expansion of banking is also partly explained by the growing use of banks by the personal sector. There has been steady expansion in the

Table 6.2 Ratios of total British employment in banking, insurance and finance, 1971–88

	1971	1974	1981	1988
Banking and finance		1.8	2.2	2.8
of which:				
Portfolio management			0.3	0.4
Building societies			0.2	0.4
Business services		3.2	4.0	6.4
Insurance		0.9	1.1	1.2
Renting of movables and dealing in real estate		0.8	0.9	1.1
Total	6.1	6.6	8.1	11.8

Source: The Employment Gazette – various issues, and the Building Societies Association

fraction of the labour force that receives monthly salaries paid straight into bank accounts rather than weekly wages in cash, and an expanding fraction of the population owns shares and houses which all involve financial transactions. This may explain some of the growth of employment in banking.

The numbers employed on portfolio management and in financial companies that organize and control other businesses where Marx predicted growth appears to be quite small in relation to employment in the financial sector as a whole. Those who work in these companies are indeed powerful and very highly paid, but they are not numerous in relation to those employed to handle more mundane banking transactions and the enormous range of business services.

There is one further element in the growth of the financial services sector which was not foreshadowed in the work of Marx or Hilferding. Both spoke of tendencies towards monopoly and concentration in industry and commerce, but the trend towards an entirely different phenomenon, 'monopolistic competition', only emerged in the economic literature in the 1930s.

A feature of monopolistic competition is that there are a considerable number of suppliers to a particular market but competition is nonetheless restricted because individual consumers of a good or service prefer some suppliers to others. Firms therefore each have a slight degree of monopoly power over those customers who currently prefer their services, but clients all have the underlying privilege of being able to choose between a number of suppliers. Hence the term 'monopolistic competition' which reflects the fact that there are elements of both monopoly and competition in the market.

This model which was originated by Edward Chamberlin and Joan Robinson in 1933–34 fits the financial services sector rather well. Consumers of financial services always have a number of bankers, merchant bankers, stockbrokers, lawyers and insurers to choose between, but each has a list of clients who have built up a preference for their company's services. Nonetheless, clients can be lost if the price charged or some aspect of the quality of the service provided becomes insufficiently competitive.

A conclusion of the monopolistic competition model that bears on the rising level of employment in the financial sector is the effect of price-fixing agreements between suppliers of a particular good or service. If they agree to fix prices at a level where their financial rewards can be expected to be very high, then if they are at the same time unable to limit the entry of further suppliers who would acquiesce in the same price-fixing arrangements, several consequences can be expected to arise.

The entry of more suppliers will gradually force the level of remuneration per firm down to a level that is competitive in the economy as a whole, but the profit margins set will at the same time remain high as a consequence of the price-fixing arrangements. High profit margins and normal overall profits will become compatible if the entry of new suppliers reduces the business that each conducts so that they all produce with a margin of excess capacity. The consequence of uncompetitively high profit margins will then be an excessive number of suppliers but not abnormal profits for individual firms. Further possibilities are that they may compete away above average profits by offering more extensive services to their clients or by marketing their services more intensively and expensively.

The fixing of prices and margins prevails in a good deal of the financial services sector in most countries. Banks commonly agree on the rates of interest they will pay to depositors and those they will charge to borrowers. Stockbrokers agree on dealing margins and the level of fees to clients. Lawyers have fixed scales of fees for arranging the conveyancing of property. The effect of such agreements will generally be, according to the monopolistic competition model, that there will be room in the market for more stockbrokers, lawyers, bankers, etc., who will each be able to achieve a reasonable income while working for far less than a full week or month. The price-fixing agreements will raise their income per transaction, so fewer transactions per week will produce an appropriate wage salary or profit return for work of the level of skill that they are able to offer. Because businesses undertake fewer transactions, there will be room in the market for more businesses employing additional workers and salary earners. The tendency for implicit or explicit price-fixing agreements which are endemic in the financial sectors of much of Western Europe and North America to multiply the numbers employed could explain some of the growth that has been so universally observed. The UK authorities have been entirely aware of this problem, and several steps have been taken since 1971 to reduce the extent of price fixing in the financial services sector. Until 1971 the major London clearing banks all offered 2 per cent less than the Bank of England's official bank rate to depositors and lent at between 1 and 2 per cent above bank rate. Building societies which lend for house purchase all agreed to charge and pay precisely the same interest rates.

Since 1971 these agreements have gradually been broken so that there are now considerable differences in the rates charged and paid by different banks and building societies. An equally significant development in London has been 1987's so called 'Big Bang' when stockbrokers abandoned the previously agreed level of commissions and fee scales that they charged, whatever the level competitive conditions called for. These moves away from price fixing and towards competition in the provision of financial services should in due course lead to reductions in the overmanning and overcapacity working that Chamberlin's theory predicts. Employment in the financial services sector may still grow if the development of the economy continues to justify a widening range of interpersonal and intercompany financial transactions, but any overcapacity and overprovision of these will no longer be a consequence of agreed prices, margins and interest rates.

If employment in the financial services sector continues to rise despite a growing level of competition within it, will the extra employment be unproductive in Marx's sense? It is important to recall that Marx regarded commercial financial transactions as indispensable to an efficiently functioning capitalist system and he made it very clear that if financial companies were not available to handle these transactions, industrial companies themselves would need to organize them, and they would do so less economically. Efficiently-managed commercial capital therefore raises the overall productivity of industrial capital. Because commercial capital does not directly produce material outputs, it is not defined as productive of value by Marx but it has a favourable indirect effect on the efficiency with which physical goods are produced and marketed so extra surplus value can be realized because of its existence. It would therefore be inefficient to curtail the extent of commercial transactions in the context of a capitalist economy, provided that competition ensures that the commercial sector itself is efficient.

There is clearly a tension in Marx between the numerous passages in which he describes commercial transactions as unproductive, and insists that commercial profits are parasitical on manufacturing, and the equally clear (though less extensive) statements that an efficient commercial sector will have the indirect effect of increasing overall business efficiency by arranging that necessary business transactions will be financed more efficiently. Marxist writers have tended to follow Marx by producing far more anti-commercial and anti-City polemicism than statements which recognize that an efficient commercial sector will actually increase a society's total surplus value. There is also virtually no recognition by Marx or by modern Marxist writers that the financial sectors of London and New York are export industries, and that the growth of any export industry must raise the rate of profit and aggregate surplus value.

Marxist writers have pointed out, of course, that many commercial transactions are only necessary in western economies in the context of capitalism. A truly socialist economy would not need to devote resources on anything approaching the same scale to the continual switching of property rights between individuals and companies. Edward Wolff, for instance, has attempted to estimate the resources the United States would save if financial and other unproductive activity peculiar to capitalism could be dispensed with, but his heroic calculations are debatable. One of his most startling propositions is that all secretaries are unproductive because they merely assist administration, while all professors of economics (and indeed sociology) are productive because they contribute to education and therefore to economic growth. It is difficult to believe that the economic growth of any society would actually be assisted by converting manufacturing industry's population of secretaries into professors and lecturers in sociology, and this example illustrates the difficulties in the way of any actual attempt to measure what capitalist economies lose by having to carry a large salaried network associated with the continual need to recycle property rights within society and the economy.

The Soviet Union has gone a good deal further than Marx's model indicates in attempting to gain more physical commodities by curtailing service sector employment. A celebrated Soviet economics textbook of the 1950s which Helen Boss (1990, pp. 161–2) quotes from and describes as 'the mid twentieth century's most imposing monument to the materialistic fallacy' insisted that:

> (The) greatest economic significance is attached to raising the share of workers engaged in the material production sphere at the expense of the share of laborers engaged in the ranks of the nonproductive branches . . . [in order to encourage] the creation of [material plenty] essential to the building of communism.

It is widely recognized that, as yet, 'material plenty' has failed to emerge from efforts to run the Russian and other similar economies without a significant financial services sector so it is to say the least unproven that the organization of production so as to minimize the need for inter-company and interpersonal financial transactions is potentially efficient.

It is to be noted that the East European command economies have indeed taken seriously Marx's definition that manufacturing where values are originally created is productive, while subsequent financial transactions which allow those values to be realized are unproductive. According to these definitions, the production of unsaleable goods is productive, while the marketing of goods which consumers actually wish to buy is unproductive. It is unsurprising that countries which have adopted this conceptual framework waste real resources to produce what no one wishes to buy, and at the same time have entirely inadequate facilities to distribute the goods which are actually in demand.

But it is also possible for financial transactions to absorb an unnecessarily high fraction of a nation's real resources. It may well be that as in so much of political economy the extremes of minimizing the extent of financial services as the Soviet 1950s textbook recommends, or alternatively allowing financial services to reach the level of a modern western market economy where they are inflated as a consequence of agreements to fix prices and dealing margins, are both less satisfactory than some intermediate position.

Modern economic theory would suggest that an optimal level of financial services may best be approached by eliminating monopolistic and uncompetitive practices. Marx and Hilferding did well to remind us that uncompetitive behaviour in this sector can never be entirely eliminated because the scale economies which Marx wrote of are bound to ensure that there will always be very large banks and finance houses with the potential to attract rents through the uncompetitive behaviour which follows naturally from their market power. The practical approach to moving towards an optimally-sized financial sector is likely to focus on the use (and abuse) of market power within this sector which is likely to have some of the adverse effects that Hilferding described.

If competitive behaviour can be achieved and if those with monopolistic power can be persuaded to behave as if competitive forces are paramount, then a modern society could attain the extensive benefits from an efficient financial sector that even Marx described when he insisted that industrial companies will function more economically when they are assisted by efficient financial companies.

References

Boss, H. (1990), *Theories of Surplus and Transfer: Parasites and Producers in Economic Thought*, London: Unwin Hyman.

Chamberlin, E.H. (1933), *The Theory of Monopolistic Competition*, Cambridge Mass: Harvard University Press.

Gilbart, J.W. (1834), *The History and Principles of Banking*, London.

Gough, I. (1972), 'Marx's Theory of Productive and Unproductive Labour', *New Left Review*, December, pp. 47–72.

Hilferding, R. (1910), *Finance Capital: A Study of the Latest Phase of Capitalist Development*, English language edition edited by Tom Bottomore, London: Routledge (1981).

Marx, K. (1867–93), *Capital*, 3 volumes, English language edition introduced by Ernest Mandel, Harmondsworth: Penguin Books (1976–81).

Robinson, J. (1934), *The Economics of Imperfect Competition*, London: Macmillan.

Wolff, E.N. (1987), *Growth, Accumulation and Unproductive Activity*, Cambridge: Cambridge University Press.

PART TWO MARX AND THE HISTORY OF ECONOMIC THOUGHT

7 On Marx's critical reading of Adam Smith's theory of prices*

Sergio Nisticò

Marx's reading of the Smithian theory of prices is centred on the distinction, within Smith's theoretical framework, of two conflicting views of the mechanisms governing exchange ratios and distribution.

On the one hand, Marx gives Smith credit for looking into 'the intimate connections' of the bourgeois economic system, i.e., for contributing, with the rest of the classical school, to the explanation of prices and distribution on the basis of an antagonism between social classes. On the other hand, Marx faults Smith for limiting his analysis to superficial appearances and for taking the point of view of the individual capitalist. This approach, Marx argues, is characteristic of 'vulgar economics', a theoretical framework whose main feature is the explanation of distribution in terms of harmony of class interests. This coexistence of two contrasting approaches within Smith's theoretical construction is what, in Marx's opinion, 'gives his book its great charm' (Marx 1969, Volume II, p. 219).

According to Marx, Smith's contribution to an understanding of the role of class antagonism in a capitalistic society, lies in his discussion of the labour theory of value. Marx sees in this discussion a recognition of the fact that 'exchange value resolves itself into a certain quantity of labour' and that therefore 'the value contained in exchange-value is resolved into that part of labour for which the labourer is paid and that part for which he is not paid' (Marx 1969, Volume II, p. 217).

The aspect of Smith's theoretical framework that Marx regards instead as an expression of the bourgeois standpoint is the 'theory of the component parts' and the associated idea that a rise in wages tends to determine a general increase in money prices, leaving the other distributive variables unaltered.

The aim of this chapter is to provide a critical evaluation of Marx's reading of Adam Smith's theory of prices, in the light of recent analytical results in the theory of value and distribution.[1] The first part discusses the analytical difficulties connected with the classical and

* I am grateful to G. Caravale and G. Mongiovi for helpful comments to a previous draft of this work. Responsibility for the opinions expressed is entirely my own.

Marxian approach, with special reference to the problem of interdependency between prices and distribution. This discussion constitutes the basis for a consideration, first, of Smith's decision to explain natural prices starting from given levels of the distributive variables; and, then, of Ricardo's attempt to find a system of prices that is somehow invariable with respect to distribution. The methodological choices adopted by Smith and Ricardo are shown to represent separate attempts to escape from the interdependency problem;[2] their approaches, based on a sequential determination of variables, are then compared with the more rigorous solution, based on a simultaneous determination of relative prices and distribution.

The second part of this chapter uses the results of Dmitriev, Bortkiewicz and Sraffa to examine the critique that Marx directed at the 'theory of the component parts'. In particular, it is argued that the foundation of Marx's critique suffers from a logical deficiency as serious as the one which he attributes to Smith.

Some recent interpreters, following Marx's reading, view Smith's idea that a rise in wages tends to determine an increase in money prices – as an expression of a 'harmonious view' of the distributive mechanism. It is shown, instead, that the Smithian relation is fully compatible with the classical-Marxian approach based on the essential role of class antagonism in the distributive process. In this perspective, the closing sections of the chapter criticize the idea that only a price theory characterized by an inverse relationship between wages and profits is consistent with the 'antagonistic view' of the functioning of a capitalist economy.

The interdependence of prices and distribution in Smith and Ricardo

Within the theoretical framework of the classical economists, the question of value, that is the search for the mechanisms governing exchange ratios between commodities, has always been linked to that of distribution. In the writings of the classicals we can distinguish two different approaches to the problems posed by this strict interdependence between prices and distribution. The first is expressed by Smith's theory of the component parts based on the idea that commodity prices can be determined by starting from the levels of wages, profits and rents given prior to, and independently of, the exchange ratios:

> When the price of any commodity is neither more nor less than what is sufficient to pay the rent of the land, the wages of the labour, and the profits of the stock employed in raising, preparing, and bringing it to market, according to their natural rates, the commodity is then sold for what may be called its natural price. (1976, book I, p. 62)

The second, which can be identified with Ricardo's theoretical research subsequent to the *Essay*,[3] aims to escape from the interdependence by making relative prices independent of variations in distribution. As Caravale (1980, 1985) has emphasized, the essential purpose – the core – of Ricardo's theory was to point out the effects of decreasing returns in the wage-goods sector upon the rate of profit, with the real wage exogenously given at its natural level. The unambiguous results Ricardo was able to reach, on this ground, within the corn-model were no longer evident when, in a multi-sectoral economy, the prices of commodities change in consequence of variations in distribution. If the labour theory of value might constitute an approximate solution, it was nevertheless true, as Ricardo himself indicates in the first chapter of the *Principles*, that its sphere of validity is extremely limited. The exchange ratios between commodities coincide with the relative labour quantities only in two cases: either when – as 'in that early and rude state of society' – the entire product belongs to the labourers, or in a hypothetical economy in which the ratios between labour and capital are equal in all sectors. Outside of this restricted sphere of validity, Ricardo recognizes that the exchange ratios cannot be determined by relative labour quantities:

> Strictly speaking . . . the relative quantities of labour bestowed on commodities regulates their relative value, when nothing but labour is bestowed upon them, and that for equal times. When the times are unequal, the relative quantity of labour bestowed on them is still the main ingredient which regulates their relative value, but is not the only ingredient, for besides compensating for the labour, the price of the commodity, must also compensate for the length of time that must elapse before it can be brought to market. All the exceptions to the general rule come under this one of time. (1951–73, Volume VIII, p. 193)

As is well known, Ricardo tried to solve this problem by searching for an 'invariable measure of value', that is a commodity which, if used as a unit of measure, would have the property of making exchange ratios invariant with respect to distribution. Ricardo's research in this direction was fruitless, and he ended by concluding that 'it is impossible to be possessed [of such a measure]' (1951–73, Volume I, p. 43).[4]

In his inquiry into the laws governing the levels of the distributive variables, Ricardo – who defines distribution as 'the principal problem in Political Economy' – is then inclined to treat the question of value as an obstacle[5] to the clear elaboration of the effects of decreasing returns on distribution.

The simultaneous determination of prices and distribution

It is by now generally agreed that the correct solution to the interdependency problem was provided by Piero Sraffa in his *Production of Commodities by Means of Commodities* (1960). This *solution requires a simultaneous* determination of relative prices and of distribution.[6] Neither the system of prices nor distribution appear in fact to be logically prior to one another; in the model constructed by Sraffa, prices are dependent on distribution to the same extent that distribution depends on prices.

Neither Smith nor Ricardo had at their disposal the analytical tools necessary to solve the interdependency problem in the same way in which it is solved by Dmitriev, Bortkiewicz and Sraffa, that is by means of a system of equations which *simultaneously* determines prices and distribution. Compared with this type of solution – the only analytically rigorous one within the classical framework – the formulations of Smith and Ricardo can both be read as attempts to solve the problem in recursive terms, that is by identifying a linear sequence, of the cause-effect type, connecting one variable to another.

Recursiveness and interdependency

A distinction can be made between *recursive* and *interdependent* economic models;[7] the latter include variables which influence each other, while in the former, variables are connected by one-way casual relations. Recursive models can be further differentiated according to whether a *logical* or a *historical* meaning is to be attributed to recursiveness. Two variables can be related to one another in a simple logical order (it can then be said that the level of one variable determines the level of another variable); or they can be related in a historical order so that one variable not only determines but also precedes, in a dynamic sequence, the other one.

Sraffa's system of prices does not give any indication about the causal links among relative prices and distribution,[8] and therefore constitutes a description of reality based on the notion of interdependency.[9]

The models of Smith and Ricardo appear, on the contrary, to be founded on the notion of recursiveness, understood in the historical sense. The search for causal links – with the cause not only determining but also preceding the effect – is, for instance, evident in Ricardo's dynamic model. Ricardo's fundamental purpose is to analyse the effect of a cause – a secular increase in the quantity of labour required for the production of wage goods – on the distributive variables. Ricardo encounters the problem of disturbances caused by variations in relative prices which tend to cloud the causal sequence that is clearly visible in a model in which relative prices do not vary with respect to changes in distribution.[10]

Since Sraffa's model is a descriptive one which does not specify the causal sequences taking place in historical time, it cannot be said that Sraffa resolves the problems which Ricardo confronted. Nevertheless, the analytical tools of von Bortkiewicz–Sraffa type can be employed (e.g. Caravale and Tosato 1980; Caravale 1985) in a dynamic context to reveal the causal link that Ricardo wished to make clear – the relation between decreasing returns in the wage-goods sector and the falling rate of profit – in a model which does not require any *ad hoc* assumption in order to make relative prices invariant with respect to distribution.[11]

Moreover, Smith's theoretical scheme appears to be characterized by an attempt to identify a causal sequence, albeit a sequence of a different sort from that of Ricardo. Smith in his inquiry into the mechanisms governing prices and distribution, seems to focus his analysis on the relation between the movement of the distributive variables – dependent on historical and institutional factors – and the variations in natural prices through which, according to Smith, the distributive antagonisms manifest themselves.[12]

It is, however, worth noting that the models of Smith and Ricardo require specific and strong assumptions in order to be expressed in terms of recursiveness. Ricardo's model requires the assumption that relative prices do not change when distribution changes; Smith's model requires the assumption that the distributive variables are given prior to and independently of relative prices.

Smith's solution based on the idea that natural prices reflect the autonomous movement of the distributive variables, and Ricardo's solution founded on the attempt to analyse the distributive set-up by assuming relative prices to be given and independent of distribution, appear then to be symmetrical in so far as they both adopt a recursive approach. Their common objective was to break the evident vicious circle between prices and distribution at a time when the analytical tools necessary to solve a system of simultaneous equations were not yet available.[13]

Marx's critique of Smith's theory of price

Smith's explanation of natural prices starting from the levels of the distributive variables is not based on a rigorous theory of distribution capable of determining wages, profits and rents independently of the exchange ratios. Smith seems simply to treat the distributive variables as given (determined by historical and institutional factors); moreover, he does not regard them as linked, one with another, by a functional relationship.

Marx's objections to Adam Smith's theory of the component parts are expressed on two different levels. On the methodological plane, Marx rejects the logical structure of Smith's procedure, arguing that the value of production (at the aggregate and at the sectoral levels) logically precedes the determination of the distributive variables. On the basis of this methodological critique, Marx goes on to reject Smith's analytical results. In particular, Marx criticizes the corollary of the theory of the component parts according to which 'the natural price itself varies with the natural rate of each of its component parts' (Smith 1978, book I, p. 64). This corollary implies that any rise in wages will be followed by a general increase in money prices. This, in turn, entails the absence of an inverse relationship between the wage rate[14] and the rate of profit, a relationship that Marx considers an essential feature of the capitalistic distributive mechanisms.

Value prior to distribution

Against Smith's treatment of the distributive variables as logically prior to natural prices, Marx asserts the logical priority of the value of the social product, which he presumes to be determined on the basis of embodied labour time:

> Adam Smith first explains that exchange-value resolves itself into a certain quantity of labour and that . . . the value contained in exchange-value is resolved into that part of labour for which the labourer is paid and that part for which he is not paid . . . Having shown this, he suddenly turns about and instead of resolving exchange-value into wages, profit and rent, he declares these to be the elements forming exchange-values, he makes them into independent exchange-values that form the exchange-value of the product; he constructs the exchange-value of the commodity from the values of wages, profit and rent, which are determined independently and separately. *Instead of having their source in value, they become the source of value.* (1969, Volume II, p. 217)

> In actual fact commodity value is the quantitative premise, the sum total value of wages, profit and rent, whatever their relative mutual magnitudes might be. In the false conception considered here, however, wages, profit and rent are three independent value magnitudes, whose total produces, limits and determines the magnitude of commodity value. (1981, p. 1002)

Here, however, Marx's own argument seems to encounter difficulties. While Marx correctly identifies the analytical deficiencies of Smith's procedure,[15] the alternative he proposes appears to suffer from the same logical shortcoming. Exchange ratios will be independent of distribution only under those special conditions within which the labour theory of value holds. Since, in general, prices depend on distribution, Marx's idea that the value of the social product has logical priority over the distributive variables seems therefore to lack coherence.

Marx was in fact aware that when commodities do not exchange according to their labour values, it is no longer evident that the value of the social product can be regarded as given prior to and independent of distribution. He believed, however, that even if exchange ratios are not directly determined by the quantities of embodied labour, it remains true that the value of the total output may be treated as logically prior to its component parts, wages, profits and rents. Marx arrives at this conclusion by virtue of the peculiar meaning which he attributes to the transformation of values in prices.

With his transformation procedure, Marx aims to demonstrate that:

a. the total amount of profits that capitalists earn by selling commodities at their prices of production is equal to the sum of the surplus values extracted from the labour process in each industry;
b. the sum of the prices of production is equal to the sum of the labour quantities contained in the commodities produced by the economy.

That is to say, Marx seeks to demonstrate that the role of the prices of production is simply to allocate the surplus value generated by production, so as to ensure the attainment of a uniform rate of profit on the total capital advanced by capitalists. The competitive process by which profit rates are equalized does not, according to Marx, alter the total amount of value that capitalists as a class have at their disposal:

> Just as little is the law of value affected by the fact that the equalization of profit, i.e. the distribution of the total surplus value among the various capitals . . . gives rise to governing average prices for commodities that diverge from their individual values. This again affects only the addition of surplus-value to the various commodity prices; *it does not abolish surplus-value itself, nor the total value of commodities as the source of these various price components.* (Ibid., p. 985, emphasis added)

> The division of the social profit as measured by this rate among the capitals applied in the various different spheres of production produces prices of production which diverge from commodity values. . . *But this divergence from values abolishes neither the determination of prices by values nor the limits imposed on profit by our laws.* (Ibid., pp. 999–1000, emphasis added)

Marx recognizes that in the presence of different organic compositions of capital, exchange ratios are not directly determined by relative labour quantities; he believes however that even in the general case, the labour theory of value continues to play an essential role in the determination of the total amount of value available to be distributed among capitalists. It is in fact on the basis of the labour quantities that Marx calculates the average rate of profit (i.e., the ratio between total surplus labour and the quantity of labour necessary to replace the capital advanced). This average rate of profit generates, in Marx's scheme, the prices of production. Marx's claim that the value of the product to be distributed is logically prior to its division into wages and profits, would be generally valid only if the profit rate can be legitimately defined in terms of ratios of labour time. Bortkiewicz (1906–7) and Sraffa (1960) have however proved that, within a system of correctly defined prices of production, the rate of profit must be determined simultaneously with the prices of production. They have also shown that:

a. the general rate of profit, correctly determined by the price equations, does not coincide with the ratio between the total surplus value and the value of the capital employed in the system;
b. the sum of surplus values is not generally equal to the sum of profits earned by the capitalists;
c. the sum of prices is not generally equal to the sum of values.[16]

Marx's idea that the transformation of values into prices does not alter the amount of value created in the production process, therefore lacks theoretical foundation. It follows then that his claim that the value of the social product is prior to and independent of its component parts, is also devoid of analytical support; and that Marx's procedure is no more coherent than that of Smith.

Wages and prices

In accordance with his idea that the distributive variables are obtained by dividing up a given value of the social product, Marx criticizes Smith's contention that a rise in wages tends to produce a generalized increase in money prices:

> The increase in wages would affect the unpaid part of the total labour, and with this the surplus-value. . . . Finally, since the value of the constant capital has remained unaltered while the value of the variable capital advanced has risen, the diminished surplus-value would be expressed in a still further reduced gross rate of profit. . . These changes in the value of wages, the rate of profit and the rate of rent, whatever the effects of the laws governing the proportions between these parts, could move only within the limits set by the newly created commodity value. (Ibid., p. 995)

> we have seen how a general rise or fall in wages, by causing the general rate of profit to move in the opposite direction, other things being equal, alters the production prices of various commodities, raising some and making others fall, depending on the average composition of capital in the sphere of production in question. (Ibid., pp. 1007–8)

Thus Marx maintains the existence of a systematic inverse relation between wages and profits, in opposition to Smith's claim that wages and prices generally move in the same direction.

In order to evaluate Marx's criticism of Adam Smith on this issue, it is necessary to specify the possible contexts in which the relation between wages and prices can be examined.

Given the size and composition of the social product, and given the technical requirements for production, an increase in the real wage will necessarily entail a reduction in the profit rate. Within the limited sphere of validity of the labour theory of value, a change in the real wage will also leave relative prices unaltered.

In Ricardo's theory an inverse relation between *money* wages and profits[17] can emerge as a consequence of decreasing returns in agriculture when the real wage is fixed exogenously. Ricardo was concerned with a dynamic equilibrium. The requirement that real wages remain fixed at a culturally-determined natural level makes a rise in money wages necessary when input requirements, and hence natural prices, increase in the wage-goods sector; this phenomenon is accompanied, in Ricardo's theory, by a rise in rents and a decline in the profit rate (Caravale and Tosato 1980; Caravale 1985). According to this interpretation, an increase in money wages when and if it occurs is in Ricardo's theory *necessarily* connected with a fall in the rate of profit. This inverse relation between the two variables has however nothing to do with the existence of a distributive antagonism between workers and capitalists.[18]

Smith approaches the question from a somewhat different angle: in a country which is undergoing neither continuous progress nor a marked decline,[19] he argues, the reward of labour will tend to remain constant over time:

> Masters are always and everywhere in a sort of tacit, but constant and uniform combination, not to raise the wages of labour above their actual rate. (1976, book I, p. 75)

The question of the relation between wages and profits becomes relevant in Smith, then, only for a country in which the rate of accumulation is steadily rising or falling.

It is interesting to observe that Smith – after having traced the origin of increases in the natural wage to increases in the rate of accumulation – points out that these increases in the wage rate are generally accompanied by (but not *causally* linked to) a fall in profits generated by the growing competition among capitalists:

> The rise and fall in the profits of stock depend upon the same causes with the rise and fall in the wages of labour, the increasing or declining state of the wealth of the society; but those causes affect the one and the other very differently.
>
> The increase of stock, which raises wages, tends to lower profits. When the stocks of many rich merchants are turned into the same trade, their mutual competition naturally tends to lower its profit; and when there is a like increase of stock in all the different trades carried on in the same society, the same competition must produce the same effect in them all. (Ibid., p. 98)

This fall in profits in a situation of marked growth will not fail, however, according to Smith, to exert a counterbalancing effect on the final price of commodities:[20]

> In countries which are fast advancing to riches, the low rate of profit may, in the price of many commodities, compensate the high wages of labour, and enable those countries to sell as cheap as their less thriving neighbours, among whom the wages of labour may be lower. (Ibid., p. 109)

It should be emphasized that in Smith's theory, the opposite movements of wages and profits do not reflect a distributive antagonism between workers and capitalists. They are not causally interrelated but represent simultaneous and distinct effects of the increase in the rate of accumulation:

> When in any country the demand for those who live by wages; labourers, journeymen, servants of every kind, is continually increasing . . . *the workmen have no occasion to combine in order to raise their wages.* (Ibid., p. 77)

The fact remains however that, in general (i.e., when no other forces counterbalance its effect) a rise in wages tends, according to Smith, to produce an increase in all money prices rather than a fall in the rate of profit. The Smithian analysis of the relation between wages and prices appears in fact to be based on the idea that:

a. for the case of an increasing rate of accumulation, a rise in wages is accompanied by a fall in the rate of profit because of the increasing competition among capitalists;

b. for the case of a rise in wages coming about from class antagonism, the rate of profit ought to be considered a rigid component of the cost of production.

The money prices would not necessarily rise in case (a); but would generally increase in case (b). Whereas in case (a) the increase which Smith has in mind is that of the *real* wage; in case (b) he is evidently referring to a rise in the *money* wage that does not imply an increase in the real wage. His failure to make clear this distinction seems to have been the catalyst for the critiques of Ricardo and Marx.

This is a crucial point. The critiques addressed to the theory of the component parts would be in effect fully legitimate if Smith's contention were that the natural price varies, *ceteris paribus*, with an increase in the real wage. It seems instead that the magnitude which Smith considers as given prior to natural prices is the money wage, with the real wage depending on the prices of the wage goods. The money wage appears then, in Smith, as the true exogenous variable. In Smith's words:

> . . . the wages of labour do not in Great Britain fluctuate with the price of provisions. These vary every-where from year to year, frequently from month to month. *But in many places the money price of labour remains uniformly the same sometimes for half a century together.* (Ibid., p. 83, emphasis added)

The possibility of treating the money wage as given is then crucially linked to the absence of an exogenously determined real wage. In effect, in Smith's discussion of the circumstances determining the reward for labour, the subsistence wage seems simply to play the role of a sort of lower floor (and not that of a long-period real wage):

> But though in disputes with their workmen, masters must generally have the advantage, *there is however a certain rate below which it seems impossible to reduce*, for any considerable time, the ordinary wages even of the lowest species of labour. (Ibid., p. 76, emphasis added)

Once the Smithian relation is reinterpreted in the perspective specified above, it becomes evident how Smith's analytical results are able to grasp the connections existing in the modern market economy, between the levels of the distributive variables and the money prices of the commodities produced.[21]

While Smith's idea that the outcome of the distributive antagonism is a rise in the price level appears to be analytically and historically well-founded, it is also true that a fundamental issue remains undetermined in his model. This is the question of the *real effects* that changes in the monetary magnitudes produced on distribution.

Given technical coefficients and the profit rate, the Smithian relation between natural wages and natural prices can be investigated on the basis of two alternative assumptions. According to the first assumption, the rise in money wages is accompanied initially by an increase in the real wage and then by a lower rate of profit. The resulting change in distribution in favour of workers would drive capitalists to react with a general increase in money prices in order to restore the original distributive set-up. The generalized increase in money prices would in this case turn out to be incompatible with a permanent rise in the real wage level.

A second possibility could be to assume that there are no temporal lags between the wage and price increases, so that wages would change only in monetary terms. The immediate proportional increase in all money prices would in fact guarantee the persistence of the original distributive scheme. According to this second assumption, the Smithian relation could then be interpreted as an analysis of the relationship between natural money wage (given the real wage) and the natural prices expressed in monetary terms. If the Smithian relation is interpreted according to this second assumption, two alternative situations could occur when money wages rise. Either

a. workers, having perceived the impossibility of obtaining an increase in the real wage, because of the higher bargaining power of capitalists, accept the existing distributive arrangement; or
b. workers, once they perceive the generalized increase in money prices, react by demanding further wage increases, thereby setting off an inflationary spiral.

Distributive antagonism and Smith's theory of price

According to Marx, Smith's determination of natural price starting from given levels of the distributive variables, is expression of a 'harmonious view' of the capitalist system. In other words, Marx believes that the determination of exchange ratios on the basis of the components of total income emerges from the 'vulgar' belief that capital, land and labour create the revenues they receive.

The idea that the components are logically prior to the sum, and the corollary according to which 'the natural price itself varies with the natural rate of each of its compenent parts' (Smith 1976, book I, p. 64) are then, Marx thinks, incompatible with the 'antagonistic view' which characterizes the models of the classical economists:

> this economic trinity as the connection between the components of value and wealth in general and its sources, completes the mystification of the capitalist mode of production . . . the bewitched, distorted and upside-down world haunted by 'Monsieur le Capital and Madame la Terre' who are at the same time social characters and mere things. *It is the great merit of classical economics to have dissolved this false appearance. . . Yet even its best representatives remained more or less trapped in the world of illusion their criticism had dissolved, and nothing else is possible from the bourgeois standpoint; they all fell therefore more or less into inconsistencies, half-truths and unresolved contradictions.* (1981, p. 969, emphasis added)

Marx's interpretation, according to which the absence of a systematic inverse relation between wages and profits represents a failure to move beyond the superficial appearance of harmony, is widely accepted and has recently been recapitulated by Garegnani:[22]

> This dependence of the value of the product upon distribution means that, . . . the constraint by which one class cannot have more without the other class having less – so evident if we could look at the product in physical terms – is no longer apparent: might not the real wage rise without affecting the rate of profit, or vice-versa? Indeed Smith himself often lost sight of the constraint and envisaged the rate of profit and the wage as determined *independently of each other*. He wrote that 'the natural price varies with the natural rate of each of its component parts'. (1984, pp. 301–2)

The argument developed here could provide the basis for an interpretation of Smith's theory that is different from the one outlined by Garegnani. The existence of a distributive antagonism need not manifest itself as an inverse relation between the distributive variables. The conflict between workers and capitalists could in fact reveal itself in terms of the capitalists' unwillingness to accept any reduction in the profit rate; this stubbornness on the part of capitalists (which, of course, is reinforced by their superior bargaining power) would produce a general increase in money prices. The Smithian relation then finds its logical foundation in the rigidity of the rate of profit:

> The commodity is then sold [when the market price coincides with the natural one] precisely for what it is worth, or for what it really costs the person who brings it to market; for though in common language what is called the prime cost of any commodity does not comprehend the profit of the person who is to sell it again, yet if he sells it at a price which does not allow him the ordinary rate of profit . . . unless they yield him this profit, therefore, they do not repay him what they may very properly be said to have really cost him. (Smith 1976, book I, pp. 62–3)

From this perspective, Smith's theory of prices can no longer be viewed as the ultimate source of the post-Ricardian (neo-classical) conception, according to which the distributive process is characterized by equitable and efficient rules, an idea expressed by Garegnani in the following terms:

> It may here be appropriate to notice how the nature of Ricardo's contribution in overcoming the error implicit in Smith's adding-up theory of prices may help us to comprehend Marx's often misunderstood position with respect to what he called 'vulgar political economy'. . . . the attempt to preserve a harmonious view of society took – Marx thought – the form of turning a blind eye upon the analytical advances of Ricardo and keeping closer to the 'appearances' by which the price of the product, seen as the *sum* of profits, wages and rents, may *seem* capable of accommodating the rise in one of these elements without a decrease in the others. (1984, p. 303)

The Ricardian inverse relation between wages and profits should not be considered an 'analytical advance' through which the distributive antagonism is finally brought to light. Rather, it is a logical consequence of the specific assumptions underlying Ricardo's model (decreasing returns in the wage-goods sector and the exogeneity of the real wage). The strict association, emphasized by Garegnani in line with Marx, between the existence of a distributive antagonism and the *w-r* inverse relation, should then be rejected. The fact that, in real terms and in a given situation, an increase in the income share accruing to one class implies a decrease in the share of the other class, is, as Bortkiewicz notes, 'a self-evident proposition' and is not linked to any specific theory of prices. In Smith's model, on the contrary, it is the very existence of the distributive antagonism – expressed by the rigidity of the rate of profit in the face of the labourers' attempt to obtain higher real wages by means of an increase in the money wages – that produces the effect of a generalized increase in money prices:

> The workmen desire to get as much, the masters to give as little as possible. . . . It is not, however, difficult to foresee which of the two parties must, upon all ordinary occasions, have the advantage in the dispute, and force the other into a compliance with their terms. The masters, being fewer in number, can combine much more easily; and the law, besides, authorizes, or at least does not prohibit their combinations, while it prohibits those of the workmen. (1976, book I, p. 74)

Conclusion

In response to the problems arising from the interdependency between prices and distribution, the classicals developed two ways to determine exchange ratios and the levels of the distributive variables. The first, associated with Smith, assumes distribution to be given, and 'composes' the price of each commodity by starting from the natural rates at which labour, capital and land are remunerated. The second approach represented by the model of Ricardo who, aware of the limits of the labour theory of value, attempts, through the search for an 'invariable standard', to re-establish the autonomy of exchange ratios from distribution.

The methodological choices taken by Smith and Ricardo are based on the concept of *causality*, in contrast to the modern simultaneous determination approach based on the concept of *interdependency*. It has been argued that since no causal links, in the historical sense, can be brought to light in Bortkiewicz–Sraffa type solutions, these models appear not to be comparable to the frameworks adopted by Smith and Ricardo.

On the basis of these methodological distinctions, an attempt has been made to evaluate the critique directed by Marx against Smith's theory of price. It has in particular been observed that Marx's idea according to which the distributive variables *must* be determined by dividing a given sum of value whose magnitude is independent of its distribution, appears devoid of analytical foundation. In order to assign logical priority to the value of production, outside of the conditions under which the labour theory of value holds, prices of production should be susceptible of determination in the way Marx determines them; that is on the basis of a process by which the total amount of profits distributed to capitalists is made equal to the total surplus value extracted from production. Marx's claim that the *sum* is given prior to and independently of the specification of its components, seems then to collapse when faced with Bortkiewicz's demonstration that the correct determination of the prices of production cannot be obtained by means of Marx's transformation procedure.

With respect to Smith's thesis that a rise of wages tends to produce a general increase in money prices, it has been argued, in opposition to Marx, that the *inverse relation* between wages and profits does not represent the necessary hallmark of the classical approach to the theory of distribution. In particular, the *Smithian relation* between wages and prices has been shown to be fully compatible with the antagonistic classical-Marxian approach, the essential feature of which is the presence of distributive conflict among social classes, whatever may be the actual relation between wages and profits.

The interpretation of the Smithian theory of prices suggested in this chapter is certainly not definitive. It has textual support in Smith's writings but these, being far from unambiguous, lend support also to other interpretative schemes. The distinguishing and specific character of the reading here proposed is that it aims at reestablishing the logical coherence and the *classical* nature of Smith's explanation of prices and distribution. An explanation that was perhaps too hastily set aside as an expression 'of the bourgeois viewpoint' by those same economists belonging to the classical tradition wherein Adam Smith is probably not only the founder but also one of the most lucid representatives.

Notes

1. The interpretative scheme supplied by Caravale (see Caravale and Tosato 1980, and Caravale 1985) for the classical school of thought and in particular for Ricardo's theory of distribution and growth has been of special importance for the development of the present work. This scheme – centred around the relation between diminishing returns and the process of accumulation – sets itself against both the revisionist interpretations proposed by Samuelson (1978), Hollander (1979, 1983) and Casarosa (1978) which interpret Ricardo's theoretical model in terms of demand and supply functions; and to the interpretative scheme of Garegnani (1981, pp. 18–26; 1984), who neglects the dynamic nature of the Ricardian model and, ignoring the presence of rent, considers the inverse relation between wages and profits to be the fundamental analytical result of Ricardo's theoretical construction.
2. It must be noted that whereas in Ricardo the search for a system of prices somehow invariable with respect to distribution coexists with a very lucid analysis of the reasons determining the interdependency, Smith was surely less aware than Ricardo of the analytical difficulties connected with this question.
3. The distributive model that Ricardo worked out in the *Essay* referred to a hypothetical economy in which corn is produced by means of corn so that there is no need to determine any exchange ratios. As is well known, this solution was criticized by Malthus who, in a letter to Ricardo of 5 August 1814, writes: 'In no case of production, is the produce exactly of the same nature as the capital advanced. Consequently we can never properly refer to a material rate of produce.' (Ricardo 1951–73, Volume VI, pp. 117–18)
4. On this point, Caravale writes: 'And this search could not be otherwise than unsuccessful: the problem as Ricardo posed it had no satisfactory solution, in the sense that the "standard measure" could have been defined *only* if conditions occurred that made it possible to do without it' (Caravale 1985, p. 155). The invariable standard would in fact have been a good unit of measure only for those commodities produced with its same ratio between capital and labour. About the nature of Ricardo's research, see also Caravale and Tosato (1980, chapter 3) and Sraffa who observes that 'the same exceptions which he had discovered in the fundamental rule determining value cropped up again in attempting to define the qualities of an invariable standard'. (Sraffa 1951, p. xli)
5. In a letter to Mill of 30 December 1815, before the *Principles* were ready for publication, Ricardo (1951–73, Volume VI, p. 348) wrote: 'I know I shall be soon stopped by the word price'. And again in a letter to Malthus of 7 February 1816: '*If I could overcome the obstacles* in the way of giving a clear insight into the origin and law of relative of exchangeable value I should have gained half the battle' (Ricardo 1951–73, Volume VII, p. 20). Sraffa (1951, p. xiv) observes that 'from this time onwards the problem of value increasingly troubled him'.
6. A solution substantially identical to the one of Sraffa can be found in the works of Dmitriev (1974) and of von Bortkiewicz (1906–7). The work of Bortkiewicz, 'Wertrechnung und Preisrechnung in Marxischen System', *Archiv fur Sozialwissenschaft und Sozialpolitik*, has been partially translated into English in *International Economic Papers*, 1952, n. 2.
7. For a detailed analysis of the questions connected with the *recursive* or *interdependent* character of economic models, see Bentzel and Hansen (1954).
8. The distinction between exogenous data (technical coefficients and one of the two distributive variables) and unknowns (relative prices and the residual distributive variable) is not, of course, sufficient to characterize Sraffa's model in 'recursive' terms.
9. The notion of 'causality', as Cavalieri (1987, p. 25) observes, should not be opposed to the notion of interdependency. Since the logical priority does not necessarily imply the historical one, it is then possible to observe phenomena of 'reciprocal causation'. The

notion of interdependency could then be understood asmutual causation. According to Cavalieri, the notions that should instead be opposed are those of 'determinism' and 'indeterminism'. Cavalieri distinguishes, for instance, between 'the logicians of economics' and 'the economists who believe in an exact science'. The former, using the logical categories of recursiveness and/or of interdependency, try 'simply' to get to a rational knowledge of the economic phenomena, with the awareness that the results can not always be of deterministic type. The latter, like all those who consider themselves scholars of a 'positive science', are drawn up along the deterministic front.

10. The assumption of the validity of the labour theory of value can thus be interpreted as a *ceteris paribus* assumption in the sense that, though Ricardo is perfectly aware that relative prices change when distribution changes, he supposes, in some passages of his work, exchange ratios to be determined by the relative labour quantities, so as to avoid the 'reciprocal causation' between prices and distribution that would deprive his policy conclusions of their theoretical rationale.
11. The analytical results obtained by Caravale and Tosato (1980) show that, though Ricardo had indicated with great clarity the circumstances which make prices dependent on distribution, his attempt to escape from the interdependency by somehow making relative prices independent of distribution, was not only destined to meet with insurmountable analytical difficulties, but was also pointless.
12. 'The natural price itself varies with the natural rate of each of its component parts, of wages, profit and rent; and in every society this rate varies according to their circumstances, according to their riches or poverty, their advancing, stationary, or declining condition. I shall, in the four following chapters, endeavour to explain, as fully and distinctly as I can, the causes of those different variations' (Smith 1976, book I, p. 71). 'In reality high profits tend much more to raise the price of work than high wages. . . Our merchants and master-manufacturers complain much of the bad effects of high wages in raising the price, and thereby lessening the sale of their goods both at home and abroad. They say nothing concerning the bad effects of high profits. They are silent with regard to the pernicious effects of their own gains. They complain only of those of other people' (ibid., 1976, pp. 109, 110).
13. It is possible also that the scientific outlook favoured by Ricardo and Smith, grounded as it was in the notion of causality, would have led them to regard the Sraffa–Bortkiewicz solution as deficient in heuristic value.
14. Although the matter will be considered in more detail later in the text, it should be noted here that much of the difficulty surrounding this point emerges from the failure of Adam Smith, and also of his critics, to clearly distinguish the relationship between the money wage and money prices from the relationship between the real wage and the rate of profit.
15. Marx writes for instance: 'In chapters VIII, IX, X' and XI of Book I, Adam Smith then seeks to determine the natural rate of these "component parts", wages, rent and profit . . . The basis from which he determines the natural rate of wages is the value of labour-power itself, the *necessary wage*. This, however, becomes meaningless again because he never asks himself how the value of the necessary means of subsistence, i.e., of the *commodity* in general is determined. And here, since he has moved away from his main conception, Adam Smith would have to say: The price of wages is determined by the price of the means of subsistence and the price of the means of subsistence is determined by the price of wages.' (Marx 1969, Volume II, p. 222)
16. In fact either one or the other of the two equalities could be added to the system in the place of the equation defining the numeraire. In general, both conditions cannot be simultaneously satisfied (Pasinetti 1977, p. 130n).
17. While the worsening of productive conditions in the wage-goods sector is *always* associated with a reduction in the general rate of profit (Caravale and Tosato 1980, chapter 2 and appendix), the effect on money wages (given the real wage bundle) will depend on the price changes of the various wage goods associated with the reduction in the rate of profit. In Ricardo's model, then, the reduction in the rate of profit is not necessarily associated with an increase in money wages. This circumstance is hinted at by Caravale (see chapter 8) and was pointed out to me by G. Caravale in private conversation.

18. Commenting on Garegnani's interpretation (1981, 1984), Caravale (1985, p. 168) observes that 'the only possible antagonism remaining in Garegnani's interpretative context is that between *real* wages and profits, a circumstance that sharply contrasts with Garegnani's own clear perception that "the specific analysis of the relationship between capital and wage labour made by Marx could not have been made by Ricardo, *interested as he mainly was in the relationship between capital and landed property at a time when the conflict between capital and labour was not yet concretely manifest.*"
19. The natural level of wage has in Smith an essentially dynamic character. This is connected, in Smith's theoretical construction, with the necessity for labour supply to adapt itself to the pace of accumulation. The natural wage would be higher in those countries which, being in a progressive phase, will require a higher rate of population growth: 'The money price of labour is necessarily regulated by two circumstances; the demand for labour, and the price of the necessaries and conveniences of life. The demand for labour, according as it happens to be increasing, stationary, or declining, or to require an increasing, stationary, or declining population, determines the quantities of the necessaries and conveniences of life which must be given to the labourer; and the money price of labour is determined by what is requisite for purchasing this quantity' (Smith 1976, book I, p. 95); 'It is not, accordingly, in the richest countries, but in the most thriving, or in those which are growing rich the fastest, that the wages of labour are highest' (ibid., p. 78; cf. also Eltis 1984, pp. 68–105).
20. Smith indicates one more counterbalancing effect, acting on the price of commodities, in the presence of a rise of wages: 'The increase in the wages of labour necessarily increases the price of many commodities, by increasing that part of it which resolves itself into wages, and so far tends to diminish their consumption both at home and abroad. *The same cause, however, which raises the wages of labour, the increase of stock, tends to increase its productive powers, and to make a smaller quanitity of labour produce greater quantity of work* . . . . There are many commodities, therefore, which, in consequence of these improvements, come to be produced by so much less labour than before, that the increase of its price is more than compensated by the diminution of its quantity' (1976, book I, pp. 96–7).
21. Leontief (1984), for example, has recently analysed the effects on prices of an increase in the money wage. Although his analytical scheme is similar to Sraffa's, Leontief does not consider the inverse relation between the wage rate and the rate of profit to be the main feature of a capitalistic system. Following a line of argument which is parallel to that of Smith, Leontief supposes that, in the presence of a rise in wages, the rate of profit remains constant. Leontief's results can in fact be obtained by closing the Sraffa–Bortkiewicz system with the Smithian assumption that both the money wage and the rate of profit are given from outside the model. In this case the money wage plays substantially the role of the numeraire and the inverse relation between the two distributive variables disappears. A similar model has been proposed by Mongiovi (1989) as an attempt to introduce money 'into Sraffa's reconstructed classical model'.
22. Positions similar to that of Marx are taken for example by Dobb (1973, p. 50) and Meek (1977, pp. 153–4). Schumpeter also sees 'two souls' in Smith's model and sees the theory of the component parts as 'the rudimentary equilibrium theory which points toward Say and, through the latter's work, to Walras' (Schumpeter 1954, p. 601). Garegnani seems, however, not to share the idea (expressed by Dobb and Schumpeter) that Smith's theory of the component parts is a truly neo-classical formulation based on the supply and demand functions of the productive factors: 'This view of Smith's approach to value and distribution seems to overlook that behind Smith's vague reference to the rate of profit as determined by the "competition" of capitalists, there lay, as we saw, the inconsistency of rates of wages, profits and rent determined independently of one another. And it was just this inconsistency that Ricardo and Marx criticized Smith for. The demand and supply forces of the modern theories, founded as they are, on the "substitutability" between "factors of production", are as absent in Smith as they are in Ricardo.' (Garegnani 1984, n. 21, p. 302)

References

Bentzel, R. and B. Hansen (1954), 'On Recursiveness and Interdependency in Economic Models', *The Review of Economic Studies*, **59**, pp. 153–68.

Caravale, G. and D. Tosato (1980), *Ricardo and the Theory of Value, Distribution and Growth*, London: Routledge & Kegan Paul.

Caravale, G. (1985), 'Diminishing Returns and Accumulation in Ricardo', in G. Caravale (ed.), *The Legacy of Ricardo*, Oxford: Basil Blackwell.

Casarosa, C. (1978), 'A New Formulation of the Ricardian System', *Oxford Economic Papers*, **30**, pp. 38–63.

Cavalieri, D. (1987), 'L'Analisi Economica tra Causalità e Interdipendenza: Elementi per una Valutazione Storico-Critica', *Quaderni di Storia dell'Economia Politica*, **3**, pp. 9–56.

Dmitriev, V.K. (1974), *Economic Essays*, edited by D.M. Nuti (first published in 1904), Cambridge: Cambridge University Press.

Dobb, M. (1973), *Theories of Value and Distribution since Adam Smith–Ideology and Economic Theory*, London: Cambridge University Press.

Eltis, W. (1984), *The Classical Theory of Economic Growth*, London: Macmillan.

Garegnani, P. (1981), *Marx e gli Economisti Classici*, Torino: Einaudi.

Garegnani, P. (1984), 'Value and Distribution in the Classical Economists and Marx', *Oxford Economic Papers*, **36**, pp. 291–325.

Hollander, S. (1973), *The Economics of Adam Smith*, London: Heinemann.

Hollander, S. (1979), *The Economics of David Ricardo*, Toronto: University of Toronto Press.

Hollander, S. (1983), 'On the Interpretation of Ricardian Economics: The Assumption Regarding Wages', *American Economic Review*, papers and proceedings, 73, pp. 314–18.

Leontief, W. (1984), 'Nuove Tecnologie e Sviluppo', *Socialismo Oggi*, 31.12.

Marx, K. (1969), *Theories of Surplus Value*, London: Lawrence and Wishart.

Marx, K. (1973), *Grundrisse*, Harmondsworth: Penguin.

Marx, K. (1976), *Capital*, Volume I, Harmondsworth: Penguin.

Marx, K. (1981), *Capital*, Volume III, Harmondsworth: Penguin.

Meek, R. (1977), *Smith, Marx and After*, London: Chapman and Hall.

Mongiovi, G. (1989), *A Note on the Development of Sraffa's Monetary Thought*, Richmond, VA, History of Economics Society.

Pasinetti, L. (1977), *Lectures on the Theory of Production*, London: Macmillan.

Ricardo, D. (1951–73), *The Works and Correspondence* (11 volumes), edited by P. Sraffa with the collaboration of M.H. Dobb, London: Cambridge University Press.

Samuelson, P. (1978), 'The Canonical Classical Model of Political Economy', *Journal of Economic Literature*, **16**, pp. 1415–34.

Schumpeter, J. (1954), *History of Economic Analysis*, New York: Oxford University Press.

Smith, A. (1976), *An Inquiry into the Nature and Causes of The Wealth of Nations*, Chicago: The University of Chicago Press.

Sraffa, P. (1951), Introduction to *The Works and Correspondence of David Ricardo*, Volume I, London: Cambridge University Press.

Sraffa, P. (1960), *Production of Commodities by Means of Commodities*, Cambridge: Cambridge University Press.

Von Bortkiewicz, L. (1906–7), 'Wertrechnung und Preisrechnung im Marxschen System', *Archiv für Sozial Wissenschaft und Sozialpolitik*, 23 and 25.

Von Bortkiewicz, L. (1952), 'Value and Prices in the Marxian System', *International Economic Papers*, 2.

8 Marx's views on Ricardo – a critical evaluation*

Giovanni A. Caravale

The considerable difficulty of communication[1] which characterizes old and new debates alike on the relation between Ricardo and Marx – from the time of Marshall to present day – is at least in part[2] attributable to the absence of a consolidated and rigorous definition of the analytical scheme in which Ricardo's research is to be placed. Under these circumstances the problem of the analytical validity of Marx's criticism of Ricardo has remained obfuscated, often prey of ideological preconceptions.

The purpose of this chapter is to contribute to dispel such confusion by looking at the question in the light of some recent theoretical acquisitions concerning Ricardo's analytical scheme of reference. By so doing, it will also be possible to evaluate two important related points.

On the one hand, the degree of compatibility between Marx's interpretation of Ricardo's theory (i.e., the theoretical model that Marx attributes to Ricardo) and his criticism of Ricardo on a number of points which are of crucial importance for both theoretical constructions.

On the other hand, the soundness of the thesis of the so-called 'continuity' between Ricardo and Marx; that is the idea – which may be placed in quite different contexts (as will be seen) – that Ricardo's and Marx's analyses are nothing but successive developments of the *same* theory.

The chapter consists of six sections. After a brief discussion of some methodological issues which appear of general relevance for the analyses in the history of economic thought, the theoretical model that Marx attributes to Ricardo is compared with the 'natural equilibrium dynamic interpretation' of the Ricardian theory. The main implications of this latter interpretation (for the points of crucial relevance for Marx's criticism of Ricardo) are then briefly spelled out. The legitimacy of Marx's main criticism is successively evaluated in the light of contemporary economic analysis, and the compatibility between Marx's interpretation of Ricardo and Marx's own criticism of the Ricardian

* I wish to thank P.L. Porta, F. Meacci and S. Nisticò for their useful comments on a previous version of this chapter. Responsibility for the opinions expressed in the chapter is of course entirely my own.

construction is examined. The final part of the chapter, on the basis of the results reached in the preceding ones, deals – however briefly – with the question of the so-called 'continuity' between Ricardo and Marx.

The conclusions arrived at can be summarized as follows:

a. most of Marx's criticism of Ricardo – in the light of contemporary analytical results based on Sraffa's work (and, of course, on Bortkiewicz's writings before him) – appears devoid of solid foundations;
b. Marx's interpretation of Ricardo (as defined above) is, on the contrary, correct in its broad lines and can be shown to coincide with the Sraffa-based 'natural equilibrium dynamic interpretation' of Ricardo;
c. Marx's criticism of the Ricardian construction conflicts with Marx's own correct interpretation of Ricardo – a fact which may be seen as an expression of his ambivalent attitude towards Ricardo, who represents an indispensable point of reference for the development of his analysis and, at the same time, an 'idol to be destroyed';[3]
d. the relationship between Ricardo and Marx cannot be described in terms of 'continuity' – their analyses cannot be viewed as the development of the same 'theory', either in the form suggested by Garegnani or in that suggested by Hollander.

Some methodological aspects

When analyses in the history of economic thought are carried out in the light of contemporary theoretical contributions, the argument often moves along, and cuts across, the subtle and ambiguous distinction between what an author of the past actually said, what he meant to say, and what he could (or should) have said.

The arbitrariness implicit in each one of the terms of this distinction can be neither denied nor eliminated. It can however be more clearly identified – thus perhaps circumscribed – with reference to Rorty's (1984) recent classification of four different 'genres' in the history of thought (these are proposed for the history of philosophy but suit well the history of economic analysis): *Geistesgeschichten*; 'historical reconstructions'; 'rational reconstructions', and 'doxographies'. The first three are, according to Rorty, 'indispensable and do not compete with one another', while the fourth may 'be allowed to wither away' (p. 67).

Geistesgeschichten 'works at the level of problematics rather than of solutions to the problem . . . [It asks questions such as] "why should anyone have made the problem of – central to his thought?" or "why did anyone take the problem of – seriously?" ' (ibid., p. 57). In other words, this is the effort to identify the central issues that the past thinker analysed, and the reasons why these issues became central to his system of thought.

'Historical reconstructions' are, on the other hand, attempts to give an account of the past thinker's system of thought 'in his own terms'. These follow the maxim that 'no agent can eventually be said to have meant or done something which he could never be brought to accept as a correct description of what he had meant or done' (Skinner 1969, p. 28). In other words, this is the effort to identify the answers that the author of past gave, or tried to give, to his central questions using the logical and/or analytical tools and terms that he had at his disposal.

'Rational reconstructions' try to move a step further. They consist of the attempt to treat the great dead thinkers 'as contemporaries, as colleagues with whom [we] can exchange views' (Rorty 1984, p. 49), since 'we are interested not only in what the Aristotle who walked in the streets of Athens "could be brought to accept as a correct description of what he had meant or done", but in what an ideally reasonable and educable Aristotle could be brought to accept as such a description' (ibid., p. 56). These reconstructions are then attempts to correct the 'mistakes' of the past thinkers and highlight their anticipations of modern doctrines – to give an account of their analyses 'in our terms', ignoring the fact that their linguistic and analytical habits may have been, and normally were, profoundly different from those of today. 'Rational reconstructions typically aim at saying that the great dead [thinker] had some excellent ideas, but unfortunately he couldn't get them straight because of the "limitations of his time" ' (ibid., p. 57). We want to be able to see, says Rorty:

> that there has been rational progress in the course of recorded history – that we differ from our ancestors on grounds which our ancestors could be led to accept . . . We need to imagine Aristotle studying Galileo . . . and changing his mind, . . . Aquinas reading Newton or Hume and changing his . . . we need to think that, in philosophy as in science, the mighty mistaken dead look down from heaven at our recent successes, and are happy to find that their mistakes have been corrected. (Ibid., p. 51)

> Such enterprises . . . are, of course, anachronistic. But if they are conducted in full knowledge of their anachronism they are unobjectionable. (Ibid., p. 53)

Although there is no pretence to reach absolute truth through this 'genre' (since, Rorty writes, 'there will be as many rational reconstructions which purport to find significant truths, or pregnant and important falsehoods, in the works of a great dead [thinker], as there are importantly different contexts in which his works can be placed' (ibid., p. 55), guidance for the choice of the 'right' context can come from the degree of coherence between the rational reconstruction proposed and the conclusions reached through the two previous 'genres' examined above.

Finally, according to Rorty, 'doxography' is 'the attempt to impose a problematic on a canon drawn up without reference to that problematic, or, conversely, to impose a canon on a problematic constructed without reference to that canon' (ibid., p. 62). It is the attempt to describe all texts in the light of some recent orthodoxy and to show that those who have worked in the field of one discipline have in substance treated exactly 'the same permanent, deep, fundamental questions' (ibid., p. 63). The notion conveyed by 'doxographies' is that each discipline is 'a natural kind' – where the 'natural' features of the kind are of course drawn from some prevailing orthodoxy – characterized by 'a few "continuing concerns" which run through all the great [thinkers]' (ibid., p. 65). This approach is not considered by Rorty as a useful one:

> we need to realize that the questions which the 'contingent arrangements' of the present time lead us to regard as *the* questions are questions which may be better than those which our ancestors asked, but need not be the same. . . We need to see ourselves not as responding to the same stimuli to which our ancestors responded, but as having created more interesting stimuli for ourselves. (Ibid., p. 63)

This approach, in other words, presupposes that some perennial truth (both for what regards the identification of the questions and some general points of the answers to be given to such questions) has been established once and for all.

Now, with reference to Rorty's distinction, what follows should be classified as an attempt at a 'rational reconstruction' for what concerns the interpretation of Ricardo's and Marx's analyses, and of their relationship; a reconstruction which presupposes of course that, through the first two approaches (*Geistesgeschichten* and historical reconstruction), the questions posed by the two great thinkers of the past have been identified and the answers they gave to these questions with their tools have been detected.

In spite of the inevitable presence of elements of arbitrariness in the analyses of economic thought and the consequent lack of an 'objective criterion' for the choice of the context in which any 'rational reconstruction' can be placed, a good indication of validity of the choice made is supplied, as I said above, by the coherence between the conclusions reached through the first two 'genres' and the 'corrections' (positive or negative) introduced with the third. It is to be hoped that this less demanding criterion is met by the following analysis.

The natural equilibrium dynamic analysis of Ricardo and Marx's interpretation

The first point I wish to make is that Marx's interpretation of Ricardo – meaning the theoretical model that Marx thought Ricardo had in mind in his research, as distinct from the criticism that the former addressed to the latter – shows relevant analogies with the Sraffa-based reconstruction of Ricardo's thought which emphasizes the inverse relation between diminishing returns and capital accumulation as the central issue of Ricardo's analysis – a reconstruction that can be termed the 'natural equilibrium dynamic interpretation' of the Ricardian construction (Caravale and Tosato 1980; Caravale 1985, 1988a).[4]

The basic elements of this latter interpretation are: (a) the central analytical role of the notion of natural equilibrium; and (b) the strict and systematic connection between changes in technology and changes in distribution.

As to the first element, it must be emphasized at the outset that Ricardo fully adhered to Adam Smith's idea that natural equilibrium represents a centre of gravity of market equilibrium positions determined by supply and demand. Natural equilibrium is thus the main object of Ricardo's analysis. In an often-quoted passage, Ricardo emphasized the role of the 'dominant' forces, as opposed to accidental and temporary forces:

> Having fully acknowledged the temporary effects which, in particular employments of capital, may be produced . . . by accidental causes . . . we will leave them entirely out of our consideration, whilst we are treating of the laws which regulate natural prices, natural wages and natural profits, effects totally independent of these accidental causes. (1951–73, Volume I, pp. 91–2)

It is important to stress:

a. the close connection that Ricardo emphasized between natural prices and natural wages (these are presented as two aspects of the same theoretical concept);
b. the reason Ricardo gives for the exclusion, from the analysis, of the deviations of market values from natural values (the term 'value' refers here to prices, wages and profits): the accidental and temporary nature of the deviations as opposed to the 'dominant' nature of the changes with which Ricardo is concerned ('lasting changes').

It is therefore of the greatest importance, in Ricardo's theory, to identify the non-accidental, non-temporary, but instead permanent and dominant forces which determine natural values. For Ricardo these forces are the conditions of production of the 'necessaries' of the workers, that is the technical conditions prevailing in the agricultural sector – the sector that produces the wage goods 'par excellence' under conditions of diminishing returns. The 'lasting changes' of which Ricardo speaks are in other words those changes resulting from the continuous worsening in the conditions of production of agricultural commodities, whose output requires ever-increasing quantities of labour.

The natural equilibrium dynamic interpretation of Ricardo thus focuses on the inverse relation between the labour content of agricultural products ('corn') and the general rate of profit, thus mirroring Ricardo's own explicit views of the problem:[5]

> Profits, it cannot be too often repeated, depend on wages; not on nominal . . . wages; not on the number of pounds that may be annually paid to the labourer, but on the number of days' work, necessary to obtain those pounds [which are in turn necessary to obtain the basket of goods representing the *given* real wage]. (1951–73, Volume I, p. 143)

> in all countries, and at all times, profits depend on the quantity of labour requisite to provide the necessaries for the labourers, on that land . . . which yields no rent. (Ibid., Volume I, p. 126)

The definition of such inverse relation for the general case of different capital–labour ratios in the various sectors (Caravale and Tosato 1980, chapter 2) can thus be seen as the solution of Ricardo's central problem.

The second element of the interpretation I am referring to is represented by the strict and systematic connection between distribution and technology, i.e., by the fact that, within Ricardo's natural equilibrium context, changes in distribution can only arise from a modification of technical coefficients expressing the conditions under which production is being carried out. This point is strongly connected with the notion of natural wage in the natural equilibrium approach (see, in particular, Caravale 1988a) and with the identification of the distributive antagonism to be considered central for the Ricardian construction.

Let us examine these points in succession. In order to concentrate on the effects that diminishing returns in agriculture determine on the set of natural prices, on the rate of profit and on the rate of accumulation, it is essential for Ricardo to make the assumption that the natural wage rate is given in terms of commodities from outside the model, by the 'habits and customs of the people'.[6] This requires in turn that an appropriate set of conditions be met for population growth and capital growth during the 'progressive phase', i.e., while the accumulation process is active. As I have tried to show elsewhere (e.g. Caravale 1985, 1988a), there are good reasons to believe, in spite of the contrary textual evidence from the chapter 'On Wages' of the *Principles*, that Ricardo did have in mind a specific set of conditions regarding the rate of growth of capital and population under which the exogenously given natural wage rate would stay constant over time. This makes it possible for the model to shed full light on the role that diminishing returns play on the pace of expansion of the economy.[7]

The assumption that the natural wage is given in real terms is crucial in its turn because it helps us in the identification of the distributive antagonism that Ricardo had in mind – that between rentiers and capitalists. To clarify this point it may be useful to recall that the analysis of changes in distribution with *no* changes at all in the matrix of the technical coefficients would be admissible in a Ricardian context only if the hypothesis of alternative distributive set-ups could be proved to be logically compatible with the idea that the situation is, in some significant sense, *given*. But, as I have tried to show elsewhere (Caravale 1988b, para. 5), it is precisely this problem of compatibility that admits no general solution within the Ricardian theoretical model: a new value of the *real* wage rate w (with respect to an initial situation of natural equilibrium defined on the basis of one level of the wage) would imply either a different matrix of the technical coefficients (the new value of the rate of profit r could thus no longer be thought of as the effect of a movement along the same w-r inverse relation, simply because this relation would not exist any more), or a different set of initial conditions (with different values of the level and/or the composition of production).

The analysis of alternative distributive set-ups (real wage-rate of profit) in a given situation finds therefore no room at all within the Ricardian context of natural equilibrium. It must then be concluded that the 'core' of Ricardo's theory cannot consist of a given inverse w-r 'relation' (which in fact would not exist[8]) meant to express the antagonism between capitalists and workers. This core consists instead, on the analytical plane, of the inverse relation between the labour content of corn (or, more generally, the labour embodied in the wage basket) and the rate of profit,[9] with a given real wage rate – an inverse relation which is the expression of the 'historical' antagonism between capitalists and rentiers.

It may be interesting to recall that, in his 'Introduction' to Ricardo's works (1951–73, Volume I, p. lvi, n. 3), Piero Sraffa hints at 'a gradual shift of emphasis from the antithesis of rent and profits to that of wages and profits' which, according to him, characterized Ricardo's theoretical research 'between the *Essay on Profits* and ed.3 of the *Principles*'. It seems clear from the general context in which the proposition is placed that Sraffa has here in mind the 'revolutionary change' introduced by Ricardo in edition 3 with 'the new chapter On Machinery in which [he] retracts his previous opinion that the introduction of machinery is beneficial to all the different classes of society' (ibid., p. lvii) and explicitly states 'that the opinion entertained by the labouring class, that the employment of machinery is frequently detrimental to their interests, is not founded on prejudice and error, but is conformable to the correct principles of political economy' (Ricardo 1951–73, Volume I, p. 392).

Although it is obvious that, in the context of chapter XXXI, Ricardo has in mind the 'antithesis' between capitalists and workers (from the specific viewpoint of the introduction of new productive techniques implying an intensified employment of machinery), Sraffa's proposition relating to the *gradual shift of emphasis* – even in its extremely careful wording – cannot be accepted as a correct representation of the development of Ricardo's theoretical research.

Having come to realize the potential distributive antagonism between capital and labour connected with the intensified employment of machinery – a specific antagonism which he had denied until the third edition of the *Principles* – certainly represents an evolution of Ricardo's thought. But to classify *this* evolution as a 'shift of emphasis' is misleading since this expression may convey the idea that the *whole* body of Ricardo's theory is shifting in focus from one type of analysis to another: from the study of the antagonism between rentiers and capitalists to that of 'the antithesis of wages and profits'. This would be a mistake.

The core of Ricardo's analysis, the main theme of his research, even in edition 3 of the *Principles* (and after, it must be added – see Caravale 1985, pp. 155–8) remains that of the relation between diminishing returns and the rate of profit; a relation whose definition would require that an adequate theory of prices be capable of eliminating the complications arising from the *differences* in the sectoral capital–labour ratios.

The question which forms the object of chapter XXXI of edition 3 (the consequences of *changes through time* in the ratio between machinery and labour) is 'added' to the above indicated body of thought. Although undoubtedly a crucial problem *per se*, it remains outside the main line of Ricardo's theoretical research: being clearly identified on the basis of a *ceteris paribus* condition and thus excluding, by definition, the analysis of diminishing returns, it is in fact placed on a totally different plane with respect to that of the main object of the Ricardian theory of value, distribution and growth.

In this latter theory, each 'state of the technology', i.e., each matrix of technological coefficients, implies – with a given natural real wage – a unique set of prices and of the rate of profit (Bortkiewicz 1952, esp. pp. 20–1; Sraffa 1960). With diminishing returns, that is with the assumption that the given real wage embodies in each year (or period) an increasing amount of labour, each new matrix of technological coefficients is associated, as I have recalled above, with a progressively lower level of the general rate of profit (Caravale and Tosato 1980, chapter 2): this is the meaning of the 'inverse relation' between the labour content of corn and the general rate of profit. (It may be worth emphasizing, although it should be evident, that this relationship holds true whatever may be the physical composition of the given wage basket, provided of course that only the agricultural components of the bundle are produced under conditions of diminishing returns, while non-agricultural goods are realized under constant technical conditions.)[10]

A change in the technical coefficients relating to the production of corn – that is, a new value of such coefficients – is thus associated with a whole new set of relative prices and with a new (lower) value of the rate of profit: changes in distribution are strictly connected with changes in the technical coefficients. Indeed, even when Ricardo seems to consider the possibility of changes in distribution *un*accompanied by changes in technology (e.g. Ricardo 1951–73, Volume I, p. 45; Volume IX, pp. 335–6; Volume IV, p. 403), he is actually considering a change in the relative price of two commodities – both produced in conditions of constant returns – brought about by a change in distribution, consequent upon a change in the production conditions of corn. Of course, this outcome depends crucially on the assumption that the two commodities (whose relative price has changed) are produced with different capital–labour ratios.

In the general version of the Ricardian model (the one in which differences in the sectoral capital–labour ratios are allowed for) an increase in the quantity of labour necessary for the production of corn is thus associated with:

a. a lower value of the general rate of profit and thus, for the 'classical savings function', with a progressive reduction in the rate of accumulation; and
b. with a whole set of new relative prices – the change of each one

> of these depending on the specific production conditions characterizing each pair of commodities as compared with those characterizing the commodity chosen as *numéraire* (Caravale and Tosato 1980, chapter 2 and appendix).

With the aid of contemporary analytical results, Ricardo's central problem thus finds a full-fledged solution.

It is, I believe, quite remarkable that Marx's interpretation of Ricardo, with no such aid, but drawing only on his capacity of capturing the essential features of Ricardo's theory 'directly' from his writings, should present striking similarities with the interpretation briefly outlined above.

In point of fact, Marx's interpretation is precisely based on the attribution of a central role to the notion of natural equilibrium, and on the emphasis laid on the systematic connection between changes in the technological coefficients (diminishing returns) and changes in distribution. Some relevant passages from Marx's work show this with great clarity:

> Ricardo defends the proposition that the permanent price is determined by the cost-price, and not by supply and demand . . . Provided that the prices of the commodities are so adjusted that they all yield a profit of 10 per cent, then every lasting change in these prices will be determined by a change . . . in the labour time required for their production. As this . . . continues to determine the general rate of profit, so the changes in it continue to determine the variations in cost-prices. If the productivity of labour decreases, the real values of the commodities rise . . . As a result of this variation, new cost-prices or, as Ricardo says, following Smith, new 'natural prices' take the place of the old. (1969, Volume II, pp. 213–15)

> Adam Smith explained the fall of the rate of profit, as capital grows, by the competition among capitals. To which Ricardo replied that competition can indeed reduce profits in the various branches of business to an average level, can equalize the rate, but cannot depress this average rate itself . . . Competition can permanently depress . . . the average rate of profit, if, and in so far as a general and permanent fall of the rate of profit, having the force of a law, is conceivable *prior to* competition and regardless of competition . . . Ricardo, for his part says: 'No accumulation of capitals can permanently reduce profits unless an equally permanent cause raises wages' . . . He finds this cause in the growing . . . unproductivity of agriculture, the growing difficulty of increasing the quantity of subsistence, i.e. in the growth of proportionate wages, so that labour's real wage is no greater, but the product obtains more labour; in a word, a greater portion of necessary labour is required for the production of agricultural products. The falling rate of profit hence corresponds, with him, to the nominal growth of wages and real growth of ground rent. (1977, pp. 751–2)

> The population grows and with it the demand for agricultural products. Therewith their price rises, as happens in similar cases in industry. But in industry, this rise in price ceases as soon as demand has become effective and brought about an increased supply of commodities. The product now falls to the old . . . level of value. But in agriculture this *additional product* . . . *costs more* and effects a constant rise in market-prices and along with that, a raising of rent. How is this to be explained if not by the fact that ever less fertile types of land are being used, that ever more labour is required in order to produce the same product, that agriculture becomes progressively more sterile? (1969, Volume II, p. 133)

The corner-stones of Marx's analytical interpretation of Ricardo are thus natural prices (natural equilibrium with a uniform rate of profit); the continuous change in the set of these prices as a consequence of the progressive decline in agricultural productivity, the reduction in the rate of profit following the working of diminishing returns in agriculture; and the distributive antagonism between capitalists and rentiers.

It is interesting to note that this interpretation differs widely from that suggested by some contemporary authors (e.g. Garegnani) who draw inspiration from Marx's 'constructive' work and tend to read Ricardo's theory mainly in terms of a distributive antagonism between capitalists and workers to the complete disregard of the role of rent and of the clash of interest between capitalists and rentiers (on this point see Caravale 1985). That this is by no means Marx's view is proved: (a) by the fact that Marx considered the theory of rent as an essential part of Ricardo's analytical scheme, and (b) by Marx's explicit recognition that the Ricardian theory is centred on the distributive antagonism between capitalists and rentiers:

> The entire Ricardian contribution is contained in the first two chapters [of the *Principles*, i.e. chapter I 'On Value' and chapter II 'On Rent'] . . . They contain the whole of his critique of hitherto existing political economy . . . and . . . produce some quite new and startling results. (Marx 1969, Volume II, p. 169)

> [Ricardo wanted] to explain the decline of profit . . . by the rising difficulty of [the] production [of agricultural goods] thereby at the same time to explain ground rent as not being in conflict with his determination of value. *This at the same time furnished a polemical weapon for industrial capital against . . . landed property*. (Marx 1977, p. 596, emphasis added)

Some implications

Before analysing some aspects of Marx's criticism of Ricardo, it is important to emphasize the implications that the above illustrated interpretation of Ricardo's theory has for some of the points that were later chosen by Marx as targets of his theoretical attack on Ricardo and that will be considered in the following section.

The role of the labour theory of value in Ricardo

The labour theory of value, it is here suggested, is relevant in Ricardo only *qua* theory of exchange and thus performs exclusively an analytical role.

Ricardo was not searching for a philosophical or metaphysical explanation of the causes of value, for the ultimate source of value. He wanted instead to define an analytically sound theory of exchange, capable of making it possible to define for the general case (in modern parlance, for a multisector model with different capital–labour ratios in the various sectors),[11] a direct and unambiguous inverse relationship between diminishing returns and the rate of profit – therefore with the pace of the accumulation process. Marx perceives the point with remarkable clarity:

> [Ricardo's] aim in asserting the [inverse] proportionality of wages and profits was not to get to the bottom of the creation of value . . . but rather . . . to explain . . . the continuing decline in the rate of profit . . . by the rise of wages, and the latter in turn by the rise in value of agricultural products, i.e. the rising difficulty of their production.[12] (1977, p. 596)

But while the goal was clearly identified by Ricardo, his journey towards it was neither easy nor totally successful. It was made up of successive steps: the so-called 'corn model' in a first stage; the labour theory of value in a second stage; the search for the 'invariable standard of value' in a third stage (the succession of these stages should not be interpreted, however, in a strictly chronological sense). In each of these last two stages his effort was to overcome the limitations of the previous one. The theoretical elaboration based on the labour theory of value is thus an attempt to generalize the sphere of validity of the conclusions reached within his corn model. The labour theory of value did attain a higher degree of validity with respect to that of the corn model (based on the assumption of physical coincidence between input and output in the sector producing the wage goods), but was still not general since it could apply only to the case of equal capital–labour ratios in the various sectors (or equivalent assumptions). Awareness of the limits of validity of this theory[13] led Ricardo to the lifelong and unsuccessful search of the invariable measure of value. It is now clear that this search could not be otherwise than unsuccessful: the problem as Ricardo posed it had no satisfactory solution in the sense that the 'standard measure' could have been defined only if conditions occurred that made it possible to do without it (this point is clarified in Caravale and Tosato 1980, chapter 3).

But Ricardo neither fully realized this circumstance (which led him to continue his misdirected theoretical efforts on this ground until the very last days of his life), nor the fact that his schema contained all the elements which were necessary to reach the rigorous conclusions he was aiming at.[14] He therefore was consciously obliged to 'settle' on approximate conclusions, and *de facto*, his analytical discourse remained at the level of intuitions – which does not mean in the least that his schema was faulty or incomplete.

The relation between relative labour quantities and relative natural prices

The problem of the relation, for Ricardo, between relative labour quantities and relative natural prices can now be seen more clearly. It is the relation between one theory of exchange – clearly defined but valid only under the very special circumstance of equal ratios between capital and labour in all sectors – and one (searched for) theory of exchange not subject to this limitation. It is in other words the problem arising from the effort to overcome such limitation. From this viewpoint it may be said that this problem is, so to speak, a 'technical' one. The divergence between the two systems (due to the presence of different capital–labour ratios in the various sectors) does open a serious problem – but only because this circumstance obfuscates the connection between the phenomenon of diminishing returns and the rate of profit. In this perspective, the search for a systematic connection between the two systems of relative prices finds no room in Ricardo's theoretical research. Even if, *per absurdum*, it would have been possible to find it, this would not have allowed *per se* (i.e., if not accompanied by the definition of the inverse relation between diminishing returns and the rate of profit) any real progress in Ricardo's analytical efforts.

The concepts of natural prices and of the rate of profit

Ricardo's theory is centred upon very clearly stated notions of natural prices and of the rate of profit.

As to the first point, Ricardo makes it clear that he identifies the notions of 'natural price', 'cost of production', and 'value':

> Mr Malthus appears to think that it is part of my doctrine, that cost and value of a thing should be the same; – it is, if he means by cost, 'cost of production including profits'. (1951–73, Volume I, p. 47)

> Mr Malthus accuses me of confounding the very important distinction between cost and value. If by cost, Mr Malthus means . . . cost of

> production, he must include profits as well as labour; he must mean what Adam Smith calls natural price, which is synonymous with value. (1951–73, Volume II, pp. 34–5)

> By cost of production I invariably mean wages and profits, Adam Smith includes rent . . . In truth then in the cost of production of all agricultural produce there is no rent, for the value of that produced from the capital last employed yields a compensation for wages, and a compensation for profits of capital, but no compensation for rent. In this sense only do I differ from Adam Smith. (Ibid., pp. 42–5)

Like Sraffa, 150 years later, Ricardo thus defines natural prices as equal to the cost of production, and makes this cost equal to the *sum* of two component parts: wages and profits. It is therefore clear that Ricardo cannot be said to have opposed a Smith-type 'adding-up' approach in a literal sense. His criticism of Smith's theory of prices related in fact only to the idea of the independent determination of the rate of profit and of the rate of wages (so that a rise in wages would invariably determine an increase in prices without affecting the rate of profit). In other words, when Ricardo spoke of Adam Smith's 'original error respecting value' (1951–73, Volume II, p. 100) he could not have in mind the presence of various component parts of the natural price, but only the lack of interdependence between these parts.

On the other hand, the rate of profit is, in Ricardo's theory, the ratio of absolute profits to the total capital advanced by the capitalists.[15] This is the crucial variable of the model; it is in fact either proportional or identical to the rate of accumulation, and therefore its magnitude determines the pace at which the economic system proceeds. Ricardo's theory cannot be understood in full if it is not seen as an effort to arrive at a general definition of the rate of profit (through a general theory of prices) – in turn a logical premise to the analysis of the path followed by it over time. The capital advanced by the capitalists consists only of wage goods in the corn model but also of other means of production in the following stages. A great part of the theoretical problems Ricardo had to face (as he explicitly emphasizes in the chapter 'On Value') derived from this circumstance. In fact, it is precisely the presence of non-wage capital that opens for Ricardo the theoretical problem he tries to solve with his reference to the labour theory of value in one stage, and with the search for the invariable measure of value in another stage.

Differences and changes

The presence of differences in the capital–labour ratios in the various productive sectors – which is the 'norm' in the real world – implies that, in the face of a change in the productive conditions of the wage goods consequent upon diminishing returns (which is in turn likely to imply a change in the nominal, or money wage rate given the real wage), the whole set of relative prices would change, thus severely complicating the analysis of the effects of the reduction of labour productivity in agriculture on the rate of profit. Clearly, this complication would not arise in the case of equal 'time structures', or capital–labour ratios, in the various sectors. A change in the productive conditions of the wage goods, i.e., an increase in the labour embodied in the given basket representing the real wage, would, *in this case*, leave relative prices equal to relative labour quantities, and display its effect directly in terms of a reduction in the general rate of profit.

The 'question of the differences' (recognition of the fact that natural prices in general do not coincide with the ratios between quantities of labour as a consequence of the difference in capital–labour ratios) and the 'question of changes' (the effects on prices of a change in distribution due to the reduction in the productivity of agricultural labour) are nothing but the two sides of the same coin.[16] In fact, in the general case (different sectoral capital–labour ratios), changes in distribution are always in Ricardo the consequence of a change in the technical conditions of production in the agricultural sector when relative natural prices diverge – because of the differences in capital–labour ratios – from relative quantities of labour.[17]

As has been emphasized above (pp. 174–6), the question of the change *through time* of the capital–labour ratios in the economy represents a totally different problem. Although extremely important in itself, this question finds, in Ricardo's general scheme of reference, only a marginal position (its treatment in chapter XXXI of edition 3 of the *Principles* is in fact independent of the problem of diminishing returns and is placed in a frame of reference which is different from that of the rest of the work).

Marx's critique of Ricardo

Marx's critical evaluation of Ricardo's theory runs through all of Marx's writings (Volume II of his *Theories of Surplus Value* (TSV) has however a special relevance in this respect) and touches upon several aspects of the Ricardian analytical construction. Here I shall briefly deal with a few (strictly interrelated) points:

a. the relation between prices of production and 'values';
b. the question of differences vs. changes;
c. the relation between the rate of profit and the rate of surplus value (i.e., the treatment of non-wage capital);

d. the role of the 'luxury sector'; and
e. the question of the resolution of prices into revenues.

These points have been examined in the literature (see, for example, Bortkiewicz 1952 and Steedman 1982). Reference to what appears to be the proper dynamic perspective of Ricardo's theory allows however, on the one hand, a more complete and accurate evaluation of the analytical foundation of Marx's criticism, and shows, on the other, the contradiction existing between this criticism and Marx's correct interpretation of Ricardo in the sense indicated above.

Prices and values

The relation between prices of production and 'values' Marx criticizes Ricardo for identifying values and 'cost-prices' (as he calls natural prices in TSV) or 'prices of production' (as he calls them in Volume III of *Capital*). The point is made repeatedly in TSV.

For instance, Marx, notwithstanding the quotation of the passage in which Ricardo clearly states that by 'value' he means 'cost of production', attributes to Ricardo

> the erroneous confusion of cost-prices and values, which he has himself refuted. (Marx 1969, Volume II, p. 199)

and writes:

> Ricardo . . . overlooks the fact that he has paid no regard at all to the constant deviations of market prices in so far as they correspond to cost-prices, from the real values and that he has substituted cost-price for value. (Marx 1969, Volume II, p. 213)

> the error Ricardo committed . . . in Chapter I 'On Value', where he identified cost-price and value. (Ibid., p. 208)

As it should be clear, there is no confusion in Ricardo who calls 'value' the natural price, or the cost of production. The confusion is in the interpretation given by Marx, who attributes to Ricardo the same meaning that the word 'value' has in his own (Marx's) writings – the labour embodied in each commodity or the relative labour quantities of any two commodities.

It can thus be said, with Bortkiewicz (1952, p. 28) that '[we] cannot . . . agree with Marx when he objects against Ricardo – as he does on innumerable occasions – that the latter had confused prices with values'.[18]

Natural prices, market prices, and relative labour quantities Marx criticizes Ricardo for not being clear enough about the distinction between the 'values'/prices of production relation (the transformation problem) on the one hand, and the natural prices/market prices relation on the other. According to Marx, Ricardo concentrates his attention on the latter relation and ignores the former:

> persistent deviations of the market-price from the cost-price . . . will bring about new migrations . . . of social capital. The first . . . occurs in order to establish cost-prices which differ from values. The second . . . occurs in order to equalize . . . market-prices with the cost-prices . . . The first is a transformation of the values into cost-prices. The second is a rotation of market-prices around the cost-price which now appears as the natural price, although it is . . . only the result of social action. It is this latter, more superficial movement which Ricardo examines. (Marx 1969, Volume II, p. 209)

Ricardo is instead crystal clear about the point raised by Marx. It is evident from the discussion made above as to the role of the labour theory of value that Ricardo has a very clear conception of the relation between natural prices, relative labour quantities, and market prices.

Ricardo in fact emphasizes, against Smith, that even after the accumulation of capital relative natural prices – called also 'values' by Ricardo – do not necessarily differ from relative labour quantities (what Marx calls 'values'). In other words, that even with positive profits it *may* happen, *under specific circumstances*, that relative natural prices coincide with relative quantities of labour. *These specific circumstances*, Ricardo then argues, *are not those that prevail in general; therefore relative natural prices do not necessarily, and do not, in general, coincide with relative labour quantities*.

Whatever natural prices may be, that is whether they coincide or not with relative labour quantities, they represent the centre of gravity for market prices which tend (through the mechanism of supply and demand described by Smith) to converge towards them.

It makes no sense to speak of a transformation problem for Ricardo in the sense of Marx. The presence of different capital–labour ratios creates serious problems in both Ricardo's and Marx's theory, because exchange ratios between commodities no longer coincide with relative labour quantities. There is however a profound difference in the meaning that these problems have in the two theoretical contexts.

In Marx, as he emphasizes explicitly, they consist of '*the essential question*' (Marx 1969, Volume II, p. 192) of the transformation of values into prices of production (or cost-prices):

> [In general] the *prices* of the commodities [are] different from their *values*. The sum total of these *cost-prices* of all the commodities taken together will be *equal to their value*. Similarly the total profit will be equal to the total surplus value . . . If one did not take the definition of value as the basis, the *average profit*, and therefore also the cost-prices would be purely imaginary and untenable. The equalization of the surplus-values in different spheres of production does not affect the absolute size of this total surplus-value; but merely alters its *distribution* among the different spheres of production. The *determination of this surplus-value* itself, however, only arises out of the determination of value by labour-time. Without this, the average profit is the average *of nothing*, pure fancy. (1969, Volume II, p. 190)

> Cost-prices remain unintelligible without values determined by labour-time. (Ibid., p. 194)

> The capitalists, like hostile brothers, divide among themselves the loot of other people's labour which they have appropriated so that on an average one receives the same amount of unpaid labour as another. Competition achieves this equalization by regulating average prices. These average prices . . . are either above or below the value of the commodity so that no commodity yields a higher rate of profit than any other . . . Competition among capitals brings about a general rate of profit *by converting the values of their commodities into average prices, in which a part of surplus value is transferred from one commodity to another*. (Ibid., pp. 29–30)

The possibility of even conceiving the central Marxian concepts of c, v, and s depends therefore on the solution of the transformation problem. In fact, since what 'appears' in a capitalist economic system is the set of 'cost-prices' characterized by a uniform rate of profit, the solution of the transformation problem performs the vital role of proving that the 'essence' of capitalist reality can be portrayed in terms of such concepts.[19] 'All science', Marx wrote (1981, Volume III, p. 797), 'would be superfluous if the outward appearance and the essence of things directly coincided.' In particular:

> Surplus value and the rate of surplus value are . . . the invisible and unknown essence to be investigated, whereas the rate of profit and hence the form of surplus value as profit are visible surface phenomena. (1981, Volume III, p. 134)

> profit is a transformed form of surplus value, a form in which its origin and the secret of its existence are veiled and obliterated. In point of fact, profit is the form of appearance of surplus value, and the latter can be sifted out of the former only by analysis. (Ibid., p. 139)

In Ricardo, instead, the problem – as it was pointed out above – amounts to that of defining a theory of natural prices capable of making it possible to draw the general conclusion that diminishing returns invariably tend to lower the rate of profit and thus the pace of the accumulation process.

In the former case, the basic concepts of the theoretical construction are at stake; in the latter, it is the need to overcome what appeared as a problem of circularity. And, as we can say now with the benefit of hindsight, the difference is also emphasized by the fact that the former problem does not seem to admit a solution *in the sense of Marx* (see, for example, Desai 1991; Napoleoni 1991; Steedman 1977), while the latter admits a perfectly general solution (Caravale and Tosato 1980).[20]

Differences and changes

A related aspect of Marx's criticism refers to the so-called question of differences and changes. Marx in fact criticizes Ricardo for having concentrated his attention on the 'changes' in distribution to the neglect of the 'differences' between prices and 'values' (the expression with which he indicated relative labour quantities). For example:

> If Ricardo had gone into this more deeply, he would have found that . . . the mere existence of a general rate of profit necessitates cost-prices that differ from values. He would have found that, even if wages are assumed to remain constant, the difference exists and therefore is quite independent of the rise or fall in wages . . . He would also have seen how incomparably more important and decisive the understanding of this difference is for the whole theory than his observations on the variation in cost-prices of commodities brought about by the rise or fall of wages. (1969, Volume II, pp. 175–6)

In order to evaluate Marx's criticism on this ground, it is useful to recall – even at the cost of some repetition (see above, pp. 181–2) – the reason why Ricardo, to use Marx's expression, concentrated his attention on the question of the changes. His primary concern, it has been pointed out, is the construction of a theory capable of explaining, in the general case, that the fall in labour productivity associated with the cultivation of progressively poorer lands (diminishing returns) implies a continuous decline in the rate of profit and hence of accumulation. In particular, he wants to clarify what are the effects, on relative prices and on the rate of profit, of changes in the productive conditions of wage goods. Since, for Ricardo agricultural goods represent the whole or at least the greater portion of the wage basket, this change will presumably result in an increase of the money wage rate, given the real wage, consequent upon the rise of agricultural prices – hence his use of the expression 'changes in distribution'. In order to do so he needs to emphasize that, in general, the situation is more complex than in the simple case in which the labour theory of value is valid. In this latter case – that is when the capital–labour ratios are equal in the various sectors – any change in the productive conditions of the wage goods (as it was pointed out above) will reflect itself directly in a change of rate of profit, while the exchange ratios between commodities continue to be regulated by the relative quantities of labour embodied in them. In the general case, i.e., when there are *differences* in the sectoral capital–labour ratios, and consequently relative natural prices *differ* from relative labour quantities, the picture becomes more complicated. The change in the productive conditions of the wage goods implies, in fact, a change in the whole set of natural prices, and in a sense obfuscates the effects on the rate of profit.

The difficulties that Ricardo encounters in the effort to reach his basic theoretical aim must not prevent us from pointing out that Ricardo has clearly seen the analytical terms of the problem, and that, in his schema, the two questions (that of the 'differences' and that of the 'changes') are strictly related to one another; as it has been said above, they are the two sides of the same coin. Marx's criticism of Ricardo on this ground is therefore founded on Marx's misunderstanding.

The treatment of 'non-wage' capital

Another criticism addressed by Marx to Ricardo is that he ignored the existence of 'non-wage' capital at the aggregate level and thus confused, or wrongly identified, the rate of profit with the rate of surplus value. For example, Marx writes:

> In his observations on profit and wages, Ricardo . . . abstracts from the constant part of capital, which is not laid out in wages. He treats the matter as though the entire capital were laid out directly in wages. To this extent, therefore, he considers surplus value and not profit . . . When we speak of his theory of surplus value we are therefore speaking of his theory of profit, in so far as he only considers profit in relation to variable capital, the part of capital laid out in wages . . . Ricardo treats the entire capital as variable capital and abstracts from constant capital, although he occasionally mentions it in the form of advances. (1969, Volume II, pp. 373–4)

> If the capital advanced consisted only of variable capital . . . then Ricardo would be right . . . a presupposition which pervades all his, and Adam Smith's observations regarding the capital of society as a whole, but in capitalist production this precondition does not exist in a single branch of industry, much less in . . . society as a whole. (Ibid., p. 414)

> Ricardo wrongly identifies surplus value with profits . . . while these are only identical in so far as the total capital consists of variable capital or is laid out directly in wages. (Ibid., p. 426)

On the first question – the 'abstraction' from non-wage capital and the relation between the rate of profit and the rate of surplus value – the evaluation of Marx's criticism can be conducted both on the ground of exegesis[21] and of that of logic. In this latter perspective, which is of crucial importance, it should be remembered:

a. that Ricardo's efforts to generalize his schema (through the labour theory of value first, and with the search for the invariable standard of value later on) stemmed precisely from his open recognition of the existence of non-wage capital at the aggregate level;
b. that Ricardo's analysis of the complex problems deriving from the presence of different capital–labour ratios would remain largely incomprehensible in the case of absence of non-wage capital.

In this latter case, relative natural prices would coincide with relative labour quantities, and a highly significant part of Ricardo's theoretical work would be meaningless. It is not only a matter of obviously recognizing that 'in nineteenth century England constant capital was being used' (De Vivo 1982, p. 91), it is a matter of logic.[22]

The 'luxury sector'

Another connected criticism of Ricardo on the part of Marx relates to the role of the 'luxury sector'.

It is well known that Ricardo maintained that the conditions of production of those commodities that do not enter in the wage bundle have no influence on the rate of profit, i.e., that only the conditions of production of wage goods are relevant for the determination of the general rate of profit:

> Suppose [that] the price of silks, velvets, furniture and any other commodities not required by the labourer, to rise in consequence of more labour being expended on them, would not that affect profits? Certainly not: for nothing can affect profits but a rise in wages; silks and velvets are not consumed by the labourer, and therefore cannot raise wages. (Ricardo 1951–73, Volume I, p. 118)

Marx criticizes this proposition arguing that the conditions of production of every single commodity in the economy are relevant in the determination of the general rate of profit:

> The rate of profit in these particular spheres of production [those in which the change of the productive conditions has occurred] would certainly fall . . . And the general rate of profit consists of the average of the particular rates of profit in all branches. (Marx 1969, Volume II, p. 431)

According to Marx, the conditions of production of all commodities, whether or not they are wage goods, influence the general rate of profit through the influence they exert on the organic composition of capital of the economy considered as a whole. Marx believes then Ricardo's thesis to be false and to be based on the 'confusion' of the rates of profit and of surplus value. Only for the latter would Ricardo's argument hold (but not for the former, which is the arithmetical average of the rates of profit in individual branches of production) since all capitals representing the total social capital play their part in the formation of that average, and therefore also those capitals which are employed in the production of luxury goods.

The analytical incorrectness of Marx's position – and the full validity of Ricardo's position – has been shown by Bortkiewicz (1952, pp. 32–3), who emphasizes in particular how Marx's errors, 'namely a confusion of values and prices, . . . led [him] to his erroneous construction of the general rate of profit, and thence to his unjustified attack on Ricardo's thesis, the essential significance of which cannot be rated sufficiently highly' (ibid., p. 33):

> The rate of profit depends *only* on those amounts of labour and those turnover periods which concern the production . . . of the goods forming the real wage rate. This theoretical result agrees entirely with Ricardo's thesis that the rate of profit cannot possibly be affected by the conditions of production of those goods which do not enter into real wages.[23] (Ibid., p. 32)

While this result is just another way of expressing Ricardo's own conception of the dependence of profit on *wages* (referred to above, see p. 173) – to be understood as 'the number of days' work, necessary to obtain [the number of] pounds [necessary in turn to obtain the basket of goods representing the given real wage]' (Ricardo 1951–73, Volume I, p. 143) – it seems useless to attempt a defence of Marx on this point based on the idea (which has been critically discussed above) that since 'Ricardo confused the rate of profits with the rate of surplus value' (De Vivo 1982, p. 197), 'Marx's critique of Ricardo on the luxury sector . . . derives from his seeing a problem which Ricardo had not even noticed' (ibid.).

The 'resolution' of prices into revenues

Marx also criticizes Ricardo for accepting Smith's thesis of the resolution of prices into revenues and argues that this may be true only if non-wage capital is ignored.

While Steedman (1982, pp. 128ff.) has conclusively shown that this is not true,[24] it seems important to stress that, in Ricardo's theory, natural prices are defined as the sum of two component parts (contrary to what happens in Smith's analysis, these two parts are, however, not determined independently of one another). The notion of natural prices, therefore, cannot be employed to suggest, even in the most indirect of ways, that in the last analysis 'value' is 'made of', so to speak, one element only

It is also interesting to note that Marx, in chapter 49 of book III of *Capital* ('On the Analysis of the Production Process') comes very close to indicate what was then proved to be (Bortkiewicz 1952, pp. 19–20; Sraffa 1960, pp. 34–40) the correct procedure for the resolution of prices into a sum of revenues.[25]

In fact Marx, setting out to analyse 'the absurd dogma that has pervaded all political economy since Adam Smith . . . that the value of commodities can be ultimately broken down into wages, profit and rent' (1981, Volume III, p. 980) concedes that, while it is 'extremely easy . . . in the case of the individual capitalist, to see that one part of his product must be transformed back into . . . constant capital which can never be transformed into income' (ibid.), 'the difficulty begins . . . when the production process is considered as a whole' (ibid.). This is because in this case 'the value of the entire part of the product that is consumed as revenue . . . actually disappears completely . . . into the sum of value formed from wages plus profit plus rent, i.e., into the total value of the three revenues' (ibid.). The difficulty cannot be overcome, Marx continues, by claiming 'that it is only from the standpoint of the individual capitalist that commodity value appears to contain a further portion of value [that of the constant capital contained in it] distinct from that existing in the form of revenue'.

What appears as an 'insoluble riddle' ('how the value of the product of each individual capital can be equal to the value sum of the three revenues plus . . . the constant capital, while the combined value sum of the products of all capitals together equals the value sum of the three revenues plus 0', ibid., p. 981) can be explained by saying, Marx emphasizes, that:

> analysis is quite incapable of catching hold of the simple elements of price and must instead satisfy itself with a vicious circle and an infinite regress. So what appears as constant capital is reducible to wages, profit and rent, but the commodity values in which wages, profit and rent are expressed are determined in turn by wages, profit and rent, and so *ad infinitum*.[26] (Ibid., p. 981)

The whole matter seems in fact a good example of 'rational reconstruction' in the sense of Rorty (1984) in which we could imagine Marx being 'brought to accept' the results reached by others along a line of thought indicated (though hesitantly) by him (see above p. 169–72), and being 'led' to correct his evaluation of Ricardo on this ground.

Some contradictory aspects of Marx's criticism of Ricardo

The preceding argument shows that, on the one hand, the interpretation that Marx gives of Ricardo (in the sense of the theoretical model that the former attributes to the latter) is to be considered correct in the light of modern economic analysis; while, on the other hand, the pungent critiques that Marx addresses to Ricardo appear analytically unfounded, when they are analysed in the light of modern economic results.

It seems interesting therefore to pose the question of the compatibility between these two different aspects of Marx's views on Ricardo in order to emphasize that Marx's criticism is in a certain sense surprising. When interpreting Ricardo, Marx was in fact perfectly clear on a number of aspects of this latter's theory – a circumstance which could have induced him to a greater prudence in his criticism of Ricardo. I wish to mention briefly some aspects that appear of special interest for the discussion carried out in the preceding part of this chapter.

In the first place, as regards the role of the theory of prices in Ricardo, and therefore also the function of the labour theory of value, Marx shows that he is perfectly aware that Ricardo's aim was not that of identifying the ultimate source of value, but rather that of defining a general theory of prices on the basis of which the inverse relation between diminishing returns and the rate of profit could be identified:

> [Ricardo's] aim in asserting the [inverse] proportionality of wages and profits was not to get to the bottom of the creation of value . . . but rather . . . to explain . . . the continuing decline in the rate of profit . . . by the rise of wages, and the latter in turn by the rise in value of agricultural products, i.e., the rising difficulty in their production.[27] (Marx 1977, p. 596)

The point is obviously connected with Marx's criticism of Ricardo on the question of the *changes*. The above-quoted passage reveals in fact Marx's clear perception that the core of Ricardo's theory is the analysis of the effects that changes in the productive conditions of the wage goods (which Ricardo often termed changes in distribution) had on the rate of profit and therefore on the pace of the accumulation process.

Criticizing Ricardo for his 'excessive' attention to the problem of *changes* (to the neglect of the *differences* between prices of production and what Marx called 'values', i.e., relative labour quantities) was, on the part of Marx, tantamount to forgetting his precise perception –

shown without any ambiguity, for example, in the passage quoted above – of the central theme of Ricardo's analytical concern.

Marx also shows his clear understanding of the relation, in Ricardo, between natural prices (or prices of production) and relative labour quantities:

> Ricardo [says that] the permanent price is determined by the cost-price and not by supply and demand: that therefore *the permanent price is determined by the value only in so far as this value determines the cost-price*. (1969, Volume II, pp. 213–15)

It is thus clear that Marx was perfectly aware that:

a. The centre of gravity in Ricardo's theory is represented by natural prices ('cost-prices', in Marx's terminology of TSV) determined by the dominant conditions of production (at the margin), and not by market prices, determined by supply and demand.
b. In Ricardo's analysis, natural prices do not necessarily coincide with relative labour quantities (which Marx calls 'values'). In the light of Marx's own discussion of Ricardo's first chapter of the *Principles* in TSV, it may be added, Marx had also a very lucid perception of the fact that in Ricardo's framework, relative natural prices coincide with relative labour quantities ('values') if, and only if, the capital–labour ratios are equal in the various productive sectors. Again, criticizing Ricardo for having neglected the difference between natural prices and 'values' (relative quantities of labour) and for having concentrated his attention on the distinction between natural prices and market prices amounts, on the part of Marx, to having forgotten what he had written in a different part of his work.

Several passages of Marx's writings show that Marx had also perfectly understood:

a. the basic role that, in Ricardo's analytical framework, the *differences* in capital–labour ratios play in determining the *differences* between natural prices and 'values' (that is, relative quantities of labour);
b. that these *differences* play an important role in the analysis of the effects determined, on prices, by *changes* in 'distribution';
c. that a major part of Ricardo's theory cannot be understood without reference to 'non-wage' capital.

He writes for instance, with reference to the first chapter of Ricardo's *Principles*:

> In Section III of the First Chapter Ricardo explains that the statement: the value of the commodity is determined by labour-time includes not only the labour directly employed on the commodity in the final labour process but also the labour time contained in the raw material and the instruments of labour that are required for the production of the commodity. Thus *it applies not only to the labour-time contained in the newly-added labour which has been bought, paid for by wages, but also to the labour-time contained in that part of the commodity which I call constant capital.* (Marx 1969, Volume II, p. 137, emphasis added)

Marx continues:

> In [a following] Section he [Ricardo] examines the modifications arising from the varying proportions in which fixed capital enters into the commodities . . . He [then] asks himself what effect the rise or fall of wages will have on capitals with different period of turnover and containing different proportions of the various forms of capital. And here of course he finds that depending on the amount of fixed capital, etc., a rise or fall of wages must have a very different effect on capitals, according to whether they contain a greater or lesser proportion of variable capital, i.e., capital which is laid out directly in wages. Thus in order . . . to re-establish the general rate of profit, the prices of the commodities – as distinct from their values [that is from their relative quantities of labour] – must be regulated in a different way. (Ibid., pp. 173–5).
>
> Thus we have: 1. A difference in the proportion of fixed to circulating capital. 2. A difference in the period of turnover of circulating capital . . . 3. A difference in the durability of fixed capital. 4. A difference in the . . . period during which a commodity is . . . subjected to the labour-process . . . before it can enter the actual circulation process . . . But *how is a change in the relative values of these commodities brought about by this difference?* . . . Ricardo says . . . that 'this difference and variety in the proportions introduce another cause, besides the greater or less quantity of labour . . . ' for the variations in their relative value – this cause is the rise or fall in the value of labour . . . [In fact, Ricardo says that] a rise in the wages of labour cannot fail to affect unequally, commodities produced under such different circumstances'.[29] (Marx 1969, Volume II, pp. 178–9)

What have been here called, for shorthand purposes, 'capital–labour ratios' are, in this passage, specified by Marx in all the forms indicated by Ricardo. This is, moreover, considered by Marx an important contribution of Ricardo to political economy:[29]

> It must be regarded as a great merit that Ricardo associates the differences in fixed and circulating capital with the varying periods of turnover of capital

> and that he deduces all these differences from the varying periods of circulation . . . of capital. (Marx 1969, Volume III, p. 176)

Once more the criticism addressed to Ricardo by Marx on the points here considered seems to imply a lack of co-ordination between different parts of Marx's writings.

Conclusion – the 'continuity thesis'

In addition to the issues briefly analysed above, Marx's criticism of Ricardo touches upon other themes which cannot receive adequate attention here (of particular importance is the conception of labour and wages in the two theories).

The argument developed so far, supplies nonetheless some elements for a provisional evaluation of what can be called the 'continuity thesis'. This thesis, that is the idea that Ricardo's and Marx's analyses are nothing but successive developments of the *same* theory, has been recently put forward with reference to quite different (indeed opposite) theoretical contexts – the 'surplus approach' (e.g. Garegnani 1981) on the one hand, and the general equilibrium theory (Hollander 1981, 1987) on the other. Briefly, a few points can perhaps be suggested.

The 'surplus approach' interpretation of the continuity thesis The basic features of the 'surplus approach' interpretation of the continuity thesis (Garegnani 1981, 1984 – who draws also on Dobb, 1973) seem to be: (i) the idea that the labour theory of value performs exactly the same role in Ricardo and in Marx; (ii) identification of the core of the theoretical construction (of both theories) in the distributive antagonism between capitalists and workers:

> The labour theory of value performs in Marx essentially the same role it had performed in Ricardo. The role is that of making it possible, in the only way practically feasible at the time, the determination of the profit rate within the classical approach avoiding the vicious circle in which the theory risked to remain entangled in Adam Smith and his immediate successors. In the terms often used by Marx, the role is to bring to light that 'intimate connection' of bourgeois economic relations, and in particular the 'inverse relation between wages and profits on capital' that reveals how 'the interests of capital and the interests of labour [are] diametrically opposed'. (Garegnani 1981, pp. 55–6, my translation)

I have tried elsewhere (Caravale 1985, pp. 166ff.) to show that the 'surplus approach' interpretation of Ricardo ('for which the real wage and the social product are given when determining the rate of profit and relative prices' – Garegnani 1981, p. 311) seems incapable of capturing the essence of Ricardo's theory. In fact, on the methodological plane, it can be said that, in the light of Sraffa's price equation method, the rate of profit (whether in a context in which changes in the technological coefficients are explicitly taken into consideration, or in a context with a given technological matrix) is in fact determined simultaneously with prices so that the requisites of Garegnani's theory of the 'core' are no longer met. In addition to this, the preceding discussion (notably pp. 178 ff. above) supplies us with further elements for the evaluation of the two basic tenets of this version of the continuity thesis.

a. In the first place, this discussion emphasizes the existence of a profound difference in the role performed by the labour theory of value in Ricardo and in Marx. In Ricardo the role of the labour theory, as we have seen, is an analytical one: that of making it possible to identify a rule of exchange between commodities on the basis of which the inverse relation between diminishing returns in agriculture and the rate of profit could be brought to light without ambiguities. (As soon as Ricardo realizes that the objective was only reached because of the special assumptions on which the labour theory is based, he tries, however unsuccessfully, other solutions, such as the search for the invariable standard of value.) In Marx, on the other hand, the labour theory of value performs the much more vital role of supplying the foundation of the crucial theoretical concepts on which his whole theory is based (*c*, *v*, *s*) and of 'revealing' the essence of capitalism behind the 'facts' (profit rate uniformity and disproportionality between prices of production and relative labour quantities). The circumstance that, as we now know on the basis of the works of Dmitriev, Bortkiewicz and Sraffa, the determination of prices and of the rate of profit can be reached with *no* prior knowledge of 'values'; and the fact that the passage from 'values' to prices of production cannot be realized in the sense of Marx, have therefore much more serious implications for Marx than for Ricardo. An analytical tool can be substituted by a better, more general, one. The very foundation of the basic concepts of a theory is not so easy to replace.[30]
b. On the other hand, the identification of a continuity between Ricardo and Marx on the ground of the distributive antagonism between capitalists and workers appears incorrect. I have tried to show elsewhere (Caravale 1985, 1988a) that, in Ricardo's theory, the central antagonism is not that between capitalists and labourers, but rather that between capitalists and rentiers, which is, in a certain sense, 'hidden' behind the inverse relation between diminishing

returns (i.e., the increase in the amount of labour embodied in the *given* wage bundle) and the rate of profit.

A certain amount of confusion is due to the fact that Ricardo often speaks of 'changes in distribution' or 'changes in wages', when referring to the worsening of the technical conditions of production of the wage goods. But, as has been pointed out above (see p. 174), the true 'core' of Ricardo's theory is the inverse relation between the labour content of 'corn' and the rate of profit. Clearly, if the wage basket consists only of corn, the worsening of the productive conditions in agriculture implies an increase in the *money* wage rate (given the real wage); and if agricultural commodities represent the greatest portion of the wage bundle it is *likely* that diminishing returns will reflect themselves, again, in an increase in the number of 'money' units needed to buy the same amount of goods constituting the real wage. But the increase in the money wage rate is not a *necessary* effect of diminishing returns. What counts then is the circumstance that the increase in the amount of labour embodied in the given real wage entails the consequence of a decrease in the rate of profit and of an increase in rent. The distributive antagonism is thus between capitalists and landowners, while workers – with a *given* real wage rate – are, so to speak, 'neutral' with respect to those changes.

This circumstance clearly marks, by itself, a profound difference between Ricardo and Marx; but there is more to add, since the Marx-type distributive antagonism would find substantially no room in Ricardo's theory. The analysis of alternative distributive set-ups, in given technical or productive conditions, appears illegitimate within Ricardo's framework of natural equilibrium and opens at the same time insoluble problems from an analytical point of view. On the one hand, it would in fact imply the total neglect of the central phenomenon of diminishing returns (thus disconnecting the analysis of distribution from the laws of motion of the system); on the other hand, the analysis of alternative distributive set-ups is incompatible with the assumption that the situation is given. This analysis would in fact imply either a different matrix of technical coefficients or a different set of initial conditions: the 'initial' inverse *w-r* relation, as pointed out above (see p. 174) would no longer exist (not even in the 'weak' sense of an abstractedly definable path – one along which it would be 'concretely' impossible to move along, for the reasons indicated in Caravale, 1988b). Movements *along* such an inverse relation could therefore not even be imagined.[31]

A parenthesis – abstract labour, concrete labour, and the notion of exploitation The idea that Marx's work represents the continuation and the development of Ricardo's analysis is stressed again by Garegnani in a recent paper (Garegnani 1986, especially pp. 173–4 and 179–85). In this paper, following a line indicated in his previous writings, Garegnani also dwells upon the relation between Marx's labour theory of value and the notion of exploitation. Arguing against the thesis that in Marx this notion *depends* on the labour theory of value, Garegnani emphasizes that the idea of such dependence derives its plausibility from the frequent and erroneous confusion between 'concrete labour' and 'abstract labour' – two concepts that Marx had kept quite distinct in his analysis.

Garegnani recalls that Marx, following Ricardo's distinction between 'value' and 'riches' in chapter XX of the *Principles*, maintained that the creation of (exchangeable) value cannot be confused with the creation of wealth, so that the fact that labour is the 'only source of value' does *not* imply that labour is the only source of riches. 'The first proposition,' writes Garegnani (ibid., pp. 175–6), 'only implies that . . . the quantities of labour necessary to produce the [different] commodities allow a correct determination of the exchange ratios between them . . . That proposition does not deny therefore that natural forces, alone or through the use of means of production, participate in the production of wealth – a thesis upon which Marx insisted emphatically.' Now, Garegnani concludes, the thesis according to which exploitation of labour in capitalist economies derives from the labour theory of value interprets this latter theory in the sense that labour is the sole source of wealth thus confounding '*abstract* labour' which explains the exchange values, and '*concrete* labour' which instead produces wealth, but only together with natural forces and means of production.

The point is important and deserves some comments.

a. It is perfectly true that Marx draws a very clear distinction between *abstract labour* and *concrete labour* viewing the former as the *only* cause of the exchangeable *value* and the latter as *one of the* 'forces' that create *wealth* (or value in use) – the other ones are nature and means of production.[32] It is on the basis of this distinction (emphasized throughout his *Critique of Political Economy* and then introduced in *Capital* from the very first pages of the very first chapter as a sort of hallmark of his magnum opus) that Marx criticizes both the draft programme of the German Workers' Party (the Gotha Program) and the position taken by the Ricardian Socialists:

> Labour is . . . not the only source of material wealth, i.e., of the use

> values it produces. As William Petty says, labour is the father of material wealth, the earth is its mother. (Marx 1981, Volume I, p. 134)

> Labour is *not the source* of all wealth. Nature is just as much the source of use values (and it is surely of such that material wealth consists!) as labour. (Marx and Engels 1968, p. 319)

b. A direct consequence of Marx's analysis of the 'dual character of labour' is that in his theory, the origin of profit and the notion of exploitation *cannot* be founded on the proposition that labour is the only source of wealth – as the Ricardian Socialists had attempted to do, exposing themselves to Marx's criticism.

In this context the main questions relating to the role of the labour theory of value are thus two: (i) the determination of exchange value, and (ii) the origin of profit and the notion of exploitation of labour.

From the first viewpoint it must be emphasized that abstract labour may be seen as the *only and ultimate* foundation of exchange value exclusively in two cases: (i) in the simple case in which the organic composition of capital is exactly equal in all sectors and therefore the labour theory of value holds true; or (ii) in the more general case (when there are different sectoral organic compositions of capital) if the transformation of values into prices of production could be solved *in the sense of Marx*; that is, if these prices could be shown to be derivable only from values, and if the two 'Marxian equalities' were satisfied.

From the second viewpoint it should be stressed that while – as I have emphasized above – Marx clearly affirmed that concrete labour is *not* the only source of material wealth, it is, on the other hand, certain that Marx – with reference to abstract labour – attributes a role of fundamental importance to the circumstance that *surplus value* (s) derives only from *living labour* (v), thus assuming the nature of *surplus labour*, that is of labour performed by the worker over and above the amount of labour necessary to produce the wage rate. The relevant passages are too numerous and too well known to justify lengthy quotations on this point. One from Volume III of *Capital* (1981) will suffice:

> The capitalist . . . can convert the value he advances into a higher value only by exchanging it with living labour, by the exploitation of living labour; . . . it is only the variable part of capital that creates surplus value. (pp. 132–3)

From both viewpoints, therefore, the solution of the transformation problem *in the sense of Marx* appears to play an essential role. From the first one, because exclusively through this solution it can be shown in the general case that abstract labour is the only and ultimate foundation of exchange value. From the second one, because it is only that solution that confers analytical legitimacy on concepts such as variable capital, constant capital and surplus value; concepts which, beyond any doubt, play a crucial role in Marx's theoretical construction and represent the very foundation of the notions of social surplus and of the exploitation of labour.

It may be concluded that Garegnani's correct insistence upon Marx's distinction between abstract and concrete labour ends up by highlighting the serious implications that the story of the transformation problem has for Marx's basic concepts and thus for the notions that are founded upon them.

On the other hand, moving the analysis on what may be called the 'institutional framework' plane[33] – in a form that (in spite of significant differences in the general framework of reference) shows a certain degree of analogy with some aspects of the approach termed 'Analytical Marxism' (Roemer 1981, 1986; see also Amariglio, Callari and Cullemberg 1988)[34] – may allow to identify an important feature of modern economic reality, but can hardly be said to leave the analysis within Marx's scientific programme. In order for this to be possible one should be able to say – against Marx – that labour is indeed the source of all wealth.

The 'general equilibrium' interpretation of the continuity thesis

The 'general equilibrium' type interpretation of the continuity thesis between Ricardo and Marx has been suggested by Hollander (1981, 1987). He believes that there is

> little justification for the attribution to Ricardo of a divorce between distribution and pricing; as in the Smithian and the neoclassical systems they are interdependent. Above all, changes in the pattern of final demand can affect the wage rate, and changes in wages can affect the structure of prices. Demand-supply analysis for Ricardo – as for Smith and the neoclassics – was the vehicle of determination in his general system . . . But . . . much of what has just been said applies also to Marx . . . the relationship between distribution and pricing which Marx had in mind was precisely that which characterizes standard Ricardian theory. Marx too is in the general-equilibrium tradition. (Hollander 1981, p. 123)

Hollander thus objects to the idea, put forward for example by Dobb (1973), of a dual development in the history of economics:

> One line turning on allocation emanating from Smith, taken up by a number of dissenters from Ricardo, and by John Stuart Mill, and re-emerging with

> the 'marginalists' and Marshall; and a second line, the Ricardo–Marx line, where distribution and pricing are divorced in some sense and demand-supply is reduced to a secondary role at best. (Hollander 1987, p. 360)

According to Hollander this distinction is false:

> The Ricardian system, like the Smithian and the neoclassical systems, can only be understood in terms of supply and demand. This statement . . . is also true of Marx. (Ibid.)

Since both Ricardo and Marx should, according to Hollander, also be considered as belonging to the general equilibrium tradition, the development of economics should then be seen as the movement along a *single line*: here the contribution of each generation of economists can be viewed as an improvement and a completion of the general construction.

In particular, for what concerns Marx, the central problem of the transformation of values into prices of production is viewed by Hollander in terms of allocation theory:

> the transfer to prices of production from values – a set of [exchange ratios] reflecting labour inputs – entails a changed distribution of resources between industries to assure that commodities indeed sell at . . . prices covering costs plus the average profit rate. The transformation in short implies an allocative readjustment of activity. It is precisely here that the adjustment mechanisms characterizing orthodox classical theory intrude . . . The transition from [values] to [prices of production] occurs by allowing the process of competition to work effectively . . . It is the process of competition – the demand supply process – which brings about that result. (1987, pp. 364–5)

In a previous work (Caravale 1985, pp. 178ff.), I have commented critically on Hollander's interpretation of Ricardo (this appears to be founded on an unjustifiable emphasis laid on the allocative mechanism in Ricardo, on the neglect of the part played by the social structure and on an erroneous conception of wages as an endogenous variable), and implicitly on his general view of the development of economics. In particular, I believe it is objectionable to identify the non-neoclassical line with the separation between distribution, the profit–wage ratio, and pricing – in the sense that the 'profit–wage ratio . . . is *prior* to the formation of exchange values or prices' – since, in Ricardo's natural equilibrium framework of analysis, the wage rate is given from outside the model (by the 'habits and customs of the people') but the rate of profit *cannot* be determined before the determination of the whole set of natural prices. (Caravale, ibid.)

What applies to Ricardo applies *a fortiori* to Marx, and Hollander's view of the continuity between Ricardo and Marx appears to be opened to some basic critiques:

a. The undeniable presence of competitive elements in both Ricardo and Marx does not by itself transform the analysis into a general equilibrium theory centred upon a problem of allocation. First, the notion of competition has a different meaning in classical and in neo-classical contexts (see, e.g., Eatwell 1982): in classical and Marxian theory this notion is restricted to the mobility of capitals in search of a higher rate of return. Secondly, in both the analysis of Ricardo and in that of Marx the centre of gravity of the system is represented by prices of production and not by market prices: the former express the dominant conditions of production in the various sectors, while the latter are determined by temporary, unsystematic phenomena. Recognition of the working of supply and demand is limited to the definition of the mechanism that brings the system back to what can be termed the natural equilibrium position. There are of course notable differences between Ricardo's and Marx's 'vision' of this equilibrium position, but the fact remains that it cannot be said that the two systems of thought 'can only be understood in terms of demand and supply' – as Hollander believes.
b. The allocation problem, in terms of which Hollander views both Ricardo and Marx, is totally static in nature because it typically deals with the question of the efficient distribution of a *given* set of resources in relation to a given structure of needs expressed by the system. Now, this specific problem does *not* occupy the centre of the stage either in Ricardo or in Marx.

   In Ricardo the emphasis is on the dynamic problem of the slowing down of the process of accumulation process caused by diminishing returns in agriculture. In Marx, the central questions, as Hollander lucidly perceives (Hollander 1987, pp. 371ff.), are (i) proving the falsehood of the conception according to which factor returns 'grow out the role played by the land, [by] produced means of production, and [by] labour' (Marx 1981, Volume III, p. 805), and showing instead that living labour alone is the source of profits; (ii) showing that as the process of capitalist accumulation proceeds there is a tendency for the profit rate to fall and to bring the system to a situation of 'crisis'. Neither of these questions seems to be identifiable with the allocation problem in its technical sense.

The rejection of the two 'extreme' versions of the continuity thesis should represent the premise for a more balanced view of the relation between Ricardo and Marx. In this view the undeniable presence of some significant common features of the two analyses (such as the antagonistic nature of the distributive process among competing social categories; the recognition of the limits of validity of the labour theory of value; the important role attributed to the prices of production; the idea of a falling rate of profit) does not induce to forget the profound differences, emphasized in this chapter, in the general structure of the two theories and in the analytical elements on the basis of which they are constructed.

Notes

1. See, for example, De Vivo 1982, pp. 87–8.
2. Another cause is obviously the disconcerting state of the theoretical discussion in the field of Marxian economics in relation to which King (1982, p. 157) speaks of 'conceptual chaos'.
3. 'Marx's discussion of Ricardo . . . redound in unjust, petty, wordsplitting remarks . . . And yet Ricardo is practically the only author who, in a certain sense, finds any mercy in Marx's eyes at all.' (Bortkiewicz 1952, p. 30, n. 56).
4. This interpretation is accepted by Porta (1986, 1988).
5. It is interesting to note that the point was perceived by Bortkiewicz with great clarity: 'in Ricardo's oft-repeated phrase that every rise in wages must necessarily be accompanied by a fall in profits and *vice versa*, one must understand by wages neither money wages, nor real wages, but that amount of labour which is needed to produce the complex of goods forming real wages . . . Furthermore, it is noteworthy that, although Ricardo does not speak of *rate* of profit, but simply of profit, . . . he . . . intends his assertion of the antagonism between wages and profit to be extended specifically to the rate of profit.' (Bortkiewicz 1952, pp. 34–5).
6. See also Bortkiewicz (1952, p. 49): 'In discussing [with reference to both Ricardo's and Marx's analyses] the connection between the productivity of labour and the rate of profit I have regarded the real wage as given'. And also (ibid.): 'it may be worth pointing out once more that, in making wages and profits move in opposite directions, Ricardo means by wages *not real wages themselves* but . . . the amount of labour embodied in real wages' (emphasis added).
7. It is interesting to note that this thesis is based on textual evidence not only from the *Essay on Profits*, but also, and I would say especially, from two chapters of the *Principles*: one is the 'strategic' (to use Hollander's expression) chapter 'On profit', while the other is the chapter entitled 'Effects of accumulation on profits and interest'.
8. What we would have instead, in connection with each possible value of the exogenously given real wage rate, is a *single point*, characterized by a couple of values of w and r.
9. The inadmissibility of a distributive antagonism, in Ricardo, between capitalists and workers (to be expressed by an inverse relation between the rate of profit and the real wage) is lucidly grasped by Bortkiewicz (1952). After having emphasized that the expression 'rise in wages' must be understood to mean in Ricardo (as it was pointed out above) '[rise in the] amount of labour which is needed to produce the [given] real wage' (ibid., pp. 34–5), Bortkiewicz states: 'We cannot, finally, stress sufficiently strongly that there is no mention in Ricardo of [the distributive] antagonism prevailing only insofar as there is no change in the value or the price of the product. Such a qualification . . . not only contradicts Ricardo's own words; it deprives his thesis – that high wages *always* go with low profits, and high profits with low wages – of its point and reduces it to triviality' (ibid.). Since it is clear that the

expression used by Bortkiewicz 'change in the value or the price of the product' means the amount of labour necessary to produce the wage goods and their price of production, this becomes a very strong assertion of the fact that Ricardo *cannot* be interpreted in terms of the antagonism between wages and profits in a given situation (that is with a given matrix of the technical coefficients). It thus coincides with my criticism of Garegnani's (1984) interpretation of Ricardo (Caravale 1985, pp. 166–78).

Bortkiewicz, in a footnote, also adds: 'Ricardo's thesis becomes a self-evident proposition also in the hands of those who interpret it in the sense that wages and profits are nothing but the worker's or the capitalist's shares in the proceeds (disregarding rent)' (Bortkiewicz 1952, p. 35, n. 83).

10. Since this can be considered a correct 'rational reconstruction' of Ricardo's way of reasoning (a reconstruction, moreover, which supplies us with the general solution of the problem, the one that Ricardo was unable to find), Marshall's criticism of Ricardo on this score seems misplaced ('He [Ricardo] does not state clearly, and in some cases he perhaps did not fully and clearly perceive how, in the problem of normal value, the various elements govern one another *mutually*, and not *successively* in a long chain of causation'. Marshall 1966, p. 672). It would in other words be more correct to say that it is Marshall who does not fully understand Ricardo's way of reasoning and does not see that in spite of the fact that Ricardo left his theoretical problem unsolved, the solution along the lines intuitively, though not analytically, indicated by Ricardo could in fact, be found. That is, he [Marshall] is not 'generous' enough towards Ricardo as he invites interpreters to be (see Marshall 1966, p. 670.)
11. Numerous passages in Ricardo's writings (e.g. Ricardo 1951–73, Volume I, pp. 46–7; Volume II, p. 337; Volume VIII, p. 149) make it clear beyond all possible doubts that his efforts were not directed to the explanation of the absolute level of prices (in terms of a given *numéraire*), but rather to the identification of a rigorous and general explanation of relative prices, that is of the exchange ratios between any two commodities produced in the system.
12. This passage supplies further evidence of the coincidence between Marx's interpretation of Ricardo and what was called above the Sraffa-based 'natural equilibrium dynamic analysis' of the Ricardian theory.
13. See also Sraffa ('Introduction' in Ricardo 1951–73, Volume I, p. xlv: 'Already in one of the letters to McCulloch . . . Ricardo had suggested that "all the exceptions to the general rule" [the labour theory of value] could be reduced to "one of time": i.e., all those deriving from different proportions of fixed and circulating capital, different durabilities of fixed capital, or differences in the "time it takes to market" (or durability of circulating capital) could be reduced to terms of labour employed for a longer or shorter time. *This conception was the one to which he finally adhered.*' (Emphasis added).
14. In the sense specified above of the possibility of identifying an inverse relationship between the labour content of corn and the rate of profit – valid in general and not only when the capital–labour ratios are identical in all sectors.
15. In chapter VI ('On profits'), after having argued that an increase in the price of corn – due to the cultivation of progressively poorer lands – will determine a reduction in the money values of absolute profits (1951–73, Vol I, p. 117), Ricardo writes for instance: 'But the *rate* of profits will fall still more, because the capital of the farmer, it must be recollected, consists in a great measure of raw produce, such as corn and hayricks, his unthreshed wheat and barley, his horses and cows, which would all rise in price in consequence of the rise of produce. His absolute profits would fall from 480 pounds to 455 pounds 15 sh. [a percentage reduction of about 7.2 per cent]; but if from the cause which I have just stated, his capital should rise from 3000 pounds to 3200 pounds the rate of his profit would . . . be under 14 per cent.'
16. Sraffa ('Introduction' in Ricardo 1951–73, Volume I, pp. xlvii–xlix) emphasizes the connection between the two questions – that of difference and that of change – but

ends by attributing greater importance to the latter: 'The two points of view of difference and of change are closely linked together; yet the search for an invariable measure of value, which is so much at the centre of Ricardo's system, arises exclusively from the second and would have no counterpart in an investigation of the first' (ibid., p. xlix). In the light of the argument developed in the text this evaluation appears to be unjustified.

17. Although Bortkiewicz (1952, e.g. pp. 34–5) is quite clear that the essence of Ricardo's theory can be expressed in terms of the inverse relation between the amount of labour required to produce the given basket constituting the real wage and the rate of profit (and was thus aware of the fact that the change in the rate of profit is accompanied by a change in the whole set of relative prices), his assertion on the point discussed in the text appears of dubious validity. He maintains in fact that the question of the differences between relative prices and relative labour quantities 'presents itself, as it were, as a special case of the . . . question [of the influence on prices of changes in the rate of profit]' (ibid., p. 30).
18. See also Steedman (1982, p. 153) who, in the same vein, concludes that this criticism stems from a mere 'verbal muddle' on the part of Marx.
19. 'Thus, although in selling their commodities the capitalists of the various spheres of production recover the value of the capital consumed in their production they do not secure the surplus-value, and consequently the profit, created in their own sphere by the production of these commodities. What they secure is only as much surplus-value, and hence profit, as falls, when uniformly distributed, to the share of every aliquot part of the total social capital from the total social surplus-value, or profit, produced in a given time by the social capital in all spheres of production' (Marx 1981, Volume III, p. 156).
20. De Vivo's interpretation of Ricardo on this ground is thus devoid of any sound foundation. He writes in fact: 'Ricardo failed to see that there was a fundamental problem in transforming values into prices. Marx, by posing this problem and finding a solution – albeit not an entirely satisfactory one – takes a substantial step . . . and faces a difficulty which threatened Ricardo's theory at its heart' (De Vivo 1982, p. 89).
21. Steedman (1982, pp. 126–39), after a careful examination of various passages from Ricardo, concludes that 'there is direct evidence that Ricardo did not ignore non-wage capital at the economy level and that, once allowance is made for Ricardo's shifting and rather confusing use of terms, all his apparent denial of aggregate non-wage capital can be seen to be just that – merely apparent' (ibid., p. 137).
22. Garegnani (1984, p. 300) takes up this criticism of Ricardo's theory almost in the same terms: 'Ricardo [in determining the rate of profit] operated *as if* capital consisted entirely of the wages advanced for the year. In fact he saw the division of the product between wages and profit as the only factor capable of influencing the rate of profit, thus ignoring the independent influence exerted by the proportion between labour and means of production'. In the footnote appended to the text, Garegnani, after having repeated his criticism of Ricardo, notes that 'Marx did not deny that Smith and Ricardo saw the existence of means of production . . . what he said was that Ricardo ignored the effects of *changes in the proportion of labour to means of production* on the rate of profit [and on prices]'. The first aspect of Garegnani's argument – that relating to the *independent* influence exerted on the prices and the profit rate by the different capital–labour ratios – has been already dealt with in the text. As to the second one – Garegnani's idea that Marx criticized Ricardo for having ignored the effect of *changes* in the capital–labour ratios (through time) on the rate of profit and on natural prices – it must be stressed again (see pp. 174–6) that this question, although extremely important *per se*, finds only a marginal position in Ricardo's *Principles*. Finally, Garegnani's recognition that 'Marx did not deny that . . . Ricardo saw the existence of means of production' seems hardly reconcilable with Garegnani's own thesis according to which 'Ricardo . . . operated

as if capital consisted entirely of the wages advanced for the year'. See also De Vivo (1982, pp. 91–2).

23. See also Steedman 1982, pp. 125–6.
24. De Vivo's objection to Steedman (De Vivo 1982, p. 92) had been answered in advance by Steedman (1982, p. 130). See also Garegnani (1984, p. 300, n. 19).
25. The circumstance that both Bortkiewicz and Sraffa abstract from rent in their resolution of prices into revenues, while Marx speaks of all three revenues including rent, does not in the least touch upon the analogy between Marx's hint and the formers' analyses.
26. See also Marx 1981, Volume II, pp. 460ff.
27. See above, note 12.
28. See also Marx's *Grundrisse* (1977, pp. 562ff.).
29. Commenting on a passage from Marx's TSV, Bortkiewicz (1952, p. 29) writes: 'One might almost be led to believe that Marx admits that Ricardo had correctly recognized the nature of the conditions which Marx calls a divergence of prices from values'.
30. The thesis that the labour theory of value, in Ricardo and in Marx, performs the role of showing – *in both contexts* – the existence of the 'intimate connection' between wages and profits is further emphasized by Garegnani, who writes (1981, p. 61, my translation): 'What matters here is however another step forward taken by Marx with respect to Ricardo: the theory of the "prices of production". Commodities in fact exchange according to ratios which do not coincide with those between the quantities of labour that were necessary to produce them, but Ricardo's analysis had remained basically tied to the assumption that the two ratios would coincide.' The preceding discussion shows instead that Ricardo was perfectly aware of the theoretical problems connected with the divergence between natural relative prices and relative labour quantities and that therefore his analysis did not remain 'basically tied to the assumption that the two ratios would coincide'.
31. See note 9 for Bortkiewicz's evaluation of this aspect of Ricardo's theory.
32. It is also correct to say that Marx's distinction between abstract and concrete labour mirrors the one made by Ricardo (in his argument against Say's theory) between value and riches – though with a certain amount of ambiguity as to the role of the forces other than labour in the determination of exchangeable value. Ricardo writes for instance: 'these natural agents though they add greatly to value in use, never add exchangeable value' (1951–73, Volume I, p. 285); 'Adam Smith nowhere undervalues the services that these natural agents and machinery perform us, but he very justly distinguishes the nature of the value which they add to commodities – they are serviceable to us, by increasing the abundance of productions, by making men richer, by adding to value in use; but as they perform their work gratuitously, as nothing is paid for the use of air, of heat, and of water, the assistance which they afford us, adds nothing to value in exchange' (ibid., p. 287).

    In fact the point is not the 'gratuitous' character of the contribution supplied by natural agents or by machinery – which is moreover of dubious general realism – but rather the assumption that the labour theory of value holds true (on which Ricardo based his argument in chapter XX) and that therefore exchange ratios are determined solely by relative labour quantities. It can well be thought that Ricardo's argument in chapter XX is carried out under this assumption for the purpose of making his point against Say emerge more clearly.
33. Garegnani 1981, pp. 84–8; in particular, p. 88: 'the proposition relating to the existence of exploitation of labour in a capitalistic society does not depend in any way on the validity of the labour theory of value. It depends instead on the theoretical approach based on the notion of social surplus, from which no other foundation emerges for profits other than the simple fact that existing economic

institutions do not allow workers to appropriate the entire product' (my translation from Italian). See also Garegnani 1986, p. 176.

34. 'The labour theory of value, for Marx, played a double role – as a theory of exchange and a theory of exploitation. Marx's approach was to use the theory of exchange as a conduit to generate the theory of exploitation. Our approach is to reject the labour theory of value in its role as exchange theory, and reconstruct the theory of exploitation on a different basis' (Roemer 1981, p. 52). 'The labour theory of value is used directly as an exploitation theory without going through the conduit of a labour theory of exchange to get there. It is by understanding that workers' power as a class is only sufficient to command a fraction of society's labour time that the locus of exploitation is exposed' (ibid., p. 160); ' . . . living labour is entitled to the product but . . . ownership of alienable factors of production (i.e. capital) does not entitle one to a share of the product' (ibid., p. 207). By way of comment, it may be said that, while the concepts of labour embodied in the given real wage and the difference between this and the amount of labour totally performed can be calculated on the basis of Sraffa's model, the problem remains of showing that surplus value originates exclusively from living labour. Roemer's direct use of the labour theory of value as a theory of exploitation does not seem to supply an answer to this problem.

References

Amariglio, J., A. Callari and S. Cullemberg (1988), 'Analytical Marxism: A Critical Overview', paper presented at the AEA Annual Meeting, New York, mimeograph.

Caravale, G. (1985), 'Diminishing Returns and Accumulation in Ricardo', in G. Caravale (ed.), *The Legacy of Ricardo*, Oxford: Basil Blackwell.

Caravale, G. (1988a), 'The Notion of Natural Wage and its Role in Classical Economics', *Rivista Internazionale di Scienze Economiche e Commerciali*, Milano: Università Bocconi e Università di Milano, July.

Caravale, G. (1988b), 'Condizioni di Domanda ed Equilibrio Naturale nelle Teorie Classiche e di Tipo Classico', *Rivista di Politica Economica*, Roma, December.

Caravale, G. and D. Tosato (1978), 'Saggio di Profitto e Merce Tipo nella Teoria di Ricardo', *Rivista di Politica Economica*, January.

Caravale, G. and D. Tosato (1980), *Ricardo and the Theory of Value, Distribution and Growth*, London: Routledge & Kegan Paul.

Desai, M. (1991), 'Transformation Problem', in G. Caravale (ed.), *Marx and Modern Economic Analysis*, Volume I, Aldershot: Edward Elgar.

De Vivo, G. (1982), 'Notes on Marx's Critique of Ricardo', *Contributions to Political Economy*, 1, pp. 87–9.

Dobb, M. (1973), *Theories of Value and Distribution Since Adam Smith*, Cambridge: Cambridge University Press.

Eatwell, J. (1982), 'Competition', in I. Bradley and M. Howard (eds), *Classical and Marxian Political Economy*, London: Macmillan.

Garegnani, P. (1981), *Marx e gli economisti classici*, Torino: Einaudi.

Garegnani, P. (1984), 'Value and Distribution in the Classical Economists and Marx', *Oxford Economic Papers*, June.

Garegnani, P. (1986), 'Valore lavoro e rapporto tra l'opera di Marx e quella di Ricardo: adcune riflessioni', *Marx e il mondo contemporaneo*, Editori Riuni ti, Roma.

Hollander, S. (1981), 'Marxian Economics as General Equilibrium Theory', *History of Political Economy*, January.

Hollander, S. (1987), *Classical Economics*, Oxford: Basil Blackwell.

King, J.E. (1982), 'Value and Exploitation: Some Recent Debates', in I. Bradley and M. Howard (eds), *Classical and Marxian Political Economy*, London: Macmillan.

Marshall, A. (1966), *Principles of Economics*, London: Macmillan.

Marx, K. (1969), *Theories of Surplus Value*, London: Lawrence and Wishart.

Marx, K. (1977), *Grundrisse*, Harmondsworth: Penguin.

Marx, K. (1981), *Capital*, Volumes 1–3, Harmondsworth: Penguin.
Marx, K. and F. Engels (1968), *Selected Works in One Volume*, New York: International Publishers.
Napoleoni, C. (1991), 'Value and Exploitation – Marx's Economic Theory and Beyond', in G. Caravale (ed.), *Marx and Modern Economic Analysis*, Volume I, Aldershot: Edward Elgar.
Porta, P.L. (1986), 'Introduzione', in D. Ricardo, *Principi di Economia Politica e dell'Imposta*, Torino: UTET.
Porta, P.L. (1988), *Valore, Distribuzione, Sfruttamento nell'Economia Classica*, Milano: Università di Milano, mimeograph.
Ricardo, D. (1951–73), *The Works and Correspondence of David Ricardo*, edited by P. Sraffa with the collaboration of M.H. Dobb, Cambridge: Cambridge University Press.
Roemer, J. (1981), *Analytical Foundations of Marxian Economic Theory*, Cambridge: Cambridge University Press.
Roemer, J. (ed.) (1986), *Analytical Marxism*, Cambridge: Cambridge University Press.
Rorty, R. (1984), 'The Historiography of Philosophy: Four Genres', in R. Rorty, J.B. Schneewind and Q. Skinner (eds), *Philosophy in History*, Cambridge: Cambridge University Press.
Skinner, Q. (1969), 'Meaning and Understanding in the History of Ideas', *History and Theory*, **8**, pp. 3–53.
Sraffa, P. (1960), *Production of Commodities by Means of Commodities*, Cambridge: Cambridge University Press.
Steedman, I. (1977), *Marx after Sraffa*, London: New Left Books.
Steedman, I. (1982), 'Marx on Ricardo', in I. Bradley and M. Howard (eds), *Classical and Marxian Political Economy*, London: Macmillan.
Von Bortkiewicz, L. (1952), 'Value and Prices in the Marxian System', *International Economic Papers*, (2).

9 Keynes and Marx

Dudley Dillard

Great economic theories begin with a vision of economic society and materialize by embedding that vision into a system of economic analysis (Schumpeter 1954, p. 41). John Maynard Keynes and Karl Marx shared a vision of decaying capitalism and a distaste for an economic system in which production is motivated by a love of money. Marx envisioned money as the symbol of alienation in capitalist society. His economic theory completely integrates money into his theory of value and capital. Keynes expressed the hope that in the future 'the love of money as a possession . . . will be recognized for what it is, a somewhat disgusting morbidity' (1971, Volume 9, p. 320). With the vision of an ageing capitalism before him, Keynes's career as an economist unfolds in terms of progressively subtle insights into the nature of money as the key institution of contemporary capitalism (Dillard 1954, p. 30).

The economic principles of Keynes and Marx may be described appropriately as monetary theories of production. The principles of economics of classical and neo-classical economists cannot be so described. A monetary theory of production focuses on the pre-eminent characteristic of capitalism, namely the motivation of those who employ labour in the private sector to make money by purchasing labour, materials, and equipment and to sell the output for money. Capitalist production is completed only when the value of output is realized in the form of money. Under these institutional arrangements the direct objective of society – the production of goods and services – is subordinated to the money-making objectives of those who organize and produce goods and services. The grand themes of Keynes and Marx centre around tensions between the public interest in employment and production and the private interest of maximizing monetary returns.

Integrating money into general economic theory

A thorough-going integration of money into general economic theory is a common characteristic of the economics of Keynes and Marx. A comparison of Keynes's *General Theory*, chapter 17, 'The Essential Properties of Interest and Money', with Marx's Volume 1, chapter 1, section 3, 'The Form of Value or Exchange Value', highlights the important, special properties of money. The thrust in both cases is a polarization of money, on the one hand, and commodities (real output), on the other. In a capitalist society, money differs from other forms of wealth not just in degree but in kind.

Keynes's views in chapter 17 are widely known but little understood. The chapter's purpose is to explain what is special about money (Davidson 1978, 1980). Every investment asset has an own-rate of interest, that is, a rate of interest measured by the difference between its spot price and its future price. There are wheat rates and house rates, as well as money rates expressed in terms of themselves. The point of the own-rate analysis is to show that the rate of interest on money stands apart from all other own-rates. The upshot of the analysis is a dichotomy between the rate of interest on money and the rate of return (marginal efficiency) on all other assets. This dichotomy lays the groundwork for Keynes's proposition that the marginal efficiency of capital adjusts to the rate of interest and not the other way round (Keynes 1971, Volume 14, p. 123).

In a significant sense, Keynes attributes involuntary unemployment to the properties of money because the rate of return on all assets other than money 'would only reach equilibrium when there is full employment' (1936, p. 235). Thus money 'rules the roost' because its rate of return falls more slowly than the own-rate of interest on any other asset.

Although money is important in determining the rate of interest, it is also important, in a somewhat different way, in determining the realized rates of return on all other assets, which depend on the expected terms on which real output can be converted into money in the more or less distant and often highly uncertain future. This will be recognized as the 'realization' problem of Marx, alluded to in Keynes's lectures on 'The Monetary Theory of Production' in 1933 (1971, Volume 13, p. 420). Money and uncertainty are the twin keys to Keynes's general theory, and the influence of shifting and uncertain views about future conversion of real output into money is what he means by a monetary economy (1936, pp. vii, 294). Money affects production directly because, if businessmen cannot convert current real output into money, the means of production will be withheld and wage earners will suffer unemployment.

Involuntary unemployment is normal in a monetary economy, but in a non-monetary economy it is impossible because 'only miscalculation or stupid obstinancy can stand in the way of production' (1971, Volume 29, p. 67). The earliest surviving draft of the table of contents of the *General Theory* carries the title 'The Monetary Theory of Production' (1971, Volume 29, p. 49). A 1933 draft of the table of contents alters the title to 'The Monetary Theory of Employment', with the first chapter entitled, 'The Nature and Significance of the Theory of a Monetary Economy' (1971, Volume 29, p. 62). In a slightly later draft (1933?) of the table of contents, the book's title is 'The General Theory of Employment', and chapter 1 is now called 'The Nature and Significance of the Contrast between a Co-operative and an Entrepreneur Economy' (1971, Volume 29, p. 63). The dichotomy between a 'co-operative economy' and an 'entrepreneur economy' is an early version of a continuing contrast between a non-monetary economy (without unemployment) and a monetary economy (with unemployment). To sum up, Keynes's central theme about involuntary unemployment is directly associated with the role of money in a monetary economy. Money is a uniquely significant asset.

Marx also establishes a dichotomy between money and commodities. In section 3 of chapter 1 of the first volume of *Capital*, he shows that money is the logical and necessary outcome in a system of commodity production. Value is traced through four stages 'from its simplest, almost imperceptible outline, to the dazzling money form' (1867, p. 55). At each of the four stages (elementary, expanded, general, and money), there is a relative (commodity) form and an equivalent (incipient money) form at opposite poles in the value relation. As soon as a commodity assumes the form of a particular equivalent in terms of which the (relative) value of another commodity is expressed, it is on the way to becoming money. In the third stage, a (once) particular commodity becomes a general equivalent, and in the fourth stage money becomes the universal equivalent of all other commodities. In the monetary economies of Marx and Keynes, the value of commodities is realized by exchanging for the universal equivalent, money.

One of the rare occasions in which Keynes praised Marx occurred in a 1933 draft of the *General Theory*. Here Keynes credits Marx with the 'pregnant observation . . . that the nature of production in the actual world is not $C - M - C'$, i.e., of exchanging commodity (or effort) for money in order to obtain another commodity (or effort). That may be the standpoint of the private consumer. But it is not the attitude of *business*, which is a case of $M - C - M'$, i.e., of parting with money for commodity (or effort) in order to obtain more money' (1971, Volume 29, p. 81).

In the paragraphs immediately following, Keynes emphasized that business firms subordinate making goods to making money:

> An entrepreneur is interested, not in the amount of product, but in the amount of *money* which will fall to his share. . . . The firm is dealing throughout in terms of money. It has no object in the world except to end

up with more money than it started with. That is the essential character of an entrepreneur [capitalist] economy. (1971, Volume 29, pp. 82, 89)

Marx presumably would have embraced these expressions by Keynes on the role of money in business decisions. The same idea is expressed by Marx on many occasions, including the following passage from the chapter 'The General Formula for Capital':

> The circulation of money as capital is . . . an end in itself. . . . It is only in so far as the appropriation of ever more and more wealth in the abstract [money] becomes the sole motive of his operation, that he functions as a capitalist. (1867, pp. 169–70)

The foregoing shows a close parallel between Keynes and Marx in integrating money into their general economic theories and emphasizes that money plays a direct, causal role in determining real output.

Effective demand and underconsumption

Effective demand is the centrepiece of Keynes's general theory. Marx did not formalize a theory of effective demand but it is implicit in much of his work, including the reproduction models of Volume 2 and the discussion of crises arising from inability to realize, as distinguished from produce, surplus value (1894, p. 286). Keynes recognized Marx's concern with effective demand when he wrote, 'The great puzzle of Effective Demand with which Malthus had wrestled . . . could only live on furtively, below the surface, in the underworlds of Karl Marx, Silvio Gesell or Major Douglas' (1963, p. 32). Marx's economics would be strengthened by a more formal treatment of the theory of effective demand.

Cognate with Keynes's division of total output (and income) into investment and consumption is Marx's division of total output (and income) into department I, which produces only capital goods, and department II, which produces only consumer goods (Marx 1885, p. 457). Each of Marx's two departments consists of three divisions: variable capital (wages), constant capital (raw materials and depreciation), and surplus value (profits). Much output is produced and sold within the same department, but, as in Keynes's model, the sale of some output depends on expenditures derived from income generated in the other department. Under simple reproduction (no accumulation), the 'great exchange', as Marx calls it (1885, p. 460), is the following:

$$C_2 = V_1 + S_1$$

where C_2 is the constant capital of department II, and V_1 and S_1 are variable capital and surplus value, respectively, of department I. In the production of consumer goods in department II, constant capital is used up and must be replaced by an equal amount of constant capital produced in department I; and this magnitude must equal the wages and surplus value received by workers and capitalists of department I, who spend their income for consumer goods produced in department II.

Since the demand for output of one department depends on the income and expenditure generated by production in the other department, the conditions of balanced money flows are delicate, more so because the interdepartmental flows, as well as the intradepartmental exchanges, involve sales for money, the payment of wages in money, and the receipt of dividends in money. Even under simple reproduction, maintaining balanced flows of aggregate demand and aggregate supply is difficult. Disequilibrium becomes highly probable, according to Marx, with the accumulation of capital under expanded reproduction. Marx had even less faith than Keynes in the self-adjusting nature of capitalism.

There is a clear parallel between Marx's 'great exchange' between departments I and II and the fundamental principle of Keynes's theory of effective demand that the amount of consumer goods and services that it pays entrepreneurs to produce depends on the amount of investment goods and services they are producing (Keynes 1971, Volume 14, p. 120).

Neither Marx nor Keynes were strict underconsumptionists. However, the following statement from Marx clearly indicates sympathy for some type of underconsumption theory: 'The last cause of all real crises always remains the poverty and restricted consumption of the masses' (1894, p. 568).

Keynes was sympathetic to underconsumptionists such as John A. Hobson but he sharply differentiated his own theory, pointing out that Hobson's was a theory of underconsumption and *oversaving* leading to *overinvestment*, whereas Keynes believed that underemployment resulted from both *underinvestment* and underconsumption.

In a footnote in the *Collected Writings*, Keynes compares Hobson to Marx and strikes a balance favourable to Marx. The note arises in relation to Keynes's discussion of Marx's formula for capital, $M - C - M'$ (see above). Keynes writes:

> Marx, however, was approaching the intermediate truth when he added that the continuous excess of M' [over M] would be inevitably interrupted by a series of crises, gradually increasing in intensity, or entrepreneur bankruptcy and underemployment, during which, presumably M must be in excess. My own argument, if it is accepted, should at least serve to effect a reconciliation

> between the followers of Marx and those of Major Douglas, leaving the classical economists still high and dry in the belief that *M* and *M'* are always equal. (1971, Volume 29, p. 82n)

The excess of *M'* over *M* is, of course, Marx's surplus value, all of which is extracted from labour but some of which may not be realized because of lack of effective demand.

Capital accumulation

Capital accumulation is as much the centrepiece of Marx's *Capital* as effective demand is of Keynes's *General Theory*. For Marx, capital accumulation is the driving force in the historic mission of capitalism. It is as much the triumph as the tragedy of capitalist civilization. Keynes's concept cognate to Marx's capital accumulation is investment, which is essentially the same economic phenomenon of current production in excess of current consumption, but with more limited side effects. Either sporadic bursts of investment or volatile capital accumulation can account for sweeping cyclical instability in production and employment. Because Keynes's model highlights investment as a source of current effective demand, it tends to neglect the long-term consequences of capital accumulation, which increase productive capacity and thereby compounds the difficulty of finding sufficient effective demand in the future. Keynes does not ignore this paradoxical role of investment, but neither does he feature it in his model.

Section 7 of Volume 1 of *Capital* is entitled 'The Accumulation of Capital'. The introduction to this section, unlike any other passage in the three volumes of *Capital*, is not included under any chapter. In five brief paragraphs, Marx recapitulates the general theme of all three volumes. Presumptively he did this in order to place the chapters immediately following in the broad perspective of his whole theory of economic development. The first chapter in section 7 on simple reproduction builds a foundation for the more realistic and dynamic conditions of expanded reproduction in which accumulation takes place.

The capstone of Volume 1 of *Capital* is chapter 25, 'The General Law of Capitalist Accumulation'. According to this general law, the accumulation of capital is accompanied by the introduction of labour-saving machinery that leads to unemployment and is an explanation of the paradox of poverty in the midst of potential plenty. In Marx's words, capital accumulation 'establishes an accumulation of misery, corresponding with accumulation of capital. Accumulation of wealth at one pole is, therefore, at the same time accumulation of misery, agony of toil, slavery, ignorance, brutality, mental degradation, at the opposite pole, i.e., on the side of the class that produces its own product in the form of capital' (1867, p. 709).

Marx modifies the classical model, which views capital as demand for labour and the accumulation of capital as an increase in the demand for labour, to allow the introduction of machinery to displace workers whenever wages threaten to rise as a result of the increased demand for labour associated with accumulation. Instead of increasing the demand for labour, capital accumulation accompanied by a change in the composition of capital (introduction of machinery) decreases the demand, throws workers out of employment, and depresses wages. Marx's paradox of poverty in the midst of potential abundance works itself out in terms of the rising organic composition of capital, that is, an increase in constant capital (machinery) relative to variable capital (wages for workers).

Marx's industrial reserve army resembles Keynes's involuntary unemployment with an important difference. Keynes's involuntary unemployment arises from a deficiency of effective demand and could be alleviated by an increase in investment, whereas the members of Marx's industrial reserve army are the victims primarily of technological unemployment associated with investment. Marx integrates technological change into his central model. Keynes's failure to do so is one of the major shortcomings of his theory. His theory of unemployment would have been strengthened if he had learned from Marx about modelling technological unemployment.

Keynes's model, does, however, account for the paradox of poverty in the midst of affluence. A rich community will have a weaker inducement to invest and therefore will be more prone to high unemployment than a poor community. The Marxian flavour of Keynes's theory is suggested by the following passage:

> Moreover the richer the community, the wider will tend to be the gap between its actual and its potential production; and therefore the more obvious and outrageous the defects of the economic system. . . . If in a potentially wealthy community the inducement to invest is weak, then, in spite of its potential wealth, the working of the principle of effective demand will compel it to reduce its actual output, until, in spite of its potential wealth, it has become so poor that its surplus over its consumption is sufficiently diminished to correspond to the weakness of the inducement to invest. (1936, p. 31)

Thus in both Keynes and Marx, capitalist wealth becomes a barrier to output and employment. Marx said, 'The real barrier of capitalist production is capital itself' (1894, p. 293). The limits of capitalism arise from the internal logic of the system and not from limitations imposed by human and physical nature, as postulated by Malthus and Ricardo. Chapter 25 contains Marx's answer to Malthus, who attributed poverty to the law of population, in conjunction with the law of diminishing returns. Ricardo denied that accumulation as such lowers the rate of profit; profits fall only because diminishing returns in agriculture decrease the productivity of agricultural labour and thus increase the price of food. Marx asserted that the limits of capitalism do not arise from nature: 'The rate of profit does not fall, because labour becomes less productive, but because it becomes more productive' (1894, p. 281). Keynes's ideas are compatible with those of Marx in explaining poverty in terms of social and economic institutions rather than human and physical nature.

The labour theory of value in Keynes and Marx

The labour theory of value is another doctrine shared by Marx and Keynes. Marx's labour theory of value is central to his system and has been the focus of a vast literature which need not concern us here. Keynes's labour theory of value is less well known and even less understood. It has been virtually ignored in voluminous discussions about Keynes and his work. Does it represent an idiosyncratic *obiter dictum* or does it have significance for his basic social philosophy and his technical economic analysis? Although incidental to his technical theory, the labour theory of value does throw light on Keynes's philosophical orientation toward capital and functional shares in the distribution of income.

On the labour theory of value, Keynes's key statement is: 'I sympathize, therefore, with the pre-classical [Smith–Ricardo] doctrine that everything is *produced* by *labour*. . . . It is preferable to regard labour, including, of course, the personal services of the entrepreneur and his assistants, as the sole factor of production' (1936, pp. 213–14). This means that labour is the only functional agent of production receiving socially necessary income. Smith and Ricardo viewed landlords as non-functional agents of production receiving unearned income because 'they loved to reap where they never sowed'. Keynes goes one step further in viewing interest, as well as rent, as non-functional, unearned income. Interest, for Keynes, is a payment for the use of money. He rejected Marshall's notion of interest as a reward for 'waiting'. Unlike Marx, however, Keynes included the services of entrepreneurs as a form of functional labour, participating in and contributing to social production. Marx viewed all three non-wage shares – rent, interest, and profits – as part of an unearned surplus value, deducted from the product of labour. Under Marx's ideal society based on thorough-going collectivism, the private receipt of rent, interest, and profits would disappear. In Keynes's ideal society, private ownership and entrepreneurship would continue. At such time in the future when capital assets cease to be scarce, they would yield no return above their cost of production. This would be the euthanasia of the rentier. This non-scarcity of capital assets need not be interpreted as a prediction of what in fact will happen; in any event it expresses Keynes's normative view of an ideal functional society.

Keynes's statement concerning the labour theory of value appears in chapter 16 on the nature of capital. He deliberately avoids speaking of capital as 'productive'. Capital equipment is viewed as 'the results of past labour, embodied in assets', which yield a return in excess of cost because they are kept artificially scarce by the rate of interest on money. For Keynes, money is a sort of institutional monopoly associated with its zero or negligible elasticity of supply in response to forces of the private market. If the rate of interest were free to fall, the production of capital assets would proceed uninterruptedly until they ceased to be scarce.

Theories of value in economics have generally been attempts to probe beneath the surface phenomena of the market to discover essential properties and relations. Marx attempted to do this with his 'abstract' labour theory of value underlying market prices and with his theory of surplus value underlying rent, interest, and industrial profits. In a similar manner, Keynes uses a labour theory of value to probe the nature of capital and the returns to its owners (capitalists) and users (entrepreneurs).

Summary and conclusions

Other comparisons between the economics of Keynes and Marx could be made if space permitted. For example, Marx as well as Keynes had a monetary theory of interest, even though interest is peripheral to Marx's main schema (Marx 1894, part 5). They had strikingly similar, and unorthodox, views concerning the relation between the quantity of money and the general level of prices (Marx 1867, pp. 135, 148–9; Keynes 1936, chapter 21). The idea of hoarding, likewise, permeates their monetary systems of analysis. There is a nice congruence between Keynes's description of money as 'a bottomless sink of purchasing power' (1936, p. 231) and Marx's statement: 'The desire after hoarding is in its very nature insatiable' (1867, p. 149). During financial crises, when hoarding increases, money reveals most visibly its subtle character as the universal equivalent, the socially recognized form of private wealth.

Perhaps surprisingly, Marx's economics had little direct impact on Keynes's thinking. In his earlier years, Keynes expressed hostility toward *Capital* (Volume 9, p. 258). Three references to Marx in the *General Theory* and additional, favourable references in the recently published *Collected Writings* suggest some moderation in Keynes's attitude toward Marx's economic analysis. What seems clear is that the similarities in the economics of Keynes and Marx resulted mainly from examining the same phenomenon, namely, capitalism as a social system of production based on private money-making, plus a sensivitity to the human cost of massive unemployment and the injustice of arbitrary inequalities in the distribution of wealth and income. In brief, the similarities of their visions account for the similarities in their economic analyses.

Visions, which are implemented by economic analysis, also contain pragmatic insights that point toward solutions of the central economic predicament of the society. Marx found the difficulty behind money to be a difficulty with private property and concluded that the problem would be solved only by eliminating private property in the means of production, that is, by elimination of the monetary system of production. Keynes sought remedies short of eliminating private property. His most heralded 'solution' to the economic problem of a monetary economy was public-sector expenditures designed to compensate for deficiencies of effective demand in the private sector.

Perhaps the highest mission of professional economists is to seek better principles at a general level of analysis. From time to time in the history of economics, significant new orientations have resulted from breakthroughs in economic theory. Meanwhile, awaiting new breakthroughs of a revolutionary character, economists can make the best use of existing theories. We have suggested, for example, that Marx's system would gain from adopting a formal theory of effective demand and that Keynes's general theory would gain from integrating technological change into the theory of investment. Some systems of theory are so incompatible that they can gain little from one another. Although the prognoses of Marx and Keynes differ fundamentally – the difference between a revolutionary and a reformer – their diagnoses have enough in common mutually to reinforce one another to provide the basis for a better theory than either of theirs separately.

References

Alexander, S.S. (1940), 'Mr. Keynes and Mr. Marx', *Review of Economic Studies*, February, 7, pp. 123–35.

Davidson, P. (1978), 'Why Money Matters: Lessons from a Half-Century of Monetary Theory', *Journal of Post Keynesian Economics*, Autumn, **1**, (2), pp. 46–70.

Davidson, P. (1980), 'The Dual-faceted Nature of the Keynesian Revolution: Money and Money Wages in Unemployment and Production Flow Prices', *Journal of Post Keynesian Economics*, Spring, **2**, (3), pp. 291–307.

Dillard, D. (1954), 'The Theory of a Monetary Economy', in K.K. Kurihara (ed.), *Post Keynesian Economics*, New Brunswick, NJ: Rutgers University Press.

Dillard, D. (1980), 'A Monetary Theory of Production: Keynes and the Institutionalists', *Journal of Economic Issues*, June, **14**, pp. 255–73.

Dillard, D. (1982), 'Money in Marx's *Capital*', paper delivered at the Western Economic Association, Los Angeles, July.

Fan-Hung, (1939), 'Keynes and Marx on the Theory of Capital Accumulation, Money and Interest', *Review of Economic Studies*, October, **7**, pp. 28–41.

Hobson, J.A. (with A.F. Mummery) (1956), *The Physiology of Industry*, reprinted, New York: Kelley and Milman.

Kenway, P. (1980), 'Marx, Keynes and the Possibility of Crisis', *Cambridge Journal of Economics*, **4**, pp. 31–6.

Keynes, J.M. (1930), *A Treatise on Money*, two volumes, London: Macmillan.

Keynes, J.M. (1936), *The General Theory of Employment, Interest and Money*, New York: Harcourt, Brace and Co.

Keynes, J.M. (1971), *The Collected Writings of John Maynard Keynes*, London: Macmillan, St Martin's Press.

Marx, K. (1904), *A Contribution to the Critique of Political Economy*, Chicago: Charles H. Kerr.

Marx, K. (1936), *Capital. A Critique of Political Economy*, Volume 1, New York: Modern Library.

Marx, K. (1933), *Capital. A Critique of Political Economy*, Volume 2, Chicago: Charles H. Kerr.

Marx, K. (1909), *Capital. A Critique of Political Economy*, Volume 3, Chicago: Charles H. Kerr.

Marx, K. (1973), *Grundrisse*, New York: Vintage Books.

Marx, K. (1974), *Economic and Philosophic Manuscripts of 1844*, Moscow: Progress Publishers.

Schumpeter, J.A. (1954), *History of Economic Analysis*, New York: Oxford University Press.

10 Marx and Keynes: the critique of Say's Law

Claudio Sardoni

Introduction: Keynes's revolution and Marx's anticipations

One year before the publication of the *General Theory*, Keynes wrote to G.B. Shaw: 'I believe myself to be writing a book on economic theory which will largely revolutionize . . . the way the world thinks about economic problems'. The new economic theory, in Keynes's opinion, would have cleared away 'the Ricardian foundations of Marxism' (Keynes 1973a, pp. 492–3). The letter eloquently shows Keynes's lack of sympathy for Marxism. However, as one of the most authoritative Keynesian economists, Joan Robinson, pointed out: 'Keynes could never make head or tail of Marx. . . . But starting from Marx would have saved him a lot of trouble' (Robinson 1965, p. 96).

In this chapter I am not concerned with a general study of the relationship between the economic theories of Marx and Keynes. My attention is instead drawn to one particular, and important, element of these theories: the critiques levelled by Marx and Keynes against Say's Law. I shall argue that there exist very important similarities between the two critiques. Keynes, however, was not aware of those similarities; had he been more familiar with Marx's work, he might have recognized that some elements of his own revolutionary theory were already present in Marx.[1]

Keynes tried to demonstrate that a capitalist economy does not necessarily generate levels of aggregate demand sufficiently high to ensure the achievement of full-employment equilibria. In order to demonstrate this, it was crucial for Keynes to reject Say's Law, which defines underemployment arising from insufficient effective demand as impossible.

Keynes held that Say's Law could apply only in an economy with characteristics far removed from those of a capitalist economy. In order for the law and all its corollaries to apply, the analysis must imply an economy where money is never kept idle, so that all savings are invested. Keynes labelled such a type of economy a 'non-monetary economy'. In contradistinction, in a capitalist economy – a 'monetary economy' – a demand for idle money can exist, implying that the level of effective demand can be insufficient to ensure full employment.

Keynes regarded his critique and rejection of Say's Law as a radical break with all the previous traditions in economic thought. For him, only Malthus and a few other minor economists questioned, though unsuccessfully, the validity of the law. As to Marx, Keynes recognized that the 'great puzzle of Effective Demand' lived furtively in Marx's underworld, but he much preferred Gesell's work to Marx's theory of capitalism (Keynes 1936, p. 355).

But Keynes's interpretation of economic theory before the *General Theory* remains unsatisfactory: he overestimated the analytical relevance of Malthus's attempts to reject Say's Law,[2] while underestimating Marx's contribution. Marx's critique and rejection of Say's Law are based on analytical concepts that in fact bring him very close to Keynes.

Marx argued that Ricardo could regard Say's Law as valid only because of his incorrect concept of money and its role in a capitalist economy. For Ricardo, money was a mere means of circulation. Under this assumption, supply necessarily creates its own demand, and effective aggregate demand can never fall short of aggregate supply.

In a capitalist economy, Marx argued, money is not simply a means of circulation. Money is also a store of value: it can be hoarded, kept idle. Capitalist entrepreneurs can be induced to hoard money instead of using it to start productive processes and to invest. If this happens, aggregate demand falls short of aggregate supply and the economy suffers the simultaneous existence of unused productive capacity and unemployed labour.

Thus Marx had already introduced some fundamental analytical concepts required for a consistent criticism of Say's Law. These concepts very closely resemble those used by Keynes.

Before turning to a more detailed exposition of Marx's and Keynes's points of view, we will look at two further issues. First, in spite of the similarities just mentioned, Marx and Keynes often used diverse terminology in their criticisms of Say's Law. In my view, this is due to the fact that they were referring to two different versions of the law: while Marx referred to the Ricardian formulation of Say's Law, Keynes referred to the law in its neo-classical version.

The two versions are different in some fundamental respects and this, quite obviously, made Marx and Keynes adopt a different terminology and perspective. However, in spite of these differences, both Marx and Keynes followed the same basic methodological and analytical path in their rejection of the law. Both argued that Say's Law can be regarded as valid only if some essential characteristics of capitalist economies are assumed away, namely if the role of money and the motives for production and accumulation are overlooked.

Second, although Marx's and Keynes's critiques of Say's Law are close to one another, it is undoubtedly true that, starting from those similar critiques, Marx and Keynes drew different conclusions with respect to the analysis of the working of a capitalist economy. Both argued that it is possible to have unemployment of labour along with underutilization of productive capacity because of an insufficient level of aggregate demand, but this phenomenon actually occurs in different ways in the analytical frameworks of the two authors.

For Marx, the economy experiences unemployment of labour and underutilization of capacity only during, and as a consequence of, general overproduction crises due to a fall in effective demand. In other words, unemployment due to a lack of effective demand can be experienced only during relevant market perturbations.

In Marx's analytical context, it is not possible to have underemployment equilibria, that is, positions of rest characterized by unemployment of labour *and* underutilization of productive capacity.

In Keynes's theory, although the economy may experience market perturbations of the kind considered by Marx, underemployment equilibria are also possible. Indeed, for Keynes, capitalist economies are likely to experience this sort of equilibrium rather than violent perturbations (see, for example, Keynes 1936, pp. 249–54).

I have argued elsewhere (Sardoni 1987, in particular chapters 4, 5, and 7) that this important difference between Marx and Keynes originated in their different microfoundations: classical for Marx and Marshallian for Keynes. However, this issue will not be considered here. This chapter is concerned with the critiques which Marx and Keynes directed at Say's Law in order to show that aggregate demand can fall short of aggregate supply. The way in which this lack of effective demand manifests itself in the economy is not taken into consideration. To use Marx's words, I concentrate only on the 'general possibility' of a lack of effective demand rather than on the way in which such possibility turns into an actual phenomenon.

Marx's critique of Say's Law

The Ricardian version of the law

Marx criticized the law in its Ricardian formulation.[3] According to Ricardo, the production and sale of commodities generates an income which is either spent for consumption or saved. What is saved is however also spent: it is invested to employ additional workers.[4] The whole income is spent and, therefore, it is impossible for a general overproduction of commodities to take place.

In Ricardo's world, for every sale there is a corresponding purchase, so that it is impossible for production and investment to be limited by an insufficient effective demand. In this context, money is merely a device which facilitates the exchange of commodities. The money income earned by selling commodities is never kept idle, since people do not draw any utility from holding money idle. For Ricardo, exchange by means of money is not different conceptually from barter: 'Productions are always bought by productions, as by service; money is only the medium by which the exchange is effected' (1951, pp. 291–2).

Ricardo's acceptance of Say's Law is related to this theory of money and money prices. It is useful to look more closely at this topic, in that it was from this that Marx started to develop his critique.

For Ricardo, there is a direct relationship between the quantity of money in the economy and the level of money prices. If (a) gold is money, (b) the velocity of circulation of money is given, and (c) the outputs of all commodities are given as well, then the quantity of money required to exchange the whole national product is

$$MD = (\Sigma\, x_i\, p_{gi})/V \quad (i = 1, 2, \ldots) \tag{10.1}$$

where p_{gi} is the price of the i-th commodity expressed in terms of the price of gold.[5]

If, for any reason, the quantity of gold (the supply of money) changes, all prices p_{gi}s (and the money wage rate) change as well. For example, if the supply of money increases, people now possess a larger quantity of money which, by assumption, will not be kept idle but is instead spent on commodities: the money value of the aggregate demand increases while the outputs x_is remain unchanged. As a consequence, prices must necessarily rise in proportion to the increase in the quantity of money.[6] Ricardo's theory of money can thus be described as a 'quantity theory of money'.[7]

Marx's criticism of the 'barter economy' and the concept of hoarding

Marx started his criticism of Say's Law by pointing out that the law would be valid if the exchange of commodities took place through barter. In such a case, a 'general glut' would be impossible.

> The only circumstance which could prevent overproduction in all industries simultaneously is . . . the fact that commodity exchanges against commodity – i.e. recourse is taken to the supposed conditions of barter. But this loophole is blocked by the very fact that trade (under capitalist conditions) is not barter, and that therefore the seller of a commodity is not necessarily at the same time the buyer of another. This whole subterfuge then rests on

> abstracting from money and from the fact that we are not concerned with the exchange of products, but with the circulation of commodities, an essential part of which is the separation of purchase and sale. (Marx 1968, pp. 532–3)

In a barter economy, the two acts of selling and buying each commodity occur simultaneously. In this context, Say's Law certainly holds: supply creates its own demand. However, provided it is assumed that money is demanded only as a means of circulation, i.e., that it is never kept idle, the same analytical results can be obtained. This is Ricardo's world, where money is only a means of circulation.

For Marx, by contrast, in a capitalist economy money is also demanded as a store of value; it may be kept idle. In Marx's terminology, money may also be hoarded. Once it is admitted that money can be kept idle, there is no longer any reason why the acts of purchasing and selling should coincide. In some circumstances, money holders may prefer not to buy commodities but to keep money hoards; in such a case, aggregate demand necessarily falls short of aggregate supply.

Marx first introduced the concept of money hoards in order to carry out his criticism of Ricardo's theory of money prices. Later, however, Marx developed the concept of demand for money hoards, that is to say demand for idle money, in order to explain why 'general gluts' are possible in a capitalist economy. Thus, Marx introduced a more general concept of the demand for money. Money is demanded not only as a means of circulation, but also as a liquid reserve (hoarded):

$$MD = MT + MH \qquad (10.2)$$

where MD is the total demand for money, MT is the demand for money as a means of circulation, and MH is the demand for money hoards.

Let us first examine Marx's criticism of Ricardo's theory of money prices. For Marx (1954, p. 115) the quantity of money demanded for the circulation of commodities is given by:

$$MT = (\Sigma\, x_i\, p_{gi})/V \quad (i = 1, 2, \ldots) \qquad (10.3)$$

which is formally identical to Ricardo's equation in (10.1).

In Marx's analysis, however, the equation does not imply that changes in the supply of money, MS, bring about corresponding changes in the price level. In (10.3) above, prices are independent of MS; prices depend only on the value of commodities and on the value of gold.[8] If the velocity of circulation of money is given, the dependent variable is therefore MT. Marx observed that 'given the sum of the values of commodities, and the average rapidity of their metamorphoses, *the quantity of precious metal current as money depends on the value of that precious metal*' (1954, p. 123; emphasis added).[9]

The fact that prices are independent of MS raises a question. If money prices do not depend on MS, how is the equality between demand for and supply of money ensured? For Marx, this equality is always ensured through changes in the level of money hoards. If, for example, MS exceeds MT, the difference (MS − MT) is hoarded. More precisely, if the circulation of commodities is to take place smoothly, a certain share of MS must be always kept idle – hoarded:

> In order that the mass of money, actually current, may constantly saturate the absorbing power of the circulation, it is necessary that the quantity of gold . . . in a country be greater than the quantity required to function as coin. This condition is fulfilled by money taking the form of hoards. These reserves serve as conduits for the supply or withdrawal of money to or from the circulation, which in this way never overflows its banks. (Marx 1954, p. 134)

Thus, the need for a smooth process of commodity circulation is the first reason for the existence of money hoards. Circulation requires that part of the existing money is kept idle.

The type of economy considered above is very simple. It could even be a non-capitalist market economy, where commodities are produced and exchanged by independent individual producers. But Marx went further in his analysis and considered a more developed economy with banking and credit; in such an economy, hoarding becomes even more necessary. People hold liquid reserves in order to be able to meet future payments at the due date:

> When the production of commodities has sufficiently extended itself, money begins to serve as the means of payment beyond the sphere of the circulation of commodities. . . . The development of money into a medium of payment makes it necessary to accumulate money against the dates fixed for the payment of the sum owing. . . . [T]he formation of reserves of the means of payment grows with that progress. (Marx 1954, pp. 139–41)

Once it has been acknowledged that money is hoarded as well as spent, the Ricardian direct relationship between the level of money prices and the supply of money no longer holds. Given the quantities of goods, their values and the velocity of circulation of money, the equality between the supply of and the demand for money (MS = MD = MT + MH) is no longer obtained through changes in the level of money prices but *through changes in the level of money hoards*.[10]

Changes in the capitalists' 'propensity to hoard'

So far, the demand for money hoards, MH, has been considered as a residual that adjusts to changes in the total quantity of money, MS. MT being given, changes in MH result from changes in MS. But Marx also considered the possibility that MH changes for other reasons; in particular, he held that *MH can also change because of variations in the 'propensity to hoard' in the economic system*. This possibility of increase in the propensity to hoard is central to Marx's criticism of Say's Law.

Let us start from equation (10.3) above and suppose that MS > MT, so that a certain quantity of money is already hoarded. With V constant, it is clear that the outputs (x_is) can exchange at the prices p_{gi} (which are assumed to be the prices which ensure a 'normal' or 'usual' rate of profit in all sectors)[11] only if the quantity of money used for circulation is MT. Were the quantity of money used for circulation less than MT, commodities could not exchange at the prices p_{gi}. This means that the quantity of hoarded money has to be MH = MS − MT, if the commodities have to exchange at the prices p_{gi}.

If the money holders decided to hoard a larger quantity MH′ > MH, it would be impossible for all the commodities produced to sell at those prices: either actual prices would fall or stocks of unsold commodities would pile up, or both. In any case, a general overproduction would occur; aggregate demand falls short of aggregate supply, that is, Say's Law does not hold.

Thus, it is the possibility of increases in the demand for idle money which renders Say's Law invalid. An increase in the demand for money hoards can be called an increase in the propensity to hoard. The question is what factors cause an increase in the propensity to hoard. Marx's answer lies in his analysis of the essential characteristics of the capitalist mode of production.

In a capitalist economy, for Marx, the capitalist class as a whole has the monopoly of money:[12] the working class receives money only in the form of wages and spends it at once on consumption goods necessary for subsistence. Only the capitalist class can hoard money, and therefore the possibility of a general overproduction comes from decisions by that class to increase its holdings of idle balances relative to the amount of money it spends in production. In other words, changes in the propensity to hoard are changes in capitalists' propensity to hoard.

Why should the capitalist class as a whole increase its propensity to hoard? The answer lies in the analysis of the motives for production and accumulation which characterize the behaviour of capitalist entrepreneurs. In a capitalist economy, entrepreneurs do not simply produce commodities in order to satisfy, directly or indirectly, their own needs;

they initiate production and investment processes in order to make profits. Only by taking account of this fundamental characteristic of the capitalist mode of production can we explain why the capitalists' propensity to hoard can increase and trigger a general overproduction crisis. Marx reasoned in the following way:

> In reproduction, just as in the accumulation of capital, it is not only a question of replacing the same quantity of use-values of which capital consists, on the former scale or on enlarged scale (in the case of accumulation), *but of replacing the value of the capital advanced along with the usual rate of profit*. . . . If, therefore, . . . the market prices of the commodities . . . fall far below their cost-prices, the reproduction of capital is curtailed as far as possible. Accumulation, however, stagnates even more. Surplus value amassed in the form of money (gold or notes) could only be transformed into capital at a loss. *It therefore lies idle as a hoard in the banks or in the form of credit money. Purchase and sale get bogged down and unemployed capital appears in the form of money*. (1968, p. 494; emphasis added)

Marx clearly refers to situations in which a significant part of the capitalist class is induced to increase its demand for hoards. Marx concentrated his attention on such situations:

> the supply of all commodities can be greater than the demand for all commodities, since the demand for the general commodity, money, exchange-value, is greater than the demand for all particular commodities, in other words the motive to turn the commodity into money, to realise its exchange-value, prevails over the motive to transform the commodity again into use-value. (1968, p. 505)

Thus, in Marx's view, capitalists' decisions to hoard are related to their ability to earn the 'usual' rate of profit.

The passage above, however, raises an issue which is worth a brief digression. In the passage quoted, Marx does not say explicitly whether he is referring exclusively to actual or to both actual and expected prices and rates of profit. However, although Marx did not use the terms 'expected prices' or 'expectations' very often, it is clear that what Marx was implicitly saying is that an actual fall in market prices induces entrepreneurs to expect future prices to be 'far below' their usual level, so that the expected rate of profit is also below its usual level. Only if expectations are introduced, in fact, does the discussion of hoarding make sense.

That a reduction in prices lowers profits and that this can lead to a reduction in the rate of accumulation is obvious – lower profits imply that less is available for investment – but, in this case, hoarding need not take place. Investment might decline but all the available money capital is nonetheless spent. Only if capitalists expect too low a rate of profit do they hoard money rather than invest.

Furthermore, Marx's concept of the capitalist mode of production is such that all relevant decisions must be based on expectations. Capitalists make production and investment decisions within a market framework which cannot be known with certainty. The division of labour itself prevents any individual firm from knowing with certainty the market for its commodities. Each firm, then, has to make its decisions in an uncertain setting.[13]

Thus, for Marx it is not possible to deal with the problem of effective demand and 'general gluts' outside an analysis of the essential characteristics of the capitalist mode of production. The capitalist mode of production is a monetary economy in which production and investment processes are initiated in order to make profits. The capitalist market constitutes an uncertain setting, in which all relevant decisions must be based on expectations. Only by abstracting from all this, is it possible to hold that 'general gluts' cannot occur.

> In order to prove that capitalist production cannot lead to general crises, all its conditions and distinct forms, all its principles and specific features . . . are denied. In fact it is demonstrated that if the capitalist mode of production had not developed in a specific way and become a unique form of social production, but were a mode of production dating back to the most rudimentary stages, then its peculiar contradictions and conflicts and hence also the eruption in crises would not exist. (Marx 1968, p. 501)

A few pages later, Marx repeated his criticism of Ricardo's approach in a way which anticipated some features of Keynes's position on Say's Law:

> All the objections which Ricardo and others raise against overproduction, etc., rest on the fact that they regard bourgeois production either as a mode of production in which no distinction exists between purchase and sale – direct barter – or as social production, implying that society, as if according to a plan, distributes its means of production and productive forces in the degree and measure which is required for the fulfillment of the various social needs, so that each sphere of production receives the quota of social capital required to satisfy the corresponding need. (1968, p. 529)

In an economic system where production is arranged in such a way as to ensure the fulfillment of all social needs, money cannot play any role other than that of a mere medium of circulation. There is no reason for social agents to hold idle money under such circumstances.

As we shall see, Keynes's critique of Say's Law follows the same approach as Marx's. For Keynes, as for Marx, the monetary nature of the capitalist economy and the motives which govern entrepreneurs' decisions and actions are the starting points for the critique of Say's Law.

However, before turning to an examination of Keynes's point of view, it will be useful to consider a further issue raised by the acceptance of Say's Law.

Say's Law in Ricardo and in neo-classical economics

The validity of Say's Law implied, for Ricardo, that any amount of capital could be employed without facing any obstacle on the demand side and that, therefore, the existing productive capacity in the economy is always fully utilized. But Ricardo never argued that Say's Law must imply the full employment of labour.[14]

Thus, Marx never had to take the trouble to demonstrate that full employment of labour is not necessarily achieved in a capitalist economy. In his critique of Ricardo, Marx was concerned only with the possibility that effective demand may fall short of supply. As a consequence of this, part of the existing productive capacity may remain unused and unemployment of labour rise. If there is unused capacity, the level of unemployment is, of course, higher than in the case of full utilization of capacity.

Keynes dealt with Say's Law in its neo-classical formulation. The law in such a formulation implies that the economy necessarily achieves full employment equilibria, and it is based on the idea that the equality between investment and saving is ensured through changes in the rate of interest.

This can partly explain why, sometimes, the similarities between Marx and Keynes remain hidden. The different formulations of the law by classical economists and neo-classical economists induced Marx and Keynes to use a different terminology in their criticisms, even though they were employing very similar concepts.

Keynes's critique of Say's Law

From a 'neutral economy' to an 'entrepreneur economy'

Keynes included all his predecessors under the denomination 'classical economists', regarding Ricardo's approach as fundamentally identical to that taken by the neo-classical school. Therefore, for Keynes, the criticism of the neo-classical version of the law applied directly to the classical version as well.[15] However, as I have already noted, Keynes's interpretation of the classicals is incorrect and, therefore, his argument must be regarded as applying only to the neo-classical formulation of Say's Law.

According to the neo-classical economists criticized by Keynes, competition would lead to the expansion of production and employment up to the level at which the supply of output is perfectly inelastic, that is to say up to full employment. For Keynes, however, there is only one level of employment which can be consistent with equilibrium. In fact,

> any other level will lead to inequality between the aggregate supply price of output as a whole and its aggregate demand price. This level cannot be greater than full employment . . . . But there is no reason, in general, for expecting it to be equal to full employment. The effective demand associated with full employment is a special case, only realised when the propensity to consume and the inducement to invest stand in a particular relationship to one another. (1936, p. 28)

In this form, however, Keynes's criticism of Say's Law bears scarcely any resemblance to Marx's criticism. But, in his writings prior to the *General Theory*, Keynes criticized Say's Law in a rather different way. There, the similarities with Marx emerge much more clearly.

In an article written in 1933 in honour of Arthur Spiethoff ('A Monetary Theory of Production' in Keynes 1973a, pp. 408–11), Keynes criticized the law by explicitly bringing in money and its essential relevance. Traditionally, money has been regarded by economists solely as a useful instrument which facilitates exchange but which is neutral with respect to its effects on the economy as a whole. An economy in which money has such characteristics is called by Keynes a 'real-exchange economy', which is very different from his conception of a 'monetary economy'. In a monetary economy, the kind of economy in which we live, money plays a specific role; it influences motives and decisions and affects the rate of interest as well as the relationship between total output and expenditure (see Keynes 1973a, pp. 408–9).

According to Keynes, most economists, though aware of the fact that we live in a monetary economy, wrote their treatises under the assumption that a market capitalist economy behaves as if it were a real-exchange economy.

Keynes developed many of these points more fully in the 1933 draft of several chapters of the *General Theory*.[16] Here, Keynes partly changed terminology, now calling a real-exchange economy a 'co-operative economy' while a monetary economy is called an 'entrepreneur economy'. Furthermore, Keynes introduced the concept of a neutral entrepreneur economy or 'neutral economy'.

A co-operative economy, though it uses money for exchange, is essentially equivalent to a barter economy in which factors of production are rewarded by a share of the real output.

> I define a *barter economy* as one in which the factors of production are rewarded by dividing up in agreed proportions the actual output of their co-operative efforts. It is not necessary that they should receive their share of the output *in specie*; the position is the same if they share the sale-proceeds of the output in agreed proportions. Since this economy does not exclude the use of money for purposes of transitory convenience, it might perhaps be better to call it a *real-wage economy*, or a *co-operative economy*, as distinct from an *entrepreneur economy*. In a barter economy (or co-operative) only miscalculation or stupid obstinacy can stand in the way of production, if the value of the expected real product exceeds the real costs. (Keynes 1979, pp. 66–7)

In so far as factors of production are rewarded in agreed proportions, money is used only as a 'transitory convenience', to buy a predetermined share of the output. In this economy, which resembles the case of 'social production' mentioned by Marx (see above p. 227), full employment of all factors is ensured: both the demand for and the supply of each factor depend on its expected reward in terms of output, and as long as the expected output exceeds its cost, production will be carried on. When the expected value of the output is no longer larger than its cost, full employment is reached.[17]

The same analytical results can be achieved even if less restrictive assumptions are made. In fact, even if some factors do not use all their rewards to buy a share of the current output but divert part of them to purchase a share of pre-existing wealth, full employment is still attained, provided that the sellers of pre-existing wealth in turn use their proceeds to buy current output (see Keynes 1979, p. 77). The latter situation depicts an economy in which income may be spent on goods or saved by each individual factor; nevertheless, what is saved is spent.

At this stage, it is easy to conceive of an economy in which the same conditions described above apply but there is a class of entrepreneurs who start productive processes in order to sell the output for money. This economy is called a *neutral economy* by Keynes. It is an economy

> where the starting up of productive processes largely depends on a class of entrepreneurs who hire the factors of production for money and look to their recoupment from selling the output for money, provided that the whole of the current incomes of the factors of production are necessarily spent, directly or indirectly on purchasing their own current output from entrepreneurs. (Keynes 1979, p. 77)

In this economy there is a mechanism which ensures that the

exchange value of the factors' money incomes is always equal, at the aggregate level, to the proportion of output which would have been the factors' share in a co-operative economy (see Keynes 1979, p. 78). Thus a capitalist economy behaves like a co-operative economy only if these restrictive conditions are fulfilled.

It is evident that Keynes's definitions of co-operative economy and neutral economy correspond to concepts which belong to neo-classical economics. However, if two qualifications are made, Keynes's criticisms apply to Ricardo as well. If we remove the idea that the validity of Say's Law necessarily implies full employment of labour and that the equality of saving to investment is ensured by a particular market mechanism, it is correct to argue that also Ricardo carried out his analysis within the context of a neutral entrepreneur economy. For Ricardo as well, money is a 'transitory convenience'.

The essential characteristics of an 'entrepreneur economy'

From a methodological point of view, the approaches of Marx and Keynes are very similar: it is possible to argue that Say's Law applies to a capitalist economy only by postulating characteristics that are not actually found in capitalism. Keynes came even closer to Marx when he described the essential features of an entrepreneur economy, i.e., a capitalist economy. Keynes even used Marxian terms:[18]

> The distinction between a co-operative economy and an entrepreneur economy bears some relation to a pregnant observation made by Karl Marx. . . . He pointed out that the nature of production in the actual world is not, as economists seem often to suppose, a case of C-M-C′, i.e., of exchanging commodity (or effort). That may be the standpoint of the private consumer. But it is not the attitude of *business*, which is the case of M-C-M′, i.e., of parting with money for commodity (or effort) in order to obtain more money. (Keynes 1979, p. 81)

In Marx's world, it is the profitability of entrepreneurs' spending which determines the dynamics of capitalist economies. Entrepreneurs start productive processes not in order to produce a larger output but to earn a profit, a profit which necessarily takes a monetary form. Keynes made the same point.

> An entrepreneur is interested, not in the amount of product, but in the amount of money which will fall to his share. He will increase his output if by so doing he expects to increase his money profit, even though this profit represents a smaller quantity of product than before. (Keynes 1979, p. 82)

Entrepreneurs will direct money to production if they expect that it is profitable (in terms of money) to do so. If production is expected to be unprofitable, money is kept idle, and, as a result, less employment is offered by entrepreneurs: 'The choice . . . in deciding whether or not to offer employment is a choice between using money in this way or in some other way or *not using it at all*' (Keynes 1979, p. 82; emphasis added).

Keynes also expressed his view in a very similar way after the publication of the *General Theory*; in his 1937 article 'The General Theory of Employment' Keynes pointed out that investment

> depends on two sets of judgments about the future, neither of which rests on an adequate or secure foundation – on the propensity to hoard and on opinions on the future yield of capital assets. Nor is there any reason to suppose that the fluctuations in one of these factors will tend to offset the fluctuations in the other. When a more pessimistic view is taken about future yields, that is no reason why there should be a diminished propensity to hoard. Indeed, the conditions which aggravate the one factor tend, as a rule, to aggravate the other. *For the same circumstances which lead to pessimistic views about future yields are apt to increase the propensity to hoard.* (In Keynes 1973b, p. 118; emphasis added)

Conclusion: Marx's and Keynes's 'entrepreneur economy'

In spite of their occasional differences in terminology, Marx and Keynes offered substantially similar arguments for rejecting Say's Law. Furthermore, their accounts of the fundamental characteristics of a capitalist economy are also very close. Here, in order to underline their similarities, I summarize their points of view by employing a uniform terminology.

Say's Law applies in an economy in which money is only a medium of exchange, a 'transitory convenience'. But in a capitalist economy, money is also used as a store of value. Capitalist entrepreneurs may spend money to start productive processes or they may keep it idle. The profitability of production and investment is the essential factor determining how money is used.

If capitalists' expectations concerning the profitability of their productive processes become pessimistic, the demand for idle money (hoards) rises while the demand for goods and labour decreases. Money is the best store of value in a system where all transactions require money. Money can be converted into goods, or labour, at any date in the future.

An increase in the demand for money is different from an increase in the demand for any other good. A larger demand for a certain commodity, along with a smaller demand for other commodities, causes a shift in employment but not necessarily a decrease in its aggregate level. On the contrary, a larger demand for money, along with a smaller demand for other goods, causes a decrease in the demand for labour in the production of goods. In fact, the increased demand for money gives rise to no increase (or no significant increase) in the level of employment in the production of money. This is true whether money is a commodity (gold) or a nominal instrument. The larger quantity of money which is demanded to be kept idle (hoarded) does not have to be produced. It is made available through the decrease in the demand for 'active money', that is, money as a medium of circulation.

Finally, all these points can be summarized by using Joan Robinson's words. An increase in hoarding occurs as a result of a 'change in sentiment', that is a change in capitalists' expectations. Hoards are

> the total quantity of money minus the active circulation ('idle balances'). An 'increase in hoarding', when the total quantity of money is constant, is then brought about by a decline in incomes and trade activity, which releases money from the active circulation of money. (Robinson 1938, p. 232)

Although Marx and Keynes addressed their criticisms to theoretical settings which were significantly different, they emphasized elements which are fundamentally the same. Both accused their predecessors of a lack of 'realism', in the sense that they assumed a type of economy, the essential characteristics of which do not correspond to those of actual capitalist economies.

Theoretical reasoning, in whatever discipline, is not and *cannot* be realistic in the sense of offering a full description of the object under investigation. Theory cannot reproduce reality on a 'one to one' scale; it has to grasp the essential and basic elements of its object of investigation through a process of abstraction. In this process, accidental and contingent elements are taken out of consideration. This is the way in which theory 'reproduces' reality.[19]

But the process of abstraction is very difficult. While contingent aspects of the object must be weeded out, no fundamental characteristic should be mistaken for an accidental or irrelevant one and therefore overlooked. If in the process of abstraction, fundamental aspects of the object get lost, theory ceases to be 'realistic', i.e., it offers a 'reproduction' of the object which no longer fits the actual 'concrete' object.

Marx's critique of Ricardo's analysis of effective demand is a logical consequence of this methodological approach. In developing his conception of the capitalist economy, Ricardo failed to understand that money, and its specific role, cannot be left out of consideration. Neglecting money, Ricardo could liken the capitalist process of exchange to barter and, consequently, he failed to see that aggregate demand can fall short of aggregate supply and give rise to all the consequences that Marx analysed.

Keynes was not familiar with Marx's methodology but it is clear that his methodological criticism of his predecessors resembles Marx's critique of Ricardo. Keynes, like Marx, stressed that his predecessors had failed to understand that the analysis of a capitalist economy cannot be carried out by assuming that it behaves like a 'neutral economy', where money does not play any relevant role. The assumption of a neutral economy is an 'unrealistic' abstraction.

Thus, a faulty process of abstraction led neo-classical economists and classical economists astray and prevented them from understanding the real nature of a capitalist economy, an 'entrepreneur economy' in which money is not 'neutral'.

Marx and Keynes played very similar roles with respect to the doctrines which were dominant in their time. Both brought about a radical break with the past, and provided a new perspective from which to observe and explain the working of the 'economic machine' – a concept first developed and used by classical political economists.[20]

Such a machine is governed by laws which can be studied in a scientific way. These laws regulate the process through which the machine can reproduce itself and grow. This process fundamentally promotes the general interest because all social actors (individuals or, rather, classes) in the system benefit from it.

In this framework, each class pursues its own specific interests and, in so doing, acts in the general interest as well. In particular, the capitalist class in pursuing its own interests enables the machine to reproduce and grow, so that it provides benefits for all classes. The laws that regulate the machine force individual capitalists to behave in this way.

Adam Smith was the classical economist most firmly convinced of this view (see, e.g., Smith 1976, p. 475). Ricardo was less confident than Smith of the compatibility of the interests of all social classes,[21] but he nevertheless believed that capitalist entrepreneurs, in the pursuit of their own interest, also work in the general interest.

At this junction Marx entered the picture and contributed a fundamental new insight. The machine cannot possibly work without using money, which has to perform several different roles. It is necessary to use money, because individual and social classes are organized in such a way that exchange (and, hence, production, reproduction, and growth) cannot take place without it.

Once money enters the scenario, the analytical framework is radically altered. In so far as money does not play a significant role, entrepreneurs are 'forced' to act in the general interest. When money is given a more general and fundamental role to play, entrepreneurs are given, so to speak, a higher degree of 'freedom'. They are no longer compelled to act in the general interest. The pursuit of their interest (to maximize their profits) is no longer necessarily associated with producing and investing at the highest possible level. The existence of money, and the possibility of keeping it idle, gives them the option of choosing not to produce and invest, so that the levels of income and employment of the working class are adversely affected.

The neo-classical vision of the economic machine was very different from the classical view. But neo-classical economists shared with classical political economists a confidence in the convergence of individual and general interest. Neo-classical economics, indeed, went far beyond classical political economy and maintained that each and every individual behaves in such a way that the general interest is realized in the form of a general equilibrium position, at which point everyone maximizes benefits and nobody can be better off. Smith and Ricardo certainly had less restrictive concepts of the general interest.

Keynes, in his critique of the neo-classical vision of the economic machine, played much the same role as Marx had done with respect to classical economics. The capitalist machine cannot function without money; and once money is made an integral part of the analytical picture, the actions of individuals may have consequences which are opposed to the general interest. While they ensure the achievement of the private interests, individual actions may prevent the economy from finding its equilibrium on the boundary of feasible optimum equilibria (see Boland 1985, pp. 185–92). Money again is the scientific 'tool' used by Keynes to discard his predecessors' theories.

Marx and Keynes, like their respective predecessors, believed that the economic system can be regarded as a machine and, then, that it is possible to study it scientifically. But they argued that the machine and its functioning could not be studied without taking account of money and its specific role. Taking account of money, i.e., building a different set of scientific abstractions, enabled Marx and Keynes to explain how individual interests and the general interest can come into conflict.

The concepts of money developed by Marx and Keynes constitute scientific discoveries: theoretical innovations that produced a new vision of the object under investigation. Marx and Keynes built theories based on abstractions which explained fundamental characteristics of the 'machine', characteristics which their respective predecessors regarded as merely secondary or utterly irrelevant.

Notes

1. Neither Marxist nor Keynesian economists have paid much attention to the relationship between Marx and Keynes. The most significant exception is Joan Robinson. In the years following the publication of the *General Theory*, some attempts to compare the two economists in a rather systematic way were made (e.g. Fan-Hung 1939, pp. 57–63; Alexander 1939). For more recent contributions see Dasgupta 1983, pp. 57–63; Dillard 1984; Crotty 1986; Heilbroner 1986; Mott 1986. As for Joan Robinson's contributions, see Robinson 1942; 1951, pp. 133–45; 1960, pp. 1–17; 1965, pp. 148–81; 1973, pp. 264–8; 1980, pp. 192–202.
2. Keynes's interpretation of Malthus has given rise to a wide debate. For example, Robbins (1952), Corry (1959), Garegnani (1978), and Milgate (1982, pp. 53–4) have all held that Keynes basically misunderstood Malthus's position and overestimated its innovative character. See, by contrast, Paglin (1961), Eltis (1980) and Costabile (1983) for a different interpretation of Malthus's theory and its relationships to Keynes's ideas. See also Sardoni (1987, pp. 11–20) for a reconstruction of the unsatisfactory criticism of Say's Law by Malthus.
3. Ricardo expressed the law in the following terms: 'M. Say has . . . most satisfactorily shewn, that there is no amount of capital which may not be employed in a country because demand is only limited by production. No man produces, but with a view to consume or sell, and he never sells, but with an intention to purchase some other commodity, which may be immediately useful to him, or which may contribute to future production' (Ricardo 1951, p. 290).
4. This was also Smith's point of view. Savings are employed as capital and consumed by productive workers. See Smith 1976, p. 359.
5. $p_{gi} = p_i/p_g$. p_g is the price of gold.
6. Relative prices, p_{gi}/p_{gj} (i,j = 1, 2, . . .), however remain unchanged. It is only the price of gold which falls.
7. The same reasoning applies if the role of money is played by a nominal instrument – for example, paper money. For an exposition of the classical theory of money see also Green 1982.
8. $p_{gi} = v_i/v_g$, where v_i and v_g denote the value of the i-th commodity and gold, respectively. The values of commodities as well as of gold depend, in turn, on the technical conditions of production, that is to say, they depend on the quantity of embodied labour.
9. Marx continued: 'The erroneous opinion that it is, on the contrary, prices that are determined by the quantity of the circulating medium and that the latter depends on the quantity of precious metals in the country; this opinion was based by those who first held it, on the absurd hypothesis that commodities are without a price, and money without a value, when they first enter into circulation, and that, once in the circulation, an aliquot part of the medley of commodities is exchanged for an aliquot part of the heap of precious metals' (Marx 1954, pp. 124–5).
10. Marx, however, was not completely consistent in his rejection of the quantity theory of money. In dealing with the case of paper money, Marx seemed to accept the Ricardian quantity theory which he had rejected in the case of gold money. See Marx 1954, p. 128. For a criticism of Marx's treatment of paper money, see Sardoni 1987, pp. 30–1.
11. The reason for this assumption will become clearer later on.
12. See Marx 1956, p. 425: 'the capitalist class . . . has a monopoly of the social means of production *and money*' (emphasis added).
13. In the following passage, Marx shows how firms try to defend themselves from uncertainty and how individual decisions, made in an uncertain setting, affect aggregate results: 'Since . . . the autonomization of the world market . . . increases with the development of monetary relations . . . and vice versa, since the general bond and all-round interdependence in production and consumption increase together with the interdependence and indifference of the consumers and producers

to one another; since this contradiction leads to crises, etc., hence, . . . efforts are made to overcome it: institutions emerge whereby each individual can acquire information about the activity of all others and attempt to adjust his own accordingly. . . . This means that, although the total supply and demand are independent of the actions of each individual, everyone attempts to inform himself about them, and this knowledge then reacts back in practice on the total supply and demand' (Marx 1973, pp. 160–1).

14. Perhaps the most convincing evidence that Ricardo did not associate Say's Law with full employment is his analysis of machinery and unemployment in the famous chapter 31 of the *Principles* (Ricardo 1951, pp. 386–97). Although Ricardo undoubtedly assumed that the law was valid, he pointed out that the process of accumulation could cause unemployment of labour to rise. On the relationship between the full utilization of productive capacity and full employment of labour in Ricardo, see also Garegnani 1978, pp. 338–41 and Milgate 1982, pp. 39–40.
15. 'The classical theory assumes . . . that the aggregate demand price (or proceeds) always accommodates itself to the aggregate supply price; so that, whatever the volume of N may be, the proceeds D assume a value equal to the aggregate supply price Z which corresponds to N. That is to say, effective demand instead of having a unique equilibrium value, is an infinite range of values all equally admissible; and the amount of employment is indeterminate except in so far as the marginal disutility of labour sets an upper limit' (Keynes 1936, p. 26).
16. In 1933, Keynes worked out two draft tables of contents and drafted several chapters of the second one. All this material was published only in 1979. On this, see the 'Editorial Note' to Volume XXIX of Keynes's *Collected Writings* (Keynes 1979, pp. xiii–iv). In the drafts of the first chapter (Keynes 1979, pp. 66–8), of the second chapter (pp. 76–87), and of the third chapter (pp. 87–111), Keynes dealt with the issues discussed here. On the theoretical importance of Keynes's drafts, see also Rotheim 1981 and Tarshis 1989.
17. In other words, the 'second postulate' of classical (neo-classical) economics holds good. See Keynes 1936, pp. 5–7.
18. However, he did not directly refer to Marx's works but to a book by McCracken on business cycles (1933).
19. Marx expressed this in the following terms. Reality 'appears in the process of thinking . . . as a process of concentration, as a result, not as a point of departure, even though it is the point of departure in reality and hence also the point of departure for observation and conception. . . . [T]he abstract determination leads towards a reproduction of the concrete by way of thought' (Marx 1973, p. 101).
20. The classical concept of 'economic machine' has been vividly described by Meek: '[I]t was they who first began consciously and consistently to visualize society as a kind of gigantic machine, a vast and intricate mechanism whose innumerable cogs and belts and levers were related to one another in certain defined ways. . . . Thus was born the truly revolutionary notion that the things which actually happened in society reflected the working of certain law-governed, mechanistic processes, "autonomous" and "objective" in the sense that they operated independently of the wills of individual men' (1977, p. 177).
21. The most obvious example is his analysis of the conflict between rentiers and capitalists.

References

Alexander, G. (1939), 'Mr. Keynes and Mr. Marx', *Review of Economic Studies*, VII.

Boland, L.A. (1985), 'The Foundations of Keynes' Methodology: The General Theory', in Lawson and Pesaran (1985).

Corry, B.A. (1959), 'Malthus and Keynes: A Reconsideration', *Economic Journal*, LXIX.

Costabile, L. (1983), 'Natural Prices, Market Prices and Effective Demand in Malthus', *Australian Economic Papers*, June.

Crotty, J.R. (1986), 'Marx, Keynes, and Minsky on the Instability of the Capitalist Growth Process and the Nature of Government Economic Policy', in Helburn and Bramhall (1986).

Dasgupta, A.K. (1983), *Phases of Capitalism and Economic Theory*, Oxford: Oxford University Press.

Dillard, D. (1984), 'Keynes and Marx: A Centennial Appraisal', *Journal of Post-Keynesian Economics*, VI, (3).

Eltis, W. (1980), 'Malthus' Theory of Effective Demand and Growth', *Oxford Economic Papers*, March.

Fan-Hung (1939), 'Keynes and Marx on the Theory of Capital Accumulation, Money and Interest', *Review of Economic Studies*, VII.

Garegnani, P. (1978), 'Notes on Consumption, Investment and Effective Demand: I', *Cambridge Journal of Economics*, II.

Green, R. (1982), 'Money, Output and Inflation in Classical Economics', *Contributions to Political Economy*, **1**.

Heilbroner, R.L. (1986), 'Economics and Political Economy: Marx, Keynes, and Schumpeter', in Helburn and Bramhall (1986).

Helburn, S.W. and D.F. Bramhall (eds) (1986), *Marx, Schumpeter, & Keynes. A Centenary Celebration of Dissent*, Armonk: M.E. Sharpe Inc.

Keynes, J.M. (1936), *The General Theory of Employment, Interest and Money*, London: Macmillan.

Keynes, J.M. (1937), 'The General Theory of Unemployment', *Quarterly Journal of Economics*, February. Reprinted in Keynes (1973b).

Keynes, J.M. (1973a), *Collected Writings, Vol. XIII*, London: Macmillan.

Keynes, J.M. (1973b), *Collected Writings, Vol. XIV*, London: Macmillan.

Keynes, J.M. (1979), *Collected Writings, Vol. XXIX*, London: Macmillan.

Lawson, T. and H. Pesaran (eds) (1985), *Keynes' Economics. Methodological Issues*, Beckerham: Croom Helm.

Marx, K. (1954), *Capital*, Volume I, Moscow: Progress Publishers.

Marx, K. (1956), *Capital*, Volume II, Moscow: Progress Publishers.

Marx, K. (1968), *Theories of Surplus Value*, Part II, Moscow: Progress Publishers.

Marx, K. (1973), *Grundrisse*, London: Penguin.

McCracken, H.L. (1933), *Value Theory and Business Cycles*, New York.

Meek, R.L. (1977), *Smith, Marx and After*, London: Chapman and Hall.

Milgate, M. (1982), *Capital and Employment*, London: Academic Press.

Mott, T. (1986), 'Marx, Keynes, and Schumpeter: A Synthesis with Special Emphasis on the Contributions of Michal Kalecki', in Helburn and Bramhall (1986).

Paglin, M. (1961), *Malthus and Lauderdale: The Anti-Ricardian Tradition*, New York: Augustus M. Kelley.

Pheby, J. (1989), *New Directions in Post-Keynesian Economics*, Aldershot: Edward Elgar.

Ricardo, D. (1951), *Principles of Political Economy*, Cambridge: Cambridge University Press.

Robbins, L. (1952), *The Theory of Economic Policy in English Classical Political Economy*, London: Macmillan.

Robinson, J. (1938), 'The Concept of Hoarding', *Economic Journal*, XLVIII.

Robinson, J. (1942), *An Essay on Marxian Economics*, London: Macmillan.

Robinson, J. (1951), *Collected Economic Papers. Vol. I*, Oxford: Basil Blackwell.

Robinson, J. (1960), *Collected Economic Papers. Vol. II*, Oxford: Basil Blackwell.

Robinson, J. (1965), *Collected Economic Papers. Vol. III*, Oxford: Basil Blackwell.

Robinson, J. (1973), *Collected Economic Papers. Vol. IV*, Oxford: Basil Blackwell.

Robinson, J. (1980), *Further Contributions to Modern Economics*, Oxford: Blackwell.

Rotheim, R.J. (1981), 'Keynes' Monetary Theory of Value (1933)', *Journal of Post-Keynesian Economics*, summer.

Sardoni, C. (1987), *Marx and Keynes on Economic Recession*, Brighton: Wheatsheaf.

Smith, A. (1976), *An Inquiry into the Nature and Causes of the Wealth of Nations*, Chicago: Chicago University Press.
Tarshis, L. (1989), 'Keynes's Co-operative Economy & His Aggregate Supply Function', in Pheby (1989).

11 Marx, Keynes, and the theory of a monetary economy[1]

Roy J. Rotheim

The focus of this chapter is to consider similar criticisms by Marx and Keynes of economic systems which were formulated such that what Marx called 'crises' and what Keynes called 'failures of the effective demand' could *logically* never occur. What emerged from their probing was that in the systems of those whom they were criticizing, money could only function as a neutral medium of exchange (or actually a useful fiction), and which therefore led to a logical separation of real and monetary phenomena.

Both Marx and Keynes wished to show that a capitalist economy was predominantly cyclical by nature, with no natural tendency to gravitate toward a prescribed state of balance. Economic cycles, especially downturns, could only be expressed in terms of a discordance between *aggregate* supply and *aggregate* demand (see Kenway 1980 and Lavoie 1983). Marx and Keynes were critical of their classical predecessors for whom such an observation was logically ruled out. Each recognized that those whom they were criticizing confused changes in relative demand with changes in aggregate demand. As such, Marx and Keynes accused those theories of being specific to a unique situation and in no way were they a general theory of economic activity. For a general theory had to to be able to explain situations when the system was in equilibrium and when it was not. Moreover, both observed that a state of over-production (explicable only under a general theory of economic behaviour) had to occur simultaneously with an increased demand for money, not as a neutral medium, but rather as a means of payment and as a store of value. These added attributes of money, each acknowledged, were not possible in a world of equilibrium where production automatically implied sale.

Keynes was not directly aware of these conclusions by Marx (although more on this below). Nevertheless, the similarities of their criticisms are striking. What accounted for this similarity was surely a unique set of common questions, that is, an alternative positive heuristic, which led them to their similar revolutionary views on the nature and scope of capitalist economies.

The concern here will be less on providing detailed exegeses on

Marx's and Keynes's theories, than on observing the commonality in approach in their views on monetary as opposed to barter economies. The significance of this investigation lies as much with the methodological insights that it offers as with the theoretical issues that are raised. The next section will focus on Marx's critique of the equilibrium theories of Classical political economy.[2] What will be shown is that the Classical political economists made no distinction between production in general and capitalist commodity production, which led to their conclusions only bearing validity at the point of equilibrium. It is in this sense that the Classical economists paid no attention to monetary variables. This summary of Marx's critique will then provide the groundwork for an analysis of Keynes's criticism of what he called Classical economics, both from the vantage point of the early drafts of *The General Theory* and from their final articulation in the book itself.

Marx's distinction between abstract and commodity production

> The capitalist economy is necessarily a monetary economy. And only if one assigns a definite economic existence to money can one separate the barter economy from the monetary economy completely and without harm to the study of production. Then one will see that hoarding meets a need and represents a conversion of value by private economic agents, marking the dividing line between the monetary and barter economies in such a way that it is impossible to analyse the equilibrium of exchanges in capitalist production in 'real' terms as if money had no economic role. (DeBrunhoff 1976, p. 21)

While Marx borrowed much from his predecessors, especially Quesnay, Smith, Ricardo and J.S. Mill, the uniqueness of his system becomes evident in the way that his analysis differed from those writers. Marx made a clear distinction between what he called Classical political economy and vulgar economics, where the former saw value relations emanating from the conditions of the creation of products whereas the latter was concerned solely with market phenomena (Marx 1867, pp. 174–5). And, while he favoured the initial emphasis of Classical political economy, Marx still found their method to be overly one-sided, in that their analysis was incapable of explaining the organic (dialectical) nature of the economy. It is common knowledge that Marx held little credibility for Say's (or Mill's) Law; that there could never be an overproduction of all commodities (see Kenway 1980). What is of importance is to see that Marx's criticism of this proposition emanated from the fact that the economy described by Say, James Mill, and subsequently Ricardo, only had ontological significance at the point where production and consumption were equivalent. To then pretend that there was a theory of movement which brought about those conclusions was methodologically incorrect. There is no real time in the Ricardian model because his categories only had meaning at the point of equilibrium.[3] So, while Marx preferred the Classical political economic approach of Ricardo, which focused initial attention at the conditions of production, he rejected the total model by which economic phenomena would be explained.

It was for this reason that Marx lodged severe criticism at Ricardo's theory of value. For Ricardo, relative exchange values for two commodities merely reflected the relative direct and indirect labour embodied by each. Relative values were something defined solely within the sphere of production, while the subsequent sale of products was taken as a given and therefore of no impact on the transformation of values into exchange values.

But, as was just indicated, while relying heavily on Ricardo's theory, especially its focus on value being created within the sphere of production, Marx saw its thrust as markedly one-sided. To see this, recall that Marx identified relative exchange value as being determined by the amount of abstract, socially necessary labour time characterizing each commodity (Marx 1867, pp. 38–9). For Marx, the idea of abstract, socially necessary labour time reflected both a quantitative and a qualitative side. The quantitative aspect of exchange value could be measured in terms of labour time itself, in a fashion closely akin to the one described by Ricardo. However, it is clear that focusing on labour time as the sole determinant of exchange value, assures the vitiation of the process of circulation as an essential factor (not to be confused with *cause*) in the equation. This would indicate that equilibrium (market clearing) was a foregone conclusion of production. The difficulty here lies in the fact that such a conceptualization identifies the circulation of commodities to be a strictly neutral process, that is, one with no effect on any outcome. And it is in these instances, as will be seen, that money is relegated to the role of what Marx called means of purchase.

Marx was critical of this one-sided view of exchange value and the consequent neutral role of money in that mind-frame. He observed that Ricardo's

> false conception of money is due to the fact that he concentrates exclusively on the quantitative determination of exchange-value, namely that it is equal to a definite quantity of labour-time, forgetting on the other hand the qualitative characteristic, that individual labour must present itself as abstract, general social labour only through its alienation. (Marx 1968, Volume II, p. 504)

In other words, the qualitative aspect of exchange value reflected the notion that the labour in whose duration value is considered is both 'social' labour and 'abstract' labour. Such forms presuppose markets and commodities. Recall that Marx saw labour as a commodity characterized by quantitative and qualitative forms. Labour power as a historical phenomenon is only nurtured by its alienation, a process which requires a market in which it can be bought and sold. A complete theory of commodity production required a focus on both the sphere of production and the spheres of circulation (input and product markets).

Marx's dissatisfaction stemmed from the fact that the Classical political economists confused capitalist or commodity production with production in general, 'that it has never succeeded, by means of its analysis of commodities, and in particular of their value, in discovering the form of value which in fact turns value into exchange-value' (Marx 1867, p. 174).

For the Classical economists, the economy was characterized as one of blissful unity. Their perception of the matter was that production and circulation were logically complementary spheres, where the latter always acted so as to equilibrate the forces that emanated from the former. This heuristic enabled them to posit the real equilibrium of the system and then to define the role of money and monetary theory in terms of the degree to which such a medium efficiently facilitates the real equilibrium exchange.

Marx was concerned that Ricardo *et al.* confused the production of goods, whose ultimate *raison d'être* is final consumption, and the production of commodities, which was unique to a capitalist mode of production, and whose motivation was not one of consumption, but rather of the expansion of exchange value, via sale in a market. Marx's aim was thus to show that the production of goods, resembled a logical, equilibrium system, which abstracted from both time and space. Production and use, purchase and sale, were coincident. It was in this vein that he criticized the theory of Ricardo in that 'the unity and not the separation of purchase and sale exists (displaying) a manner of thinking the criticism of which belongs to the sphere of logic, and not to that of economics' (Marx 1859, p. 96). Here every purchase is considered as a sale, and every sale a purchase; the equilibrium of the entire system is assured from the outset.

Circulation, the process of commodities trading for money which in turn traded for commodities, or C–M–C, revealed itself in the classical schema as being reduced to one of direct barter, where products traded directly for products

> that overproduction is not possible or at least that no general glut of the market is possible, is based on the proposition that products are exchanged against products or as Mill put it, on the 'metaphysical equilibrium of sellers and buyers', and this led to (the conclusion) that demand and supply are identical. (Marx 1968, Volume II, p. 493)

Use value ultimately trades for use value,

> the outcome of the circuit C–M–C shows that it dissolved into the exchange of C–C. Commodity has been exchanged for commodity, use value for use value, and the transformation of the commodity into money, or the commodity as money, is merely an intermediary stage which helps to bring about this metabolism. (Marx 1859, p. 95)

Money, in other words, acts solely as a medium of exchange.

But Marx did not consider such money to be 'real' money, as Arnon observes, but as something more akin to 'accounting' money. Arnon cites Marx as saying in this regard: 'Money is needed here only as a category, as mental relation' (Arnon 1984, p. 560). The economic theories of his predecessors in which money played this unique role were thus considered by Marx to be logical constructs, rather than models of an ongoing real-world economy. He rightly observed that the implications of their models had ontological validity at and only at the point of equilibrium. Such models, based on 'the unity of forces must imply that those forces are in balance, not that they cease to be forces' (Marx 1968, Volume II, p. 500). And this dual perspective was ruled out by the assumption that the laws of value could only be conceived from the vantage point of the equilibrium. As Lunghini puts it:

> According to Marx, when demand and supply are equal to each other they cannot explain anything because they exert no influence on market value and shed no light on the reasons why the market value is expressed by precisely one sum of money rather than another. The true intrinsic laws of capitalist production cannot be explained on the basis of the reciprocal action of demand and supply because these laws show themselves in their pure form only when demand and supply cease to act because they are in equilibrium. (1985, p. 55)

Marx was keenly aware that the intellectual framework of the Classicists allowed certain questions and precluded others. As Marx noted, Ricardo made the careful distinction between the overproduction of a particular commodity and overproduction in general, accepting the former and ruling out the latter. In fact, the latter simply made no sense for Ricardo's schema. In this same vein, such a heuristic ruled out any other function for money besides a neutral means of circulating commodities. An excess supply of any one commodity did not imply an excess demand for money, only an excess demand for another commodity. It was possible for one commodity to be temporarily over-supplied only so long as another was undersupplied.[4] Protecting the core of the Classical metaphor required a positive heuristic that focused on equilibrium, not on how it came about, and on the acceptance of Say's Law, and the neutrality of money. All of these foci are necessitated by the confines of the programme. But such a myopic perspective was not to Marx's liking:

> That only *particular* commodities, and not *all* kinds of commodities, can form 'a glut in the market' and that therefore over-production can always only be partial, is a poor way out. In the first place, if we consider only the nature of the commodity, there is nothing to prevent *all commodities* from being super abundant on the market, and therefore all falling below their price. We are here only concerned with the factor of crisis. That is all commodities, apart from *money* [may be superabundant]. (Marx 1968, Volume II, p. 504)

Crisis, in the aggregate, implies that there is not an overall demand for commodities, but rather an overall demand for money. Money, in this case, must be demanded for purposes other than neutrally facilitating exchange. We shall return to this shortly.

Because of the heuristical devices just described, it is no surprise that Ricardo was able to include a quantity theory of money into his overall framework. By positing an equilibrium system in which relative prices would automatically be equivalent to relative embodied labour time, there was no other possible explanation for the price level as a whole except in terms of the quantity of money (see Kregel 1974). Just as the 'metaphysical equilibrium of purchase and sale' were figments of a logical, rather than an economic mind, so too was a theory of the price level which required this abstraction from the economic process.

For Marx, this result followed from the 'speculative' impetus of the Classicists to confuse abstract production and commodity production. As Kenway so aptly observed: 'Ricardo has a theory, but Marx argues that it is not a theory of capitalism' (Kenway 1980, p. 152).

What is meant by the phrase 'not a theory of capitalism'? Ricardo's is 'not a theory of capitalism' because it does not recognize the contradictions (crisis tendencies) inherent in the conversion of value into exchange value. Such a conversion, in the aggregate, is necessary of production in the economy if it is to be renewed on at least a constant scale. For Marx, the conversion of value into exchange value (or seen from the other direction, the valorization of the process of production) requires a certain distribution of income which will cause aggregate spending to purchase all the consumer and capital goods which have been produced. As is well known, Marx perceived the fundamental contradiction to be that the rate of exploitation in production motivated by individual capitalist's impetus to extract as much labour from labour power caused overproduction to be a regular occurrence of the capitalist productive process. Here the historically defined interests of the individual capitalists, the need to extract surplus labour so as to put the most on the market for the least cost – 'the process of production appears merely as an unavoidable intermediate link, as a necessary evil for the sake of money making' (Marx 1885, p. 58) – has resulted in a distribution which is in fundamental conflict with the requirements of the renewal of capital.

But in the world of Classical political economy it was impossible for there to be an overproduction of all commodities. Production was to satisfy the demands of the producers; how could the demand in the aggregate not be there if it existed at every point of production? Individuals, however, do not normally purchase what they produce and their ability to purchase (as opposed to their desire to purchase) is linked by their source of income from selling their products and/or their labour-services. Marx contended that the conditions of production could only be renewed in the aggregate under the Classical schema if it were either merely assumed at the outset, or if some grand social contract were constructed which assured that the correct distribution of income was obtained to allow society to be able to afford the products which it has produced. In this latter instance he observed:

> All the objections which Ricardo and others raise against over production., etc. rest on the fact that they regard bourgeois production either as a mode of production in which no distinction exists between purchase and sale – direct barter or as social production, implying that society, as if according to a plan, distributes its means of production and productive forces in the degree and measure which is required to satisfy the corresponding need. This fiction arises entirely from the inability to grasp the specific form of bourgeois production and this inability in turn arises from the obsession that bourgeois production is production as such, just like a man who believes in a particular religion and sees it as the religion, and everything outside of it only as false religions. (Marx 1968, Volume II, p. 529) (See also Lunghini 1985, pp. 52–4)

Marx observed that positing equilibrium at the outset was an absurd way of conducting economic inquiry. Its focus emanated from the specific conditions of equilibrium in the system without regard for those processes which brought the equilibrium about – *and which might potentially undermine this equilibrium*. Requiring there to be a social contract to assure the correct distribution of income might be a unique answer to the problem of avoiding crisis but it certainly had nothing whatever to do with capitalist production.

Thus, while possibly serving the needs of some ideological prerequisites, Classical political economy was incapable of addressing, let alone solving, the problems that characterized specifically commodity producing economies. For the requirements of the capitalist and the requirements of capital are not always confluent, the culprit here being distributions of the product which emerge from anarchistic production processes, not socially predetermined ones:

> In society, however, the producer's relation to the product once the latter is finished, is an external one, and its return to the subject depends on his relations to other individuals. He does not come into possession of it directly. Nor is its immediate appropriation his purpose when he produces in society. (Marx 1973, p. 94)

What should be obvious to this point is that Marx's criticism of Classical political economy was that it was a singular, specific theory rather than a general theory. Its focus emanated from the conditions of equilibrium in the system without regard for those processes which brought about the equilibrium or which might undermine it. By means of its particular heuristical configuration Classical political economy was able to separate real from monetary factors, preventing any interaction by means of the logic of the system itself. For Marx, an economic theory required an investigation into the 'general' nature of what he called 'the metamorphosis of commodities – which include the separation of purchase and sale just as it does their unity. . .' (Marx 1968, Volume II, p. 504).

Unlike the Classical system which confused abstract production in general and historical commodity production, which permitted them to make the dichotomy between real and monetary factors, Marx's system posits from the outset that with the evolution of commodities comes the requirement of a universal equivalent in money form. In this regard commodity production *causes* money relations to develop, although the existence of money relations reveals the 'contradiction imminent in the money relation, in the relation of the product to itself as money' (Marx 1973, p. 146). (See also Arnon 1983.) Here there is no concept of separating (dichotomizing) the commodity from the monetary sectors. The existence of money relations which naturally emanate from commodity production allow there to be a separation of purchase and sale C–M . . . M–C which act as the structure from which crises are possible.

This separation of purchase and sale is not the cause of crisis, but rather the objective circumstance under which crises are possible.

A *general theory* for Marx needed to explain the forces which caused purchase and sale to flow into each other (unity of forces) as well as those that clogged the process (crisis).[5]

The separation of purchase and sale in time and space admits to the possibility of crisis '[b]ut this is never the cause of crisis' (Marx 1968, Volume II, p. 515) (see Kenway 1980). Marx's theory of crisis, instead, is premised on the fact that disruption in the economy occurs from capital working itself out in its own reproduction. For him, 'the very nature of capital leads to crisis' (Lebowitz 1976, p. 470). Indeed it is the very nature of the production and reproduction of capital which creates its own barrier.[6]

> [Ricardo] cannot therefore admit that the bourgeois mode of production contains within itself a barrier to the free development of the productive forces, a barrier which comes to the surface in crises and, in particular, in over-production – the basic phenomenon in crises. (Marx 1968, Volume II, p. 527)

We've seen that Marx is careful to distinguish between abstract production and commodity production, the latter being unique to a well developed market economy. It was his belief that under a system of capitalist commodity production money took on forms, other than a mere medium of exchange, which signalled the possibility of crisis: viz., store of value and means of payment. Each occurs as a consequence of the possibility of crises occurring in the abstract, in the metamorphosis of the commodity:

> The most abstract form of crisis (and therefore the formal possibility of crisis) is thus the metamorphosis of the commodity itself; the contradiction of exchange-value and use-value, and furthermore of money and commodity, comprised within the unity of the commodity, exists in metamorphosis only as an involved movement. The factors which turn this possibility of crisis into [an actual] crisis are not contained in this form itself; it only implies that the framework for a crisis exists. (Marx 1968, Volume II, p. 509)

Let us take each one of these contradictions in turn.

Contradiction of exchange value and use value

In a barter economy, there is no contradiction between exchange value and use value. Everything is produced with an equivalent purchase in mind, and, therefore, exchange value is only an ephemeral moment between the sale and purchase of use values. In such cases, money, the social equivalent of all exchange value, also takes on an ephemeral existence, merely facilitating the exchange between two use values. However, with commodity production, the motivation to sell is not the same as the motivation to purchase. During the metamorphosis of commodities, the system can get bogged down. It is the nature of commodity production that the conflict between production and circulation is reflected in a separation of purchase and sale which lends itself to the possibility that exchange values will not be converted back into use values. This fundamental contradiction between the requirements of individual production and the social requirements for aggregate reproduction was described above. Of course such an occurrence can not logically exist if aggregate supply and aggregate demand are coincident. Rather, it is a prerequisite for crises to occur to admit that the two may deviate, especially in the case where the latter is less than the former:

> At a given moment, the supply of all commodities can be greater than the demand for all commodities, since the demand for the general commodity money, exchange value, is greater than the demand for all particular commodities, in other words the motive to turn the commodity into money, to realise its exchange-value, prevails over the motive to transform the commodity again into use-value. (Marx 1968, Volume II, pp. 504–5)

Here the circuit of industrial capital is broken, exchange value may not be used to renew the productive and capital accumulation processes. Money winds up not as a temporary abode of purchasing power, but rather as a hoard; where goods lie dormant on the other end of the balance sheet, i.e., as a situation of overproduction.[7]

Contradiction of money and commodity

The last part of the immediate quotation signals yet another function for money when the separation of purchase and sale is allowed, i.e., the contradiction between money as a medium of exchange and as a means of payment:

> The crisis in its second form is the function of money as a means of payment, in which money has two different functions and figures in two different phases, divided from each other in time. (Marx 1968, Volume II, p. 510)

Assume there exist three businesses: the first sells to the second; the second to the third; while the third sells on the market to final consumers. Business has been good, and each sells to the next on a 90-day credit basis. The third business anticipates to sell its output to be paid for at the end of 90 days. The second, expecting to realize its surplus value in 90 days, and anticipating a healthy future, contracts to purchase new capital goods from the capital goods sector. The second business also purchases circulating capital in advance, part of which comes from business one. Business one, now also expecting to realize its surplus value at the end of the credit period, does the same as business two and contracts with the capital goods sector for more capital goods:

> Thus the production of surplus value and with it the individual consumption of the capitalist, may increase, the entire process of reproduction may be in a flourishing condition, and yet a large part of the commodities may have entered into (final) consumption only apparently, while in reality they may still remain unsold in the hands of the dealers, may in fact still be lying in the market. (Marx 1885, p. 78)

In other words, suppose that the final sales of business three never materialize:

> Now one stream of commodities follows another, and finally it is discovered that the previous streams had been absorbed only apparently by consumption . . . Their owners must declare their insolvency or sell at any price to meet their obligations. This sale has nothing whatever to do with the actual state of the demand. It only concerns the demand for payment, the pressing necessity of transforming commodities into money. Then a crisis breaks out. It becomes visible not in the direct decrease of consumer demand, the demand for individual consumption, but in the decrease of exchanges of capital for capital, of the reproductive process of capital. (Ibid.)

With the crisis, each producer is caught with shelves full of commodity capital. 'The means of production lie without functioning on the one side, while labour-power remains unemployed on the other' (Marx 1885, p. 50). In addition, for the producer of final consumers' goods, 'piles of unsold commodities accumulate and clog the flow of circulation' (ibid.). The credit link has now been broken, and all capitalists will be unable to pay their debts. The crisis 'concerns the demand for payment, the pressing necessity of transforming commodities into money' (ibid.).

Money acting as means of purchase functions so as to facilitate the transformation of commodity into commodity. In this function it is but the temporary link between purchase and sale. Money as means of payment occurs when the link is broken and when it is money, itself, that is demanded. In both this case and in the case of money as hoard (store of value), the demand is for money itself rather than for money as facilitator of exchange. These functions of money are not aberrations from a normally smooth functioning system where commodities trade ultimately for commodities. Such a perspective is consistent with the

Classical view which is capable of dichotomizing between real and monetary phenomena. Under Marx's method, the organic nature of commodity production requires that some thing exists which satisfies the latter two functions of money. It is not possible to conceive of commodity production without the existence of a money which functioned as a store of value and means of payment which could be demanded to satisfy these criteria. This is because it is not possible to conceive of commodity production in which crises are not regular occurrences.

Keynes's monetary theory of production

At the core of Keynes's system stood the capital accumulation decision over time, one which facilitated economic growth when expectations were fulfilled, and one which caused the system to fall apart when expected prospective yields were disappointed. Keynes wished to show that when considering the world in which we lived, it was illogical to posit an equilibrium system where money did not exist. The thrust of his attack was not at the results of an existing tradition in monetary theory, but instead it focused on the necessary inextricable relationship between monetary and real factors in, what he referred to as, a monetary economy. In fact, for Keynes, a monetary economy was not an equilibrium barter economy which could be disturbed by the introduction of money. Money was an essential part of the system *ab ovo*, and needed to be defined within the context of such a framework.

Like Marx, J.M. Keynes had a vision, an intuition of an economic system which could best be characterized as one which organically moved in time. And even though they needed to fix time long enough to establish categories by which that system could be specified and identified they always recognized that every moment was the embodiment of forces which either balanced for a period of time or interacted so as to cause the system to move. Change was not something which only occurred by some unforeseen exogenous shock to the equilibrium. For when Keynes spoke of equilibrium, he used the phrase in the same sense as Marx, as the unity of forces, not just the unity.

Keynes was also critical of what, in *The General Theory*, he called Classical economics. Included in his definition of the Classical economists were not only 'Ricardo and James Mill and their *predecessors* . . . [but also] the *followers* of Ricardo, those that is to say, who adopted and perfected the theory of the Ricardian economics, including (for example) J.S. Mill, Marshall, Edgeworth and Prof. Pigou' (Keynes 1936, p. 3). Although there are clear differences between the theories of the predecessors and followers of Ricardo, what caused them to be lumped together in Keynes's mind was that they all adhered to a similar method, language and discourse focused about the Classical dichotomy between real and monetary forces. As he observed in the very first chapter of *The General Theory*:

> I shall argue that the postulates of the classical theory are applicable to a special case only and not to the general case, the situation which it assumes being a limiting point of the possible positions of equilibrium. Moreover, the characteristics of the special case assumed by the classical theory happen not to be those of the economic society in which we actually live . . . (1936, p. 3)

Keynes believed that this dichotomy was a fair representation of an economy at the point of full employment equilibrium. There, increases in the stock of money would affect the general price level because the elasticity of supply of commodities in the aggregate would be zero. In other words, aggregate output could not change, and movement in the system would only occur internally, that is, intersectorally, but not in the aggregate. Subsequent changes in relative prices had no effect on the aggregate level of prices. But the language and method of full employment equilibrium was neither the language or the method of states other than at full employment equilibrium.[8] In addition, Keynes was keenly aware that the classical theory described an economy that had nothing whatever to do with the characteristics 'of the economic society in which we actually live'.

In contrast, Keynes, like Marx, wished to describe an economics of a capitalist system, where output in the aggregate was liable to fluctuation, and where money played a unique and integral role:

> This book, on the other hand, has evolved into what is primarily a study of the forces which determine changes in the scale of output and employment as a whole; and whilst it is found that money enters into the economic scheme in an essential and peculiar manner, technical monetary detail falls into the background. A monetary economy, we shall find, is essentially one in which changing views about the future are capable of influencing the quantity of employment and not merely its direction. (Keynes 1936, p. vii)

For reasons which are beyond the scope of this chapter the final product of *The General Theory* appears markedly different from the pre-1934 drafts (see Rotheim 1981). Keynes excluded from the final product chapters which dealt with methodological issues of the differences between the economic systems of his predecessors (co-operative and neutral economies) and that reflecting his newly developed beliefs (an entrepreneur economy). It is indeed unfortunate that Keynes omitted these clarifying chapters from the book; anyone who reads them will be persuaded of their importance to the clarity of his thesis. Perhaps their inclusion would have headed off many of the erroneous interpretations of the book. The importance of these chapters will not be overlooked in the present essay, for they contain what, indeed, are the paradigmatic links to the same heuristic employed so successfully by Marx.

Keynes's attempt to integrate a theory of money in a theory of value led him, as early as 1932, to draft a table of contents of a new book which he then wished to title 'The Monetary Theory of Production' (Keynes 1979, p. 49). By December 1933 Keynes intended to open the book with a chapter bearing the title 'The Distinction between a co-operative economy and an entrepreneur economy'. A draft of what was the second chapter of the December 1933 table of contents, bearing that heading, was discovered in 1976. Here Keynes made the fundamental distinction between the roots of classical economics and 'the economic society in which we actually live', i.e., an entrepreneur or monetary economy.

In this chapter, Keynes differentiated among three types of economies: a real-exchange economy, a neutral economy and a monetary economy. He also called the first type a co-operative economy and a real-wage economy, while the monetary economy was also referred to by him as a money-wage economy. Each of these designations had attached to them certain key ideas and perspectives which when taken together yield a criticism of the premises of Classical economic method, one surprisingly similar in nature to Marx's critique of Classical political economy.[9]

In a real-wage economy, Keynes assumed that factors would be paid in real output. A 'neutral economy', according to Keynes, was one where factors, instead of being paid in output, could be paid in money, 'provided that all of them accept the money merely as a temporary convenience, with a view to spending the whole of it forthwith on purchasing such part of current output as they choose' (Keynes 1979, p. 77).

The neutral economy differed from a real-wage economy only in that the latter implied that factors would be paid in terms of product while in the former they would be paid in money. But, so long as there was some 'mechanism of some kind to insure that the exchange value of the money incomes of the factors is always equal in the aggregate to the proportion of current output which would have been the factor's share in a cooperative economy' (ibid., p. 78), then the two would yield the same results. This was so because the motivation for starting up production was the same in both economies, the only difference being that there was no money in the one, while money was a 'veil' in the other.

The key idea, here, is that the economy is focused on the exchange of real goods and services. Money either does not exist, as it is redundant, or if it does, then it is only a neutral element, one that facilitates exchange. Now, it is not a barter economy in which we actually live. So then, if money does exist, and if it is to be neutral, then this result could only occur if certain specifications about distribution held so that all that was produced would be sold. Keynes had some very serious doubts that distribution in the real world would consistently yield this result. In fact, the only way he was convinced that it would be the logical outcome of the economic process was if it was assumed from the outset (more on this later) or if, like Marx, there were some social contract which assured that there existed the correct distribution of income to bring it about. This, he concluded, could only occur in a 'co-operative situation', one where the motivation of the producer and that of the consumer were confluent and where society, as a whole, came to some agreement about the production and distribution of that output. And thus, he defined the real-exchange economy as a co-operative economy in that a co-operative economy was one in which 'the factor of production are rewarded by dividing up in agreed proportions the actual output of their co-operative efforts'.

It should be noted that Keynes uses the phrases co-operative and entrepreneur economy as the result of his exposure to Marx through reading a book by an American economist, H.L. McCracken, called *Value Theory and Business Cycles* (1933), where in a not too brilliant chapter on Marx, McCracken briefly describes Marx's two types of economies. Keynes consequently writes in the drafts:

> The distinction between a co-operative economy and an entrepreneur economy bears some relation to a pregnant observation made by Karl Marx – though the subsequent use to which he put his observation was highly illogical. He pointed out that the nature of production in the actual world is not, as economists seem often to suppose, a case of C–M–C′, i.e., of exchanging commodities (or effort) for money in order to obtain another commodity (or effort). But it is not the attitude of *business*, which is a case of M–C–M′, i.e., of parting with money for commodity (or effort) in order to obtain more money. (1979, p. 81)

From this perspective, Keynes argued that the premises of the real-exchange economy were such that unemployment was not an aggregate phenomenon, but rather something that could be explained by sectoral imbalances – an over-supply of labour in one market implying an under-supply of labour in another. This conclusion would be valid so long as there was never a change in the aggregate level of output, i.e., that effective demand could never fluctuate. And this, according to Keynes, required that 'sales proceeds exceeded variable costs by a determinate amount (therefore) effective demand cannot fluctuate; and it can be neglected in considering the factors which determine the volume of employment' (ibid., p. 80). This led Keynes to write in this same draft chapter:

> It is, I surmise, a conclusion of the classical theory that, given the amount of capital equipment and the supply schedule of labour in terms of output, the volume of output and hence the ratio of aggregate quasirent to the price of output tends to be *constant*. I cannot point to any passage where this is stated . . . but the above must, I think, be considered as following from the second postulate. Output will be pushed to the point at which the utility of the marginal product is equal to the disutility of the marginal employment; and aggregate quasirent in terms of output must, therefore, by such (an) amount as corresponds, given the supply function of the capital equipment (i.e., the quantity of output corresponding to the application of any given quantity of employment to the given capital equipment), to the quantity of output. If this is correct, then it is the case that, given the capital equipment and the supply schedule of labour, aggregate quasirent, divided by the price of output, is constant. (1979, p. 70)

Keynes concluded, then, that a co-operative economy was consistent with the assumption of full employment. Here, the marginal unit of output is just equal to the variable cost of that output where the factors receive their 'reward in terms of output in general'. This flow of output could only be distributed in 'agreed proportions' so long as 'the marginal utility of output is equal to the marginal disutility of effort' (Keynes 1979, p. 77). In this case, the value of expenditure is always equal to the value of income. Thus, as Keynes observed:

> [T]he conditions required for the 'neutrality' of money . . . are, I suspect, precisely the same as those which will insure that crises do not occur. If this is true, the real-exchange economics . . . is a singularly blunt weapon for dealing with the problem of booms and depressions. For it has assumed away the very matter under investigation. (1973a, p. 411)

What this all leads to is the same conclusion which Marx reached in his criticism of Classical political economy: that it only had ontological significance at the point of equilibrium, which in Keynes's case was characterized by full employment. As Devillers noted with regard to Keynes: 'The theory of relative prices based on market mechanisms cannot explain the determination of the level of production and thus employment without having assumed it from the beginning' (Devillers 1990, p. 168).

And this is the key to understanding Keynes's choice of the phrase 'real-wage' when referring to the co-operative, real-exchange economy. For according to the Classical theory, the level of employment could be considered within the metaphor of an aggregate labour market where the decisions to supply and demand labour were specified in terms of a real-wage. But for Keynes, a real-wage was an organic phrase, not a static entity (see Rotheim 1988, 1989). In the numerator was a money wage while in the denominator was the price of wage goods or the aggregate price level. In Keynes's system, as in Marx's, the aggregate level of output was permitted to fluctuate. What that implied was that workers could not bargain in terms of real wages by manipulating their money wage because if output and prices could fluctuate in the aggregate, then it might be possible that the change in money wages would *cause* the aggregate level of output and prices to change. As such, the subsequent real wage would be uncertain, and therefore beyond the control of labour as a bargaining tool.

What Keynes recognized was that there would be only one instance at which the money-wage and the aggregate price level would be independent, that being the point of full employment equilibrium. Thus Keynes found it appropriate to designate the neutral, co-operative economy as a real-wage economy because at the point of full employment equilibrium, there is a unique money wage and aggregate price level, that is a unique real wage at which the supply and demand for labour are equated. Only existing at the point of unity meant, as Keynes remarked, 'that the postulates of the classical theory are applicable to a special case only and not to the general case, the situation which it assumes being a limiting point of the possible positions of equilibrium' (1936, p. 3). But as aggregate output was not capable of changing, then the Classical metaphor described only the balance, not the forces which caused or undermined that state.

Finding the characteristics of Classical model totally out of synch with the real world, Keynes offered in its place a model of an entrepreneur (or money-wage or monetary) economy. He called it an entrepreneur, as opposed to a co-operative economy, because while the classical C–M–C model 'may be the standpoint of the private consumer, . . . it is not the attitude of business, which is a case of M–C–M′, i.e., of parting with money for commodity (or effort) in order to obtain more money' (1979, p. 81). He called it a money-wage economy because relative money wages were the only convention by which workers could bargain. And it was considered a monetary economy because when the scale of output and employment as a whole was the *modus operandi*, then 'money enters into the economic scheme in an essential and peculiar manner' (1936, p. vii).

In the co-operative or neutral economy, some labour could be temporarily unemployed in one sector only if there was an excess demand for labour in another. There could be no general unemployment because everything that was earned was spent. In contrast to this, Keynes wished to consider a general state of unemployment. Such a state could only occur if there were what he called fluctuations in effective demand, where some portion of current output remained unsold. His position was that 'fluctuations of effective demand can be properly described as a monetary phenomenon'. (Keynes 1979, p. 85):

> In a real wage and co-operative economy there is no obstacle in the way of the employment of an additional unit of labour if this unit will add to the social product output expected to have an exchange value equal to 10 bushels of wheat, which is sufficient to balance the disutility of the additional employment. Thus the second postulate of the classical theory is satisfied. But in a money wage or entrepreneur economy the criterion is different. Production will only take place if the expenditure of 100 in hiring factors of production will yield an output which is expected to sell for at least 100. In these conditions the second postulate will not be satisfied, except in the limiting case of a neutral economy. (Ibid., p. 78)

Unlike the co-operative and neutral economies where no chosen volume of output can ever be unprofitable, 'in an entrepreneur economy . . . the volume of employment, the marginal disutility of which is equal to the utility of its marginal product may be 'unprofitable' in terms of money' (ibid., p. 79). Such an outcome can only occur, according to Keynes, if there could be fluctuations in effective demand. These fluctuations in effective demand reflected the relationship between expected sales receipts and variable costs. Aggregate employment would alter as these two fluctuated.

> It is only when we waive the second postulate that aggregate quasirent, divided by the price of output, can be supposed to fluctuate, apart from changes in capital equipment or in the supply schedule of labour in terms of output. . . . This is fundamental. For it is the fluctuations of aggregate quasirent, such as the classical theory has not contemplated as possible, which lead to fluctuations in employment, in spite of there being no change either in the supply function of the capital equipment or in the supply schedule of labour in terms of product. (Ibid., pp. 70–1)

Fluctuations of aggregate demand were only possible in an entrepreneur economy, and therefore, it was only within such a framework that 'the quantity of employment and not merely its direction' could be explained. The reader should be careful to note that Keynes is not identifying the causes of fluctuations in effective demand. All he is saying is that effective demand will not fluctuate if the aggregate output is distributed among workers and capitalists in such a way that their expectations are fulfilled. If this is not the case, then distribution of income will fluctuate as aggregate output fluctuates and the interests of entrepreneurs (that is money making) will diverge from the interests of consumers and a crisis of overproduction will ensue.

Once such fluctuations were admitted into the general framework of his economic analysis, the next concern for Keynes was the role of money in effective demand failures. His intention was to show that 'fluctuations of effective demand (could) be properly described as a monetary phenomenon' (1979, p. 85). In a neutral economy, money could have no meaning beyond a means of circulating equilibrium goods to satisfy definite wants. However,

> It is the essence of an entrepreneur economy that the thing (or things) in terms of which the factors of production are rewarded can be spent on something which is not current output, to the production of which current output cannot be diverted (except on a limited scale), and the exchange value of which is not fixed in terms of an article of current output to which production can be diverted without limit. (1979, p. 85)

In the entrepreneur economy factors are paid in a thing that must be durable, difficult to produce, and whose exchange value is not fixed in terms of something to which resources can be diverted. If these properties are particular to an entrepreneur economy, then it follows that it is only in an entrepreneur economy that money can serve the function as a store of wealth. And it is because of the possibility of money being a store of wealth that it is a further feature of our actual monetary system which makes a deficiency of effective demand a more frequent danger than the opposite; namely the fact that the money in terms of which the factors of production are remunerated will 'keep' more readily than the output which they are being remunerated to produce, so that the need of entrepreneurs to sell, if they are to avoid a running loss, is more pressing than the need of the recipients of income to spend (ibid., p. 86). Unlike the Classical system in which no one would ever demand money except as a temporary abode of purchasing power,[10] in Keynes's system, as in Marx's, it was possible for there to be a deficiency in demand for *all* commodities balanced on the other side by an excess demand for money. In Keynes's case, because of the essential properties of money (as he eventually referred to them in chapter 17 of *The General Theory*), the excess demand for money would not call for an increase in production of money nor an increased substitution of reproducible assets for money as the money rate of interest rose. The economy was not self-correcting, and the unemployment caused by the deficiency of aggregate demand could persist.

With the generalization of the economy by Keynes, money could also take on a form similar to what Marx called a 'means of payment'. Keynes revealed such a likelihood in his November 1931 reply to the first instalment of Hayek's review of Keynes's *Treatise on Money*. Keynes pinpointed his difference with Hayek as follows:

> Dr Hayek holds himself, and implies that I also hold, that an act of monetary expansion – meaning by this a transference from the inactive deposits to the active deposits to the total quantity of money being unchanged, or an increase in the total quantity of money the quantity of the inactive deposits being unchanged – is not merely a possible cause of investment exceeding saving, but (1) that it is a necessary cause of this and (2) that the amount of the monetary expansion exactly measures the excess of investment over savings and hence is exactly equal to the amount of profits (in my terminology). . . . Dr Hayek's theory comes to the same thing as the theory that the excess of saving over investment is measured by the increase of the inactive deposits. . . . [W]hen I first began to work on Book III of my *Treatise* I believed something resembling this myself. My ceasing to believe it was the critical point in my own development and was the germ from which much of my eventual theory was worked out. . . . The point, put very briefly, is, firstly, that money may be advanced to entrepreneurs (directly by the banks, or through the new issue market or by the sale by them of their existing assets) either to meet losses or to provide for new investment, and that statistics of the quantity of money do not enable us to distinguish between the two cases; and secondly (to indicate a general principle by means of an illustration), that, if, desiring to be more liquid I sell Consols to my bank in exchange for a bank deposit and my bank does not choose to offset this transaction but allows its deposits to be correspondingly increased, the quantity of money is changed without anything having happened either to saving or to investment. (1973a, pp. 246–8)

Indeed Keynes's point here is that Hayek's conclusions only follow if we assume full employment and no leakages; a situation where money will always be 'neutral'. Thus Hayek is assuming what he wishes to prove. However, in a monetary economy, an increase in savings *may not and probably will not* increase investment, increasing rather inactive balances in the banks and increased indebtedness by producers of consumption goods while the money supply may not only increase because of an increase in monetized demand for industrial circulation (true, if money is seen only as a medium of exchange) but also because of a change in the state of bearishness (store of value function)[11] or 'to meet losses' (acting as a means of payment).

To sum up this section, we can note that Keynes's criticism of Classical economics enabled him to establish a method by which questions of real variables, especially employment and output, could no longer be considered independently of the role of money in the system. In an entrepreneur economy, money is a means of payment. But, because money possesses those essential properties which permit it to act as a store of wealth, there is an inherent tendency for fluctuations in effective demand and employment. That is, 'Money is par excellence the means of remuneration in an entrepreneur economy which lends itself to fluctuations in effective demand' (1979, p. 86).

Some final observations

It has been shown that while Keynes had no knowledge of Marx's analytical differences between systems of barter and commodity production it was the nature of questions that were primary to his analysis which caused him to travel down a path remarkably similar to that pursued by Marx. Neither asked what would happen to the system when money was tacked on to barter, as it has been traditionally done. It was for this reason that their conclusions were radically different from the norm. The relevance of this exercise is not in the fact that their answers were similar, but rather that they asked different questions from their predecessors. What makes their systems of analysis unique is that their positive heuristic (which could be considered the negative heuristic to their antagonist's models) set the tone from which their similar conclusions followed quite naturally.

It is also intriguing that it is this element of Marx's, and to a lesser extent Keynes's, analysis that is least emphasized. Just as it has been common practice to read Keynes through the Hicksian ISLM set of spectacles, a filtering mechanism which explicitly separates the real from the monetary sectors, so too has it been common to read Marx and compare him to others through the transformation problem. It is that if the transformation problem cannot be 'solved', then there is no relevance to Marx's theory of commodity production. Indeed, the relevance of Marx's theory is that it surpasses all others within the Classical tradition because it develops a theory of 'commodity' production. Criticisms of Marx never focus on this, his 'model' of a capitalist system, his dialectical heuristic. Rather, they focus on a technical notion, which only has relevance if one never moves his realm of inquiry beyond the pure value form of the commodity. In other words if they perceive Marx as the minor post-Ricardian that modern economists insist is his true label.

The same can be said for critics of Keynes. For them, who employ a general equilibrium set of spectacles, Keynes's analysis fails because of specification errors: his workers suffer from money illusion and his investors fall into liquidity traps.

In both cases, the critics of Marx and Keynes, employing a non-monetary based criticism, completely miss the paradigm switch that each is attempting, not out of ignorance, nor obstinacy, but because their training is such that the fundamental questions being raised by Marx and Keynes are so totally out of their intellectual set, their positive heuristic, that they are unable to envision the nature of the paradigm that is being proposed. Thus the criticisms that ensue, which may be logically coherent within the critic's positive heuristic, is totally off the mark with respect to the model that is being criticized.

For the systems of Marx and Keynes, money is not the cause of capitalism nor the cause of capitalist dislocation. Rather it is the instrument, the institution, by which those characteristics peculiar to a capitalist mode of production are revealed. As we have shown, in such a case, the role of money transcends that of a mere medium of exchange. For in a monetary theory of commodity production, it functions also as a means of payment and as a store of value. And it is these two functions that money plays which are the revelation of an economy which cannot be characterized by a real equilibrium with a means of circulation appended as an afterthought. This was the message that Marx and Keynes wished to impart with regard to their money theory of commodity production.

Notes

1. Thanks to Mark Blaug, Tim Koechlin, Michael Lebowitz, and Michael Perelman. This chapter is dedicated to Professor Alexander Balinky.
2. It will not be comprehensive as so much has been written on this subject in the last few years (see Arnon 1984, Chiodi and Messori 1984, Crotty 1985, Kenway 1980, Lavoie 1983, Lunghini 1985, Panico 1980 and Sardoni 1986).
3. This is an ironic accusation especially with regard to Ricardo in that he [Ricardo] rejects the scarcity theory of value as encompassing a small portion of the total quantity of goods in society and replaces it with a theory which can explain the value of reproducible commodities. See Ricardo (1970, chapter 1).
4. 'If physicians increase too much in number, what is wrong is not that their services are available in superfluity, but perhaps that the services of other producers of immaterial products are in short supply – for example, prostitutes' (Marx 1968, Volume I, p. 268).
5. Some of the impetus to Marx's ideas on the separation of purchase and sale, the distinction between barter economies and those in which money intercedes, and their relation to general overproduction come from John Stuart Mill (1844). I am grateful to Mark Blaug for this reference. Marx's reliance on J.S. Mill's distinction between

barter and money economies, however, seems only to go so far. For in his discussion of the nature of crisis, Marx lumps Mill together with others 'who . . . want to explain the crises by these simple possibilities of crisis contained in the metamorphosis of commodities – such as the separation between purchase and sale' (1968, Volume II, p. 502).

6. It is not the purpose here to lay out Marx's (or Keynes's) theory of crisis. For Marx's, see Sweezy (1942), Itoh (1975), Lebowitz (1976), and Sardoni (1986). For Keynes's, see Davidson (1972).
7. See DeBrunhoff (1976), Arnon (1984) and Crotty (1985).
8. In the 'Preface' to *The General Theory* Keynes clearly directs his attack by saying that, 'For if orthodox economics is at fault, the error is to be found not in the superstructure, which has been erected with great care for logical consistency, but in a lack of clearness and of generality in the premisses' (1936, p. v). See also Carabelli (1988).
9. The distinction between monetary and non-monetary economies has a long history in the history of economic doctrine and certainly would have been known to Keynes. The notion of neutral money played some significance in the interchanges between Keynes's public and private interchange with F.A. Hayek on the latter's review of the *Treatise on Money* (see Hayek 1931b, 1932 and Keynes 1931), Keynes's corroboration with Kahn and Sraffa with whom he shared his correspondence with Hayek as it was unfolding, and through Sraffa's review of Hayek's *Prices and Production* (Sraffa 1932). For example, Sraffa in the review of Hayek notes:

   > [T]he difference between a monetary and a non-monetary economy can only be found in those characteristics which are set forth at the beginning of every text-book on money. This is to say, that money is not only the medium of exchange, but also a store of value, and the standard in terms of which debts, and other legal obligations, habits, opinions, conventions, in short all kinds of relations between men, are more or less rigidly fixed. . . . It would be idle to rehearse these platitudes had not Dr Hayek completely ignored them in his arguments. The money which he contemplates is in effect used purely and simply as a medium of exchange. (1932, pp. 43–4)

   Among his many talents, Sraffa was a Marx scholar. The influence that Marx's criticism of Classical political economy had on Sraffa's critique of Hayek and on the formulation of Keynes's understanding of the key issues as his own mind-frame evolved is something that will never be known as there does not appear to exist any correspondence between the two on this review. Still, the similarity of ideas contained in the Sraffa review and Keynes's subsequent distinction between monetary, neutral and non-monetary economies surely lends itself to the conclusion that Sraffa's understanding of the issue had a strong influence on Keynes.
10. Recall Keynes's observation in his famous 1937 *Quarterly Journal of Economics* article that in the classical world only someone in a lunatic asylum would hold money as a store of value.
11. Later called 'liquidity preference'.

References

Arnon, A. (1984), 'Marx's Theory of Money: the Formative Years', *History of Political Economy*, **16**, (4).

Carabelli, A. (1988), *On Keynes's Method*, Basingstoke: Macmillan.

Chiodi, G. and M. Messori (1984), 'Marx's Analysis of the Relationship between the Rate of Interest and the Rate of Profits: a Comment', *Cambridge Journal of Economics*, **8**.

Crotty, J. (1985), 'The Centrality of Money, Credit, and Financial Intermediation in Marx's Crisis Theory: An Interpretation of Marx's Methodology', in Resnick and Wolff (eds), *Rethinking Marxism*, Automedia Press.

Davidson, Paul (1972), *Money and the Real World*, Basingstoke: Macmillan.

DeBrunhoff, S. (1976), *Marx on Money*, New York: Urizon Press.

Devillers, M.-H. (1990), 'Finance and Adjustment in a Monetary Production Economy', in Alain Barrère (ed.), *Keynesian Economic Policies*, New York: St Martins Press.

Hayek, F.A. (1931a), *Prices and Production*, London.

Hayek, F.A. (1931b), 'Reflections on the Pure Theory of Money of Mr J.M. Keynes', *Economica*, August.

Hayek, F.A. (1932), 'Reflections on the Pure Theory of Money of Mr J.M. Keynes: II', *Economica*, February.

Itoh, M. (1975), 'The Formation of Marx's Theory of Crisis', *Bulletin of the Conference of Socialist Economists*, February.

Kenway, P. (1980), 'Marx, Keynes, and the Possibility of Crisis', *Cambridge Journal of Economics*, **4**.

Keynes, J.M. (1931), 'The Pure Theory of Money: A Reply to Dr Hayek', *Economica*, November.

Keynes, J.M. (1933), 'The Monetary Theory of Production', reprinted in *The Collected Writings of John Maynard Keynes* (hereafter cited as CW), Volume 13, Cambridge Press.

Keynes, J.M. (1936), *The General Theory of Employment, Interest, and Money*, London, reprinted as CW, Volume 7.

Keynes, J.M. (1937), 'The General Theory of Employment', *Quarterly Journal of Economics*, reprinted in CW, Volume 14.

Keynes, J.M. (1973a), *The General Theory and After: Preparation*, CW, Volume 13.

Keynes, J.M. (1973b), *The General Theory and After: Development*, CW, Volume 15.

Keynes, J.M. (1979), *The General Theory and After: Supplement*, CW, Volume 29.

Keynes, J.M. (1982), *Social, Political and Literary Writing*, CW, Volume 28.

Kregel, J.A. (1974), 'The Post-Keynesian (Radical) Approach to Monetary Theory', *Bulletin of the Conference of Socialist Economists*.

Lavoie, D. (1983), 'Some Strengths in Marx's Disequilibrium Theory of Money', *Cambridge Journal of Economics*, March.

Lebowitz, M. (1976), 'Marx's Falling Rate of Profit: A Dialectical View', *Canadian Journal of Economics*.

Lunghini, G. (1985), 'Capitalist Equilibrium: from Soho to Bloomsbury', in Fausto Vicarelli (ed.), *Keynes's Relevance Today*, London.

Marx, K. (1913), *Contribution to a Critique of Political Economy*, 1859, Chicago.

Marx, K. (1973), *Grundrisse*, Vantage Press.

Marx, K., *Capital*, Volume I (1867), Volume II (1885), Volume II (1890), Moscow: Progress Publishers.

Marx, K. (1968), *Theories of Surplus Value*, 3 Volumes, Moscow: Progress Publishers editions.

McCracken, H.L. (1933), *Value Theory and Business Cycles*, New York.

Mill, J.S. (1844), 'Of the Influence of Consumption on Production', Essay II in *Some Unsettled Questions of Political Economy*, reprinted in J.M. Robson (ed.) (1967), *The Collected Works of John Stuart Mill*, Volume IV, Toronto.

Panico, C. (1980), 'Marx's Analysis of the Relationship between the Rate of Interest and the Rate of Profits', *Cambridge Journal of Economics*, December.

Ricardo, D. (1970), *Principles of Political Economy and Taxation* (1817), Sraffa edition, Cambridge Press.

Rotheim, R.J. (1981), 'Keynes's Monetary Theory of Value (1933)', *Journal of Post Keynesian Economics*, Summer.

Rotheim, R.J. (1987), 'Marx's and Walras's Theories of Capital Accumulation', *International Journal of Social Economics*, Summer.

Rotheim, R.J. (1988), 'Keynes and the Language of Probability and Uncertainty', *Journal of Post Keynesian Economics*, Fall.

Rotheim, R.J. (1989–90), 'Organicism and the Role of the Individual in Keynes' Thought', *Journal of Post Keynesian Economics*, Winter.

Sardoni, C. (1986), 'Marx and Keynes on Effective Demand and Unemployment', *History of Political Economy*, Fall.

Sraffa, P. (1932), 'Dr. Hayek on Money and Capital', *Economic Journal*, March.

Sweezy, P. (1942), *Theory of Capitalist Development*, New York: Monthly Review Press.

12 Observations on Marx's and Kalecki's approaches to the theory of effective demand

Mario Sebastiani

The purpose of this chapter is to investigate the relationship between the stream of thought bound to Marx and the ideas conceived by Kalecki in the 1930s. Accordingly, attention is devoted to an evaluation of the Marxist ascendancy over Kalecki and to an assessment of whether and to what extent his work has contributed to problems in the Marxist tradition.

Kalecki and the Marxian theory of exploitation

This task is complicated by the 'ubiquity' of Marx's thought, both on account of the variety of themes which he tackled, and on account of the multiplicity of ramifications in which is has manifested itself, or in which it has left (sometimes unnoticed) seeds.

This vitality is a sign of the greatness of Marxian *system* – a greatness in no way undermined by possible weaknesses of its elements – and it is confirmed in that this system has permeated modern economic thought.[1] Thus it would be a mistake to evaluate the Marxian system purely on the basis of what Marx actually said. Similarly it would be inappropriate to assess its influence on modern thought solely on the basis of those who profess to be Marxists; all the more so because, as has been observed,[2] perhaps the richest fruits of Marx's doctrine are to be found in the works of scholars who have no explicit ties with its ideology.

Among the questions left open by Marx, the most controversial ones concern the relationship between values and prices of production, and the problem of effective demand. That is, the two moments which countersign the Marxian analysis of profit – the *origin* of profit and the condition for its *realization*. The former relates to the production sphere, to the exchange between capital and labour, to the difference between the use value and the exchange value of labour force; the latter to the attitude of economic agents to spend. Each aspect corresponds to a feature of capitalism that Marx denounces but whose theoretical basis he is unable to demonstrate: the exploitation of workers and the systematic waste of resources.

Several generations of scholars have debated these themes, yet with a significant division of tasks. The professed Marxist component has mainly (and unsuccessfully) concentrated its attention on the transformation problem, convinced that this is the crucial element required to validate the theory of exploitation. The second theme has been developed by economists of different extractions, frequently unrelated to Marxism but sharing the aim of setting up – by drawing on hints scattered throughout Marx's works – ideas and tools by which the working of modern capitalist economies could be explained.

Kalecki belongs to this second group. Indeed his undogmatic attitude and his intellectual independence from Marxian doctrine are apparent. Kalecki's Marxism is not avowed, and he generally avoids making use of the categories and the language typical of this approach. Thus the concepts of labour-value and of exploitation (in Marx's meaning) do not occur in Kalecki's work, and no attention is paid to notions such as prices of production or the general rate of profits. Kalecki sticks stubbornly to the field of market prices (determined by the cost of production and by that hazy creature called degree of monopoly), so that his conception of profit appears entirely within the sphere of realization.

Kalecki's silence on the existence of a *causa causans* of profit, prior to the realization sphere, could naturally be interpreted either as a tacit acceptance of Marxian premises or as a tacit rejection of them. In the first case, Kalecki would merely have limited his attention to the 'phenomenal reality', to the condition for the realization of surplus value, while accepting, as the ultimate causes of the latter, that provided by Marx (i.e., the law of value and the theory of exploitation). If such were the case, however, it would be necessary to verify the compatibility of the categories used by Kalecki and those of Marx, which would entail switching from market prices to prices of production and then – through any of several paths, according to a still unsettled debate – to the notion of exploitation.

Kalecki's complete silence on the matter suggests a second interpretation whereby the origin of profit rests entirely on the power of firms to set prices over costs; that is, profits originate in the power relationship between producers and workers, the latter regarded as consumers rather than as suppliers of labour. The realization of profits then depends on the propensities to consume and invest. Thus the whole problem of income distribution finds its answer in the market, which means dropping the Marxian analysis of distribution. Naturally, this does not imply that the notion of exploitation was foreign to Kalecki, but rather that he does not follow Marx in attempting to pass from a purely ideological conception to one having a basis in scientific verification. Considering his pragmatism, it is hardly surprising that Kalecki took no steps in this direction; for he would have viewed the attempt to provide a 'scientific' demonstration of exploitation (i.e., of the 'origin' of surplus value) as an escape from a *reality* which requires no demonstration.[3]

Anyway, whatever his opinion might have been, Kalecki's silence allows us to focus on the effective demand and to argue that it is in this field that the main elements of convergence with Marx can be traced. Indeed Dobb remarked that Kalecki's work 'could be regarded as a formalization of the "realization problem" ' (1973, p. 212). This assertion overstates the case somewhat in that, although Kalecki's research undeniably centres around the realization problem, it should not be regarded (as we shall see below) as a contribution which is entirely internal to Marxian theoretical analysis.

Reproduction schemes and the theory of effective demand

It has been written that Marx's schemes of reproduction probably mark the origin of macroeconomics[4] and that with these schemes Marx set up an analytical tool whose potential was to become evident only after the advent of Keynesian theory.[5]

According to a widely accepted view,[6] Marx was unable to follow up his perception of the problem of effective demand with a theory of it, because he lacked (i) a theory of investment decisions, and (ii) a theory of the effects of investment on the overall level of production.[7]

As far as investment decisions are concerned, Marx is inclined to identify saving and accumulation in the long run, i.e., he considered profit and investment as inseparable over the long period. Saving and investment are in point of fact *separate* acts, and they can also be *widely separated* in time (hence the hoarding of money as cause and consequence of crises); but they are basically *non-independent* acts. Once the distrust which accompanies crises vanishes, the struggle for survival induces capitalists to accelerate as much as possible the pace of investment.[8]

On the other hand, a theory of aggregate output would have been all the more necessary to Marx inasmuch as he appears to deny that the level of production is normally determined by the productive capacity of the economy. Indeed, though overproduction becomes manifest only under particular circumstances (namely, the crisis), this does not seem to imply that in normal conditions the economy operates at full capacity. To the contrary, Marx observes:

> The periods in which capitalist production exerts all its forces regularly show themselves to be periods of over-production; because the limit to the application of the productive powers is not simply the production of value, but also its realization. (*Capital*, Volume II, p. 391n)

Marx's description of the 'industrial cycle', where 'high pressure' production is but a phase, further confirms this view.[9]

Without describing the schemes in detail, it is perhaps sufficient to recall that the outputs that can be exchanged between the two sectors which form the system[10] must be equal in value,[11] and that the mutual demands must also be equal. To achieve this Marx specifies the expenditure function of all the wage earners, whereas the expenditure behaviour of capitalists is set forth only for those operating in sector I. The behaviour of the capitalists in sector II is determined as a residual, so as to ensure the existence of equilibrium.[12] Marx furthermore maintains that surplus value must be completely spent, so that the share consumed is immediately determined once the share accumulated has been fixed; accordingly, the possibility of insufficient aggregate demand is ruled out *ex hypothesi*.

Thus, from the standpoint of the modern theory of effective demand, Marx's approach suffers a two-fold limitation: first, it does not consider independent consumption and investment functions; second, the expenditure decisions of the capitalists of one sector are taken as fully dependent on the decisions of the capitalists of the other sector.

Nevertheless, Marx's reasoning is consistent with his own purpose, which was to specify the *conditions* by which the system can reproduce itself – on an unchanged or on a growing scale – without encountering sectoral disproportions or shortfalls in aggregate expenditure; he wanted, moreover, to demonstrate that the possibility of the existence of equilibrium rests on the co-ordination of the behaviour of agents (a co-ordination which in turn he considered beyond the reach of capitalism). Indeed, Marx argues that 'on the basis of the spontaneous pattern of this production, this balance is itself an accident' (*Capital*, Volume II, p. 571). Anyway, the reproduction schemes at least provide a framework of compatibilities which can be developed into a theory of income, once some definitional and equilibrium conditions are replaced by functional relations, i.e., by behavioural equations.[13] Once we fill the gap and add *independent* consumption and investment functions for the capitalists of *both* sectors, then equilibrium must be achieved by the adjustment of other variables. Alternatively: (i) *given distribution*, sectoral outputs must adjust so as to reach levels and proportions which coincide with the demands – in this way we obtain a theory of output;

or else (ii) *given the levels of production*, it is the distribution which, through changes in prices, and then their divergence from values, adapts itself in such a way as to bring the structure of demand into line with production. In this way we have a theory of distribution along 'post-Keynesian' lines.[14, 15]

'Kalecki,' Joan Robinson observes,[16] 'began at this point', i.e., by assuming the distributive setting as a given and the output as a variable. It has already been said that Kalecki cannot be considered an orthodox Marxist, though it is widely agreed that the Marxist formation made his theoretical effort far easier; whereas Keynes was committed to a revolution against the ideas with which he was brought up, for Kalecki, the approach to the theory of effective demand came about as a natural extension of his own cultural tradition.[17] This continuity is reflected in several aspects of Kalecki's work (to be examined below), where Marx's influence worked mainly through Rosa Luxemburg.

Yet, Robinson's statement implies more than a cultural affinity; it entails that the relationship between Kalecki and Marx can be seen as one of theoretical derivation. Besides prompting the problems to be taken up and providing a background free from on-principle preclusions, Marxian theory would have given Kalecki the tools needed (i.e., the reproduction schemes) to tackle these problems; it was precisely by virtue of the reproduction schemes that Kalecki would have succeeded in reaching his goal.

This view rests on an *ex-post* interpretation of Kalecki's work, which finds no confirmation in the manner in which his thought developed over the years. Indeed, the starting point of Kalecki's theory of effective demand is an essay (1933) which presents an analysis based on the *classical* hypothesis of zero propensity to save from wages and in which no explicit connection with Marx's theory is put forth.[18] Only at a later stage does Kalecki seem to focus the affinity between his approach and that put forward by Marx in the reproduction schemes; this awareness was reached after he fully realized (also thanks to Keynes) the importance of the concept of underemployment equilibrium v. the business cycle, and after he came to the conclusion that his theory provided a solution to a problem left unresolved by Marx. Furthermore, the incidental manner in which Kalecki (in his major works) aligns his reasoning to Marx's reproduction schemes appears as an implicit denial that he considered these schemes as his source of inspiration.

The first time Kalecki recalls Marx's schemes is in the *Essays* (1939), when he observes that the relations whereby investment brings about an equal amount of saving 'are contained in the famous Marxian scheme of "extended reproduction" ' (p. 45). However, he adds, Marx

> is interested in finding out, with the help of exchange equations, the pace of investment in investment and consumption goods industries respectively, which is necessary in order to secure a steady expansion of output . . . He does not pay attention to the problem of what happens if investment is inadequate to secure the moving equilibrium, and therefore does not approach the idea of the key position of investment in the determination of the level of total output and employment. (p. 45)

In his *Theory of Economic Dynamics* (1954), Kalecki goes on to translate his own arguments into Marx's terms. After dividing the economy into three sectors (investment goods, capitalist consumer goods and consumer goods for wage earners), he argues that the sectoral outputs ultimately depend on the expenditure of capitalists.[19] This reasoning is later formalized in a model (Kalecki 1969)[20] in which Kalecki concludes that

> The national income (or product *Y*) which can be sold, and the profits *P* which can be realized, are in every circumstance determined . . . by the level of investment *I* and by the consumption of capitalists C_k (for a given distribution of income between wages and profits). (Kalecki 1969, p. 329)

The novelty of this result stems from elements which Marx essentially lacked (or which he handled in a rather confused manner). Marx would certainly have conceded that profits, i.e., *realized* surplus value, are affected by capitalists' expenditure and that the latter has a certain degree of autonomy with respect to profits.[21] Nevertheless, (i) this autonomy appears to Marx to be confined to the short period (since in the long run, saving governs investment); (ii) the amount of produced surplus value (as distinct from the amount realized, i.e., from profits) and the overall level of output continue to rely on factors which are prior to the realization sphere.

The autonomy of capitalists' expenditure is instead clearly asserted by Kalecki, who argues that it rests ultimately on the working of the banking system, which creates financial resources upon request, so that investment is made independent of any previous accumulation of profits and savings.[22] Kalecki makes it very clear that it is not the flow of saving in itself, but the supply of financial resources which is the prerequisite for expansion of investment; and that it is the latter which, by raising the level of activity, brings about an equal volume of saving.[23] Thus, Kalecki's concept of the role of money and financial resources brings to mind Marx's circuit of money capital and his conviction that capitalists as a whole are able to produce the amount of liquid assets needed to realize the surplus value.[24] Indeed, it is most likely that the immediacy with which Kalecki perceived both the 'revolving' nature of financial capital and the endogeneity of money supply, derives precisely from his familiarity with the Marxian reasoning.

Undoubtedly, however, the notion of capitalism as a system grounded in class barriers, which Kalecki shares with Marx, is fed by the nature of the financial system, by that circuit of capital which both of them hold irremediably closed to non-capitalists. In no way can workers 'break their chains' and become entrepreneurs themselves, since the ownership of capital is a pre-condition for carrying out investment activity, all the more so inasmuch as it is an essential requisite for obtaining credit.[25]

Kalecki on Tugan-Baranowski's and Luxemburg's positions on capitalist development

The different conclusions which can be drawn from the reproduction schemes led Kalecki to differ with *both* Tugan-Baranowski and Rosa Luxemburg on the effects of capitalist accumulation. Tugan-Baranowski argued for the necessity of dynamic equilibrium (provided that exact proportions between sectors are ensured); while Luxemburg attempted to prove that capitalism exhibits instead an opposite tendency. These contrasting conclusions are, for Kalecki, consequences of the same distortion with which Tugan and Luxemburg view the accumulation process, and of the absence of a definite theory of investment decisions. Both of their theses are based on the idea of the accumulation as a process *co-ordinated* within the capitalist class. Thus one can argue that individual investment decisions (precisely because they are co-ordinated) mutually support one another; while the other can maintain that the excess capacity potentially brought about by these decisions would (for the very same reason) be anticipated by the entrepreneurs and hence lead to a check in investment. Kalecki however argues that the weaknesses of these arguments are in both cases due to deficiencies in the investment theory.

The objection which Kalecki directs against Tugan is that

> The fundamental idea of Tugan rests on an error that what *may* happen is actually happening, because he does not show at all why capitalists in the long-run are to invest to the extent which is necessary to contribute to full utilization of productive equipment. (1967, p. 147)

Kalecki is nevertheless sympathetic to the 'deeply anticapitalistic' ideological basis of Tugan's conclusions, that is, to his conviction that the 'absurdity of capitalism' is such that it would justify the production of machines as an end in itself, in this way making 'its development immune against the problem of finding markets for its products' (ibid., p. 148).

Kalecki applies a symmetrical argument to refute Luxemburg's conclusions on the inevitability of a halt in the accumulation process due to the lack of a 'third element' which is represented by extra-capitalist markets. This thesis too would appear to reflect deficiencies in the analysis of investment decisions, since underlying Luxemburg's reasoning is the idea that accumulation is the fruit of decisions made by the capitalist class taken as a whole. Since capitalists are aware that there is no final market for the growing output made available by the new equipment, why would they bother to invest at all?[27] Here, Kalecki objects that

> capitalists do many things as a class but they certainly do not invest as a class. And if that *were* the case they might do it just in the way prescribed by Tugan-Baranowski. (1967, p. 152)

He concludes, then, that while on the one hand the lack of co-ordination of investments brings about crises, it, on the other hand, permits capitalism to contain the consequences of its own internal contradictions. This lack of co-ordination, in fact, is not only an expression of the anarchy of the market, but also an effect of the competition among entrepreneurs, which takes place by means of innovations, product diversification, the search for new sources of raw material, the introduction of new processes of production: in short, by means of a non-stop investment race. It therefore cannot be ruled out *a priori*, according to Kalecki, that the capitalist economy is in fact able to generate tendencies towards extended reproduction; but this conclusion does not in any way imply a denial of the existence of the problem of effective demand, as in Tugan.[28] Hence the recognition of the important but not necessarily vital role played by external markets in supporting the process of accumulation.[29]

Such are Kalecki's objections against the determinism of the conclusions of the two authors. He rejects both the 'neo-harmonicists' and the 'catastrophists' views; for he recognizes that capitalism is such a versatile Protheus that it has the capacity to overcome (at least temporarily) its own limits; and, paradoxically, to succeed in doing this precisely by virtue of its own contradictions

Unemployment and crises in Marx and in Kalecki

But what then can be said about the *ultimate causes*, the very origin of unemployment (as distinct from the principle of the effective demand, i.e., from the *possibility* for income to adjust at equilibrium levels which are independent of full-employment capacity)? Here, Kalecki's view strongly resembles that of Marx.

According to Marx unemployment is a 'permanent' feature of capitalism, a phenomenon deeply rooted in it, even though it appears more or less striking according to the phases of the industrial cycle. The fundamental, primitive and endemic cause of unemployment, Marx argues, is mass underconsumption – a cause just as permanent as is the poverty of the working class:

> It is no way a contradiction, on this contradictory basis [the increase in the productive forces *versus* the limited basis for consumption], that excess capital coexists with a growing surplus population; for although the mass of surplus-value produced would rise if these were brought together, yet this would equally heighten the contradiction between the conditions in which this surplus-value was produced and the condition in which it was realized.[30] (*Capital*, Volume III, p. 353)

Incidentally, Marx's reasoning here provides further evidence that he does not believe that, as a rule, the level of output is established by the productive capacity of the economy, or that unemployment is due to insufficient accumulation of capital.

Also for Kalecki, beyond the lack of investment which is at times the immediate and most evident cause of unemployment, the basic problem is the chronic underconsumption of the masses. This factor is revealed and emphasized by another factor (also acknowledged by Marx): the asymmetry of the effects of investment, which affects productive capacity more heavily than demand. This would entail two noteworthy consequences. On the one hand, it would be contradictory over the long term to base unemployment policies on the expansion of investments.[31] (Kalecki denies that the accumulation process is able to 'stand on its own feet', i.e., can, as Tugan-Baranowski maintains, provide itself with the necessary outlets for its products.) On the other hand, this asymmetry, inasmuch as it leads to the alternation of situations of over-accumulation and of underaccumulation, lies at the basis of cyclical fluctuations. The *causa causans* of the business cycle, i.e., of the instability of capitalism, is therefore an intrinsic feature of accumulation, which marks its limit and internal contradiction – the *productive character* of the investment:

> We face here one of the most remarkable paradoxes of the capitalist system. The expansion of the capital equipment, i.e., the increase in the national wealth, contains the seed of a depression in the course of which the additional wealth proves to be only potential in character. (Kalecki 1935a, p. 32)

Again, with the particular strength deriving from its being the closing remark of the *Essays*:

> The tragedy of investment is that it causes crises because it is useful. Doubtless many people will consider this theory paradoxical. But it is not the theory which is paradoxical, but its subject – the capitalist economy. (Kalecki 1939, p. 149)

The similarity of this view to that of Marx is evident; the quotation would appear to repeat almost word for word Marx's epigram 'the *true barrier* to capitalist production is *capital itself*' (*Capital*, Volume III, p. 358). Where the 'contradiction' or the 'barrier' to accumulation lies in the fact that the mechanisms governing accumulation and income distribution enter into conflict with each other as far as the realization of the surplus value is concerned. That is, in the fact that in a capitalist regime income distribution is governed by forces acting in a direction which is diametrically opposed to that of guaranteeing a relationship between consumption and investment suited to the growth of productive capacity.

In this sense, Kalecki would certain adhere to Marx's statement (which Marx himself has difficulty in arguing) according to which:

> The ultimate reason for all real crises always remains the poverty and restricted consumption of the masses. (*Capital*, Volume III, p. 615)

As far as the *immediate* causes are concerned, to Kalecki the crisis arises because of excess capacity installed, and the recovery takes place once this excess has been eliminated by a period of negative net investment. In Marx's view these phases are determined rather by fluctuations of the general rate of profits, due to the swinging of the industrial reserve army.[32]

Marx's linking of the fluctuations of the general rate of profits to the up and down of the *production* of surplus value (i.e., to changes in wages and in the organic composition of capital), rather than to those of its *realization*, directly follows from his own definition of the rate of profits. Yet, this reasoning makes it difficult for him to argue that the 'ultimate cause' of crisis is underconsumption. The inadequacy of consumption can no longer be regarded as the factor which pushes the rate of profits downward: rather, it must be the latter which negatively affects the former *via* a breakdown of investment and employment.[33] Thus Marx is deprived of the link connecting the belief that overproduction *ultimately* originates in underconsumption, with the interpretation of the latter as an *actual cause* of crises.[34]

Kalecki and Marx also share the idea that, ultimately, unemployment has political roots; the Kaleckian theory of the political cycle has clear Marxian roots. Unemployment goes hand in hand with capitalism, first of all inasmuch as it performs a function of social control, by safeguarding the values and relations on which the system is grounded. Any development which threatens those values can only be temporary: in particular, income distribution may indeed undergo changes during the business cycle,[35] but in the long run it is subordinated to the safeguard mechanism of accumulation (a safeguard which is however misconceived, bearing in itself the seeds of the contradiction).

Thus, Marx argues that over the long run the dynamics of wages and employment must be 'confined within limits that not only leave intact the foundations of the capitalist system, but also secure its reproduction on an increasing scale'; whence he concludes that 'the rate of accumulation is the independent, not the dependent variable; the rate of wages is the dependent, not the independent variable' (*Capital*, Volume I, pp. 770–1). Reasoning in this way, Marx seems to upset the relation between wages and accumulation which we have seen earlier to be the basis of the industrial cycle. Indeed, the *status* of independent or dependent variable depends on the time horizon considered. Every time the rise in wages appears to threaten the accumulation process, these are violently pulled down by the restoration of the unemployed army; in the long run, therefore, it is the rate of profits which capitalists regard as 'normal' (then the ensuing rate of accumulation) that determines wages, and not vice versa.[36]

The share of wages, rather than the real wage, is for Kalecki the most meaningful measure of the state of class relations. Obviously, this does not mean that the real wage level is unimportant, but its gradual increase over the course of time is a historically observed fact. However, inequalities in the diffusion of welfare persist and there is no frame of reference whereby the level reached can be evaluated.[37] The distributive shares, instead, reveal more immediately the conflictual nature of income distribution – the 'size of inequality'. This is the 'hard core' over which the social parties struggle, and it is here that the short-sightedness of the capitalist class emerges. Because the capitalist class is more interested in its own *relative* condition (the share of profits), rather than the *absolute* condition (the level of profits), it prevents the whole of society from benefiting from a larger level of output.[38]

It is precisely this defence of the bitter hand of vested interests – disguised as a defence of a general interest, namely of not disturbing *favourable conditions* for private accumulation of capital – which Kalecki identifies as the source of the failure which all attempts to reform the capitalist system would ultimately encounter.[39]

Conclusion

Beyond their shared broad vision of capitalist society, the convergence between Marx and Kalecki occurs on the issue of effective demand.

Mark provided Kalecki with the idea (though devoid of theoretical demonstration) that the deficiency of effective demand is rooted in the normal working of the capitalist economy. For his part, Kalecki believed himself to have solved a problem left open by Marx, by showing that the equations determining the level of total output are 'contained' in the scheme of extended reproduction.

It is obviously a different matter as to whether Marx would have considered Kalecki's solution appropriate to his system. As we have seen, Kalecki shifts the emphasis from the production to the realization of the surplus value, and from the conditions of exploitation to the conditions of the markets. It is a change that Marx would hardly have accepted, and it was precisely his reluctance to follow this route which had driven him away from that solution to the problem of effective demand toward which the reproduction schemes pointed. Taking into account also Kalecki's interest in market prices (as opposed to prices of production) and his 'strong distaste' for the theory of value, we can easily conclude that the correct answer to the preceding question is that Kalecki has not been a diligent exegete of Marx and his conclusions are not those at which Marx was aiming.

Thus it is quite understandable that intransigent advocates of Marx's purity should oppose this kind of exercise.[40] The problem remains, of course, whether it is preferable to protect a system from infection by spurious elements, though it be incomplete and unable to interpret relevant aspects of the real world;[41] or, alternatively, to leave the system open to integration and modification, so as to permit the construction of a new theoretical *corpus*, distinct from the original contributions. This latter method of building a new theoretical system, free from exegetical cures, is for some writers not only *legitimate*,[42] but also *necessary* in order to avoid dissipating Marx's insight.[43]

Notes

1. See Schumpeter's view: 'Most of the creation of the intellect or fancy pass away for good after a time that varies between an after-dinner hour and a generation. Some, however, do not. They suffer eclipses but they come back again, and they come back not as unrecognizable elements of a cultural inheritance, but in their individual garb and with their personal scars which people may see and touch. These we may well call the great ones – it is no disadvantage of this definition that it links greatness to vitality. Taken in this sense, this is undoubtedly the world to apply to the message of Marx. . . . We need not believe that a great achievement must necessarily be a source of light or faultless in either fundamental design or detail. On the contrary we may believe it to be a power of darkness; we may think it fundamentally wrong

or disagree with it on any number of particular points. In the case of Marxian system, such adverse judgment or even exact disproof, by its very failure to injure fatally, only serves to spring out the power of the structure' (1954, p. 3).

2. See, for example, Graziani 1982, p. 703.
3. In this connection see Brus (1977, p. 59): 'He felt, for example, a strong distaste for the Marxian theory of value, which he considered metaphysical and (if I am not mistaken) never wanted to discuss.'
4. Klein 1947, p. 118.
5. It is widely agreed that with his schemes of reproduction Marx was a forerunner of moderns approaches to macroeconomics, from dynamic equilibrium theory to Leontief's input–output analysis. In this connection see Samuelson (1967) who, after defining Marx as 'a not-uninteresting precursor of Leontief's input–output' (p. 616), allows that 'Marx's model of expanded reproduction is perhaps the first example of those golden-age paths of compounded interest which Cassel, D.H. Robertson, Von Neumann, Harrod, Domar, and all the rest have made so fashionable in modern economics' (p. 618). Though the contributions of these authors were developed independently of Marx, nevertheless 'we all might well have benefited earlier from study of the Marxian tableaux' (p. 617).
6. See Robinson (1949, 1951), Sweezy (1942), Klein (1947) and Kaldor (1960).
7. Kalecki also shares this opinion. Marx, though 'deeply aware of the influence of effective demand on the dynamics of the capitalist system . . . never examined systematically the process described in his reproduction schemes from a point of view of the contradictions intrinsic to capitalism on account of the problem of effective demand' (Kalecki 1968, p. 78). Such a step, Kalecki adds (ibid., p. 78), was precluded by his failure to develop a theory of the motivations of investment decisions, or an explanation of the consequences of the same on the level of production (see also Kalecki 1939, p. 45).
8. On more than one occasion Marx seems to confirm the idea that capitalists invest what they can save: 'One part of the surplus-value is consumed by the capitalists as revenue, the other part is employed as capital, i.e., it is accumulated. With a given mass of surplus-value, then, the larger the one part, the smaller the other. Other things being equal, the ratio of these parts determines the magnitude of the accumulation' (*Capital*, Volume I, p. 738). Marx's emphasis on the *coeteris paribus* condition could give rise to doubts about whether he was indeed convinced that the surplus value could really be regarded as a datum, i.e., an amount independent of capitalist's consumption and investment; but this seems to concern once again the field of realization of the surplus value rather than that of its creation.
9. Marx suggests the idea of a 'characteristic cycle of modern industry . . . which takes the form of a decennial cycle . . . of periods of average activity, production at a high pressure, crisis, and stagnation, [which] depends on the constant formation, the greater or the less absorption, and the re-formation of the industrial reserve army or surplus population' (*Capital*, Volume I, p. 785). See also the following passage: 'The market expands more slowly than production; . . . there comes a moment at which the market manifests itself as too narrow for production. This occurs at the end of the cycle. But it merely means: the market is glutted. Over-production in manifest' (Marx 1969, Volume II, p. 524).
10. Marx considers two sectors: sector I produces capital goods, and sector II produces consumer goods.
11. It should be recalled that Marx assumes that exchanges occur according to labour values.
12. Initially Marx (*Capital*, Volume II, p. 582) considers the share of surplus value that is accumulated by the capitalists (in both sectors) as given. This hypothesis is soon abandoned because it is incompatible with equilibrium, and the propensity to invest of capitalists in sector II is made an endogenously determined variable. This reasoning has been sharply criticized by Rosa Luxemburg, since 'there is no rule in this accumulation and in this consumption [of capitalists of section II], both being

only justified with the requirements of accumulation in section I'; hence Luxemburg's conclusion that Marx set up a 'wholly arbitrary picture of the relations within the section II' (1960, pp. 108–9). See also Morishima: 'The unnatural adjustment of the rate of accumulation by capitalists of department II to the exogenously determined rate of accumulation in department I was invented by Marx merely as a *deus ex machina*' (1973, p. 125). It is perhaps worth noting that Marx's argument can be seen from two distinct angles: (i) that of the conditions under which *initially given* productions are fully realized (i.e., the equilibrium at a given point in time); (ii) that of the conditions for a *steady* equilibrium. With numerical examples, Marx came close to defining the conditions for the first case; but he did not specify the conditions for dynamic equilibrium. Nevertheless, his examples depicted a system tending towards an equilibrium path characterized by uniform rates of growth of the two sectors, steady rates of accumulation, and fully realized production. From the viewpoint of Kaleckian (as well as Keynesian) theory, the first characteristic is most interesting.

13. See Klein (1947): 'Actually, Marx made the groundwork for a complete equation system to determine the level of income (effective demand) but did not build the complete system' (pp. 126–7). Again: 'However, imbedded in Marx's literary discussion and numerical examples, there are several hypothesis and assumptions that can be used to build a system of equations' (pp. 118–19).
14. In particular see Robinson 1956 and 1962.
15. The change in relative prices will necessarily alter the 'organic composition of capital', i.e., the ratio between constant and variable capital expressed in terms of prices. Alternatively, given the price structure, one can imagine that the adjustment runs through changes in techniques, that is, changes in what Marx calls the 'technical composition of capital'. Marx, however, does not even consider this eventuality, since his analysis of the reproduction schemes is grounded on the hypothesis of given techniques.
16. 'Kahn, at the "circus" where we discussed the *Treatise* in 1931, explained the problem of saving and investment by imagining a cordon round the capital-goods industries and then studying the trade between them and the consumption-goods industries; he was struggling to rediscover Marx's schema; Kalecki begun at this point' (Robinson 1965, p. 96). Similarly Lange: 'The model worked out by M. Kalecki is often wrongly reckoned with those based on Keynes's theory; in fact it is derived from Marxist theory of reproduction and accumulation' (Lange 1963, p. 309n).
17. Paradoxically, the fact that he was trained in a cultural milieu where the persistence of unemployment was not regarded as a theoretical puzzle, may have played a part in his own undervaluation of the novelty and the importance of the ideas he was developing. This would help to explain why, in the works preceding Keynes's *General Theory*, Kalecki treated the problem of underemployment together with that of economic fluctuations (undoubtedly a contributing factor in the profession's failure to appreciate the originality of his ideas). Besides, it is likely that the greater interest which Kalecki seems at first to have in economic fluctuations (although he was perfectly aware that unemployment could not be reduced to a mere aspect of the business cycle) was due to the fact that in these he found reflected his fresh Marxian readings on the ineluctability of *crises* as a 'supreme expression' of the contradictions of capitalism.
18. The debt is instead to Aftalion and Tinbergen.
19. 'Imagine that following Marxian "schemes of reproduction" we subdivide the economy into three departments: department I producing investment goods, department II producing consumption goods for capitalists, and department III producing consumption goods for workers. The capitalists in department III, after having sold to workers the amount of consumption goods corresponding to their wages, will still have left a surplus of consumption goods which will be the equivalent of their profits. These goods will be sold to the workers of department I and department II, and, as

the workers do not save, it will be equal to their incomes. Thus, total profits will be equal to the sum of profits in department I, profits in department II, and wages in these two departments: or, total profits will be equal to the value of production of these two departments – in other words, to the value of production of investment goods and consumption goods for capitalists. The production of department I and department II will also determine the production of department III if the distribution between profits and wages in all departments is given. The production of department III will be pushed up to the point where profits earned out of that production will be equal to the wages of departments I and II. Or, to put it differently, employment and production of department III will be pushed up to the point where the surplus of this production over what the workers of this department buy with their wages is equal to the wages of departments I and II' (Kalecki 1954, p. 47).

20. Given the shares of wages in each sector's output, and with $P = I + C_k$, from the equilibrium condition of the expanded reproduction (restated as $P_3 = W_1 + W_2$, i.e., the profit of the wage-goods sector equal to the demand for wage goods originating in the other sectors), Kalecki derives the equation whereby the overall level of production is made to depend on capitalists' expenditure and on the share of wages:

$$Y = I + C_k + \frac{w_1 I + w_2 C_k}{1 - w_3}$$

where I and C_k are investment and capitalists' consumption; and with:

$$\frac{w_1 + w_2 C_k}{1 - w_3} = C_w$$

consumption of wage earners equal to the wage bill $(W_1 + W_2 + W_3)$.

21. On this point see Sardoni 1989.
22. See Sebastiani 1985.
23. 'Now it is possible for the capitalists to step up their investment, even though their profits have not increased . . . nor have they curtailed their consumption *ad hoc*. . . . The financing of additional investment is effected by the so-called creation of purchasing power. The demand for bank credits increases and these are granted by banks. . . . The entrepreneurs who engage in additional investment are "propelling" into the pockets of other capitalists profits which are equal to their investment, and they are becoming indebted to these capitalists to the same extent *via* banks' (Kalecki 1935a, p. 29). J. Robinson reports that: 'This was the point [the fact that the availability of financial means must precede investment, while saving follows it] over which Keynes stumbled when we showed him the *Econometrica* article [of Kalecki (1935b)]' (Robinson 1977, p. 13). It is worth noting that the distinction between the concepts of finance and saving formed the core of a debate (in *The Economic Journal*) on the theory of interest contained in the *General Theory*, among Keynes, Ohlin, Hicks and Robertson.
24. The circuit of money capital (*Capital*, Volume II, chapter 1) starts with capital advanced by the capitalists (their own or credit) to purchase labour power and means of production; once the product has been manufactured and sold, the capital resumes its money form and, with the accrual of surplus value, returns in the hands of those who advanced it. The circuit of the capital thus includes its transformation, from financial capital into capital incorporated in labour power and means of production, then into real assets and, finally, into accrued financial capital.

As for the adjustment of monetary circulation to the requirements of production, in Marx this takes place by virtue of the behaviour of the capitalists themselves: 'In relation to the capitalist class as a whole, the proposition that it must itself cast into circulation the money needed to realize its surplus-value . . . is not only far from paradoxical, it is in fact a necessary condition of the overall mechanism' (ibid., p. 497). The increase in monetary circulation, continues Marx, can take place in three ways: (i) through an increase of velocity of circulation ('a more economic use of the quantity of money in circulation', p. 419); (ii) through a drop in the capitalists' liquidity preference ('the transformation of money from the hoard form into the circulating form', p. 419); (iii) ('to the extent that all these means together are not enough') through an increase in money supply ('there must be an additional production of gold', p. 420).

25. Cf. the following passage, the Marxian roots of which are transparent: 'Many economists assume, at least in their abstract theories, a state of business democracy where anybody endowed with entrepreneurial ability can obtain capital for starting a business venture. This picture of the activity of the "pure" entrepreneur is, to put it mildly, unrealistic. The most important prerequisite for becoming an entrepreneur is the *ownership* of capital' (Kalecki 1954, pp. 94–5).
26. The same criticism Kalecki probably opposed to the 'austro-marxist' scholars (Kautski, Hilferding, Bauer), who claimed to see in Marx's schemes the demonstration of the unlimited possibility of survival of capitalism.
27. See Kalecki 1967, p. 151 and 1968, p. 335.
28. Indeed 'Innovations break the impasse of a simple reproduction only to some extent and they do not warrant the utilization of resources in the sense of Tugan-Baranowski' (Kalecki 1967, p. 151).
29. Among the reasons inducing Kalecki to reject Luxemburg's thesis in its rigid form is that it is in part the fruit of an error. For Luxemburg identifies the driving factor of demand to be the *volume* of exports to non-capitalist sectors, instead of the trade *balance*: this mistake, according to Kalecki, is the origin of the overestimation of the role played by external markets. Kalecki's criticism is correct on both theoretical and historical grounds, but in a prospective sense the thesis of the inevitability of general overproduction emerges strengthened by this correction; indeed, what hinders the development of capitalist economies *taken as a whole*, is not their inability to increase the volume of exports but the irreconcilability of the need common to all to maintain an active (and increasing) balance of trade.
30. '*Over-production* is specifically conditioned by the general law of the production of capital: to produce to the limit set by the productive forces . . . without any consideration for the actual limits of the market or the needs backed by the ability to pay' (Marx 1969, pp. 534–5). And further: 'The word *over-production* in itself leads to error. So long as the most urgent needs of a large part of society are not satisfied, or *only* the most immediate needs are satisfied, there can of course be absolutely no talk of an *over-production of products* – in the sense that the amount of products is excessive in relation to the needs for them. On the contrary, it must be said that on the basis of capitalist production, there is constant *under-production* in this sense. The limits to production are set by the profits of the capitalists and in no way by the needs of the producers. But over-production of products and over-production of *commodities* are two entirely different things' (ibid., p. 527). Finally: 'The sale of commodities, the realization of . . . surplus-value, is restricted not by the consumer needs of society in general, but by the consumer needs of a society in which the great majority are always poor and must always remain poor' (*Capital*, Volume II, p. 391n).

    There is a passage in *Capital* (Volume II, pp. 486–7) where Marx attacks the 'ingenuous' version of underconsumption (expressly connected with Rodbertus): 'It is a pure tautology to say that crises are provoked by a lack of effective demand or effective consumption. The capitalistic system does not recognize any forms of consumer other than those who can pay. . . . If attempt is made to give this tautology the semblance of a greater profundity, by the statement that the working class receives too small a portion of its own product, and that the evil would be remedied if it received a bigger share, i.e., if its wages rose, we need only to note that crises are always prepared by a period in which wages generally rise. . . . From the standpoint of these advocates of sound and 'simple' common sense, such periods should rather avert the crisis. It thus appears that capitalist production involves certain conditions independent of people's good or bad intentions.' It would, however, be a mistake to interpret this passage as a proof that the volume of consumption is not relevant as a cause of crises; it should instead be understood in the sense that any attempt to overcome realization difficulties, by modifying the distributive order, generates reactions (a drop in investment) which are converted into causes of crises.

31. Kalecki deals with this aspect mainly in (1944) and (1945). His thesis rests partly on empirical observations, and partly on the belief that the propensity to save is bound to rise together with pro-capita income (1945, pp. 84–5). His conclusion on the ground of economic policy, is that the pace of investment should be adjusted in such a way as to create jobs according to the growth of active population, while the *additional demand* needed to raise this to its full employment level should be promoted by public expenditure, especially in the field of mass subsidies.
32. Marx, however, is aware of the impact of the 'disruption' and of the 'devaluation' of capital in prompting the recovery (see *Capital*, Volume III, pp. 355–7).
33. See Marx, *Capital*, Volume III, p. 350.
34. In this connection see the criticism put forward by Robinson (1949).
35. Both Marx and Kalecki hold the view that real wages move according to the business cycle. In Marx, wage negotiations seem to be carried out in real terms, and he argues that 'Taking them as a whole, the general movements of wages are exclusively regulated by the expansion and the contraction of the industrial reserve army, and this in turn corresponds to the periodic alternations of the industrial cycle' (*Capital*, Volume I, p. 790). For Kalecki, real wages show a similar course during the cycle, though negotiation is conducted in nominal terms; his reasoning is that the power of trade unions (which is subject to changes in the course of the cycle) works in two directions: in obtaining nominal increases and in dissuading the firms from making good through price increases (see, especially, 1971).
36. Marx's position here has also been interpreted as a prefiguration of what we call now the 'post-Keynesian' approach. Indeed Steindl suggested: 'In the Marxian long-run analysis the adjustment concerns the distribution of income between workers and capitalists: . . . this distribution of incomes in the long-run is adjusted in such a way as to provide just the necessary saving to finance the *given* trend rate of accumulation' (1952, p. 237; emphasis added; see also Wood 1975, pp. 11–12).
37. Obviously, Kalecki rejects the theory of marginal productivity.
38. As is known, for Kalecki the level of profits depends solely on capitalists' expenditure, whereas the profit share depends on the degree of monopoly. Given the level of profits, production varies inversely to their share; consequently (except for the case of full employment) any improvement in the workers' position does not affect the level, but only the share of profits.
39. On this aspect, see Kalecki 1943.
40. A further example of this difficulty can be found in the debate on the compatibility of Sraffa's price system with Marxian theory.
41. Again, Schumpeter glimpses a reason for this attitude towards Marx's thought: 'For the friends [of Marx] he was so much more than a mere professional theorist that it would have seemed almost blasphemy to them to give too much prominence to this aspect of his work' (1954, p. 21).
42. See, for example, what Hobsbawn wrote of Marx: 'Inasmuch as a system of ideas survives its author, it is no longer confined to the bounds of content or original intents. Within the sweeping bounds traced by the exegetic capacities of men, or even by human willingness to recognize a link with a well-loved or a favourite predecessor, that block of ideas is subject to an unforseeably extensive series of changes and of practical and theoretical transformations' (1982, p. 6).
43. See Robinson: 'With the light that Sraffa has thrown on the theory of value and

Kalecki on the process of realization of the surplus, we can develop a complete system, not of *neo* Marxism but of *intelligible* Marxism' (1979, p. 253). This operation, Robinson adds (ibid., p. 252), is all the more legitimate since: 'Considering the political use that has been made of [Keynes's ideas as revised by "bastard Keynesians"], it is natural enough for Marxists to be suspicious of Keynes, but what is the objection to Michal Kalecki, who set out almost exactly the same analytical system as the *General Theory* on the basis of the schema of expanded reproduction in Volume II of *Capital*?'

References

Brus, W. (1977), 'Kalecki's Economics of Socialism', *Oxford Bullettin of Economics and Statistics*, **39**.

Dobb, M. (1973), *Theories of Value and Distribution since A. Smith*, Cambridge: Cambridge University Press.

Graziani, A. (1982), 'L'analisi Marxista e la Struttura del Capitalismo Moderno', in AA.VV., *Storia del Marxismo*, Torino: Einaudi.

Harris, D. (1972), *On Marx's Schemes of Reproduction and Accumulation*, New York: Penguin Books (originally published in *The Journal of Political Economy*, **80**, 1972).

Hobsbawn, E.J. (1982), 'Il Marxismo Oggi: un Bilancio Aperto', in AA.VV., *Storia del Marxismo*, Torino: Einaudi.

Kaldor, N. (1960), 'Capitalist Evolution in the Light of Keynesian Economics', in his *Essays on Economic Stability and Growth*, London: Duckworth.

Kalecki, M. (1933), *Proba Teorii Koniunktury*, Warsaw: Institute of Research on Business Cycles and Prices.

Kalecki, M. (1935a), 'The Mechanism of Business Upswing', republished in Kalecki (1971).

Kalecki, M. (1935b), 'A Macrodynamic Theory of the Business Cycle', *Econometrica*, July.

Kalecki, M. (1939), *Essays on the Theory of Economic Fluctuations*, London: Allen and Unwin.

Kalecki, M. (1943), 'Political Aspects of Full Employment', *Political Quarterly*, (4).

Kalecki, M. (1944), 'Three Ways to Full Employment', in AA.VV., *The Economics of Full Employment*, Oxford: Oxford University Press.

Kalecki, M. (1945), 'Full Employment by Stimulating Private Investment?', *Oxford Economic Papers*, March.

Kalecki, M. (1954), *The Theory of Economic Dynamics*, London: Allen and Unwin.

Kalecki, M. (1967), *The Problem of Effective Demand with Tugan-Baranowski and Rosa Luxemburg*, republished in Kalecki (1971).

Kalecki, M. (1969), 'Le Equazioni Della Riproduzione di Marx e L'economia Moderna', in AA.VV., *Marx Vivo. La Presenza di K. Marx nel Pensiero Contemporaneo*, Milano 1969 (originally published in *Social Science Information*, 1968).

Kalecki, M. (1971), *Selected Essays on the Dynamics of the Capitalist Economy*, Cambridge: Cambridge University Press.

Klein, L.R. (1947), 'Theories of Effective Demand and Employment', *Journal of Political Economy*, **60**, April.

Lange, O. (1963), *Political Economy*, Volume I, London: Pergamon Press.

Luxemburg, R. (1960), *L'Accumulazione del Capitale*, Torino: Einaudi.

Marx, K. (1969), *Theories of Surplus Value*, London: Lawrence and Wishart.

Marx, K. (1977), *Capital*, Volume I, New York: Vintage Books Editions.

Marx, K. (1981a), *Capital*, Volume II, New York: Vintage Books Editions.

Marx, K. (1981b), *Capital*, Volume III, New York: Penguin Books.

Morishima, M. (1973), *Marx's Economics. A Dual Theory of Value and Growth*, Cambridge: Cambridge University Press.

Robinson, J. (1949), *An Essay on Marxian Economics*, London: Macmillan.

Robinson, J. (1951), 'Marx and Keynes', in her *Collected Economic Papers*, Volume I, Oxford: Blackwell. (Originally published in *Economic Journal*, June-September 1941.)

Robinson, J. (1956), *The Accumulation of Capital*, London: Macmillan.

Robinson, J. (1962), *Essays in the Theory of Economic Growth*, London: Macmillan.

Robinson, J. (1965), 'Kalecki and Keynes', in her *Collected Economic Papers*, Volume III, Oxford: Basil Blackwell. (Originally published in AA.VV., *Essays in Honour of M. Kalecki*, Warsaw, 1964).

Robinson, J. (1977), 'Kalecki and Keynes and the Economics of Capitalism', *Oxford Bulletin of Economics and Statistics*.

Robinson, J. (1979), 'Who is a Marxist?', in her *Collected Economic Papers*, Volume V, Oxford: Basil Blackwell.

Samuelson, P. (1967), 'Marxian Economics as Economics', *American Economic Review*, May.

Sardoni, C. (1989), 'Some Aspects of Kalecki's Theory of Profits: Its Relationship with Marx's Schemes of Reproduction', in M. Sebastiani (ed.), *Kalecki's Relevance Today*, London: Macmillan.

Schumpeter, J.A. (1954), *Capitalism, Socialism, Democracy*, London: Allen and Unwin.

Sebastiani, M. (1985), *L'Equilibrio di Sottoccupazione nel Pensiero di M. Kalecki*, Rome: Nuova Italia Scientifica.

Steindl, J. (1952), *Maturity and Stagnation in American Capitalism*, New York: Monthly Review Press.

Sweezy, P.A. (1942), *The Theory of Capitalist Development*, New York: Monthly Review Press.

Wood, A. (1975), *A Theory of Profits*, Cambridge: Cambridge University Press.

Index